DATE DUE

MR 4 98			
AP 26 98			

DEMCO 38-296

Katherine Anne Porter and Mexico

Katherine Anne Porter and Mexico

The Illusion of Eden

by Thomas F. Walsh

University of Texas Press, Austin

For acknowledgments of permission to reprint manuscript
and previously published material, see p. 267.

First Edition, 1992

Requests for permission to reproduce material from this work should be
sent to Permissions, University of Texas Press, Box 7819, Austin, Texas
78713-7819.

∞ The paper used in this publication meets the minimum requirements
of American National Standard for Information Sciences—Permanence
of Paper for Printed Library Materials, ANSI Z39.48-1984.

Library of Congress Cataloging-in-Publication Data
Walsh, Thomas F. (Thomas Francis), 1925–
    Katherine Anne Porter and Mexico : the illusion of Eden / by
Thomas F. Walsh. — 1st ed.
      p.   cm.
    Includes bibliographical references and index.
    ISBN 0-292-74311-4
    1. Porter, Katherine Anne, 1890–1980—Knowledge—Mexico.
2. Porter, Katherine Anne, 1890–1980—Journeys—Mexico.
3. Mexico—Description and travel.   4. Mexico in literature.
5. Authors, American—20th century—Biography.   I. Title.
PS3531.0752Z846   1992
813'.52—dc20   91-24381

For my wife and sons

Contents

Photographs following page xvi

Preface

The subject of this study inspired it. I met Katherine Anne Porter at the first of several delightful Sunday lunches at the Georgetown home of Marcella Comès Winslow in the summer of 1960. Those encounters led me back to Porter's works, which I then began to include in my courses, especially the three stories of *Pale Horse, Pale Rider*. After pursuing my interest in Mexican history a few years later, I wished to know more about Porter's life in Mexico and the origins of her Mexican works. In Mexico City I met Mary Louis Doherty, Porter's friend from 1921 and model for Laura in "Flowering Judas," who generously shared with me her memories, photographs, and letters from Porter. She persuaded me to describe my project to Porter, who responded on October 29, 1976:

> I am very sorry I am so late answering your letter of last April. I hope you have not disappeared into Mexico or a Precolumbian "dig" by now. I was and am very interested to hear from you and I should like for you to call on me on whatever date we could manage between our several occupations, for it is seldom indeed that I hear from anyone who remembers my time in Mexico which was I do believe after later experiences in several countries, the most exciting, memorable, tragic and honest country—mind you I didn't say government as there aren't any honest ones.
>
> I have survived and outlived almost everyone that I knew and worked with and formed lasting friendships with such as Covarrubias—Felipe Carrillo—oh I won't go on: they are dead and gone. But I do have a fairly full memorable record and I should like to talk with someone who knows what it was like there in my time.

When we did begin our talks in 1977—thanks to her nephew Paul Porter—she proved that her memories of her time in Mexico were incredibly sharp even though she was in extremely poor health, having suffered a stroke earlier that year. The combined memories and papers of Porter and Doherty are the essential material out of which my study grew.

When I finally realized that I could not encompass my investigation in a series of articles, the National Endowment for the Humanities came to the rescue with a year's grant in 1988–1989, supplemented by Georgetown University at the urging of English Department chairman James Slevin. Without that aid I could never have completed my work.

The list of others to whom I am indebted is long. I am especially grateful to colleague Raymond Reno, John Edward Hardy (who also supported my grant proposal), Ruth (Beth) Moore Alvarez, Arthur S. Healey, Marie C. Walsh, Joan Reuss, and Joseph Kahl for reading and making valuable suggestions on my whole manuscript. My thanks also to colleagues Roland Flint, Keith Fort, John Glavin, John Hirsh, Eusebio Rodrigues, Jason Rosenblatt, Janis Stout, and Mary Titus, who read sections of my work, to Dorothy Brown for her knowledge of American history of the twenties, and to James Foy for his psychological knowledge.

My file of her letters is proof of the unselfish expert help on Porter's life Joan Givner gave me over the years. George Hendrick also promptly answered all the questions I put to him, while Beth Alvarez, who knows her way around Porter's papers better than anyone, frequently advised me about details of Porter's life and brought to my attention several previously unrecorded publications.

In Mexico, Susannah Glusker graciously allowed me to read the letters and diaries of her mother, Anita Brenner. Constantly helpful, she also introduced me to Malcolm Niven, who allowed me to read the diaries of his father, William Niven. I am also indebted to Rita Lynch, who has searched among friends and libraries in Mexico for information about Porter and who supplied me with important information about Alma Reed. My thanks to Samuel O. Yúdico, Jr., for showing me photographs of his father and to Jaime Shelley for information about his grandfather. I thoroughly enjoyed meeting Manuel Alvarez Bravo, Mexico's most famous photographer, who took Porter's passport picture in 1931. In this country, John Doherty discussed his sister's life in Mexico and supplied me with postcards she had sent her family, Robert S. Wicks gave me important biographical and bibliographical information about William Niven, while María Amelia Heath taught me my way around the National Archives, where archivists of the State Department's Military and Naval Intelligence files were extremely helpful.

I am grateful to the staff of the McKeldin Library of the University of Maryland, especially Helen Olszewski and Blanche Ebeling-Koning, for making Porter's papers and photographs available, and to Isabel Bayley, Porter's literary executor, for permission to quote from them and from letters held in the special collections of other libraries. These include Princeton University Library (Allen Tate Papers); Mugar Memorial Library of Boston University (Carleton Beals Papers); Beineke Library of Yale University (Josephine Herbst and Matthew Josephson Papers); the Newberry Library (Malcolm Cowley Papers); and the Harry Ransom Humanities Research Center of the University of Texas at Austin ("Holiday" manuscript). I also wish to thank Peter Blodgett of the Huntington Library for discovering letters of Pablo González in the Albert Fall Collection; Katharine Vogel of the George Meany Memorial Archives for information about and photographs of Samuel Gompers and Mexican labor leaders; the staff of the New York Public Library for permission to examine the papers of Genevieve Taggard, and the staffs of Hemeroteca Nacional de México and the Library of Congress for making Mexican newspapers available to me. *American Literature, Wascana Review, College Literature, Studies in Short Fiction,* and the *Journal of Modern Literature* have granted me permission to draw from my articles that appeared in their publications.

This book would never have come into being without the constant support of my wife, María. Her knowledge of her native land has also made a difference in my interpretation of Porter's Mexican works. It was she who identified the words of the song "A la Orilla de un Palmar," embedded in the text of "Flowering Judas."

T.F.W.

Note to the Reader

My husband, Thomas F. Walsh, died on November 2, 1991, while this book was passing through the press. He had corrected and returned the galleys, and then made some subsequent corrections, and these were entered on the page proofs, which have been read and corrected by a group of my husband's colleagues: Roland Flint, Philip Herzbrun, John Hirsh, Raymond Reno, Eusebio Rodrigues, Jason Rosenblatt, and Roger Slakey. The index was prepared by our friend Beth Alvarez, herself an accomplished student of Katherine Anne Porter, who also assisted with the proofreading. This book is my husband's masterwork, the culmination of many years' work on Katherine Anne Porter and on Mexico, and I am most grateful to all who helped bring it to completion.

Maria A. Walsh
January 19, 1992

Introduction

In 1920 Katherine Anne Porter, an unknown journalist, first settled in Mexico. After four visits totaling three years, she left her "familiar country" in 1931, the celebrated author of *Flowering Judas*. Her Mexican experiences inspired nine published stories and sketches, three unpublished stories, and the opening section of her novel, *Ship of Fools*. A recognized authority on Mexican culture, she published ten essays and numerous book reviews on the subject over the years. Although Mexico failed her as the Promised Land she vainly sought, it released her creative energy, beginning with "María Concepción" in 1922.

My study of Porter is biographical and literary. It attempts a full account of her experiences in Mexico, some of them heretofore unknown, and interprets her Mexican works in light of those experiences.[1] Knowing the autobiographical sources of her fiction, one may determine how their emotional and intellectual content survives in the text and deepens the understanding of it. The study also explores imagistic and thematic links between Porter's notes, letters, essays, and fiction, Mexican *and* non-Mexican. Since she first revealed herself as person and artist in Mexico and since her Mexican experiences triggered memories of her Texas past and influenced her non-Mexican works, it is crucial to interrelate all her works. For example, Violeta in "Virgin Violeta" and Miranda in "Old Mortality" have in common painful experiences of Porter's youth, while her terror of death, felt in Denver and Mexico City, informs both "Flowering Judas" and "Pale Horse, Pale Rider." Taken together, they more clearly reveal Porter's mind and personality, an additional concern of this study.

It is a commonplace that the mind is divided by conflicting emotions and ideas, but Porter's mind was inordinately in conflict with itself. She wrote her friend Kenneth Durant about reserving "the right to have changed my mind, my feelings and my point of view as I went. . . . Yet I am the same persons (!stet) (that is much too good a typographical slip to set right. In fact I am not sure that I was at least two regiments of people inside, always at civil war)."[2]

Her mind did battle between hope in an earthly paradise and despair at its impossibility, between temptations to quit this world and grim but stronger determination to hold on, between desire for and rejection of love, between defiance of conservative conventions and nostalgic devotion to the old order. She often oscillated between these polar extremes and knew she would repeat the pattern in the future. She was also aware of her capacity for self-delusion, dramatized it in her fiction, and at times defended it as a survival technique. She attempted in self-analytical notes to account for frequent periods of depression or melancholia—she used both words. The alarm with which she viewed her condition, sometimes in Freudian terms, might have persuaded her to seek professional help, yet there is no evidence that she ever did and considerable evidence that she should have. Her alarms were not merely overdramatized expressions for future fictional use, but signs of a troubled personality which her occasionally erratic behavior confirmed.[3]

Porter's self-analyses and her letters to her father and sisters often turned back to her unhappy childhood. When she read in Joseph Grasset's *The Semi-Insane and the Semi-Responsible* that a child's earliest impressions sometimes manifest themselves later in obsessive fashion, she wrote in the margin, "So my horror and pain here and now from that old terrible time."[4] When she was almost two years old, her mother died shortly after the birth of her fifth child. Porter's father, melancholic even before the death of his wife, never recovered from the blow, using it and other misfortunes to curse his unlucky stars. He and his young children moved into the small two-bedroom house of his mother, who supported them until her death, when Porter was only eleven years old. Porter remembered living in humiliating poverty which her father was unable to dig himself out of. Worst of all, she remembered, in an unfinished autobiographical essay, "Pull Dick, Pull Devil," his blaming himself and his children for his wife's death and wishing they had never been born. Describing herself as neurotic, she in turn blamed her father as the principal cause of her problems, her blame-shifting reflecting the very weakness she found in him. Indeed she recognized uncanny similarities between their personalities, reenforcing her resolve not to be a failure like him. Although those similarities accord with psychological theory that depressive states are hereditary, Porter's Oedipus relation to her father may best explain her preoccupation with frigidity, rape, fear of pregnancy, revenge, and hatred between the sexes that recur in her notes, essays, and fiction.[5]

That relation may also explain her oscillating desire for and fear of human contact. She fell in and out of love, calling it, in one of her early Mexican notes, an illusion and, in her letters and fiction, an illness she and her characters hoped to recover from. At times her principle of rejection, as she called it, sprang from her fierce determination to prevent anybody from interfering with the practice of her art. She defined herself first and foremost as artist, a self-image that buoyed her up during fits of depression and justified her behavior in failed human relationships.

Her frequent depressions influenced her pessimistic view of life but interfered with the practice of her art. It is tempting to think that she sank into depression when she could not force herself to write, especially under pressure of a deadline, but it was more likely the other way around. Her depression either drove her into feverish activity in an effort to overcome it or submerged her further in its doldrums as she tried to analyze it. When she could write, it meant that incidents in the present or out of the past took shape in her imagination and objectified and justified her mental state. The failed Mexican Revolution confirmed her pessimistic view of the world, but, ironically, rewarded her with subject matter for her art. She never formed any consistent philosophical position, but struggled to reconcile her sense of the pervasive power of evil with the individual's power to overcome it.

The difficulty of reconstructing Porter's life in Mexico is complicated by the limited number of sources. An almost compulsive letter writer and careful curator of her correspondence by the thirties, she left few letters from the most important period of 1920–1921. The tattered, fragmentary notes that do survive are in such a jumbled state that their significance and precise date of composition are often a puzzle. And many notes that recall past events, even shortly after their occurrence, are semifictions, partly because she always tended to transform reality into a subjective version of it. Versions of her life given in interviews, especially after publication of *Ship of Fools* in 1962, over forty years after her first visit to Mexico, are particularly unreliable, for in them she attempted to claim as biographical fact almost everything that appeared in her published fiction. She stated in a 1972 lecture, "You see, my fiction is reportage, only I do something to it. I arrange it and it is fiction but it happened." "Arrangement" is indeed a modestly understated definition of the act of literary creation. In contrast, she had told Josephine Herbst (August 3, 1934) that it was impossible for her to make a "report"; instead she invented for her characters "characteristic" experiences that "might have happened to them."

Porter predicted to Kenneth Durant (December 8, 1954) regarding the possible revelation of indiscreet letters written over the years: "I shan't mind anything at all twenty-five years from now, when I shall be rising ninety-ish, with a wig and false teeth and a stick: why no, I'll probably be telling everybody the most disreputable stories on myself and friends, making them up when the real ones give out, doing my best to get a reputation as a real hellion in my day!" Her biographers, then, must attempt to distinguish between what happened and what Porter said happened, between truth and what she wanted to pass as truth. Faced with her uncorroborated statements about her life, they may have to rely on intuition to determine the degree of truth contained therein. Occasionally they will perpetuate her fictions about herself or invent new ones of their own, but her fictions, when recognized as such, can reveal as much of her personality as her truths and lead to an appreciation of her creative powers, which were much more prodigious than she would have us believe.

Note: Transcribing Porter's unpublished letters and manuscripts for purposes of quotation poses a challenge to the scholar. There are misspellings of geographical place names, diacritical marks are omitted for personal and place names, and marks of punctuation such a periods, slashes, and parentheses are used arbitrarily, a result of Porter's composing at the typewriter. I have retained Porter's misspellings and omissions of diacritical marks in transcribing for quotation. Her use of British spellings and unconventional use of marks of punctuation has been silently emended. Specifically, for Porter's use of from two to numerous periods either three of four periods have been substituted. In one case, I have substituted dashes for the series of periods (p. 45).

Roberto Turnbull's "Camera Study" of Porter, Manuel Alvarez Bravo's portrait of Porter, Porter's drawing of Luis Hidalgo, and photographs of Porter's maid Eufemia, Eugene Pressly, Hart Crane, Porter dressed as a Mexican Indian, and Porter with her geese are reproduced courtesy Special Collections, University of Maryland at College Park Libraries. Other photographs not otherwise credited are from the author's private collection.

Members of the Pan-American Federation of Labor at San Angel Inn, Mexico City, in January 1921. Plutarco Elías Calles, then minister of Gobernación, sits in the middle of the front row, with Samuel Gompers to his right and Luis Morones second to his right. Mary Doherty is third from the right in the second row; Thorberg Haberman is to her left. Felipe Carrillo Puerto is second to the right in the third row, and behind him is Robert Haberman. Porter is first left in the third row.

Samuel Gompers sits front center. Standing to his right is Robert Haberman and to his left is Samuel Yúdico, Porter's first model for Braggioni in "Flowering Judas." Courtesy The George Meany Memorial Archives.

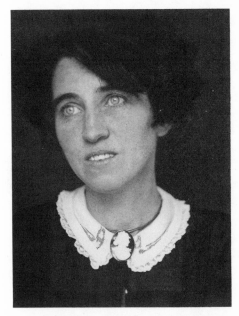

In Edward Weston's 1926 photograph, Mary Doherty wears the lace collar and blue serge that became Laura's "uniform" in "Flowering Judas."

Nicaraguan poet Salomón de la Selva was Porter's lover and the object of her satire in "Virgin Violeta" and the unpublished "Legend of Rosita."

Roberto Turnbull's "Camera Study" of Porter in 1922. His photographs appear in Porter's Outline of Mexican Popular Arts and Crafts.

In 1930 Porter had her maid Eufemia dress up in a Tehuana costume, although she seemed to approve of her going modern in "Leaving the Petate."

Eugene Pressly, whom Porter met in Mexico in 1930 and later married in Paris. Her melancholic pictures of Pressly were the inspiration for Miranda's view of Adam in "Pale Horse, Pale Rider."

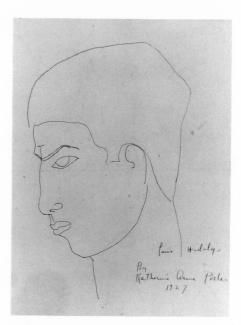

Porter's ink drawing of caricaturist Luis Hidalgo, who was Porter's lover in 1927-1928. At this time her works revealed her flair for literary caricature.

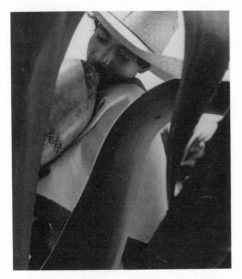

One of G.V. Alexandrov's stills taken at the Hacienda Tetlapayac. It is similar to the ones Andreyev shows the narrator in "Hacienda." Courtesy of the Lilly Library, Indiana University, Bloomington Indiana, and the estate of Upton Sinclair.

Porter's caption for this picture reads, "Hart Crane in my garden, Spring 1931." Crane is wearing a bridle that Moisés Sáenz gave him.

Porter dressed as a Mexican Indian.

Manuel Alvarez Bravo took this portrait of Porter in 1931.
He later became Mexico's most renowned photographer.

Porter and her geese, part of her menagerie in Mixcoac in 1931.

*Marcella Winslow, the author, Luis Dupre, and Porter in
Winslow's Georgetown home in 1960.*

Katherine Anne Porter and Mexico

1. Porter and Mexican Politic

Porter's Politics before Mexico

Explaining her interest in the Mexican Revolution to Archer Winsten in 1937, Porter claimed that she had always been a "rebel," making a "revolt" against the "confining society" of her native Texas by fleeing from it. In Mexico, therefore, she "plunge[d] in on the side of Liberty, Equality and Fraternity" and was "a so-called Fellow Traveller for many years," but never joined the party because she valued her "mental freedom."[1] She had made much the same point about freedom to Caroline Gordon (January 6, 1931), stating she had run away from the South because she had no intention of "not thinking what I please, nor of conforming where conformity would cramp and annoy me." The pattern of her life was to escape anything and anybody that threatened her "mental freedom," but that pattern does not sufficiently explain why she became as seemingly radical as she pictured herself to Winsten.

In "Pull Dick, Pull Devil," Porter identified her youthful rebellion against "confining society" with socialism. Contradicting Malcolm Cowley's assertion that "Mexico City was her Paris and Taxco was her South of France,"[2] she claimed she published "a violent defense of Woman Suffrage" when she was fourteen, "was converted to Socialism at the age of 15" after hearing Eugene Debs, and took "all social and political problems for [her] province at 18." One might doubt the accuracy of this claim, but not Porter's early interest in the woman's vote. In 1909 her brother Paul wrote her that "poor old J. H." [John Henry Koontz, whom Porter married in 1906] is probably a "suffragist at home anyway if merely for the sake of peace." In the rest of the letter he lectured her on the proper place of women: "You say women are slaves, bound by routine and unappreciated labor. I should call them the White Man's burden," adding that a woman's intelligence does not function in the realm of politics. There is no record of Porter's reply unless it appeared years later in "Old Mortality" when Cousin Eva, who went to prison for suffragist activism, complains, "In our part of the country, in my time, we were so provincial—a woman didn't dare to think or act for herself. . . ."[3]

It is unlikely Porter underwent an instant conversion to socialism after nearing Eugene Debs speak, but certainly she knew who he was and what he stood for. She wrote Kenneth Durant (March 30, 1936) that her father took her to hear Debs when she was about fourteen years old: "I remember the southern newspapers were still referring to him as a raging, blood thirsty monster of revolution, and describing his famous 'tiger crouch'. . . . He was a tall, pale colored thin man who did lean over as near as he could get to his hearers; he talked very urgently and gently, and the things he said seemed mild and reasonable." Porter was not alone in her estimate of Debs. Between 1906 and 1912 he and Mother Jones spoke at Texas camp meetings that attracted thousands of farmers. In the elections of 1912 the Socialists won 20 percent of the vote in some counties and 17 percent in the East Sabine region, the setting of Porter's "Holiday."[4]

The main issue was the high percentage of land tenancy, one that would concern Porter in Mexico. In fact, Texas Socialists in 1914 warned that tenants would become more "enslaved" than Mexican peasants who were fighting a "bloody revolution" to liberate their land.[5] Although Porter complained to Josephine Herbst (October 16, 1933) of government neglect of the farmer and wished she were in the South "to help the farmers fight," in "He" and "Noon Wine" her concern is not tenancy but the moral fiber of the Whipples and the Thompsons, tested in their hard struggle to scrape a living from the land. In "Holiday," however, Father Muller, an armchair Socialist who reads *Das Kapital* as if it were the Bible, offers Texas tenant farmers interest rates lower than those of the bank so that they can buy their own farms, but when his wife dies in her attempt to rescue the livestock during a ferocious storm, he can only bemoan the futility of a "hundert tousand tollers in the bank" (431). The story tells us that economic systems are little compensation for the unpredictable calamities nature inflicts.

We can reconstruct Porter's political attitudes as a journalist for Denver's *Rocky Mountain News* in 1918–1919 from "Pale Horse, Pale Rider" even though it was published in 1938 and influenced by later experiences in New York and Mexico. Early in the story, Miranda and her friend Mary Townsend are genuinely fearful of losing their jobs or going to jail for not buying Liberty Bonds they cannot afford. Earlier two bond salesmen had attempted to intimidate Miranda into buying bonds. The Kafkaesque stare of one of the men, "really stony, really viciously cold, the kind of thing you might expect to meet behind a pistol on a deserted corner," prompts her to think to herself, "Suppose I were not a coward, but said what I really thought? Suppose I said to hell with this filthy war?" (272–273).

The answer is that she would probably have been convicted under the sedition laws and imprisoned. Miranda had heard of "stories of personal disaster, of outrageous accusations and extraordinarily bitter penalties that had grown monstrously out of incidents very little more important than her failure—her refusal—to buy a Bond" (278). The stories were true. In an all-out campaign to force people to buy bonds, Councils of Defense in some states created elaborate schemes to check up on subscribers. People were called on during the night and told they must buy more bonds; others were threatened with loss of jobs; and in some communities the houses of "bond slackers" were painted yellow.[6] Senator Norris, arguing against U.S. entry into the war, had stated amid cries of "Traitor!" that "belligerency would benefit only the class of people . . . who have already made millions of dollars, and who will make hundreds of millions more if we get into the war."[7] This argument was shared by the Socialists, but became dangerous to express during the war. Porter's hero, Eugene Debs, was sent to prison for ten years for an antiwar speech in Canton, Ohio. Through Miranda's view of the "filthy war," Porter makes clear she sides with the opponents of war for the classic reasons. While a bond sales-man makes his pitch in a theater, Miranda whispers, "Coal, oil, iron, gold, international finance, why don't you tell us about them, you little liar?" (293). In a letter of January 1932 to Eugene Pressly, Porter made her antiwar stance explicit: "Certainly we should have stayed out [of the war], and would have, except for the flood of lying propaganda, the appeals to false sentiment, the hysterical nagging and yelping of the Allies for us to come in."

Although these remarks have the advantage of hindsight, "Pale Horse, Pale Rider" seems to reflect Porter's feelings toward the war in 1918 and the guilt she felt, either then or later, at her own timidity in not speaking up, especially since freedom of expression was so crucial to her. She might also have felt guilty about her contributions to the war effort. Before coming to Denver, she worked for the *Fort Worth Critic*. Also a volunteer for the Red Cross and mem-ber of the Social Service Club's Cheer Funds Committee, she wrote a piece about visiting the hospital at Camp Bowie: "After only three visits the men have begun to look forward to Friday, dolling all up for the occasion and appearing nicely shaved and brushed and polite. The ones who are really sick—they have a good many of these now—complain and tell their little-boy grievances and troubles, sure of sympathy and understanding and real interest. It's too bad so many of them had to go and get measles and mumps and such like ailments of extreme youth."[8] The tone of this passage, especially in the last sentence, casts doubt on the value of the cheery social visits; assuming the point of view of the visitors, Porter gently mocks their gushy and insincere attitudes. In the Red Cross scene in "Pale Horse, Pale Rider," drawn from the Fort Worth period, the narrator, also assuming the point of view of the Red Cross volunteers but now with a clearly mocking bite, makes Porter's attitude clear: "With this loot they were now setting out, a gay procession of high-powered cars and brightly tinted faces to cheer the brave boys who already, you might very well say, had fallen in defense of their country. It must be frightfully hard on them, the dears, to be floored like this when they're all crazy to get overseas and into the trenches as quickly as possible" (275–276). As the young women scatter about the ward, "uttering girlish laughter meant to be refreshingly gay," Miranda feels "miserably embarrassed at the idiocy of her errand" (276) and soon flees when a patient with a "hostile" face rejects her overtures. When another woman wonders what good such visits do, Miranda replies, "I hate it" (277). The ambiguous tone of the *Critic* article masked what Porter did not have the courage to reveal about the war in general.

In her story Porter also manipulated history to stress the police-state tactics of the government. Miranda wonders if a threat to fire her "isn't a kind of blackmail. I don't believe even a Lusk Committeeman can get away with that" (271). Later she thinks, "The worst thing about the war for the stay-at-homes is there isn't anyone to talk to any more. The Lusk Committee will get you if you don't watch out" (290). On another occasion she speculates that a member of the Lusk Committee probably spread the rumor that the Germans caused the influenza outbreak. But the Lusk Committee did not exist during the war. Created by the New York legislature, it operated mainly in New York City from May 1919 until April 1920, when Porter was living in Greenwich Village. Invoking the Red Scare, state senator Clayton Lusk claimed, "More than 20,000 alien enemies in the Communist Party of New York alone are openly organized for the overthrow of the Government by force and violence."[9] The committee raided seventy-three "Red Centers" and jailed almost a thousand "radicals." Eventually a few aliens were deported and the rest were freed for lack of evidence. Remembering such violations of the principle of freedom, Porter turns "Liberty Bonds" into an ironic oxymoron. When Miranda recovers consciousness amid the celebration of the armistice, she hears voices singing "My country, 'tis of thee": "Sweet land . . . oh, terrible land of this bitter world where the sound of rejoicing was a clamor of pain, where ragged tuneless old women, sitting up waiting for their evening bowl of cocoa, were singing, 'Sweet land of Liberty—'" (312–313). The passage reveals how influenza ravaged Miranda's mind and body, but the ironic use of "liberty" suggests that fate and state have conspired to deny it to Miranda and Adam.

Following in the footsteps of her close friend, Eva Chappell, who was probably the model for Mary Townsend in "Pale Horse, Pale Rider,"[10] Porter left Denver in the fall of 1919 and settled in Greenwich Village. Texas for Porter was "the native land of [her] heart"[11] and the setting of half her collected stories, but New York was her intellectual home, where she could freely develop her art among fellow artists. She could easily have subscribed to "the system of ideas" that, according to Malcolm Cowley's *Exile's Return,* characterized Bohemia of the twenties—for example, "the idea of liberty"; "the idea of female equality"; and "the idea of changing place" whereby "the artist can break the puritan shackles" through repatriation (60–61). If her radical friends are any indication, Porter found the Village to her liking politically. Bessie Beatty, at whose home Porter celebrated Christmas in 1919,[12] was editor of *McCall's,* had been an active suffragist in California, lectured on feminism, and published in 1918 *Red Heart of Russia.* Ernestine Evans, whose college graduation photo is among Porter's papers, had been a Balkan correspondent for the *London Chronicle* and the socialist *New York Call.* She frequented 12 St. Luke's Place, home of poet Genevieve Taggard and Helen Black, both writers for the *Nation* and Porter's close friends later in the twenties. Porter first met Floyd Dell, novelist and editor of the *Nation,* in 1919 and later at the Union Square apartment of Alex Gumberg, a Russian-born American Socialist.[13] Kenneth Durant, who married Ernestine Evans in 1923, was also among Porter's friends, reminding her in 1936 of his remark in 1920 that she wrote like an angel. Porter wrote Robert McAlmon (August 21, 1934) that she considered Durant one of her best friends, claiming that as his assistant on ROSTA, the Russian news agency that evolved into TASS in 1923, she wrote the daily news story while he wrote the cable.[14] Although I have found no evidence of her work on ROSTA, undoubtedly her New York friends contributed to her radical ideas, making revolutionary Mexico politically attractive to her.

According to Porter's July 1923 note to the *Century,* "Why I Write About Mexico," the country was familiar to her because her father, who had lived there, told her "enchanting stories" about it. She also claimed she "watched a street battle between Maderistas and Federal troops from the window of a cathedral" while an old Indian woman explained to her, "It is all a great trouble now, but it is for the sake of happiness to come," not in heaven but "on earth" (CE 355). Yet Porter confessed to Robert McAlmon (July 28, 1934) that though she had lived through revolution, major strikes, and the Sacco-Vanzetti affair, "in spite of my frantic endeavors to be everywhere at once, take part in everything, and see all, the battle always takes place nine miles away." She invented the incident with the didactic Indian woman to dramatize and justify her presence in Mexico because she had "been accused by Americans of a taste for the exotic, for foreign flavors" (CE 356).[15] (The incident is the first example of Porter's practice of placing herself in a fictitious eye of the storm while hiding her real adventures in Mexico.)

However natural the interest of Texans in Mexico, as Porter claimed in her *Century* note, it was in New York that two Mexicans, musician Tata Nacho (Ignacio Fernández Esperón) and painter Adolfo Best Maugard persuaded her to visit their country in 1920.[16] In December 1919 Best exhibited his paintings at the Knoedler Gallery in New York and in early 1920 began to create stage settings for a new ballet of Anna Pavlova, with whom he had collaborated in Mexico in 1918. In a long appreciation of his work, poet Babette Deutsch mentions the "ballets for which Mr. Best did the stage settings," adding, "And the pantomimes were written by Miss Katherine Anne Porter."[17] Best was nobody's idea of a revolutionary, as his early self-portrait in three-piece suit with walking stick suggests, but his European training, talent, and art theories, developed out of his study of pre-Columbian art with anthropologist Franz Boas, intrigued Porter. She originally planned to continue their ballet collaboration in Mexico.

Porter had more important irons in the fire. Ernestine Evans, feature editor of the *Christian Science Monitor,* asked her for "sketches" of Mexico (March 23, 1920). Porter wrote her family (December 31, 1920) that she came to Mexico "fortified by letters from editors and publishers like Scribner's and MacMillan, with an agreement with the United Press that I might write them a series of stories." At this crucial time in Mexican history she planned to write a book of her impressions of Mexican culture and develop in that fertile soil her talent as creative writer. Everything was falling into place. Like her Village friends, she would earn a living by her pen in an exciting foreign country with political aspirations to her liking.

On July 4, 1920, she wrote her sister that her ballet pantomimes were delaying her, but her passport was in order and, because an outbreak of bubonic plague had closed the port of Veracruz, she planned to travel to Mexico by land. Pavlova's ballet had been held up and was finally canceled altogether in October because the sets that Best designed did not pass fire inspection.[18] Also in October a friend, Ira Patchin, gave Porter letters of introduction to "Mr. Robertson," the consul at Nuevo Laredo, and to George T. Summerlin, U.S. chargé d'affaires in Mexico City, pointing out Summerlin's Louisiana roots. (She would soon have reason to be wary of both men.)

Porter began her journey in late October. According to the fanciful account she gave Hank Lopez in 1965, when she boarded the Mexican train at the border, "the whole roof was covered with soldiers and rifles and young women with charcoal braziers and babies." When she asked what was happening, a man told her, "Well, we're having a little revolution down here" (I 121–122). She warned Kenneth Durant she would tell such a story in her old age, one that, as with the *Century* note, retrospectively placed her in danger. The fact was that not even armed guards had accompanied trains from the border for months, as an acquaintance of Porter pointed out in 1921.[19] She probably derived her description of train roofs covered with soldiers from photographs included in Anita Brenner's *The Wind That Swept Mexico,* which she reviewed in 1943. Her notes never mention the Mexican train, but include an account of her journey to the border, later incorporated in a fictional fragment:

> At every station long boxes lay in stiff rows with a red white and blue flag over each one. All the way there was the October rain taking the color out of the air, and there was never even one person walking among those rows at any station, lifting the cloth and looking and saying, "This one is mine." There was no one, and I began thinking that these boxes full of mould dug up in France and brought back with newspapers sobbing aloud over them, were meant to travel from place to place until they had made all the possible journeys. And then they would be part of side shows in country fairs and the private rooms of museums for the consolation of a people that had not fumbled death as much as it wanted to during the war.

This chilling picture of death and abandonment is an ominous prelude to Porter's Mexican experience.

Mexico 1910–1920

In "The Mexican Trinity" (1921) and "Where Presidents Have No Friends" (1923), Porter tried to make sense of Mexico's complex political situation. To understand her experiences, we must see them in the context of Mexican history, of which she became a serious student and in which she played a minor role. Since she met heads of government in Mexico, including President Alvaro Obregón, whose inauguration she attended, it is important to know, beginning with the outbreak of the revolution, who they were and what they stood for.

In November 1910 Francisco Madero, thwarted in his attempt to campaign for the presidency, headed a general uprising against aging dictator Porfirio Díaz that ended with his election as president in May 1911. Those who rose up were wealthy northern hacendados, like Madero, who were excluded from power in the Díaz regime; small middle-class landowners, like Alvaro Obregón of Sonora, who in a time of economic decline bore the brunt of new taxes while foreign landowners benefited from much lower taxes[20]; and, finally, peasants like Emiliano Zapata, who continued to lose communal lands to foreign investors and hacendados. Zapata's state of Morelos had almost become one vast hacienda as town after town disappeared off the face of the earth. In Yucatán around 125,000 Mayan Indians were slaves along with 8,000 Yaquis of Sonora, captured and forced to work in the hot coastal flatlands.[21] Thus three revolutionary groups existed at the same time, divided by social and economic class and at cross purposes with each other. When Madero, more interested in modifying than changing the old system, didn't move toward land reform, Zapata continued to fight for Land and Liberty.

The still-powerful old oligarchy and foreigners, fearing that Madero would carry reforms too far, conspired to remove him. General Victoriano Huerta, encouraged by U.S. ambassador Henry Lane Wilson, overthrew the regime and on February 18, 1913, had Madero and his vice-president murdered.[22] Coahuila governor Venustiano Carranza, joined by the forces of Obregón and Pancho Villa, overthrew Huerta in August 1914. Then the power struggle between the proletarian Villa and the autocratic hacendado Carranza began. Obregón and other Sonorans, among them Plutarco Elías Calles and Benjamín Hill (Obregón's nephew), sided with Carranza out of their own economic interests. In April 1915 Obregón soundly defeated Villa in the bloody battle of Celaya, reversing Villa's political fortunes.

To consolidate his power, Carranza called a convention that produced a constitution not particularly to his liking nor to that of foreign governments and the church. The constitution of 1917, like that of 1857, restricted church ownership of property and operation of religious schools. Article 27 also declared that all subsoil resources belonged to the nation, giving it the right to nationalize any mining or petroleum property, and provided for the breakup of the great haciendas and restoration of illegally seized Indian land. Article 123 established for the first time a labor bill of rights and eliminated debt peonage. Although provisions of Article 123 have been more honored in the breach ever since, the new constitution marked significant advances in social structure and working conditions in contrast to the brutal feudalism of the Díaz regime.[23]

Article 123 was influenced by anarchist-socialist ideas, mainly imported by Spanish émigrés, in the late nineteenth century. Early in the twentieth century, the socialist-influenced Liberal Party helped organize workers of the Anaconda-owned Cananea Copper Company in Sonora, but in 1906 government forces put down a violent strike against low wages and racial discrimination, killing at least thirty miners. In 1908 the government put down another strike at the Rio Blanco textile plant in Puebla, killing 200 workers, and continued to suppress strikes all over the republic up to 1910. In 1911 typographers formed a model labor union and carried out socialist organizing activities, ideologically combatting capitalism through its organ *El Tipógrafo Mexicano.*[24] Porter's close association with labor leaders in 1920–1921 and sympathy with socialist ideas explain why the young man who attempts to court Laura in "Flowering Judas" is "one of the organizers of the Typographers Union" (96).

In 1912 the Casa del Obrero Mundial was founded. Cleaving to anarchist principles of complete independence from government, it successfully organized many unions but was suppressed by Huerta just before his overthrow. In 1914 Obregón made friends with labor leader Luis Morones and his follower Samuel Yúdico, both prototypes of Braggioni in "Flowering Judas." Obregón's motives were not altruistic since he needed more troops in his fight against Villa; 7,000 Mexico City workers in 1915 formed six Red Battalions and joined Carranza's forces in exchange for the Casa's right to organize workers throughout the country.[25] The same year, the Casa obtained the House of Tiles as its meeting place. Built in the sixteenth century as the home of the Count del Valle, it became the Jockey Club in 1895. In an elegant travel book dedicated to Porfirio Díaz, American author Marie Wright devoted a chapter to the Jockey Club, describing its tile façade, bronze railings brought from China in Spanish galleons, and "gilded lamps with snowy crystal globes, afire with the witchery of electricity"–the place where one could encounter "the four hundred" of Mexican society.[26] The symbolism of their new quarters was not lost on members of the Casa, who enjoyed "the novelty of seeing a proletarian group installed in a luxurious mansion." Priests passing the House of Tiles, "situated on the edge of the most bourgeois and antirevolutionary part of Mexico City," would curse the revolution and workers would shout back, "Viva la Casa del Obrero Mundial!"[27]

Before Porter arrived in Mexico, the House of Tiles became Sanborn's restaurant, as it still is today. In a fictional fragment she describes Braggioni, Laura, and "their crowd" taking tea there, just as she and others, including Samuel Yúdico, used to. In "Flowering Judas" Braggioni confides to Laura that he likes "to indulge his love of small luxuries. 'I have a taste for the elegant refinements,' he said once, flourishing a yellow silk handkerchief before Laura's nose. 'Smell that? It is Jockey Club, imported from New York'" (93). The narrator again refers to Braggioni's cologne: "Now he perfumes his hair with Jockey Club, and confides to Laura: 'One woman is really as good as another to me, in the dark. I prefer them all'"(99). Knowing that Yúdico, the last general secretary of the Casa, negotiated to house the labor union in the exclusive Porfirian Jockey Club,[28] Porter, stressing Braggioni's pride in his perfume, ironically recalls the Casa's pride in their luxurious quarters and suggests that corrupt labor leaders slavishly imitate the elite whose privileges the revolution was supposed to have eliminated.

The Casa's tenure in the House of Tiles was short-lived. Pablo González soon tossed it out because its successful strikes and national organization angered Carranza.[29] After the Casa called a second general strike in July 1916 to protest a serious loss in the workers' standard of living, the government declared martial law and General Benjamín Hill arrested the Casa's leaders, forcing the organization to disband when it received little support from Obregón. Two years later Luis Morones and followers created, with the government's permission, a new labor union, the Regional Confederation of Mexican Workers (CROM). In November 1918 the Pan-American Federation of Labor was created with Samuel Gompers as president and Morones as vice-president, angering Mexican Socialists because Gompers was strongly antisocialist and supportive of the U.S. entry into the war.[30]

Obregón, after Carranza's election to the presidency in May 1917, resigned his government and military posts in order to prepare for the presidential election of 1920. He traveled extensively in the United States and held many press interviews to attract American business to Mexico and to make himself politically acceptable in advance of his anticipated success as presidential candidate. During his campaign of 1919–1920 he made a secret pact with Grupo Acción, the inner circle of CROM leaders, whereby they would form a labor party to support him while he, in turn, promised to include them in his government. He also gained support from regional chieftains and was extremely popular among the common people.[31]

When Carranza realized that his hand-picked candidate, Ignacio Bonillas, had little popular support, he sent troops into Sonora and called Obregón to Mexico City to answer charges of conspiring to overthrow the government. When the Sonorans declared against federal authority on April 11, Obregón was forced to flee Mexico City for his life, disguised as a railroad engineer with lantern in hand, aided by such allies as Luis Morones.[32] Obregón's supporters quickly mobilized a large army, causing Carranza and his government to entrain for Veracruz. He was murdered in transit by one of his own army in the mountain town of Tlaxcalantongo, Puebla. In "Where Presidents Have No Friends" Porter describes the stubborn old man's flight and death, the moral of which is "A President of Mexico can trust no one" (CE 407).

Interim president Adolfo de la Huerta found that he could not trust Pablo

González, who was tried and condemned to death in July for his part in an insurrection in Monterrey.[33] González, the subject of several of Porter's cryptic notes, was dubbed the general who never won a battle. "His only handicap was a fear of failure that had numbed his brain and left him as stupid as he was ambitious."[34] It also left him utterly ruthless. Sent to Morelos by Carranza in 1916 to defeat Zapata, he annulled all reforms and treated as the enemy those he was supposed to protect. He became wealthy from all the goods his army looted, but he did not bring down Zapata until 1919 and then only by treachery after influenza had decimated the population. After his conviction for treason, he was pardoned by De la Huerta and fled to the United States, where he plotted the overthrow of the Mexican government. Six weeks later Obregón was elected president and two months after that Porter arrived in Mexico City.

Mexico 1920

When Obregón took power, the economy was in a shambles. In need of foreign capital, he sought U.S. recognition of his government that was withdrawn at Carranza's death. The principal problem was oil, which Porter stresses in her two political essays, calling U.S. oilman Edward L. Doheny the "most implacable of Mexico's interior enemies" (CE 410). Doheny was the first to raise a well in Mexico in 1901. By 1907 his company was capitalized at fifteen million dollars. Despite revolutionary violence, oil production increased from 3.5 million gallons per year in 1910 to 157 million gallons in 1920.[35] However, when Carranza invoked Article 27 in 1919 to prevent new drilling by companies without permits, Doheny, Senator Albert B. Fall, and others mounted a vociferous campaign for U.S. intervention. Doheny, exploiting the Red Scare, even claimed that "prominent Mexicans were trying to stir up revolution and bolshevism in the United States." Secretary of State Robert Lansing, working closely with the oil companies, threatened Mexico with intervention and recommended sending the navy into Mexican waters, an action President Wilson rejected.[36] After Carranza's overthrow, oil companies pressured Obregón to be more flexible concerning Article 27.

Fearing intervention by newly elected President Harding, especially with Fall in the cabinet, Ernest Greuning of the *Nation* sent Paul Hanna, correspondent for the *New York Call* and the *London Daily Herald,* to write a series of articles on Mexico that appeared in the *Nation's* March and April issues of 1921. Porter soon became a close friend of Hanna, describing him as "an enlightened human being of a rare order," who "saw Mexico perfectly straight, without hysteria, prejudice or any other objectionable attitude." In his last article (April 27), Hanna accused the oil companies of obduracy that would "lead us straight into bloody war and the conquest of Mexico" through "highly financed intrigue." Porter later made the same point in "Presidents": oil people "cheerfully admit it is cheaper to keep a few minor revolutions going than to pay taxes" and so assure Pablo González "support and aid" (CE 411). In their articles Hanna and Porter, who benefited from his knowledge of the oil companies, shared the same political position, but Hanna was optimistic about Mexico's future while Porter was skeptical and fatalistic. Hanna praised Mexico's unified determination to strengthen "The House Set in Order" whereas Porter lamented a nation split by multiple opposing factions, with the traditional enemies of progress in danger of prevailing.

Both Hanna and Porter worried that pacification of the nation after ten bloody years of warfare had splintered it into autonomous regions under generals who operated like warlords. De la Huerta and Obregón compromised with generals too powerful to be replaced in return for recognition of the new government and pensioned hundreds of other generals out of work. Disgruntled Carranzistas fled across the border or bided their time in Mexico, waiting for the opportunity to rebel. And rebel they did. In a pronouncement against the government in 1922, General Francisco Murguía listed over eighty military men executed in the first two years of the Obregón regime.[37] That year his own name was added to the list when he was executed for crossing the U.S. border and creating a tiny insurrection. "A. A. Seraphic," chief of Naval Intelligence in Mexico City, wisely predicted in August 1920, "Carranzistas with all other disgruntled elements will not be able to direct any successful revolutionary movement,"[38] but newspapers preyed on public fears with sensational reports of each new flare-up.

As if to justify U.S. intervention and Carranzista rebellions, conservative newspapers carried on "fevered discussion . . . as to the best means of stamping out Bolshevism," which was, according to Porter, "the inclusive term for all forms of radical work" (CE 399). The Red Scare she had witnessed in New York had made its way to Mexico. *Excelsior* constantly attacked foreign radicals and Mexican Socialists. One headline read, "The Bolsheviks in Mexico Hope to Receive 18 Million Dollars," while another accused Felipe Carrillo Puerto of Yucatán of trying to set up a Bolshevik republic. Not that the press wasn't given enough fuel for its fire. Speaking before a large Labor Day gathering on September 27, 1920, Luis Morones railed, "We have but one watchword – organization; but one purpose – the destruction of the capitalistic system and all that it stands for."[39] Morones was not a Bolshevik although Porter wrote Paul Hanna (April 19, 1921), "It is not a defamation of character to call a man that in this country." But, of course, it was if *Excelsior* was doing the calling, and it was not when friends like Porter wished to praise him for his apparently radical stance. Firmly in Gompers' camp, he had no relationship with the tiny Communist party in Mexico, composed mostly of foreign propagandists. On September 5, 1920, a reporter for the *New York Tribune* concluded that "there is small fear that Bolshevism will go far in Mexico."[40] Just to be sure, Obregón expelled several foreign agitators associated with the movement in May 1921.

CROM, with Luis Morones at its head, was, Marjorie Ruth Clark points out, entirely "practical and opportunistic"; the organization concerned itself "little with the ultimate transformation of society," preferring an "'equilibrium' between labor and capital" to "destroying capitalism" (68). In accordance with Grupo Acción's secret pact with Obregón, Cromistas were on the government payroll, Yúdico as head of the Central Garage and Morones as chief of Military Manufacturing with an annual budget of fourteen million pesos, a large reserve of men under his orders, and access to arms and ammunition.[41] Although Porter praised her employer's enlightened treatment of munitions workers (CE 414), CROM was more interested in guarding its turf against the incursions of rival unions. In light of its agenda, Morones's brave words against capitalism, uttered before he entered Obregón's cabinet, were heated rhetoric in competition with other speakers that day to tell the crowd what they wanted to hear. And newspapers reported in full the alarming evidence of Bolshevism.

On that same day in 1920, Felipe Carrillo Puerto outdid Morones, waving a red and black flag and telling the crowd that they should sack business places and dynamite the Government Palace if that was the only way to put food in their mouths.[42] In "Presidents" Porter wrote, "Felipe Carillo [*sic*], a Maya, was elected governor [1922] by sixty thousand majority, and if he lives to take the chair, we shall see revolutionary theory practiced freely in Yucatán" (CE 412). It is easy to understand Porter's fascination with the handsome, charismatic Carrillo. Imprisoned and exiled for championing the Maya cause as newspaper editor when the henequen barons were in power, he later fought under Zapata, returned to Yucatán to form the Socialist party, and in 1917 organized socialistic Leagues of Resistance, whose membership grew to over 72,000 by 1922. He sided with Obregón against Carranza and in 1920 became a member of the House of Deputies in Mexico City, where Porter first met him, noting that "he made speeches standing on chairs and shaking his fist–in the name of Christ they took our land, in the name of Revolution I give them back again." Porter's fear of his survival was well founded, for he was assassinated along with three of his brothers in the rebellion of 1924. Diego Rivera painted his portrait in a mural, and Porter made him the principal subject of a Mexican novel she never completed.

Carrillo Puerto and other radicals who had supported Obregón's candidacy under dangerous circumstances tested his tolerance with their inflated rhetoric and weakened his position in the conservative press and U.S. State Department. Although Chargé d'affaires Summerlin reported that Obregón "seemed to appreciate the necessity of clearing up all misunderstandings with us and intimated that he wished 'to play the game,'"[43] he was persistently distrustful of his motives. Porter's comment in "Trinity" that "one of the conditions of recognition by the United States is that all radicals holding office in the Cabinet and in the lesser departments must go" (CE 402) reflects Summerlin's complaints, but the real issue remained the land-oil controversy. On March 25, 1921, Seraphic reported his plan to stress, at an oil conference in Galveston, Texas, "unalterable opposition to the confiscatory provisions of Article 27" and insist that "the entire matter be left in the hands of the State Department" (NID 13023 D).

However, Seraphic, unlike Summerlin, praised Obregón's efforts to resolve labor strikes without antagonizing the working classes (NID: 13023 B). Seraphic's estimate was sound. Although Obregón won the confidence of agrarians and labor leaders, he slowed down radical labor and land reforms and assured American businessmen that he would restore "an attitude of fairness to Americans and their interests."[44] It is unsurprising, then, that many American businessmen, despite the scare tactics of the oil companies and State Department, supported him. Governor Hobby of Texas was prominent at Obregón's inauguration and later gave a sumptuous banquet in his honor, declaring, "We do not feel as though we are strangers in a strange land."[45] By the end of 1920, six states had recommended recognition, which oil companies managed to stall until 1923.

History justifies Porter's pessimistic analysis of all the factions that made radical change in Mexico impossible. However, when she asserted that the professional politicians of Mexico "are pathetically unanimous in their belief that big business will save the country" (CE 400), she never placed Obregón in that group nor mentioned the efforts of American businessmen in his favor. Compromised by her close association with the ambitious Morones, she showered him with praise while her radical friends were condemning him for his sellout to the American Federation of Labor.

2. Porter in Mexico, 1920–1921

El Heraldo de México

"The smoke emitted by Popocatepetl is said to have become thick and voluminous creating the impression that the famous volcano inactive from time immemorial is getting ready for an eruption and villagers are getting ready to move." So wrote (September 1, 1920) A. A. Seraphic, indefatigable recorder of petty uprisings and natural disasters. While Popo made headlines, *El Heraldo de México* of November 9 announced: "Miss Katherine Anne Porter, a young writer of much charm and promise, has just arrived in Mexico from New York. She is here to study Mexico, and to gather material for a book and a great pageant-play on the stirring history of this romantic land." The report also stated that she had collaborated with Best Maugard in producing Aztec-Mexican pantomimes for Pavlova (true), had written for the magazine *Asia* (true), and had also been "music and art critic on several of the largest New York newspapers" (untrue). On the following day *El Heraldo* repeated the same information along with the date of her arrival, November 6, and reprinted Babette Deutsch's appreciation of Best Maugard that mentions Porter's pantomimes. Porter had apparently acted as her own press agent. After registering at the Hotel Regis, she sought out Thorberg Haberman, editor of the English-language section of *El Heraldo*, who obtained a job for her on the newspaper.

Thorberg also found an apartment for her at 20 Calle Eliseo, close to the Haberman residence at number 16, within walking distance of downtown Mexico City. The two women had much in common. While living in Greenwich Village in 1917, Thorberg had joined the Socialist party and actively participated in the New Feminist Alliance and in the People's Council for Peace, which opposed U.S. entry into the war.[1] She soon invited Porter to a feminist meeting, conducted by the "beautiful" Elena Torres, "her eyes glittering with that excitement that seems to burn in her all the time." Torres, a native of Yucatán who helped develop Carrillo Puerto's rationalistic schools, was employed by the Mexico City chief of police to work full time as a feminist organizer.[2] Porter guessed that this must be "the first time in the history of woman suffrage they ever had any sort of official help, especially in the beginning of their fight. How civilized these radicals are. They see the just thing and do it with no fuss at all." She became the seventy-ninth member of the Woman's Party and planned to "get the complete history of Elena and her crowd for a future story."

Thorberg also introduced Porter to CROM leader Luis Morones, a "huge bodied, swarthy man, dressed in a gray business suit. Keen eyes, with a glint of impatience in them. Heavy dark face, thick mobile mouth. He talks with restraint, very rapidly, holding his ground in a business argument." In a long newsy letter to her family (December 31, 1920), she wrote of attending the lottery ticket seller's ball in his company, dancing "until two o'clock with one eyed men, and marvelous carbon colored Indians with scarlet blankets, who dance divinely – and one staggers home in the gray of the morning with vine leaves and confetti in one's hair." She also planned to teach dancing in the Institute of Social Sciences and write a revolutionary English textbook for the institute in collaboration with the Habermans.

Robert Haberman, born in Romania and raised on New York's lower East Side, was a lawyer who in 1916 contracted with agents of Military Governor Salvador Alvarado to attract colonists to Yucatán. In 1917 he settled in Yucatán, where he helped Carrillo Puerto write the state's new constitution and develop its rationalistic schools, and in 1918 directed all state cooperatives. When Carranza replaced Alvarado with a new governor to crush Carrillo's socialist programs in early 1920, Haberman fled to Mexico City where he joined CROM, becoming the only foreign member of Grupo Acción, probably through his friendship with Samuel Yúdico, who had been a Casa organizer in Yucatán.[3] (By then Alvarado was owner of *El Heraldo*.) Conservative newspapers often blasted Haberman as a dangerous radical because of his support of Carrillo Puerto while U.S. Intelligence compiled a thick, unfavorable dossier on him, but Porter more accurately described him as "an old-line Socialist" who "has had a marked effect on the attitudes of Morones, Calles and other politicians in combatting the Communists."

On January 16 Porter and Haberman co-authored in the *New York Call* "Striking the Lyric Note in Mexico," which praised the Mexican government's aid to strikers harassed by foreigners celebrating Armistice Day in 1920. In contrast, "One remembers similar demonstrations in America, with police riding down the marchers" and "the militia lounging about, guns in hand, during strikes, in the streets of Denver." Porter wrote the article while Haberman, the *Call*'s Mexican correspondent, supplied background information – their first and last collaboration. She soon came to hate his partisan cynicism – he told her he would like to control all propaganda ("semi-official lies") to the United States and to reward favorable press criticism – but he opened doors for her into the exciting world of Mexican politics. On November 30, she participated in Obregón's inaugural ceremonies, where "deputies and senators in their London-made clothes rose at taking of oath, their pistol butts bumping under their coat tails." Later she attended a party at Chapultepec Castle and drank tea and champagne with the president himself. In her December letter, she told her family she had met "all the holders of government reins" and later expected "to be connected by a small thread to the affair, and now I dabble a bit at times, for it is very amusing."

But what Porter published in *El Heraldo* was not amusing. On November 22 she wrote a scathing review of Vicente Blasco Ibáñez's *Mexico in Revolution,* accusing him of gathering "together the most trivial and scandalous untruths ever put between book covers as a serious account of a nation" to tickle "the ear of the white man who indirectly made it worth his while to write this book." (In three separate notes, Porter later retold the story of Obregón's regret at turning down Blasco Ibáñez's proposition, originally made to Carranza, to write a favorable account of Mexico for fifty thousand pesos.) She had him in mind when she wrote in "The Mexican Trinity" of those who dash in, "gather endless notes and dash out again and three weeks later their expert, definitive opinions are published. Marvelous!" (CE 399). Although he viewed himself as an "impartial observer" of Mexico,[4] Porter charged him with sitting at cafe tables to discover "the truth about Mexico in Revolution" and writing "a delightful, an informing, a profoundly truthful mental autobiography of Blasco Ibáñez." Nevertheless she soon shared his jaundiced view of Mexican politics and drew from his book in "María Concepción."

Porter's review of W. L. George's *Caliban* (December 15) reveals her own "mental autobiography." As if describing herself, she wrote that the novel's heroine has "that deadly female accuracy of vision that cannot be deceived. That would believe if it could, and knows it cannot do so." And she approvingly states that George finds "no remedy for the world's wrongs," for

> his conclusions are rooted in the profound pessimism of a thoughtful man who looks on a world in chaos, and hears the shrieking of a million Messiahs bent on setting it to rights each in his own way. He looks back on a world clamorous with war, and looks forward to a world clamorous with war pursued in many causes into the Glacial Age. And out of it all the solitary victory that any of us can wring from life is the triumph of having achieved birth and the right to our day of sweat and confusion and half attained desires.

Even without the shift to the first person plural, this passage is a personal statement of the reviewer who goes beyond George's ideas to express her own "profound pessimism." The mood sharply differs from the exuberance of Porter's letter to her family, written two weeks later, which began, "If we could have dreamed . . . of how nearly I would achieve plain sight of the things I had set my heart upon, all those years would have been not so seemingly inutile and desolate." Perhaps Porter, anxious to impress her family, exaggerated her prospects in Mexico and hid her true emotional state or had just emerged from one of her depressions. She had complained of her unhappiness to Babette Deutsch, who alludes to it in a letter of November 16.

The pessimism of the George review also informs "The Fiesta of Guadalupe," written two days before. It appeared in *El Heraldo* on December 13, 1920, although Porter dated it 1923 in her *Collected Essays*. Thus it is her earliest literary effort based on her Mexican experience and the earliest recognized work in her canon, antedating "María Concepción" by two years. Since it is based on Porter's visit to the basilica of Guadalupe on December 12, feast day of the Virgin, it was written in the space of several hours to appear in *El Heraldo* the following day, a remarkable accomplishment for a work of such literary merit.[5] The 1920 date also disproves assumptions of critics that the sketch was written after Porter had become disillusioned with Mexico.

The sketch resembles those of Nathaniel Hawthorne, such as "Sights from a Steeple," in which a first-person narrator situates himself in a particular place for a short, continuous period of time – generally the course of a day – and recounts what passes before his eyes, creating in the process a unified emotional impression. In "The Fiesta of Guadalupe," the place is the basilica of Guadalupe on the northern outskirts of Mexico City. The narrator follows Indian pilgrims to the gate of the basilica where she witnesses native dances, crosses the plaza to view pilgrims drinking at the sacred well, enters the basilica where the congregation venerates the sacred tilma on which appears the image of the Virgin, then ascends the hill of Tepeyac where a small chapel contains another image of the Virgin, and finally descends the hill as the light of day begins to wane.

Since the narrator follows the Indian pilgrims, visiting the holy places where they worship, she describes her own journey as a pilgrimage, but it is that of an unbeliever, a dismayed witness of their devotions. The first sentence of the sketch, "I followed a great crowd of tired and burdened pilgrims, bowed under their burdens of potteries and babies and baskets, their clothes dusty and their faces a little strained with long-borne fatigue," firmly establishes the tone. The plodding sentence with its long *o* sounds expresses the narrator's pity for the Indians' "long-borne fatigue," which suggests a permanent state of suffering. They make a joyless pilgrimage to the Virgin of Guadalupe to seek relief that only a miracle can bring. At the sacred well, where people pray "to be delivered of their infirmities and sins," "a girl weeps as she drinks, her chin quivering." In the chapel of Tepeyac, during the recital of a "doleful litany," "a man reached up and rubbed the glass [encasing the image of the Virgin], then gently stroked the head of his sick and pallid wife, who could not get near enough to touch for herself. . . . A mother brought her baby and leaned his little face against the glass for a long time, the tears rolling down her cheeks." Even the exotically costumed Indian dancers in the plaza perform in "utter solemnity": "Not a smile. Not a sound save the mad hysteria of the old bells awakened from their sleep . . ."

The insistent point of the sketch is not just the Indians' suffering, but also their attempt to relieve it through the Virgin of Guadalupe. The narrator tells us, "Great is the power of that faded virgin curving like a new moon in her rigid blue cloak, dim and remote and immobile in her frame above the soaring altar columns." In the chapel on the hill, "a later Virgin, grown accustomed to homage . . . has progressed to the role of Powerful Intercessor. Her eyes are vague and a little indifferent, and she does not glance at the devout adorer . . ." In both descriptions, the virgins' concern for the afflicted is belied by the series of adjectives beginning with "faded" and ending with "indifferent." In the face of such indifference, the Indians have "a terrible reasonless faith," like that of their ancestors, "early victims of Faith who went up (how slowly and heavily, let the old gods themselves tell you) to give up their beating hearts in order that the sun might rise again on their people." The narrator sees "the awful hands of faith, the credulous and worn hands of believers; the humble and beseeching hands of the millions and millions who have only the anodyne of credulity," "anodyne" resembling Marx's "opium." Porter implicitly attacks the Catholic Church as she attacks it explicitly in "The Mexican Trinity," citing its constant alliance with foreigner and landowner to deny the Indians the land stolen from them. A month of Robert Haberman's rationalistic socialism must have influenced her, but it is hard to believe that Porter, reared as a Methodist and officially converted to Catholicism in 1910, could have referred to Christ as a "magnificent Egoist who dreamed that his great heart could redeem from death all the other hearts of earth destined to be born" unless she had rejected Christian dogma and probably religion itself before coming to Mexico.

The sketch also doubts the success of the revolution. As the sun disappears and shadows lengthen, the narrator seems "to walk in a heavy, dolorous dream," not unlike that of the blind children of faith:

> It is not Mary Guadalupe nor her son with his bleeding heart that touches me. It is Juan Diego I remember, and his people I see, kneeling in scattered ranks on the cold floors of their churches, fixing their eyes on mystic, speechless things. It is their ragged hands I see and their wounded hearts that I feel beating under their work-stained clothes like a great volcano under the earth and I think to myself, hopefully, that men do not dream forever.

The image of hearts beating like a volcano that might one day erupt seems immensely ironic. It was suggested by Popocatepetl, "that monster belching forth his smoke and thunder," as she described it in her December letter: "The legend has it that when this occurs, Mexico is about to change dominion. I wonder." Well she might since the new government in which she expected to participate was in place after ten bloody years of war. Yet in the last paragraph of "The Fiesta of Guadalupe," the narrator hopes for a revolution because the misery of the Indians makes it seem to her that it has not taken place.

Porter's description of the fiesta sharply contrasts with *El Heraldo*'s front-page report of the "sumptuous religious ceremonies, decorations in all the streets and churches, and typical dances with rare costumes." During mass celebrated by the archbishop, "a Franciscan priest gave the sermon, recalling the gifts and graces that the patroness of Mexico had showered on her children," a sermon Porter would have found bitterly ironic had she understood Spanish. The report describes "typical" activities of the day: "Stands sold refreshments, typical breads and sweets. More than 20,000 persons filled the streets and the Hill of Tepeyac, enjoying the day in the open air and eating in the shade of the trees of the area," with "somersaults, cock fights and legal games" in the afternoon.

One wonders whether the reporter of *El Heraldo* and Porter witnessed the same fiesta. He does not mention the "long-borne fatigue" of Indian pilgrims. In fact, "Indian," "poverty," and "suffering" never appear. But Porter, newly arrived and pessimistically inclined, was so overwhelmed by the bowed and burdened Indians she could see little else. From "The Fiesta of Guadalupe" in 1920 to "Hacienda," based on experiences of 1931, the Indians' condition was a constant preoccupation. She warmly admired their art but, except for "Xochimilco" and "María Concepción," saw them as eternal victims. In "The Mexican Trinity," she described them as "this inert and slow-breathing mass, these lost people who move in the oblivion of sleepwalkers under their incredible burdens; these silent and reproachful figures in rags, bowed face to face with the earth" (CE 401–402), precisely the same images as in "The Fiesta of Guadalupe," including that of the Indians living "in a deathly dream." In "Hacienda," the image reappears: " . . . all over Mexico the Indians would drink the corpse-like liquor" (pulque) and "swallow forgetfulness" (168). Pulque *and* religion contribute to their somnambulism: "Both are anodynes: pulque and the merciful goodness of María Santísima. The Indians drink pulque and call upon the Mother of God."[6] "Anodynes" recalls the image of "The Fiesta of Guadalupe" ten years before.

In "The Mexican Trinity" Porter laments that "there is no conscience crying through the literature of the country," no "literature of revolt" (CE 401). "The Fiesta of Guadalupe" almost qualifies in that it exposes an intolerable condition that cries for change, but the addition of "hopefully" in the last line of the sketch doesn't convince us that men won't "live in a deathly dream forever."

"The Fiesta of Guadalupe" and her review of George's novel, written within two days of each other, reveal a "mental autobiography" of Katherine Anne Porter in her first days in Mexico City. She did not create a tissue of malicious distortions of Mexico for the delectation of an anticipated audience, as she accused Blasco Ibáñez of doing, but did reveal her pessimistic cast of mind before entering Mexico. The hitherto unknown pages of *El Heraldo* force us to reevaluate, not just the sequence of events that changed her attitude toward Mexico, but the very nature of her psychology. Like George's heroine, she had "that deadly female accuracy of vision that cannot be deceived," at least not for long, and "would believe if it could, and knows" sooner or later "it cannot do so." The Indians at Guadalupe justified her pessimism. Although the Indians of Xochimilco inspired her with hope, she always returned to her original view of the individual's unhappy prospects in this life.

On December 14 Porter became editor of the English-language section of *El Heraldo,* changing the name of her column from "Social Notes" to "Talk of the Town": "Being feminine, our mind makes itself up brand-new every hour or so, and though it keeps life from being dull, it also complicates things a trifle now and again." Through her column she raised funds for an orphanage and a free school with clinic and child-care facilities for the poor. She visited the school and admired its attempt to assist working mothers who "are burdened in their struggle for existence." She also urged the American community to sign a petition to the governor of New York to commute the death sentence of two Mexican nationals convicted of murder in New York City. Although the fairness of their trials was at issue, Porter argued that "capital punishment, for any reason, is an abominable thing." Among the twenty-one signers were Porter, the Habermans, and Mr. and Mrs. Fortmayer. Mr. Fortmayer listed by Military Intelligence as a "notorious radical" who attempted to smuggle arms into Yucatán while living in Mérida (MID 10058-0-6). After the governor ordered new trials, Porter poked fun at those who refused to sign the petition, reporting that one woman, "well known for her independence and freedom," gave as excuse "I will have to ask my husband," impelling "a hearer to remark that while Adam certainly hid behind the skirts of Eve, Eve had been hiding in Adam's vest pocket ever since."

On December 17 Porter wrote an account of the funeral of General Benjamín Hill, Obregón's nephew and minister of war, who mysteriously died of food poisoning after a banquet. Her report is worth quoting in full:

> Under a brilliant morning sky, clean-swept by chill winds straight from the mountains; with busy people thronging the streets, the vendors of sweets and fruits and toys nagging gently at one's elbow; with three "ships" circling so close above the trees of the Alameda one could see the faces of the pilots; with the air live with the calls of bugles and the rattle of drums, the Minister of War, General Hill, passed yesterday through the streets of the city on his final march, attended by his army.
>
> Life, full and careless and busy and full of curiosity, clamored around the slow moving metallic coffin mounted on the gun carriage. Death, for the most, takes his victories silently and secretly. And all the cacophony of music and drum and clatter of horse's hoofs and shouts of military orders was merely a pall of sound thrown over the immobile calm of that brown box proceeding up the life-filled streets. It sounded, somehow, like a shout of defiance in the face of our sure and inevitable end. But it was only a short dying in the air. Death, being certain of Himself, can afford to be quiet.

When the Pale Rider was the topic, Porter responded with eloquence.

Dwindling from two full pages in early November to a mere quarter-page in December, the English-language section of *El Heraldo* disappeared altogether and without warning on December 25, 1920, but not before giving us our only accurate contemporaneous account of Porter's first weeks in Mexico.

Adventures in Mexico

The other source of Porter's activities of 1920 is her aforementioned letter of December 31, in which she informed her family she had become managing editor of *Magazine of Mexico,* had sipped champagne with the president, attended bullfights and dances, participated in archaeological digs, and on Christmas Day met at the Habermans' Felipe Carrillo Puerto and her "beloved," J. H. Retinger. The whirl of activities continued in 1921. Besides digging at William Niven's archaeological site at Azcapotzalco, she visited the pyramids of Teotihuacán with Manuel Gamio, often visited Xochimilco with her friend Mary Doherty, attended the Pan-American Federation of Labor conference in January, attended land partition ceremonies with Lincoln Steffens in February, edited the March and April issues of *Magazine of Mexico,* took a walking tour with artist Winold Reiss in March, visited J. H. Retinger in the Laredo jail in April, survived the deportation crisis in May, taught dancing in public schools, and climbed Popocatepetl with artist Xavier Guerrero probably in June. Throughout the period she enjoyed Mexican nightlife and attended parties at the U.S. Embassy. Besides editing *Magazine of Mexico,* she completed three Mexican sketches, "The Mexican Trinity," and recorded the revolutionary adventures of both Carrillo Puerto and Roberto Turnbull.

The spirit with which Porter entered many of the above activities and relationships is reflected in her desire to tell her family "a thousand delicious things" about life in Mexico, which "is a continual marvel to the eye, and to the emotions," and the perfect place for romantic adventure. It was "amusing" to participate in the new government, to fly over and take pictures of smoking Popo, to meet Zapata's former companion, Antonio Díaz Soto y Gama, who "rode his mountains with his gang for seven years with a copy of Karl Marx and the Bible in his pocket," but her adventures are related to her endemic unhappiness. In "St. Augustine and the Bullfight" (1952), Porter defined adventure as "something you seek for pleasure . . . for the illusion of being more alive than ordinarily" (CE 92) and is earmarked by "violence of motives, events taking place at top speed, at sustained intensity, under powerful stimulus and a willful seeking for pure sensation" (CE 101). The definition may explain Porter's December account of her top-speed activities. She had sought "pure sensation" to create the "illusion of being more alive," for the adventurer, according to Georg Simmel, attempts to satisfy a psychological need to give life a "momentary splendor," to experience "the intensity and excitement with which [adventure] lets us feel life in just this instant," but such "self-abandonment to the powers and accidents of the world" can delight and also destroy us.[7] Porter's almost manic activities were an attempt to escape states of depression in which she felt less than alive, but the adventures themselves ironically returned her to the very despondency she attempted to escape. The exotic dances at Guadalupe were "a continual marvel to the eyes and to the emotions," but they couldn't hide the Indians' hopeless condition nor Porter's own.

On November 6, 1920, the day of Porter's arrival in Mexico, *El Heraldo* reported that Roberto Turnbull had returned to Mexico to give an exhibition of his films about Mexico, among which was "a moving picture of the excavating going on at Azcapotzalco under the direction of Professor William Niven." Porter soon met both Niven and Turnbull. She recorded Turnbull's first-person account of his hair-raising adventures as photographer for the Constitutionalist army in 1913, among them witnessing a battle over a water hole, an episode Porter later used in her uncompleted Mexican novel, *Thieves' Market.*[8]

William Niven fascinated Porter even more than Turnbull. He became the model for Givens in "María Concepción" (1922), the subject of a book review, "Enthusiast and Wildcatter" (1927), and the unnamed "Old Man" in "The Charmed Life" (1942). Soon after her arrival, she started visiting his shop and his excavations at Azcapotzalco. Years later, while rummaging through her "dear hoarded trash heap of the past," she came across a snapshot in "the buried city of Azcapotzalco where I often went to dig for little clay faces and other curiosities. I am sitting on a heap of human skulls, smiling at a little Indian boy-baby wearing a straw hat and a breech clout of flour sacking." She added, "My packing box was a heap of skulls, that I shook death from . . . when I stood up and let the letters fall, that we carry the dust of the dead on our shoe soles into our houses which indeed are built of bones." As Niven had dug bones from the pre-Columbian past, so has Porter, in this Düreresque passage, dug up bones from the graveyard of memory.

Why would memories of Azcapotzalco and William Niven cause her to portray herself as goddess of death? Seemingly "The Charmed Life" offers no clues. The sketch, originally published in *Vogue,* is in the genre of "The Most Unforgettable Character I've Met," the precise words Porter used in her notes. Porter tells us, "I enjoyed the company of the Old Man, his impassioned singleness of purpose, his fervid opinions on his one topic of conversation [the Chinese origins of Mexican culture], and the curiously appealing unhumanness of his existence. He was the only person I ever saw who really seemed as independent and carefree as a bird on a bough." Because her own "life was full of foolish and unnecessary complications," she "envied him his wholeness," as he rode "his hobby-horse in triumph to the grave" (CE 427). Porter sharply focused on the Old Man's single-minded passion, but at considerable expense to Niven's complex character and to truth in general. She claims that the Old Man was "nearly eighty" when she met him, that he had five sons because, he said, his wife "was just too proud to have anything but boys," and that she refused to come to Mexico. However, in 1920, he was seventy years old, he had eight sons and one daughter, most of whom were born in Mexico, and his wife was living in Tampico, where her oldest son worked. Increasing his age and isolating him so completely from his family, Porter can better make the claim that, in his self-absorbed pursuits over a very long life, he "was completely free of family ties and not missing them, a happy, devoted man who had known his own mind, had got what he wanted in life, and was satisfied with it" (CE 427–428). In contrast, Porter was never free of family ties, did not know her own mind, could not devote her whole attention to art, and was not happy. Although she clearly suggests a serious flaw in the Old Man's "unhumanness," there were times she wished she could pay the price for such perceived simplicity and single-minded devotion to profession.

The real William Niven, however, had led a much more exciting life than Porter suggests. A professional mineralogist, he arrived in Mexico in the early 1880s and prospected for gold in the state of Guerrero, but his interest turned to archaeology when he discovered the prehistoric ruins of Omitlan near Chilpancingo. Porter pictures a harmless man who never carried a gun, but Niven's diaries tell a different story. In 1901 he and his workers helped government forces in Guerrero put down a rebellion, and he bragged of his expert training in the use of firearms in his native Scotland. In 1911 he was sentenced to be hanged by a rebel force in Morelos, but was freed through the intercession of the U.S. Embassy.[9]

However, when Porter wrote that the Old Man "bore a charmed life, nothing would ever happen to him" (CE 430), she was not referring to the incident of 1911 but to a failed plot to overthrow the government that supposedly had occurred three months earlier. After spending a long afternoon reading his letters from "his international big bugs," she learned that "hair *can* rise and blood *can* run cold. There was enough political dynamite in those casually written letters to have blown sky-high any number of important diplomatic and financial negotiations then pending between powerful governments." Assured that he had not shown the letters to anyone else, she advised him to "Get rid of them. Don't even be caught dead with them" (CE 429), but when he refused, she dropped the subject. Porter's notes to the sketch harp on the letters:

> A business man wrote cheerfully that a Mexican rebel general was being furnished with money and guns to raise troops, and they were expected to march against their government on such and such a date. I said suddenly at this, "And they've done (did) it too." I reminded him of a certain revolt which had been suppressed with slaughter of troops and the execution of three generals about a month before and that all the plans for it were given in this letter nearly three months old.

Another version has five generals "shot at dawn, as usual." When she asked, "What about your own skin? How would you explain? This looks as if you were plotting against the government," the Old Man replied, "I know Generals and archbishops and big Oil Men and mine owners and financiers." Another note ends the sketch differently: "And after some years, I had heard that he had died alone and quietly in his sleep in the bare room where he slept. . . . I often wonder what became of all those letters from conniving internationalist politicians, but I imagine his family saw that they were destroyed."

Like the sketch itself, the notes are a blend of fact and fiction. The fact is that since Niven had little concern for revolutionary change, it is unsurprising that he would have friends of like mind. His oldest son, William Niven, Jr., protégé of oilman William Buckley, Sr., and breadwinner of the Niven family, was an official of the Texas Oil Company and, reported *El Heraldo,* arrived in Mexico City from Tampico on the same day as Porter to negotiate an oil contract with the U.S. government. However, the statement that the Old Man died alone in his Mexico City shop is fictional; Niven left Mexico City in 1929 and lived in Texas with his family until his death in 1937. But even as Porter imagined his lonely death, she still wondered whether the family had disposed of the letters, as if it mattered then what their contents were. She was inordinately concerned about them because she had read them probably as early as January 1921, months *before* the Mexican government executed the plotters in June.

Joseph H. Retinger, whom Porter met at the Habermans' on Christmas Day, also became involved in her discovery of Niven's letters. His career as extraordinary adventurer made him the perfect accomplice. He was born in Cracow, Poland, and educated in Paris, where, according to his account, he came to know Ravel, Giraudoux, and Mauriac, among others. While head of the Polish Bureau in London, he became fast friends with Joseph Conrad, later publishing *Conrad and His Contemporaries.* He worked for Polish independence and also consulted with Clemenceau and Northcliffe about his idea of persuading Austria to sign a separate peace to hasten the end of World War I. When he resisted the attempt to repatriate captured Polish soldiers so that they could fight for the Allies, he became persona non grata in France and England and made his way to Spain, then finally to Cuba, where he met and was befriended by Luis Morones, returning from a trip to Europe. He arrived in Mexico in 1919, visited his brother in the United States, and returned to Mexico in 1920. All this Retinger claimed in an uncompleted autobiography and in conversations with John Pomian.[10] However, some of his claims about his activities in Mexico as adviser to Morones are exaggerated or inaccurate.

U.S. Intelligence had a less favorable view of him. Reports state that he was, in 1917, an Austrian agent, friendly to the Japanese. He tried to convince British and French authorities that he was employed by the other. "He exploited to the utmost the advantage of his glib tongue and good manners; boasted of his acquaintance with distinguished persons; and represented himself as a man of influence." His political views were "obscure" and varied with the situation, but "definite evidence" associated him with "the Austrian peace intrigue." In May 1918 he was expelled from France because he proved himself a "menace" by intriguing with the Polish army in France. An order of 1918 was to "arrest this party should he attempt to enter the U.S." But enter it he did in 1920 and made friends with a Lieutenant Colonel Stuart, telling him he was writing a history of the political movements in France during the war. In "financial straits," he was "incapable of earning a living except through his knowledge of political secrets or his writing." "Boastful of his acquaintances with distinguished persons," he would probably trade in Mexico on his casual acquaintances in the United States (MID 812.00/24877, 28641).

The prediction was accurate. Retinger introduced himself to Summerlin, telling him he was attached to the Polish Mission in Washington and had come to Mexico to recover his health. According to Summerlin, Retinger, claiming friendship with Colonel Stuart, "got off on Bolshevism and Socialism in Mexico. I am a little suspicious of the gent."[11] In his memoirs, Retinger states that Summerlin had "a second-rate intelligence," disliked Mexicans, and "favored the 'Big Stick' policy," adding, "I felt in him a violent antipathy toward me, which was later translated into action" (55).

When Porter and Retinger met, it was collaboration at first sight. She would help him with his biography of Luis Morones and do other odd jobs for CROM while he would fascinate her, for a time, with his old-world sophistication, his stories of Polish counts, Paris artists, Joseph Conrad, and Jane Anderson, a beautiful American writer he had become infatuated with in England and whom Porter had later met in Denver.[12] He represented to Porter "Europe" in all its Jamesian connotations. In her notes she credited him with thoroughly educating her in international politics, but later described him as "an Austrian Pole much given to international intrigue" and "a complex and fascinating liar," confirming U.S. intelligence reports.

In January, Mary Louis Doherty joined Porter and Retinger. A social worker on Staten Island, she met journalist Agnes Smedley, Thorberg Haberman's former sister-in-law and later apologist for Red China, who persuaded her to go to Mexico. Upon her arrival, Doherty stayed at the Habermans' and remained there until August, briefly losing her bed to the legendary labor agitator Mother Jones.[13] It was there that Samuel Yúdico came to entertain her with his guitar, inspiring Porter to create the scene between Laura and Braggioni in "Flowering Judas." Doherty became the second gringa to work for CROM and also taught Indian children twice a week in Xochimilco, just south of Mexico City. She was less self-centered and ambitious than Porter, more consistently committed to Mexico's social progress, and, above all, more willing to serve in whatever capacity. For that last quality, Porter ridiculed her in her notes, calling her "a kind of virgin office wife," "the hanger-on and born gooseberry" because she would keep Retinger company in a hotel lobby until the party he was to meet appeared, at which point he would dismiss her. Doherty, on the other hand, deferred to her more talented friend, even rescuing pieces of writing Porter had crumpled up and thrown into the wastepaper basket. For her, life in Mexico was a delight, as a 1921 letter to her sister indicates: "We passear every day in Chapultepec Park in a coché–those nice old family coaches with either one nice, sleek fat horse or 2 smaller ones—with their nice clank, clank on the pavement. To-day being Sunday everyone passears from 12 to 2 all in their best—you get in the procession & the cars barely move along–up one line & down another–much bowing etc. You see everyone from Obregon down & since most of the people we know are gov't officials & they all come out in their cars–it is great fun." [14]

It was also great fun to attend the annual convention of the Pan-American Federation of Labor in early January and have her picture taken with all the delegates and guests, among them Calles, Morones, Gompers, Carrillo Puerto, the Habermans, and Porter. It must also have been fun for Porter, who was invited by the Habermans to a social gathering, where she eventually fell asleep at the feet of one of the U.S. labor delegates. She was among those who saw Gompers off at the train station, giving him a farewell kiss.

While radicals attacked Gompers's domination of the convention, he left Mexico, satisfied that it had been a success. Although he lamented the "emotional side" of the Latin American mind that "has developed . . . a philosophical background redolent of socialism, syndicalism and their various allies," he was gratified that the Mexican labor movement had developed along trade union lines "more identical with those of the American Federation of Labor" and gave his stamp of approval to the Obregón regime. [15] In sympathy as she was with radical idealists, Porter never criticized at the time Morones's close ties to the American Federation of Labor, which she later called a gang of thugs. In "Flowering Judas," she would dramatize Laura's impossible choice between inoperative idealism and corrupt pragmatism.

Perhaps Retinger, with his understandably strong anti-Russian bias, had temporarily cooled Porter's radical ardor. He was among Morones's party that had traveled to the border to greet Gompers just before the convention (although Randolph Robertson, the U.S. consul at Nuevo Laredo, prevented them from entering the United States, thereby prompting a convention resolution to protest his action). In 1922 Porter wrote that Retinger "is a reactionary, and has succeeded in modifying many of Morones' revolutionary views," advising him against "any sort of alliance between Russia and Mexico, especially an alliance of workers." But, according to Mary Doherty, in the first months of 1921, they frequently met at the famous Café Colón on the Paseo de la Reforma. Although Porter, in her notes, referred to herself as his mistress, all indications are that their relation was more intellectual than sexual.

Soon after her arrival, Porter wrote that she had completed a "cartoon" of Adolfo Best Maugard. Although nothing came of creating ballet pantomimes with him, she continued to see him frequently, sometimes refusing to go out with Doherty because she was waiting for him to drop by. He introduced her to his brother-in-law, artist Jorge Enciso, director of the National Museum. As she insisted in interviews years later, she was familiar with other Mexican artists, Miguel Covarrubias and Xavier Guerrero among them, before Diego Rivera's return from Europe in late 1921. In 1978 Porter told me that she had been very fond of Guerrero and wished she had accepted his offer of marriage, confirming Doherty's report of their close relationship.

Porter told Hank Lopez of her fondness for Felipe Carrillo Puerto, recounting an incident that occurred while they were rowing in the shallow lagoon in Chapultepec Park. When their boat sprang a leak, she managed to jump to the bank, but he sank up to his neck. After changing clothes, they danced that night at their favorite Salón Mexico, where he taught her the latest dance steps, including the "low-bending tango."[16] The boating accident seems not worth repeating, but Porter dramatized it in her notes three times; in one version Carrillo jokingly accuses her of trying to drown him. Possibly she wanted to turn it into an ominous forecast of his untimely death in 1924. Among her papers is a photograph of Carrillo, inscribed, "To my dear friend, Catarina, from Felipe," along with Trinidad's "story to Felipe as he repeats it to me." Unlike the raw transcription of Turnbull's account, this story is in fictional form with several scenes rewritten. In it the narrator tells of picking up in Mexico City and falling in love with Trinidad, who tells him she was taken from a convent in Yucatán by the leader of a rebel band, who then passed her around among his troops. When she later learns that the narrator sought out and killed the rebel, she has a mass said for the rebel's soul and eventually leaves the narrator, who is befuddled by her mysterious behavior. It is Porter's first story of an exploited young woman, whom her servants call La Niña.

Magazine of Mexico

Although her Mexican labor friends strongly condemned U.S. policy toward Mexico, Porter was in frequent contact with the American Embassy. In her notes she mentioned conversations with chargé d'affaires George Summerlin and described to Ernestine Evans (June 12, 1949) a gown she used to wear to Embassy parties. Through Robert Haberman we have a broader view of activities she never mentioned in interviews.

On July 26, 1921, Haberman met with the special assistant to the U.S. attorney general to answer such questions that he "might care to ask." He cared to ask about Agnes Smedley (imprisoned in 1918 for aiding Indian nationals in their struggle against British rule[17]). Haberman "admitted" that she was his sister-in-law, but objected to libelous newspaper attacks on him just because Hindus had used his name without his knowledge to order gun shipments to India. The special assistant wrote, "In brief, Haberman would lead one to believe that he has been the butt, as well as the target of all forces antagonistic to his interests and that they have deliberately engaged in a campaign of vilification against him," an appraisal not unlike that of Porter, who referred in her notes to his "romantic yarns of personal treason." After denying charges that Lincoln Steffens had negotiated a secret treaty between Russia and Mexico and confirming Obregón's intolerance of "any pernicious communist activities" and determination to deport all foreign agitators, Haberman told the special assistant the following:

> A MISS KATHERINE ANNE PORTER, a writer who has been in Mexico for a year and who is stated to have been born in Texas, is on intimate terms with many of the leading radicals in Mexico, as well as a few of the Mexican officials. She is a writer of the magazine "Asia." She is also intimate with one RETINGER who Haberman stated is well supplied with funds. Retinger was believed to be in the German secret service during the period of the war and is now suspected of activities of a similar nature. Miss Porter is also on intimate terms with COLONEL MILLER, the representative of the Military Intelligence Division in Mexico City, and according to Haberman receives a great deal of inside information from Colonel Miller, as that individual is stated to be addicted to strong drink and to give many parties in which the fair sex participate. . . . Haberman emphasized the activities of RETINGER, particularly, as he believed he should be thoroughly watched. (MID 10058-0-79, 91)

Haberman's slander of Retinger, his arch-rival for the favor of Morones, casts doubt on his portrait of Porter as Mata Hari, but the special assistant took Haberman's revelation seriously. Miller was transferred to another post in September (MID 2345-645-2), and Porter's 1922 visit to Mexico was duly recorded (MID 10058-0-106). The special assistant signed himself "J. E. Hoover."

The chief of Military Intelligence soon wrote to Colonel Miller, who replied, "The subject of this letter is personally known to the writer. The young woman in question is an attractive, clever and cultured young woman of about 35. To all appearances she is a lady born and bred." He then identified her as the author of *My Chinese Marriage,* stated that she "associated with radicals," especially with Natasha Michaelova (who was deported from Mexico with her friend, Charles Francis Phillips), and that she occasionally "appeared at social functions by the American colony in Mexico City." Miller thought it "a fair inference" that Porter had "been on intimate terms with a few of the Mexican officials" and "in this connection" mentioned Luis Morones. He closed with a fairly lengthy discussion of Porter's editorship of *Magazine of Mexico,* about which little was previously known.

Besides giving the earliest record of Porter's sexual activities, Miller sheds light on *My Chinese Marriage.* While in New York, Porter contracted to record the story of Mae Franking, an American who had married a wealthy Chinese student and completely adapted to his traditional way of life in China. Porter finished the project in Mexico, the story appearing serially in *Asia* (June to

September 1921) and later that year in book form. She later claimed that it was
"a mere setting down of someone else's story, nothing of my own,"[18] and
scribbled in a copy of the book at the University of Maryland that she wrote it
"from the dictated words of Mae Tiam Franking." Miller's version of author-
ship is more accurate: "She wrote under this unusual nom-de-plume [M.T.F.]
because the story is a true account of an actual marriage . . . written as though
told by the wife herself. Naturally Miss Porter could not write under the name
of the protagonist of the story, a real character, and, in order to present the
story in a thoroughly realistic manner, the author could not well write under
her own name."

This complex explanation suggests more than mere ghostwriting. Some
passages reveal how Porter's experiences in Mexico worked their way into the
writing of the story. For example, Porter writes of "tile-roofed houses surrounded by arched verandas" and of "trees in winter foliage, not the brilliant
green of summer, but the sage-green and pale tan of November" through
which "the houses shone in dull blue and coral pink and clear gray. Jagged
cacti shot up among the bulbous rocks and everywhere the scarlet poinsettia
set the hills aglow with patches of brilliant color" (*Asia*, August 1921, 718).
Porter arrived in Mexico in November, over a month into the dry season when
the poinsettia, native to Mexico and lands to the south, begins to bloom. The
coincidence of Porter's writing in Mexico the story of another woman's encounter with an "alien" culture–the word appears at regular intervals in the
work–guaranteed Porter's emotional involvement. Substituting "Mexico" for
"China" in the following passage, we have a good idea of her vain hopes about
her adopted land: returning students "come home brimming with hope and
filled with aspirations toward their country's betterment. And gradually they
are forced to acknowledge one enormous fact–that China has been her
glorious, grim old self for too many centuries, her feet are sunk too deeply in
the earth of her ancient traditions to be uprooted by one generation of youth–
or two or three or a hundred" (July 1921, 616).

In her December 1920 letter to her family, Porter wrote that *Magazine of
Mexico* was to appear soon, "backed by a frightful set of rich American bankers
who love oil and silver and coal and gold–love the very sound of those unctuous words, and can think of nothing else by day or by night, drunk or sober."
Thanks to Miller, we know that the magazine's promoter was G. A. Hole, "a
capitalist of Seattle," and the managing director was W. D. Outman of San Antonio. A promotional ad in the March issue states that "Katherine Anne Porter,
who has done some very clever work for 'Asia' and other publications of international reputation, will begin a series of articles on the really interesting
phases of Mexican life." Undoubtedly the series was to constitute a book Porter
was planning to write. In a later note, she listed such topics as Turnbull's story;
Atl; Teotihuacán in three parts; folklore, legends, and superstitions; story of
marihuana; pulque shops; Christmas custom of Posada; potteries of Puebla,
Oaxaca, and Guadalajara; and Covadonga bullfight.

Porter wrote the issue's lead article on Obregón, whose picture appears on the cover. Entitled "The New Man and The New Order," it presents "the high adventure" of Obregón's entry on the national scene, dramatically caught at his inauguration: "A blare of trumpets sounds in the streets. Nearer. A great muffled shout, a sustained mellow roar soaks through the walls of the Camara. Another and milder roar inside, as the people rise to their feet. The clock hands point straight to twelve. The main portal swings back ponderously, and two men in plain dress suits, one wearing a white and green and scarlet ribbon across his chest, enter." Porter will not predict Obregón's success, for there are "plots for prestige, there are plots for political preference, there are plots for graft, great business interests are at stake, international problems of growing importance, and interweaving of selfish, private and governmental problems without end." She even repeats the language of her letter to her family, originally directed, ironically, against the magazine's promoters: "Here are silver and gold, coal and oil – the air is redolent with the sound of these unctuous words. Men mouth them lovingly, and stare at vague and varied horizons." Nevertheless, there is the "unbreathed hope that this nation will take its rightful place in the commonwealth of the world," led by a man "with a detached legal passion for setting disorder to rights." She even hopes that the "capital of the world would come to [Mexico's] aid and capital is the one and only material need of this retarded, stunted and potential giant" – a hope in stark contrast to the pessimism of "The Mexican Trinity," in which she equates oilmen with all foreign exploiters.

The magazine, amply illustrated with full-page photographs as well as three reproductions of Best Maugard's paintings, also contains an article on picturesque Mexico City, assuring potential U.S. tourists and investors that streets are safe, shops display finery for "a finery loving people," restaurants are crowded until late hours, and strawberries are available at the breakfast table ten months of the year, while another article assures the reader that "Mexico is the best field for land operations in the Western hemisphere." An editorial, entitled "KEEP DOWN THE PLOTTING," identifies U.S. border states as "constant headquarters for juntas of various factions" who send arms and ammunition "across the lengthy boundary in shifting streams," making the United States "an accessory before the fact" if it permits its soil to be violated by such activities. Porter probably wrote it, already aware of the contents of the letters written to Niven.

The April issue of *Magazine of Mexico* was the last because requested subsidies from the Mexican government were not forthcoming. This we know from Colonel Miller, on whom we also have to rely concerning its contents since a copy of it has not surfaced – a pity since Porter claimed she wrote the whole issue. The cover features a portrait of Luis Morones while Porter's lead article especially praises him for his efficient management of the munitions factories, about which Miller disagreed. The issue also contains "In a Mexican Patio," "an unusually clever literary effort." Luckily the sketch is among Porter's papers along with a rejection letter from Paul U. Kellogg of *Survey Graphic,* where she tried to republish it in 1924.

"In a Mexican Patio" brilliantly records in rich sensual detail sights and sounds of Porter's guest house on Calle Eliseo to create the character of a Mexican household. Like "The Fiesta of Guadalupe," it observes unity of place and time, recording the events of a day from waking to falling asleep. Upon awakening, the narrator begins to interpret the house's sounds and smells, the slapping of hands meaning that Maria is making tortillas, the splash of water that Manuel is washing the paving stones of the driveway, and the roasting coffee and carbon smoke that Lupe is fanning the blaze in the red-tiled brasero. The point is not just to register first sense impressions but to stress the servants' many activities that begin before daybreak, for they define the character of the house.

As the narrator passes to the dining room, she sees Heraclia hanging bird cages on the outer wall. "Her blue reboso falls back straightly almost to her feet as she stretches up her neck. The black bands of her hair bind her forehead and cheeks in a sleek curve. Her eyes are fixed with curious intensity on her simple task." Here the narrator lovingly establishes a presence most other guests would not notice at all. In the dining room, a little boy brings the narrator her coffee, the "strangled yelp" he gives when it spills on his thumb assuring her that it is hot. As she eats her breakfast, she notices that a "mirror framed in a confusion of carved oak roses and bulbous Cupids over-sophisticated of eye and posture reflects in its ravelled silver three dying annunciation lilies, shrivelled pale ochre at the edges. I think calmly of death as I butter a roll and examine the lilies." Casually and humorously death slips into the sketch.

After breakfast, the narrator decides to visit doña Rosa, the proprietress of the house, to complain about the grieving young coyote temporarily tethered to a drain pipe on the roof. On the way, she observes "pictures of obscure saints, their upturned eyes glazed with highly specialized agonies. A shrine lamp is blood colour before a pallid Virgin gazing into the mysteries of a paper-flower bouquet." As in "The Fiesta of Guadalupe," and other Mexican works, religious artifacts, mockingly unreal, serve as ironic counterpoint to the human activity going on around them. In the next sentence, doña Rosa, sitting "in a vast bed overflowing with puffy quilts riotous with strange blossoms," obscurely evokes the virgin.

The matter of the coyote settled, the narrator notes that the "general air of freshness" of the well-furnished house is due to "the natural industry" of the servants, but at a price to them. Lupe, who brings her ten o'clock chocolate, "is an overworked, distracted woman with three children at her skirts. Life is a tragic business for her" and soon will be for young Consuelo: "She is very beautiful, with finely formed hands and feet. In a decade, she will be like her mother, a seventeen year old girl already haggard, who works with a baby on her arm, wound in her reboso. In two decades she will resemble her grandmother, who cannot be older than forty years. But she has the look of some-

thing agelessly old, that was born old, that could never have been young."
Three generations of females, their aging process frighteningly accelerated, are
graphic witness to the loss of beauty and promise that haunted Porter during
all her stays in Mexico. Social conditions made her perception of mortality
painfully sharper:

> One may have the complete use of a human being here for eight or ten
> pesos a month. They carry water in huge jars to the stone washing tubs,
> where they kneel at their work. They toil up and down endless flights of
> stairs: to the roof to hang linen, down again for another load, crossing
> long courts on hundreds of small errands. If I go to sleep at twelve, it is
> to the sound of their voices on the other side of the wall, still gathering
> together the ends of the day's labour. If I wake at six, they are pattering
> about, their bare feet clumping like pony hoofs.

The point of the opening paragraph is clear. As long as the narrator lives in
this house, she is the guilty beneficiary of the labor of other women.

In the next scene, a small child informs the narrator of the death of her
"Gatito de Oro," the only cat "who required to be loved," but now he is dead,
and the child insists on details: he was "lying twisted, so, with his head
so,—and the ants were at him. His teeth were showing, and he seemed very
angry. But he was not angry—of course not, he was only dead. Pobrecito!" Poor
little one, his love for the narrator is ended. A bit later fifteen-year-old Dolores
enters with the narrator's dinner. She calls her collie "Pobrecita" but calls herself "Yo solita," causing the narrator to think she is in love. And she is. In the
dark of the patio, a young man writes her name and "Yo te amo" in the air with
a lit cigarette: "How practiced are those fingers, turning delicately on a steady
wrist, scrivening in ash-veiled flame upon a wall of air!" But his love may be as
ephemeral as his expression of it or as short-lived as Gatito de Oro.

Then there is doña Rosa's chihuahua, his surface "tinted emerald green" that
a few days before was "painted a watermelon pink" with "a blue ribbon on his
tail," making the narrator think she "had never sufficiently understood the
phrase 'local colour.'" Despite such details, the local color of the sketch is de-
cidedly somber, ending with the narrator's fear of death and unrequited love.
At night she remembers another night when she danced "until the moon went
down." She had listened to a guitar player sing about "love, how it is cruel,
because life devours us, a day at a time, and a dream at a time, until we are
ended utterly." The song affects one of her companions who views the grey
faces of others against the grey sky: "She touched her own face. 'I am a ghost
too!' she cried out in a high shocked voice. Her mouth became a turned down
crescent moon. She began to cry. 'I am a ghost, a ghost! I can never dance
again!" As the narrator attempts to sleep, she hears a woman play Chopin, her
music taking "the place of tears" as if she "weeps in a dream." Identifying with
the woman, the narrator concludes, "In the sunlight one may laugh, and sniff

the winds, but the night is crowded with thoughts darker than the sunless world." The sketch ends on a Hawthornian note. Eight years later, its configuration of deathly and lovelorn images appeared again in "Flowering Judas."

Xochimilco

In one scene of "In a Mexican Patio," the narrator admires Indians from Xochimilco who have come to build a thatched hut on a neighboring roof. "The women are quite nice," with their red and green embroidered blouses and wide skirts wrapped across their hips. So they prove in "Xochimilco," Porter's only unmixed joyous response to Mexico and her third published sketch, based on one of her visits to the village where Mary Doherty taught school.[19]

"Xochimilco" is a sympathetic rendering of the daily activities of the Xochimilcan Indians, viewed from a "canoa" that carries the narrator and her companions through the village's canals. She describes children at play, women bathing in the canals or selling food from their dugouts, and men plying their barges filled with vegetables grown in the "chinampas" (small islands) around which the canals flow. In an earlier version of the sketch, "The Children of Xochitl," Porter establishes a mythic basis for the reader's sympathetic response. Accompanied by a village patriarch, she and her friends visit a roofless church protected by the Virgin in four manifestations, including that of Guadalupe. Again exhibiting her anti-Christian bias of "The Fiesta of Guadalupe," Porter tells us that "these Indians have suffered the benefits of Christianity to an unreasonable degree," but in Xochimilco it doesn't matter because the guide is at heart a "pagan" who sings the praises of Xochitl, the patroness of this church, "more abundant with her favors than all the others together." He expands: "Xochitl sends rain. Xochitl makes the crops grow – the maguey and the maize and the sweet fruits and the pumpkins. Xochitl feeds us!" The narrator informs us that "Xochitl is the legendary Aztec goddess of the earth, of fruit, of abundance, who discovered pulque – especially the strawberry flavored kind! – and also made known the many other uses of the maguey plant, by which the Indians can live almost entirely." Like the guide, she prefers Xochitl to her Christian counterparts: "In a race where women sowed and reaped, wove and spun and cooked and brewed, it was natural that a goddess should be fruitful and strong. We looked with intense sympathy and interest at the decaying and alien stronghold where Xochitl had set her powerful foot, there to compete with usurping gods in caring for her strayed family."

The Indians of Xochimilco are indeed the children of Xochitl, for "they get all material for their needs from the earth; vegetables and flowers from the chinampas are their wares offered to the outer world." They in turn spring from Mother Earth like vegetables and flowers: "They seem a natural and gracious part of the earth they live in such close communion with, entirely removed from contact with the artificial world." One Indian is an "independent human being, vending his small wares, under a kindly sky, in company with the poplars," while another "lives as a tree lives, rooted in earth, drinking in light and air." The "artificial world" creates neurotics, but one of the food vendors serves her customers "without haste or nervousness in competent silence. Her face will be smooth and untroubled, her voice not edged. Primitive woman cooks the greater part of her time; she has made of it, if not a fine art, then a most exact craft. There are no neurotics among them." A beautiful girl reveals in her motions a "trance-like quality . . . as if she had never awakened from the prenatal dream." One of the narrator's companions, "tormented with neuroses," admires the girl's "inner repose," speculating that she "should live for a century." She shares the immortality of Xochitl, whom the guide describes as "saint of the body."

Porter eliminated all references to Xochitl in her published version, perhaps because her anti-Christian bias was not appropriate for the readers of the *Christian Science Monitor* or because she rejected the pure fiction of her guide preaching Xochitl's virtues. A fragmentary note indicates that the "guide" was an old man "warmly drunk," who whispered to Retinger, "If you will come again, without your sister, I will present to you the very prettiest girl in Xochimilco." Several years later, Porter wrote, "I have not met one [Indian] who recognized the names of their ancient gods, or realized that there was a time when their race was not Catholicised" and "ruled by their old and terrible superstitions of God and Hell." Porter chose Xochitl—who was not an ancient goddess but a seventeenth-century literary invention later popularized in art—because she is "the goddess of the flowers and fruit" while "Xochimilco means in Aztec 'the place of the flower.'"

Although Xochitl doesn't appear in "Xochimilco," Porter envisions the Indian town as an "Island of the Blest," a term used in *My Chinese Marriage* to describe a transported Mexican landscape, or an Eden whose prelapsarian dwellers enjoy a perfect harmony with beneficent nature. She overidealized them as if to escape the reality she experienced elsewhere in Mexico. Whereas the Indians of Calle Eliseo are trapped in a daily round of servitude, a Xochimilcan could "be a servant in a rich house, but depend on it, he will not." The women of Eliseo seem old at birth, but the women of Xochimilco seem immortal. The Xochimilcans do not suffer from neuroses although, in a 1931 note, Porter described the Indian as a "neurotic creature," "warped and twisted in a thousand ways, worn down by his burdens" and "inhibited and prohibited at every turn by his inner compulsions and the outer forces pressing slowly, interminably upon him." Porter does "not presume to feel pity" for the Indians of Xochimilco, although she felt nothing but pity for the suffering, burdened Indians at Guadalupe, some of whom were probably from Xochimilco. Out of her visit to Xochimilco in the spring of 1921, Porter created another kind of "mental autobiography," a wish fulfillment of the perfect world where she could feel whole instead of the "neurotic creature" she felt she was, "warped and twisted in a thousand ways." "Xochimilco" is the first and most complete of the Edens that appear in Porter's fiction. It expresses her hope in Mexico as the promised land, but, juxtaposed with "The Fiesta of Guadalupe," it reveals the oscillation between hope and despair that characterized her entire life.

Porter's notes on artist Winold Reiss, whom she met in the spring of 1921, prove how brief her Edenic vision was and how changeable her moods. Reiss invited her to walk to Tepotzotlán, fifteen miles north of Mexico City. On the way, they viewed "the silent mottled fields of maguey" spreading towards the mountains and "encroaching on the small village gardens at our backs. The sky was veiled smoothly from edge to edge with gray mist, and all the shadows were ghostly." When Porter blurted out, "It is so black," Reiss "turned puzzled painter's eyes" on her. "Black? in this? I think I never [saw] so much depth of color, layer upon layer—it is almost shocking to the eye," to which Porter responded, "I meant the mood." Both tried to see "from the other's point of view," but Porter gave up the effort: "'It is black,' I decided, 'because there is so much death in it.'" Reiss responded that in "the collision of life and death," death always came out "a bad second." Temperamentally the two artists were poles apart; for Porter, death seldom came out a bad second, no matter how much she wished otherwise.

The Plot

All of Porter's experiences described above, including her discovery of Niven's letters, occurred in late 1920 and early 1921. Retinger, who accompanied her on at least one visit to Xochimilco, mysteriously left Mexico City in late February. Since his departure is related to the letters, it is necessary to return to their contents.

Among Porter's papers is a letter to Niven from a man named Bryan:

> I am glad to hear of your good business during the inauguration. I suppose it won't be long now until there will be another inauguration. Since Obregon's side partner, Hill, is gone, it is only natural to suppose that the very sudden and severe illness of Obregon and death of Hill were *not* entirely accidents and that the illness of Obregon must be the last.
>
> In spite of the million dollars that have been spent in favorable propaganda for Obregon here in the States, there is not much confidence felt here in his ability to bring order to Mexico. *This is not the way it is going to happen.*
>
> You have been told just what is going to happen. There won't be any monkeying with conditions there after March 1st. That is a cinch. I've been here nearly two weeks and am doing something. Two of my closest friends will be secretary and assistant secretary of war, and I have their assurance that they will give me what I want.

> Business conditions are fierce here. It's harder to get money here for
> investment than it is to find an honest man in Mexico.

The original letter was written in late December after the mysterious death of
General Hill, whose funeral Porter covered in *El Heraldo*. More important, it is
written on Niven's own stationery in Porter's distinctive scrawl. She copied it
and other letters to expose a plot to overthrow Obregón before it took place
and revealed their contents to Paul Hanna, who left Mexico City in February
1921. A passage from his last *Nation* article on Mexico (April 27) proves what
Porter had done:

> Rumors of such inspired mischief fill the days and nights of an in-
> quiring visitor to Mexico City. I have read extracts from letters written to
> a friend in the Mexican capital by a gentleman who was travelling on the
> special car of President-elect Harding during December and January last.
> This gentleman referred to a forthcoming complete reorganization of the
> Mexican Government, by force of arms, assisted or entirely accomplished
> by the United States. . . . this letter writer stated that under the Harding
> Administration "the Secretary and Assistant Secretary of War will both
> be friends of mine, and I know exactly what they will do." Was this
> private correspondent telling the truth or merely painting his own im-
> portance to a distant friend? I don't know. . . . Another statement . . .
> explained that several millions of dollars had recently been expended in
> the United States to create opinion favorable to the Obregón Administra-
> tion. But all in vain, he added; the problem would not be adjusted by
> friendly negotiation: "You have been told how it will be done, and it will
> happen just that way." (615)

Uncertain whether Bryan was blustering, Hanna, without naming names,
exposed the contents of Porter's copy of the letter to Niven before the plot went
into effect. Porter must have shown him copies of other letters as well. A typed
note, on which she had later scribbled "1921–Notes from letters to Niven,"
states that Bryan met Pablo González in Laredo and accompanied him to
Washington, where he introduced him to Albert Fall and others; at the meeting, González promised church liberty and elimination of Article 27; Bryan
then went to Mexico with messages from González to General Sidronio Méndez, who sent word back that 4,500 troops scattered around Villa Guadalupe
were ready for action "in case Summerlin and Obregon failed to come to
terms." The note closes, "Sidronio Méndez, apparently serving Obregon, is the
general of these plans, confidante of González."

There is solid evidence that Bryan was not blustering. In 1919 Albert B. Fall
officially recommended intervention as a last resort against the Carranza regime while encouraging Félix Díaz, the incompetent nephew of Don Porfirio,
to form an alliance with other dissident generals to overthrow Carranza.

Charles Hunt, a close associate of Fall, claimed that in 1921 oil companies encouraged González and others to provoke an incident in Tampico that would precipitate intervention.[20] U.S. Intelligence reported that González had amassed arms in Texas and planned to enter Mexico in May 1921. Sidronio Méndez, who had risen from colonel to brigadier general in González's army, had been commander of the plaza in 1920. Suspected of disloyalty to Obregón, he was moved out of harm's way as consul in Chicago, where González sought him out (MID 8321 EO; 10640-2177). González wrote his brother that Méndez would aid him in his plan, "but it must be without compromising himself." A translation of his letter is among Fall's papers along with González's 1921 "Plan of National Reconstruction," in which the election of Obregón is pronounced void and González is declared "Supreme Chief of the Reconstruction Movement."[21] Among the sixteen provisions of the plan, the only one scored in the margin, presumably by Fall, concerns Article 27.

Niven's informant, retired major Harry S. Bryan, had been a resident of Mexico City, where he manufactured raincoats. In a letter of June 21, 1921, to Undersecretary of State Henry P. Fletcher, Randolph Robertson, U.S. consul of Nuevo Laredo – the same man whom Porter was asked to contact on her way to Mexico and whom Gompers criticized for refusing Luis Morones entry into the United States – reported that Bryan and González visited him "some weeks past" to tell him they were to retain an attorney to represent González in Washington "should the General decide to cross the Rio Grande and 'start something.'" Alfredo Robles Domínguez, a presidential candidate in 1920, also reported to Robertson that he had consulted with Fall, who suggested that if all factions unfriendly to Obregón should unite and cross the border, then the United States would recognize their belligerency, a development that sent Bryan to Washington to consult with his friends. The consul also reported that William Buckley, Sr., was acting as go-between for Robles and Fall (SD 812.00/25118). Robertson's report justifies the panic that made Porter's hair rise and blood run cold when she first read Niven's letters.

Porter's discovery must have appealed to Retinger's conspiratorial nature, although what exactly Porter told him is unclear from the eight brief fragments scattered among her papers that connect him to the letters. The briefest reads, "Retinger – the story of his imprisonment; my getting of the letters, our story," while a fuller account reads, "His way of getting the letters which involved Lord Beaverbrook, Archbishop Burke of Canada, Harry Bryan, General Wood, Lucio Blanco, and who else? The revolution against Obregon for the fifteenth of May. His betrayal of Niven and me – 'What's the life of one old man against a world of cause?'" And another: "A prominent American citizen, a friend of a very prominent American citizen, wrote a lot of foolish letters to a Mexican counter-revolutionist in sympathy with the American Intervention. Counting on the aid of L. B. [Lucio Blanco], a bandit with a few hundred followers, they plan counter-revolutionary uprising for about May 15. Letters intercepted, copied, handed over to Government officials." And a fourth version: "'You are perfect,' he would say, 'But perfect, you never make a mistake,' and she knew then that he would want an impossible thing of her–to steal Paul's letters, or go to the Munitions and beg money for him."

These versions raise more questions than they answer. Did Niven permit Porter to copy the letters or to read them in the first place, especially since in 1918 Carranza officials raided his shop in search of a letter of safe conduct from Zapata? Did Retinger betray Porter by informing government officials of the letters or did she show him the letters so that he would inform? What the four versions do show is her attempt to blame Retinger for her actions. Her "getting of the letters" in the first version becomes in the second his "way of getting the documents," resulting in his betrayal of her and Niven. In the third version she hides behind the impersonal passive voice of the last sentence. The fourth version is, of course, a fictional rendering of her experience that obscures her responsibility for stealing–that is, copying the letters. Two versions give the date of the uprising as May 15, Porter's birthdate, as if Pablo González had her in mind when he created the plot. Another note states that he and others were designing "to make a revolution coincident with the flower fiesta," celebrated on May 15. For obscure reasons, Retinger made a trip to the United States in February. Porter's notes frequently link his journey to the letters, implying a causal rather than merely chronological connection. For instance, her mention of his "betrayal of Niven and me," quoted above, is followed by "His grand preparation for a secret diplomatic journey of investigation to Washington. (His pretext, buying saddles for Morones, who was head of munitions and army supplies in general.)" This whole fragment is apparently a reworking of the chain of events for fictional purposes, but Retinger's adventurous past and love of intrigue make it plausible that he planned a trip to Washington to thwart González's plot without telling anyone in Mexico of his intentions. On February 28 he was denied a visa in Nuevo Laredo (SD 811.111). On April 2, 1921, Hanna informed Porter of Retinger's latest adventure. When he and Retinger met in San Antonio on March 3 to take a train to Washington, Retinger told him he had had trouble with the consul in Nuevo Laredo, who kept his Polish passport. The consul, Randolph Robertson again, turned up on the same train and had Retinger arrested in St. Louis for illegal entry. (In his report to Military Intelligence [PF10471], Robertson remembered that Retinger was Morones's interpreter when the party requested entry into the United States to greet Gompers *and* to buy saddles.) Robertson, according to Hanna, resented the fact that Morones, "a Bolshevik," had signed all of Retinger's credentials as translator. Although State Department officials in Washington told Hanna that Retinger's transgression was merely technical, showing him his dossier in which he was accused of trying to contact the *New Republic*, Retinger was still not set free. Hanna also referred to his *Nation* articles on Mexico, adding, "I am convinced that the interventionists mean to have their way. Of course I should like to know what you have learned since you gave us that glimpse of portentous private correspondence. The interventionist plot thickens fast here." The "us" may include Retinger.

Retinger's illegal entry may have been a mere technicality, but he languished in wretched jails in Houston and Laredo for over four months. When he wired for bail money, Porter borrowed four hundred dollars from, of all people, Summerlin, a fact recorded by Colonel Miller and admitted by Porter many years later. But each time money was raised, U.S. Immigration officials increased the bail. After Morones failed to persuade Lincoln Steffens to stop at Laredo on his way back to the States, he sent Porter in April, but she could do nothing and later complained of Retinger's "plain and fancy lying all the way through." In a draft of a letter to Hanna, she wrote that Retinger "has dramatized himself and his adventures until life is now only a fog in the midst of which he moves fevered with visions." She thought the situation "entertaining to watch at a distance," but resented having to take part in it, "even remotely." Retinger often wrote from his cell, grumbling about his plight. A Porter note reads, "My friend R., who is in prison in Laredo (. . . for various political complicities, a born mischief maker and genius of intrigue) writes that his cell is very hot, the place is full of cockroaches, and the food abominable. He would be pained to know how very little I care." After visiting him, she wrote, "Let me know, please, what has happened since I left you. I am an indefatigable taker of notes these days, and the idea of publishing the incident, with all its rich and racy detail, is growing on me."

February to June

Porter responded callously to Retinger out of pique at his refusal to confide in her and embarrassment that Hanna's information about him reflected on her, but, most of all, out of preoccupation with her own troubles. Retinger's case, she wrote Hanna, "is a small part of our troubles here—we are having deportations, riots, arrests . . . " Her letter was a rehearsal for her essay "The Mexican Trinity," which begins:

> Uneasiness grows here daily. We are having sudden deportations of foreign agitators, street riots and parades of workers carrying red flags. Plots thicken, thin, disintegrate in the space of thirty-six hours. A general was executed today for counterrevolutionary activities. There is fevered discussion in the newspapers as to the best means of stamping out Bolshevism, which is the inclusive term of all forms of radical work. Battles occur almost daily between Catholics and Socialists in many parts of the Republic: Morelia, Yucatán, Campeche, Jalisco. In brief, a clamor of petty dissension almost drowns the complicated debate between Mexico and the United States. (CE 399)

The essay attempts to give an objective view of Mexico's political climate of mid-1921 but is also veiled autobiography, the enumerated events contributing to Porter's own growing "uneasiness." A long note entitled "A Month of Uncertainties," several fragmentary notes, a letter to Retinger in prison, and a recapitulation of events of 1921 published in "Where Presidents Have No Friends" in 1922 also highlight her anxiety. To the events listed in the first paragraph of "The Mexican Trinity" can be added the related mysterious bombings of Catholic edifices. Porter squeezes all into the month of May, but they occurred from February to July and need examination in order of occurrence.

February: the piecing together of two bits of information leads to the identity of Angel Gómez, who appears under his own name in Porter's "The Dove of Chapacalco" and *Thieves' Market* and in her notes as "the bomb-thrower." At 3:30 A.M. of the sixth, two bombs were thrown from a speeding Ford within an hour of each other, the first shattering the windows of the archbishop's residence and the second destroying the interior of El Recuerdo, a factory that made artificial jewelry. The inspector general of police attributed the second bombing to the intransigence of the owners of El Recuerdo, who had closed shop rather than bargain with the workers. One of the negotiators in that labor dispute happened to be Angel Gómez, delegate of the Federation of Workers.[22] In "The Mexican Trinity," Porter mentions that "now and then a stick of dynamite has been hurled at a bishop's palace by a radical hot-head" (CE 403). She could have informed the inspector that the hothead was Gómez.

March: Although Obregón told reporters, on the fifth, that favorites of the Díaz regime who had annexed whole towns to their haciendas and then taxed citizens for use of water should be forced to return that land to their former owners, Governor Francisco Múgica of Michoacán complained that his government, in the process of repartition, had great difficulty disarming the large haciendas' hired guns who were killing Indians and threatening nearby towns. Aiding Múgica's land-reform efforts was Agrarian Commission president J. Isaac Arriaga, "an incorruptible and exemplary revolutionist," who admitted that one of his greatest difficulties was resistance from those the government was trying to help.[23] In "The Mexican Trinity" Porter explains why: "The peons are further assured by the priests that to accept the land given to them by the reform laws is to be guilty of simple stealing, and everyone taking such land will be excluded from holy communion—a very effective threat. The agents who come to survey the land for the purposes of partition are attacked by the very peons they have come to benefit" (CE 403). As if to prove her point, Archbishop Francisco Orozco y Jiménez told Mexico City reporters on May 8 that people didn't want communal land "because they know the Commandments of the Law of God."[24] The archbishop was known to Porter, who modeled the bishop in "The Dove of Chapacalco" after him. Her extensive notes to "The Mexican Trinity" precisely describe the situation in Michoacán. Tracing the history of communal land, she states that a handful of hacendados "have the entire state of Michoacan, one of the largest and richest states in

Mexico" and that "the Catholic Church, owner of land administered in the name of a third party, is working with the hacendados." Michoacán was for Porter the place where the principles of the revolution would be realized or not.

April: On the second, the American Federation of Labor resolved to oppose any propaganda in favor of U.S. intervention. The union anticipated Pablo González's announcement on the twelfth that his Plan of Reconstruction, mentioned above, was in effect. The fifteenth was "the day in which all discontented elements place themselves under the leadership of Pablo González in the Northern States and orders have been sent by the Government here to Generals in command to use the iron hand in putting down any revolutionary movement." González had his secret agent in Mexico City supply money to his former officers who wished to join others in Tamaulipas and Nuevo León (NID: 13023 C; MID 10640-2512).

May: Socialists in Michoacán postponed their May Day demonstrations for a week so that their followers could participate in the election of local judges; if the wrong judges were elected, they could, according to Porter, refuse to carry out the paperwork necessary for repartition of land. During demonstrations of the eighth, some Socialists, angered at resistance to land reform, flew a red and black flag from the tower of the cathedral of Morelia and, when it was removed, beat up the sacristan and slashed a venerated image of the Virgin of Guadalupe.[25] Newspapers were full of this provocative act and the subsequent chain of events. When the city government, on May 11, refused Catholics permission to hold a demonstration, they decided to disobey the order, thereby assuring a clash with the Socialists. Porter wrote that Haberman and Yúdico were "polishing their pistols" for the showdown on May 12, a detail later used in "Flowering Judas." The attempt of the police to break up the demonstration on that day resulted in ten dead, among them J. Isaac Arriaga. His death, which Porter lamented in her notes, was graphic evidence to her that traditional forces would defeat revolutionary reforms.

When a delegation from Morelia solicited aid from organized labor in Mexico City on May 13, workers broke into the House of Deputies, planted the red and black flag, and gave vent to their anger over the death of Arriaga. After they left the chamber that evening, Carrillo Puerto and others spoke against the bourgeoisie from the chamber's balcony.[26] The next day, Obregón condemned the invasion of the Camera and called for disciplinary action against Carrillo and Díaz Soto y Gama for exploiting the situation. On May 15 Obregón issued a decree that foreigners "who meddle in our political affairs against the provisions of the Constitution" would be expelled.[27] Porter noted that she had been warned to stay indoors on this day, her birthday and the festival of the flowers: "A pleasant, red-minded sculptor is modelling my head. Our birthdays are identical, and we planned to celebrate with a noble party," but he never appeared. On the same day, several foreigners, among them Charles Francis Phillips, were deported. Porter learned later that when her friend Natasha

Michaelova denounced herself in protest, she was forthwith deported with only the clothes on her back and that F. W. Fortmayer, cosigner of the petition to the governor of New York, disappeared while walking in a downtown street. The General Confederation of Workers (CGT) bitterly complained that six foreign members of their federation had been expelled, including Michaelova and Fortmayer.[28] Newspapers reported that the government was searching for Angel Gómez, identified as a Cuban radical, for his part in the invasion of the Chamber of Deputies,[29] but he was probably hiding in Haberman's house.

On May 17 Socialist delegates held a demonstration in front of the chamber to denounce Obregón's Liberal Constitutional Party, but police ordered firemen to turn on their hoses, knocking the speaker, Aurelio Manrique of the Agrarian Party, off his feet and dispersing the large crowd of listeners.[30] In "Where Presidents Have No Friends" Porter's version is that the firemen turned hoses through the open windows of the Chamber of Deputies and "the disorderly deputies were drenched to the bone" (CE 412). That night the body of Arriaga was brought to Mexico City, mourned in the offices of CROM and buried the next day.

On May 19 *Excelsior,* pursuing its anti-Bolshevik campaign, attacked Haberman, "yelping his name freely." According to Porter, he "went into hiding on advice of his Mexican political protectors," presumably Morones and Yúdico. "His wife begins to pack up her precious Mexican jars and rugs. I visit Bob. He sits in a tumbled bed, pale and bitter. Has written a long piece about the way the American government cracks the whip over Mexico." In a later version, she describes a "certain Roumanian Jew agitator" who pens "a curious thesis on the crime of giving into the hands of one man, Obregón, absolute power," adding, "I possess that document now, and when I wish to smile, I read it." Another note describes the "instinctive mournful melancholy of his eyes, like an ape in a cage. The sneering impatient underlip could not nullify the misery of those poor, pathetic eyes . . . poor little Jewish drug clerk who had read too much, and let his day dream possess him." If Porter allowed her bias against him to surface, it may help explain why he did not scruple to inform J. Edgar Hoover against her.

Even more unsettling than Haberman's plight was Summerlin's information that Porter herself was on the deportation list. He told her, "with a manner that reeked of self-righteousness, that, thanks to him, it had been removed," but somebody else from the Embassy told her it was on again. Taking no chances, she had her bags packed for two days, "determined not to be sent away without a coat," as Natasha Michaelova had been. In another version, she recites what she will tell the police in order to give herself enough time to pack. In the meantime, her money had run out and she began to feel hunger. She walked past secret service men sitting on the curb in front of the Habermans' house, not caring whether they seized her because in jail at least she would be fed. Not finding Thorberg inside, she stole a dozen tortillas and a bowl of mole. In a separate note, she wrote of crying a great deal and feeling sorry for herself: "Starvation is very hard on the flesh, and the idea of death is very hard on the nerves; I should like to deny that I am terrified but I am." She wrote many notes and drafts of letters to Retinger and Hanna about her predicament. Some are overdramatized versions of her ordeal, but she wasn't making it all up. Mary Doherty's letter to her sister gives us another view of the deportation crisis:

> Of course all of our crowd is on [the list]. . . . Bob is hiding with the papers . . . yammering daily for his head. . . . Secret service people guard the house–all mail held up. All the Mex[icans] are with us all the while because they don't want us deported–Obre[gon] would change his mind & cancel the order but the Amer[icans] keep up the rumpus & won't stop until they get B[ob]. It has been over 2 wks. now. . . . Strangely enough–no doubt due to the nervous tension & suspense–we who are still around loose are having a very good time—we go forth gayly with the leaders of the very gov[ernment] that has us on the list for deportation. Kathryn, Thorborg & I have very hilarious times. Of course we are really quite safe in a way for they won't take us until they get the more important ones & as yet we have done nothing because we can't speak Spanish–only in disrepute because of our beliefs & our associations & Kath. espec[ially] because she has refused to associate with the Amer[ican] colony. She is very pretty & very clever & they would like to have her & she is not very radical. . . . It will all be very funny to laugh at a yr. from now–just now a little nerve wracking . . .

Doherty's mention of living in a state of tension for two weeks puts her undated letter around May 29, the date of Porter's draft letter to Paul Hanna, in which she stated that Haberman was still in hiding. She began her letter, "Things happen so quickly here, I have not been able to record them," making it sound like her December letter to her family, in which she recorded all her exciting adventures. The rapid series of events in May also qualify as adventure, but of a different kind. The possibility of being whisked off the street by an unknown force "terrified" her because it had "the idea of death" in it. One of her diary entries reads, "I think the truth is that I do not wish to die. And yet I have set my sails for death, rather than to ask for help, the whole experience here has set me a little mad, I think. I was worn out when I came here, and." The passage ends in mid-sentence, but begins again with an account of street riots, pitched battles in Morelia, and occasional bombings that blend with street noises she hears as she drifts off to sleep: "I have such a sense of horror, of continual movement of the lights and shadows at my back, of long supernatural silences which are broken suddenly with a roar of strange noises which I recognize as the street clamor below." In her patio sketch, Porter had written,

"In the sunlight one may laugh, and sniff the winds, but the night is crowded with thoughts darker than the sunless world."

Mary Doherty had written that her May experiences "will be very funny to laugh at a year from now," but sunlight or passage of time never totally dispelled Porter's nightmare sensations of death-threatening adventures. She returned to them a year later in "Where Presidents Have No Friends" and almost ten years later in "Flowering Judas." Her later description of Haberman in hiding reflects her own responses to deportation. In that reconstructed scene, she has him bemoan, "Always I wished to escape from the realities of life–When I reached one state of being I immediately could not endure–I wished only to go to another country. . . . Now, this is the only country I have not wished to leave. . . . I can make for myself exactly the sort of life I want. . . . and they will not have me." Escape from reality became a major theme in Porter's fiction. Her own adventures in Mexico were a form of escape from depression, but they gave only temporary relief or, worse, turned dangerous, causing her to escape from them. Escape was not a solution but a vicious circle.

June: On the fifth, General Fernando Vizcaino was accused in Oaxaca of plotting against the government and was shot at dawn of the next day, the first casualty of what was called "the Oaxaca conspiracy." On that same day, González attempted in Washington to obtain recognition of belligerency on behalf of his followers. On the fifteenth, General Carlos Greene, former private secretary of González, and Major Carlos Méndez were arrested. Méndez was accused of transferring a considerable quantity of arms to his father, General Sidronio Méndez. On the twenty-fourth, in La Palma, San Luis Potosí, Sidronio Méndez, in command of an armed band, offered resistance to government forces and was forthwith killed. On that day, González was listed as a deserter and his property was confiscated. Several other generals formerly associated with González were arrested and later released, but Carlos Méndez and his brother were executed.[31] Porter refers to the Oaxaca conspiracy in "Where Presidents Have No Friends"; after noting that the hosing in the Chamber of Deputies "would be absurd, comic, if death were not in it," she began her next paragraph, "Wherever generals playing the counterrevolutionary game are captured, there they are executed, usually within twelve hours. Pablo González has escaped so far, but only one of his numerous forays recently resulted in the execution of five men, two of them being generals in the president's army" (CE 413). In "A Month of Uncertainties," she wrote, "Letters intercepted, copied. Handed over to government officials. Five conspirators, all they could lay hold of, executed within three days," to which she added, "How on earth can this concern me? Yet it does." The appearance of Méndez's name in Niven's letters explains her concern.

It is impossible to know what information the government had about Sidronio Méndez, but Porter implicated herself in her fictionalized version of his death:

As I drive along, letters in pocket, I consider the step I am about to take. What, after all, am I doing, except committing an act of opera bouffe treachery calculated to bring death to several other opera bouffe traitors? Why then, do I do it? I have no grudge against them, no, nor their cause. It is as fully ridiculous, fantastic and unnecessary as the one with which I am so strangely allied. But I am, for once, and by accident, on the side of the strong—when I joined them, I had no idea they would be—Am I, then, so bored with my own existence? I had scarcely suspected it—why did not my fancy turn me toward some harmless pastime—wasn't there some object I could collect—those little clay faces from Teotihuacan—I had really meant to dig there some day—I am well aware of the enemy within me: hidden and powerful. He lives upon Sensation. He loves this furtive flight by night in a closed car, he loves the sense of power implied in the possession of these letters—letters silly, so futile and so potent—Five men will die at last on the word of these letters—

I deliver them to a fellow player, whose pantomime and words are dramatically apt and appropriate—he will give them in turn to the star of the show—As I pass through the lines of soldiers with rifles at rest, I bow when they touch their caps—I cannot resist drawing my veil over my eyes before I make the little dash across the pavement that will lift me safely into my taxicab—I will drive to a certain cafe. There some one will meet me—we will drive immediately to another—I shall spend the evening dancing—

At dawn the executions began—Five in all, at intervals during the next three days—Three of them at least were the wrong men. The ones they really hoped to get got away.

These five whom I never saw in life take their ghostly and ironic revenges—Sleeping is even more peopled than waking hours with their reproachful images—They are not to fade entirely for almost three years. It is as well I could not foresee this at the first. [Dashes substituted for ellipses of varying lengths in the original.]

The second to last sentence suggests that Porter composed this page no earlier than 1924. A curious blend of melodrama and first-person confession, it is the only fragment in which the "I" takes responsibility for her actions, although she is split into two selves and gives way to "the enemy within," who is masculine and loves to be associated with the powerful and to wield power even at the cost of five lives. We may dismiss the night journey itself as fiction, but not the psychology of the narrator, who closely resembles Katherine Anne Porter in her association with the powerful who undermined her revolutionary idealism and in her love of adventure or "sensation" that ends in guilty nightmares "crowded with thoughts darker than the sunless world." It doesn't matter that those executed were traitors to the revolutionary cause; she depicts herself as a traitor like them because her motives were not pure and because her powerful associates may be as reprehensible as Méndez and his sons. On a personal rather than political level she betrayed Méndez, Niven, and herself.

Porter attempted to exorcise the ghost of Méndez in "The Evening," an unfinished short story also written about 1924. One passage reads: "It was a perfect story, and in it he glorified somewhat the history of that soiled packet of letters he had just placed in the hands of General Mendez, they being merely a half dozen intercepted letters from minor trouble makers in the opposite camp, and a manifesto to which several leading generals had foolishly set their names; an act they might be much troubled to explain later, in case their cause failed." Although the military activities in this death-haunted story are confusing, Porter's resurrection of Sidronio Méndez is not. She made him an honorable revolutionary and placed in his hands a packet of letters identical to those she copied, thus giving him, as if in an act of propitiation, the opportunity to save himself by disposing of the evidence that had condemned him.

Once the true history of Niven's letters is known, it is difficult to read "The Charmed Life" as Porter intended it. As with Méndez, she resurrects Niven and attempts to save him by persuading him to destroy the damning letters. But to rewrite history and nominate oneself potential savior when, in fact, the opposite was true seems inordinately self-protective. But then she knew that Niven did not suffer from her mischief, dying at the advanced age of eighty-seven. Returning to the letters twenty years later, she couldn't entirely suppress the truth nor could she entirely tell it by revealing the real reason for Niven's charmed life.

Among Porter's papers is a contract, dated June 14, from the minister of education, José Vasconcelos, appointing her to teach dancing in several girls' schools on the meager salary of four pesos a day. She taught for a while, but lost her job, she told me, when it interfered with her work for CROM. And she continued to enjoy the company of Carrillo Puerto and Xavier Guerrero. Carrillo's signed photograph to her appeared in the May 28 issue of the Yucatán feminist magazine *Redención*. She visited Popocatepetl with Guerrero, probably in June since she wrote in May about postponing the trip because of the deportation scare and ill health. Several scattered notes reveal that she bathed with Guerrero in a mountain pool fed by melting snow and visited the Sacromonte overlooking the plaza of Amecameca. The town made a lasting impression:

> I shall come back some day to live in Amecameca, at the foot of the
> volcano, in a house of adobe with an adobe wall around it, and mottled,
> copper-green moss will cover it over within a year. There shall be a tiled
> fountain in the garden, with ducks and ferns and figs and pomegranates
> growing along the walks. There shall be a tiled fireplace in the room

where I keep my books, and the design shall be made by Adolfo Best
Maugard. A silence will be over the place, so enormous that any spoken
word shall sound quite unnecessary.

This, no matter what end is prepared for me in the stead, is my
dream.

This is Porter's first description of her dream house, an almost attainable
Edenic refuge away from death-threatening adventures in Mexico, but the
silence inside its moss covering is that of a tomb-womb. Porter often tried
to make her dream house come true. In "Now at Last a House of My Own,"
she tells of lugging her furniture, which she calls "my personal equivalent of
heaven and earth," from "Mexico to Paris to New York to Louisiana and back to
New York" in search of the place where she belonged, but she failed to find it
because in her life "there was never permanency of any sort, except the permanency of hope" (CE 175). At least there remained the permanency of memory:
in 1977 Porter told me she wished she had settled in Amecameca, one of the
pleasantest images salvaged from her first visit to Mexico.

On July 18 the Habermans were deported, or so Mexican newspapers and
the U.S. government reported (MID 9140–6651), but in New York Robert represented Mexican interests, took time to polish his image at Porter's expense in
his August interview with J. Edgar Hoover, and returned to Mexico in 1922.
On July 20 Retinger, expecting deportation to Poland, wrote Porter, praising
"In a Mexican Patio" and asking her to visit him in Laredo so that she could
help him with his memoirs, but upon his release from jail returned to Mexico.
With the threat of deportation still in the air, Porter appealed to her friend
Kitty Barry Crawford to finance her return to the United States.[32] When the
money arrived, she left Mexico in late August, Retinger and Mary Doherty
seeing her off at the train station. (Doherty left Mexico late in October.)

Porter's eleven months in Mexico constitute one of the most important periods of her long life. Never again would she have such an insider's view of the
workings of government and such a close association with those in power.
Never again would she be so personally involved in political intrigue. Porter
came to Mexico with a deep-seated pessimism about the human condition, a
pessimism that her early exposure to the Mexican Indian confirmed, but her
new acquaintances strengthened her feminist-rooted socialist ideals and gave
her occasional hope of the possibility of radical change. A diary entry of early
1921 marks a midpoint in her struggle between hope and despair:

I am in touch with the revolutionists, mostly, for they are the idealists—at first, I thought this was a true social revolution, but now I see it
is half political, but it is a beginning, though halted in its advance by a
thousand crushing forces from within and without. Within there is the
hideous ignorance of the poor lost darkened people, without the com-

> bined forces of politics, diplomacy, and money of the world. I realize
> more plainly than ever that war and conquest are great games played out
> by a few powerful men, with the lives of all the little people as wagers.

The first sentence retains faint hope in revolutionary idealism, but the second invokes the somber image of the Indian of "The Fiesta of Guadalupe," while the last returns to the fatalistic perception in her review of George's novel "of war lords and the politicians," who "play the great games of molding public destiny." "The Mexican Trinity" later particularized the players as church, foreign oilmen, and hacendados. Thus Mexico confirmed on the spot Porter's worst fears of the irresistible powers of the world that make radical change next to impossible. In her total assault against the Mexican Trinity, Porter identified with the "idealists," whose "cause is so hopeless" (CE 400). The events of May and June made that hopelessness personal. In notes to her essay, she made her birthday the focal date of Pablo González's uprising, the tragic events in Morelia, and her own deportation, dramatizing herself as the terrified pawn of all those forces conspiring to thwart revolutionary goals. Yet her own idealism was undermined by the very revolutionaries with whom she associated. She held Retinger responsible for modifying the radical politics of Morones, but his pragmatic realpolitik had influenced her own views. Her friendliness to American Federation of Labor leaders during the Pan-American convention gave tacit approval to political expedience. Although she typified Haberman as one more concerned in preserving power than in adhering to revolutionary goals, her theft of Niven's letters revealed to her the impurity of her own motives—she too was corrupted by the love of power. In "The Mexican Trinity" she flays "international finance," but as editor of *Magazine of Mexico,* she worked for U.S. financiers. Her three sketches, taken together, express the tug between ideal and real, hope and despair. All the conflicting forces at work in Mexico formed a battleground in her psyche and, ten years later, found expression in "Flowering Judas," whose theme, she stated, is self-betrayal.

3. Porter and Mexican Art, 1922 and 1923

"The Dove of Chapacalco"

Kitty and Garfield Crawford not only financed Porter's return to the United States but welcomed her into their home in Fort Worth.[1] She worked on Garfield Crawford's *Oil Journal,* wrote a column, "Let's Go Shopping with Marie," for the *Fort Worth Record,* and joined a newly formed Little Theatre, acting in its productions over the next five months. These activities took time from her writing, a story called "The Dove of Chapacalco" and a longer Mexican work. "The Dove of Chapacalco" was Porter's first attempt to write a Mexican story, one dealing with the Indian experience. Its setting, like that of "María Concepción," was based on visits to Teotihuacán with Manuel Gamio, honored today as one of the intellectual heroes of the Mexican Revolution.[2]

Porter, who hardly mentions Gamio in her uncompleted essay "Gamio and the Cafe," often accompanied him to Teotihuacán and elsewhere while never sharing him with her other friends, according to Mary Doherty. The opportunity to draw from his vast knowledge of Mexican Indian culture, ancient and modern, explains her possessiveness. With the publication of *Forjando Patria* in 1916, he is credited with launching social anthropology in Mexico.[3] As the title suggests, he writes of forging a new nation that would integrate all the country's diverse elements since harmony cannot exist when the privileged few live in plenty while most of the country suffers from hunger and ignorance. His chapter "The Redemption of the Indigenous Class" argues that sociological studies of the Indians' strengths and needs can help overcome centuries of mistreatment since knowledge of them becomes self-knowledge. Anticipating the muralist movement, he recommends creation of an Office of Fine Arts that would encourage a nationalistic art reflecting "the joy, the anguish, the life, the soul of the people."[4] He also praises the Aztec woman as the prototype of "la mujer femenina," adept in the social and fine arts as well as in the culinary arts, creating Mexican food and nutritive drinks, even pulque, "whose discovery tradition attributes to the famous Xochitl" (124). He clearly influenced Porter's idealized description of the Xochimilco woman and her culinary skills in "The Children of Xochitl."

Gamio began work in Teotihuacán in 1917 and in 1922 expanded the ideas of *Forjando Patria* in the monumental two-volume *La población del Valle de Teotihuacán,* which studies the ancient civilization and modern inhabitants of the region. In "Where Presidents Have No Friends" Porter praises him for his restoration of the pyramids and for "studying race sources in Mexico with the sole aim of discovering the genuine needs of the Indian, and the most natural method of supplying them" (CE 414) and reflects his ideas in her uncompleted essay, "Teotihuacán," begun in 1921. He also fueled her anticlericalism. After documenting the church's early mistreatment of the Indians, he found that present curates of the valley, with one exception, had demoralized them.[5] Such information prompted Porter to write in "Teotihuacán," "Scientific men of the country are beginning hastily to enclose these churches, and to restore them, and to place their relics in museums, in order that the next age will know what it has freed itself from" since "the souls of men were once in slavery to a belief in God."

Porter didn't go to Teotihuacán just to view churches: "Indians live there, uncorrupted by one drop of white blood. I wished to see what four centuries of civilization had done for them." Like her alter-ego Miranda, Porter wanted to see for herself, but Gamio, acting as guide, showed her the dismaying results of those four centuries. In 1920 seven hacendados held 90 percent of the land while 95 percent of the population was landless. Workers on the haciendas earned up to one peso for ten hours of labor. Seventy-three percent of the population was totally illiterate and most were poorly nourished. The infant mortality rate was "alarming," but there was no doctor in the region. Gamio characterized the population as spiritually demoralized, melancholic, and passive as well as economically destitute.[6]

So Porter characterizes the Indians in "The Dove of Chapacalco," transporting the Valley of Teotihuacán to the southern state of Chiapas, which she never visited. In one scene a "listless crowd gathered slowly, drifting in on the bloodless impetus of a curiosity long since divided from faith in the possibility of a change for the better." In another, "Babies with large stomachs and emaciated heads crawled about mutely on the hot baked earth, women stooped over fires and stirred in their cooking jars, or patted tortillas between their palms, all wordless, as still of feature as if they were not yet awakened from their prenatal oblivion." In contrast, the narrator of "The Children of Xochitl" describes "a trance-like quality" in the motions of a woman washing clothes "as if she had never awakened from the prenatal dream." The slight shift from "prenatal dream" to "prenatal oblivion" almost dissolves the vast difference between Edenic bliss and deathly somnambulism.

Since Gamio describes Teotihuacán as a place where revolutionary ideas never penetrated, Porter had to transport them into her story. Her one-page summary of the plot shows how she did it. Listing the three main characters,

"Gomez, revolutionary dynamiter," "Archbishop, extorter of money from the Indians," and "Vicenta, mistress of the archbishop," she noted that Gomez, while planning to blow up "the holy statue which is chief source of fame and revenue to the church," meets and falls in love with Vicenta, arousing her sympathies about "freedom, about liberty, about the freeing of the enslaved Indians." "She plans with him destruction of palace, murder of the archbishop, general uprising of the Indians. Plans are carried out."

Porter based the political situation in "The Dove of Chapacalco" on the events of mid-1921 that had so impressed her. In the second section of the story we learn that a "fallible group of mestizos and Indians, half idealistic, half petty politician, had set up, after appropriate and necessary bloodshed, a proletarian government," with the intention of putting "into immediate practice the theories of justice, liberty, equality, fraternity, land division, freedom for all and forever. And the chief beneficiary of these changes should be the downtrodden feeblest brother, the Indian." But when "the latest set of saviors" in the House of Deputies propose land distribution and arming the Indian in self-defence, a riot ensues that the fire department quells by thrusting hoses through the chamber's broken windows—a fictitious account of events that began with the land partition controversy in Morelia in May 1921. Porter's fictitious cabinet of five radicals and three conservatives, reflecting her description of Obregón's divided cabinet in "The Mexican Trinity," decides to defuse the issue by sending an investigative commission and troops to a remote state in the "Hot Lands," where it was reported that the archbishop of Chapacalco had attacked an Indian village with his "army of bow and arrow fighters," exacting a whole year's tribute as an offering to "the miraculous image, María La Soledad, who had averted a plague of the Rotting Fever from the cathedral town."

Porter modeled her archbishop after Archbishop Francisco Orozco y Jiménez, whose negative views of land partition on May 8 are cited above. Her notes to "The Mexican Trinity" read:

> The palace of the archbishop in Guadalajara, Jalisco, was dynamited a few days since by unknown enthusiasts for liberty. This archbishop is worth a story in himself. He is Orozco Jimenez, of Chiapas. If he had not been a priest, he would have been an excellent bandit of the old style. In Chiapas he armed his Indians with lances and arrows against a village that had refused to pay him extortionate contributions to the church. Later, he formed an association in his church, raised funds for certain charitable works, and departed with the money. It was said he would be shot by his own congregation on his return. Nothing of the sort. He came as Bishop. He is fearless, clever, cunning, lettered, dangerous. Of the Inquisitor type. Dominating spirit of the clergy in Mexico. This dynamite episode . . . gives the Catholics an opportunity and excuse for reprisals of the most ruthless sort.

Orozco y Jiménez had been bishop of Chiapas, where, according to one source, he attempted in 1911 to stir up an Indian revolt against Madero, while, according to another, he used part of a large inherited fortune to build schools and give San Cristóbal its first power and light system.[7] He survived Constitutionalist anticlerical violence in Jalisco from 1914 to 1919 and, when church-state relations improved, had a private audience with Obregón on April 28, 1921,[8] perhaps attracting Porter's attention then.

Porter's animus against the church culminated in "The Dove of Chapacalco." Making the former diocese of Orozco y Jiménez the setting of her story, she depicted her archbishop as "mestizo with the arrogance of a Castilian grandee," who "loathed that part of himself which claimed kinship with these earth stained people," apparently to reflect her model's reputation as condescending to the lower classes who were expected to obey church authority unquestioningly.[9] Porter also made her archbishop fat, like most of her male villains, although Orozco y Jiménez was slender.

In the first section of the story, the archbishop, traveling in his carriage drawn by four white mules and protected by his Indian bodyguard, stops at La Merced convent, where he discovers Vicenta, a fourteen-year-old servant girl. "'Soft and warmly colored as a ripe mango,' thought the Archbishop, who loved food. And other appetites recurred to him in the simile." Although the mother superior tells him that Vicenta is "all Indian and therefore stupid," he decides to "take this kitten home" to "amuse" his aging servant, Antonia. In the carriage he forces the terrified girl to lie at his feet. When she finally drifts off to sleep, he contemplates his prize:

> This one was charming, a soft reddish color all over, like a painted clay
> jar; round arms set strongly on broad shoulders netted with firm flat
> muscles. Her head thrown back left her throat naked—sharply modelled
> under the chin, swelling a little at the base, a round deep hollow accent-
> ing the line above the sloping wing-like collar bones. The slanted eyes
> seemed smiling in sleep, though they were grave and timid when awake.
> A pretty soft girl, an obedient child who would not trouble him.

Vicenta's youthful body stimulates the archbishop's lust, her naked throat serving as metaphorical proof. At age fifty, he feared he was "dying of impotence" with his Indians "growing restive" and revolution "eat[ing] away . . . his privilege," but now "he forgot his rages in the touch of this child who slept at his feet. He became young again, sweetened, renewed." Delighted "at the breath of her terror, laboured and short, against his face when he held her with both powerful arms, implacable as his desire," he asks his "little dove" to put up her mouth and learn to kiss him.

In the fourth section of the story, we view the archbishop through the eyes of Vicenta, now nineteen, as she surveys his quarters with walls "covered with red plush faded in spots to brown the color of dried blood," with leering cupids gazing down from the ceiling "with eighteenth-century sophistication" and with a life-size ivory crucifix, "a treasure of his collection," dominating "the tawdry, gilded panels facing the bed." The details are obviously symbolic: "Over all the palace there breathed a silent decay, a creeping death, the tatters of grandeur waiting for the final blow of time."

In contrast to the aging decadent archbishop, Vicenta is young and strong, "with cleanly savage instincts," "the simmer of joy in her veins" responding to the sunlight and to "the smell of hay and warm breathing animals from the stables." Her vivacity distinguishes her from the apathetic Indians of the area, making her kin to the Indians of Xochimilco, but the archbishop has compromised her by educating her and giving her power in the palace because of his love for her. Without him she recognizes she would be no better off than Mariposa, an Indian like her, scrubbing clothes in the patio. Still she is not happy. His palace is a "prison" from which she longs to be free, even imagining herself as a soldadera, but Antonia in her wisdom warns her of her naivete: "Hunger is not happiness, and a soldadera carries her pack on her back and her cub inside of her, and is beaten by whatever man she belongs to, and eats what is left after the man and sleeps when he is done with her, and life is a long trouble." Antonia's depiction of a worse form of male domination may alter Vicenta's image of freedom, but it won't placate her. Porter has invested her with her own "feverish desires," her love of adventure, search for freedom, and her despair at not finding it, creating in her an anticipation of the young Miranda of "Old Mortality," who looks on her family's house and her convent school as a prison. In Vicenta's "feverish desire to have done with one small task and hurry on to another," she is open to the larger task Angel Gomez will soon propose.[10]

Angel Gómez became Porter's model of the mad bomb-throwing anarchist. Aware of his involvement in the bombing of El Recuerdo and the archbishop's residence in Mexico City, she accuses him in her notes of other terrorist acts:

A. G. Blowing up churches–months and months on his knees in Guadalupe cathedral, studying the situation with a view to bombing the famous Tilma, etc. Where is he now? Nobody knows. We just follow the trail of blown up churches and bishop's palaces. Failed in mission–four great spotlights kept playing over the Tilma. In desperation went over and dynamited two bishop's palaces.

As a matter of fact, on November 14, 1921, after Porter had left Mexico, a bomb did go off in the basilica of Guadalupe, shattering the glass that protected the Tilma, but at the time Catholics identified the perpetrator of all the bombings as Juan M. Esponda, a member of Obregón's staff.[11] As the Catholics chose Esponda, so Porter chose Gómez. A fragment of a letter, dated September 8, 1921, lists him as one of the subjects of four portraits she planned to create. His portrait probably led to the writing of "The Dove of Chapacalco."

Part three of the story introduces Gomez, lying "on a tumbled bed in the closely shuttered back room of a house in the Calle del Cielo," where "Liebemann, the Austrian Jew, had been sheltering him ever since his attempt to blow up the National Palace, a week previous. Liebemann was a socialist with a love of the spectacular. He desired to be a respectable part of a respectable proletarian government, but a fantastical twist in his mind craved the feverish importance of intrigue." The passage reveals how Porter transformed fact into fiction. Eliseo became Cielo, while Haberman became Liebemann, but an Austrian rather than a Romanian Jew to make him blend with Retinger since she found the "fantastical twist" of both their minds similar. (In "Flowering Judas" Haberman simply became "the Roumanian," with "Jew" discreetly dropped, and Retinger became "the Austrian.") Taking fictional revenge on those she didn't like, she has Gomez think of Liebemann as "a good sort of fool, but not intelligent enough to be dangerous." Angel Gómez, on the other hand, retains his own name, minus the accent. Described in the text as "pure Spanish lately banished from Barcelona" (but as Cuban in U.S. government files), he had a kind of anonymity in real life that made him fictitious to Porter. The change from rioting in the Chamber of Deputies, the original reason for his hiding, to attempting to blow up the National Palace makes him appropriately dangerous in the story. Gómez probably did hide in Haberman's house, where Porter met him. He, like Porter, would have witnessed the Haberman-Liebemann quarrels–their "monotonous, bitter voices grinding away in an interminable duet" make their fictional name ironic. (Porter told me that Thorberg "was as tough as hell" and once knocked a book out of Haberman's hands. The Habermans were divorced in 1925.)

Boasting that he always falls asleep over the "verbose and windy" revolutionary theories of Karl Marx, Gomez is a man of action and catalyst in the story's plot. Hearing that a special commission is to investigate the archbishop, he smuggles a ride on their special train and fanatically plans to do what they only talk of doing:

> He was in love with his own dreams of destruction. His own ecstasies nibbled at his nerve ends deliciously. Better than love was a long night of lying awake, blazing with his desire to destroy, with his own hands, every church, every miraculous image, and every monastery in the republic. That was to be his glorious achievement, his unanswerable argument to the awful faith of the peones. "See friends!" he would cry in his imaginings, "Here is your wonder working plaster image with painted eyes. I, Gomez, a man like yourselves, take it in my hands, so, and set a little flame to it . . . . pouf! Where is your god now!" Ah, he would cleanse a whole race of superstition, he would awaken the minds of ten million enslaved peoples!

His reasoning accords precisely with that of some Constitutional commanders. For instance, in 1915, after Salvador Alvarado ordered all churches of Yucatán closed, a mob burned the principal images of Mérida's cathedral to the tune of "La Cucaracha." Alvarado later stated that generals wanted to show Indians that "lightning would not strike" when they rode their horses into churches and publicly smashed statues of venerated saints.[12]

Porter, giving Gomez Alvarado's motivation, planned a scene of image-burning in Chapacalco's cathedral similar to those in Yucatán. Working toward that end, Gomez provokes a woman by wishing her luck in the land partition, but she rejects it: "No, hombre – do not tempt us with dreams. The cura has told me if I accept this land, I am a thief and my soul shall not see God," to which Gomez responds, "Maria la Soledad is only a plaster image with glass eyes, and a little lighted match would set her ablaze! Yet you pray with reverence to a thing no more miraculous than your cooking pots! Oh, simple woman!"

In a long emotionally charged passage, the narrator shares Gomez's view. In it black-shawled women pray to Soledad, her robes "stiff with silver embroidered sprays of wheat, sterile image of fecundity" and her coronet adorned with golden rays "dagger-sharp about her face":

> La Soledad! All the sorrows of the poor, the ineffectual, the sick, the desolate believers of the world had been brought to those primly covered feet, had been held up before those inconsolable clasped hands and lonely forsaken brows. All day the step of her shrine was dark with the shawled forms of women, the air heavy with the breath of their murmurings. "Surcease from sorrow, oh sweet little Mother Mary! Ease us of our pain, give us rest and light! Oh, lonely and stricken Lady, pray for us!"

But they pray in vain: "For three centuries Maria La Soledad had stood in her niche, her agate eyes gazing upward, lighted by day and night with the pale fires of devotion. Dust lay in the folds of her gown, on her fingers, on her head. Dust."

Porter's choice of Nuestra Señora de la Soledad's name is appropriate since it commemorates Mary's desolation at the foot of the cross on Good Friday, and the story is set during "the time of the Easter festivals." She planned to make the burning of the cathedral an ironic nonliturgical festival. Soledad is also appropriate since the shawled women who darken the step of her shrine identify with her desolation just as the "Mexican venerates a bleeding, humiliated Christ . . . because he sees in him a transfigured image of his own identity."[13] But the narrator views such identification with a dusty false image of fertility as futile, for it only perpetuates woman's role as suffering passive victim of male domination, symbolized principally by the archbishop for whom Soledad is a money-making scam. Despite her own victimization by the archbishop, Vicenta is an exceptional woman because the archbishop has raised her up and given her insight into his operations: "She cared nothing for Maria La Soledad. She knew by what agency those hands lowered themselves in benediction on the first day of May. She knew what miracle brought tears of blood to those agate eyes at three o'clock every Good Friday." In Porter's plot outline, the domesticated dove turns activist and joins Gomez in the burning of Soledad.

Porter's anticlerical identification with Gomez hardly makes him the hero of "The Dove of Chapacalco." She mocks his fanatical, egotistical savior complex: "In love with his own dreams of destruction," he would singlehandedly "cleanse a whole race of superstition, he would awaken the minds of ten million enslaved peoples!" And his concept of freedom is seriously flawed; he advises Liebemann to beat his wife "once a week until she learned a woman's place in life." When Vicenta learns that his freedom applies only to men, she leaves him. Porter further undermines his revolutionary credentials through his love of romantic poetry, "evoking with the easy song of the words, his own picture of the blonde princess, pale, sighing through her little strawberry mouth, sitting in her golden chair, dreaming of love . . . longing to be a swallow or a butterfly, to flutter out and find love . . . ah." Such sensibility recalls Porter's complaint in "The Mexican Trinity" that "A small group of intellectuals still writes about romance and the stars, and roses and the shadowy eyes of ladies, touching no sorrows of the human heart other than the pain of unrequited love" (CE 401). Gomez is a false revolutionist, trapped in his own fantasies, without any compassion or respect for those he would liberate. Only Vicenta develops consistent ideas about freedom—rejecting both the archbishop and Gomez, her antagonists on the right and left, united in their sexism.

In 1931 Kitty Crawford urged Porter to finish "the 'Dove' thing you started ten years ago," but she never did, its twenty-nine pages of uninterrupted narrative remaining among her papers. Not allowing herself enough time to digest the raw experiences of a few months before, she may have felt the story too melodramatic, the anticlericalism too explicit, and the motivation of the three principal characters too simplistic. Nevertheless, "The Dove of Chapacalco" enabled her to make more effective use of the same setting and to manage the less spectacular triumph of another Indian heroine in "María Concepción." It also helped her solve the problem of placing her heroine in the center of a revolutionary situation, resulting seven years later in "Flowering Judas," which also portrays a virgin endangered by an obese adversary.

Our only other evidence of Porter's creative work in Fort Worth is the aforementioned fragment that states, "Yesterday I began work on my Mexican book, all to be done in the form of the Patio story. I have it in Four parts, and the third part is called 'Four Portraits of Revolutionaries.' The four are Yudico, Bob [Haberman], Angel Gomez and Felipe [Carrillo Puerto]. You can imagine what they will get from my point of view. The portrait of Yudico is almost completed." The book might have included the following topics: "Revolutionaries. Reactionary Mexicans. The Spanish element. The British. The French. The American. The Middle Class Mexicans (Mestizos mostly). The Indians. The politicians." Scattered notes, mostly about Haberman, reveal her interest in the anatomy of the revolutionary. Her almost completed portrait of Yúdico did not survive except in the character of Braggioni in "Flowering Judas," to which Angel Gómez contributed.

Outline of Mexican Popular Arts and Crafts

In 1920–1921 Porter was caught up in Mexico's political revolution. In 1922 she was more happily involved in its idealistic cultural revolution. Ironically, that political intriguer, J. H. Retinger, was responsible for the opportunity. Following his return from Laredo, he was temporarily out of favor with Morones, thanks to his arch-enemy, Haberman. While in Fort Worth, Porter replied to his "brotherly note," commiserating with him on his lack of money and "no effective friends" in Mexico, lamenting that she was in no position to help him: "Ay dios! I could wish you a better instinct of self preservation, a little power of forecasting tomorrow's weather. Then you would strip yourself today and perish of cold the next. Both of us do it, but you are the more incorrigible." She promised to write to Morones, but "still I must see how he behaves where you are concerned," prefacing her promise by a quotation from Machiavelli about one "who in the cause of another's greatness is himself undone." Retinger persisted in writing to her nevertheless. On October 16 he complained that he had not heard from her in over three weeks and informed her that the "horrid clarinette player" (Haberman) was soon returning to Mexico to cause more trouble and that Doherty would leave in late October with Porter's papers. Encouraged by her plans to return to Mexico in January, he wrote a gushy letter in December, hoping that they would be united by Christmas Day, the anniversary of their first meeting, and closing, "I kiss your microscopic hands and humbly pray for your prompt arrival." But his real intention was "a great plan of work, which we could do in common," including "the intime autobiography of the modern St. Theresa, which you are writing." Porter's real intention was not to see him at all but to visit Carrillo Puerto, elected governor of Yucatán in November 1921. Retinger advised against the trip. Complaining that Porter never answered his telegram about his illness in which he begged for a reply, he reminded her, on January 10, of the time in Mexico when she kept him waiting a whole day without bothering to give him news of her whereabouts. He also repeated his wish for "a literary partnership," she helping him with his works in English and he helping her in "knowing things European"–otherwise he would soon have to sail for Europe.

Retinger did not leave Mexico but regained favor with Morones because of his work in public relations. In March he sent Porter a telegram about another kind of collaborative effort she could not resist: "GOVERNMENT APPOINTS YOU AMERICAN ORGANIZER OF MEXICAN ART EXHIBITION IN WASHINGTON TO BEGIN MAY STOP TOTAL SALARY THREE THOUSAND PESOS AND EXPENSES STOP DURATION TWO MONTHS APPROXIMATELY STOP IMMEDIATE PRESENCE MEXICO INDISPENSABLE . . ." Porter arrived in Mexico on April 5 and remained approximately two months. U.S. Military Intelligence reported that she "was cabled for recently by the Mexican Government," was staying at the Hotel Imperial, and would take an exhibit of Mexican art and industry to the United States, adding, "While it is not known whether Miss Porter is a radical or not, it is believed she is more or less of a socialist" (MID: 10058-0-106). She would have preferred the identity of artist, working with some of the most creative minds in Mexico. In 1934 she wrote Robert McAlmon that the Mexican Renaissance began with Diego Rivera's return to Mexico and that in her more than four years' involvement she knew everybody in it. In fact, she was involved in it four months altogether, but did indeed know everybody in the movement, naming several in "Where Presidents Have No Friends" and acknowledging their help in her *Outline of Mexican Popular Arts and Crafts.*

Porter praised José Vasconcelos, like Manuel Gamio, another intellectual hero of the Mexican Revolution, for instituting "an intensive program of school funding among the Indians": "He claims in his calm way that the true purpose of higher education is to lift the souls of men above this calamitous civilization" (CE 414). Seeking to bring about the social, economic, and principally educational "redemption" of the country, he initiated "a crusade of public education" to assimilate indigenous peoples and forge an ethical-linguistic-cultural unity because Mexico's strength was in "mestizaje" (racial mixing). As minister of education under Obregón, he brought about the construction of 50 percent more schools in the republic, established Indian cultural missions, and appointed Mexican painters to stimulate production of folk arts. To undo centuries of humiliation the Indians suffered in their own country, he commissioned the painting of public murals that celebrated their prehispanic past and their rich cultural traditions. He was father of the muralist movement, encouraging a remarkable group of artists who shared his fervor.[14]

In her 1929 review of Anita Brenner's *Idols Behind Altars,* Porter praised the muralists because they "exhumed . . . the art of the Indian in Mexico" and "restored the Indian himself, a perpetual exile in his own land, to the status of a human problem before a world that had almost ceased to regard that race as a living force in Mexico." Although Dr. Atl (Gerardo Murillo), Diego Rivera, Roberto Montenegro, Adolfo Best Maugard, David Siqueiros, and Jean Charlot were all European trained, they "adopted habits of thought and adapted methods of working, and went, in the process, very consciously 'primitive,' imitating the Indian miracle paintings, delving among ruins, searching in the archives, attending Indian fiestas, using the native earths for their colors."[15] They could have been born in Europe, so great was the difference in background between them and the rural Indian. Montenegro returned to Mexico to discover to his delight an "unknown land" wherein lay the inspiration for the expatriate Mexican artists. Although Porter had been shocked by the Indian's crushing poverty in 1920, as self-defined exile herself, she identified with the Indian as artist and "perpetual exile in his own land."

The relation of talent and race raised uncomfortable questions in Porter's mind. In her 1929 review she wished that "some one as well equipped for the work might do for the United States of North America what Miss Brenner has done for Mexico. Surely this country . . . might also be discovered to have some common, unifying source. Explained in terms of creative vitality and racial intermixtures, we might find ourselves justified in being 'with pleasure and talent' Americans."

The question of race was very much on Mexican minds as Vasconcelos's affirmation of mestizaje shows. When Guatemalan artist Carlos Mérida opened his one-man show in Mexico City in September 1920, he defended the Mayan motifs in his work by insisting on the need to produce "a totally American art," racially "original in character." The Indian motifs of his work anticipated the mural decorations of others. As if to emphasize Mérida's point, David Siqueiros issued a manifesto from Barcelona in May 1921, stating that Mexican artists must come closer to the works of ancient Indian painters and sculptors. Entitled "Three Appeals of Timely Orientation to Painters and Sculptors of the New American Generation," it marked, according to Jean Charlot, the beginning of the Mexican Renaissance.[16] Siqueiros wrote it after discussions with Rivera, who at the urging of Vasconcelos returned to Mexico in July 1921. He received his first mural commission in December and began work in early 1922. Porter first met him in April.

The exhibition to which Porter contributed grew out of the Exposition of Popular Art of the Centenary, conceived and organized by Roberto Montenegro and Jorge Enciso to celebrate the centenary of independence on September 19, 1921. The first of its kind in Mexico, it reflected the nationalistic spirit of the artistic renaissance in Mexico. Dr. Atl, who published *Las artes populares en México* in conjunction with the exposition, wrote that indigenous art revealed "a true national culture," characterized by profound melancholy, strong artistic feeling and imagination, admirable manual dexterity, and individualistic spirit that could "assimilate, transform, and place a personal stamp on new materials."[17] Public response to the exposition far exceeded the calculations of its creators. The National Museum established a department dedicated to indigenous arts and collected specimens of contemporary pottery to place beside those of ancient Mexican cultures. After centuries of neglect, native craftsmanship had gained recognition. In September 1922 the manifesto of the Syndicate of Revolutionary Artists, Sculptors, and Engravers, formed by Rivera, Siqueiros, and Guerrero, dogmatically declared that the noblest "expression of our race blooms" from the Indian's "special talent to create beauty"; his art "is the healthiest spiritual expression there is in the world and his tradition is our greatest possession."[18] This fervid nationalism lay behind the decision earlier in 1922 to enlarge the collection of folk art for a new exhibition to be shown outside the country. Also at issue were the economic potential of native crafts and the favorable propaganda effect in the United States, which still hadn't recognized Mexico.

Porter later told Hank Lopez that she had conceived the idea of the exhibition, Gamio had seized upon it, and Best Maugard had carried it through, persuading Obregón to appoint her as North American representative. They all collected the artifacts "in about six months" and she did the monograph "in about the same time" (94). But most of the artifacts had been gathered long before she arrived, giving her two months rather than six to write her monograph. Ignoring the exposition of 1921, she once more placed herself in the center of a national adventure. Nevertheless, her monograph was a significant contribution to the exhibition. It also contains the first record of her aesthetics and her enthusiastic response to the art of the Indian whom she viewed so pessimistically in 1921.

The work is divided into three parts, "Pre-Hispanic," "Colonial Art," and "The Present." Drawing in the first part from William Prescott's account of the myths of Quetzalcoatl and Huitzilopochtli, she comments, "The Mexicans carved the images of their deities in stone, and left them for us to see and touch and wonder at, and to make our own legends about them."[19] Deriving her knowledge of Aztec women from Gamio, she states with satisfaction that "they enjoyed a cleanly human equality in society utterly foreign to the ideals that governed the relations between men and women of the European and Asiatic races" (13). But the most important influence on her in this section is Adolfo Best Maugard. From his study of pre-Columbian art, he had identified seven art motifs from which he derived a method of teaching children to develop their artistic potential. He successfully proved the method's efficacy in 1921, training over 150 teachers, among them artists Carlos Mérida, Rufino Tamayo, and Miguel Covarrubias, who, in turn, trained many others to carry instruction back to the classroom. In *A Method for Creative Design,* which Porter later edited, he asserts that when the child is aware of "the stored wisdom accumulated in Time," he will give testimony to a "new faith in himself as the instrument of beauty." The key to wisdom is the seven motifs, such as the spiral, circle, and wavy line, found in all early primitive art and proof of man's attempt to "materialize his emotion and make a record of his imagining." Conscious of these motifs, the child will no longer need to copy from others, but "will dream his work out of his own imagination and his production will be unique."[20]

Without citing Best Maugard in *Outline,* Porter notes that the motifs are "the universal expressions of emotions and perceptions that animated the awakening soul of man, the natural idiom of primary understanding." She expounds on Best's ideas but with a shift of emphasis:

> A child of today, fragrant of civilization that he is, yet sees his world first with the eyes of innocence. He draws by instinct a straight line. A wavy line is water, a round circle serves variously to express his feelings for a flower, a head, a moon. He draws these things because they are the first planes and outlines the human eye apprehends.
>
> In his terrors the child is primitive man. He fears flood, fire, lightning,

the mysterious and awful portents of nature. He creates superstitions about his birth, his emotions, his sex. I submit that these instinctive gropings make all men akin, and that they derive from within the individual. (6)

Whereas Best Maugard, in seeking the universal "archetype" out of which the seven motifs develop, stresses the human need to go beyond art and comprehend the "noumenon" itself, Porter remains earthbound, linking childhood "innocence" and "terror"—her words, not Best Maugard's. She later explored her memories of childhood from that perspective.

In the second part, Porter relies on Dr. Atl's knowledge of the regional origins and characteristics of popular arts and stresses his idea of the Indian artist's assimilative powers. Pointing out that he transformed ceramics and weaving of wool, introduced by the Spanish, she praises his "ability to adapt and use strange forms" and lay "the foundation for his new art, destined to become racial and genuinely expressive." The Indian, she claims, derived his ideas from foreign art and from "his own magnificent traditions, filtered them through his own understanding, translated them into his own common speech: the result is a thing of superb beauty and strength." Unlike the Mexican-born Spaniard, "the native added always more and more of his own feeling and psychic reaction, until at once the thing was his own, an interpretation of beauty, national, personal—even more, absolutely individual" (28–29). Throughout her monograph, she identifies the Indian's race with an innate appreciation of beauty. Although the Indian has remained "static" during the country's "political and social" changes, he is of a "race that expresses itself in terms of beauty." He is the model artist, transcending the wretched condition of his life in his art, if nowhere else.

Porter's idealization of the Indian as artist was also expressed in a letter to the *Christian Science Monitor* (June 5, 1922) that gives us our only contemporaneous view of her activities:

> I spend my time in an old house of the seventeenth century in an immense hall littered with beauty and great windows opening on the patio garden. Diego Rivera comes there at times, and Best, and Vasconcelos, and Toledano. Indians from the country help to assort pottery and painted boxes and serapes more beautiful than ever I imagined serapes could be, and great silver embroidered saddles and spurs that glitter like jewels. The stirrups are of dark blue polished steel encrusted with silver flowers and leaves and birds. A horseman's dream of saddles and stirrups!
>
> There is pottery from Puebla, done in the old style, Chinese blue on cream color, dragons and birds and leaves. In other colors, too, pale yellow and orange and green with that dark blue. It touches the heart to see how these people have persisted in their instinctive need to create

beauty, and how they have taken the humble materials of their own earth at their very doorsteps, and have contrived lovely things that make you remember all beauty.

Everything is a delight to Porter's eye: "Baskets woven fine as cloth, with geometric designs, come from a dozen places, each with its own designs. In all these things I have never seen two objects that bore the identical pattern. Every man makes a thing with his own hands, after his own thought." Everything that touches his life, "from head to foot, in all his household and his work, every object created for his daily use, he makes as beautiful as he can in his own incorruptible fashion. The thing is his own. . . ." She ends her letter because she must "go to Diego's studio—an old ruined church—to select drawings. There are gardenias in my room and two bright green baby parrots are quarreling amiably over their breakfast of banana. It is early morning and summer in Mexico." The last two sentences are a little poem as colorful as a serape to express the sheer joy she felt in being surrounded by Indian art. On that early summer morning she entered Eden as she did over a year before in Xochimilco.

In the second part of *Outline,* Porter mentions Xochimilco: the florists there "fashioned flowers into decorative shapes with a long patience of execution which is still the most remarkable thing about the flower arrangement of the Mexican" (17). Their art is literally a product of nature and can serve as metaphor for all native art; because "artists are one with a people simple as nature is simple: that is to say, direct and savage, beautiful and terrible, full of harshness and love, divinely gentle, appallingly honest," they create an art which is "a living thing that grows as a tree grows, thrusting up from its roots and saps, knots and fruits and tormented branches"(33). The passage recalls the bargeman in "Xochimilco" who "lives as a tree lives, rooted in earth, drinking in light and air." So intimate is the relation between man and nature that the wearer of a serape containing the colors of the land "seems not merely in sympathy with the trees and hedges of cactus and the gray road, he literally is one of these"(42). Native artists give "instinctive obedience" to the laws of nature and thus achieve "innocently, without premeditation, the perfect speech of their hearts" (39). Her notion seems to derive from Emerson's "Nature": "Thus in art does Nature work through the will of a man filled with the beauty of her first works."

But, Porter warns, if "the artist were removed from his fructifying contact with his mother earth, condemned daily to touch instead the mechanics of artifices of modern progress, he might succumb, as do the aristocratic arts, each in turn, to the overwhelming forces of a world turned dizzyingly by a machine" (38). The passage explains why Laura in "Flowering Judas" "will not wear lace made on machines" (92). For Porter, not only is nature essential to the artist, but also his particular place in nature, his "tierra," his "earth": "There he belongs, and there he will return inevitably, no matter how far he goes

away, nor how long he must stay in foreign places." Porter applied these perceptions to her own life as artist. Even though she stayed in "foreign places,"
she must "inevitably return," if not in body then in spirit, to her "tierra," her
Texas, where she could practice "the perfect speech" of her heart. Like the
carver of walking sticks in San Esteban Titzatlán, she will carve out stories and
each will be "a chapter in [her] life's experience, a record of what [she] has
seen and felt" (47–48).

Rivera and Others

The most illustrious participant in the exhibition was Diego Rivera,
who had identified with the folk artists of Mexico by calling himself a pul-
quería painter. His work fascinated Porter, as her *Christian Science Monitor*
letter attests:

> Rivera, whose paintings we are bringing, I think is one of the great artists
> of the world, though he has had to live down the fact that he founded
> Cubism, and gave the first Cubist exhibition in Paris ever so long ago.
> But now he is simple and splendid and paints like a god in a mood of
> repentance of the hurts he has given his creatures.
>
> When I first went to see his Indian fresco, still half finished, in the
> National University here, I was struck with the certainty that I was in the
> presence of an immortal thing. And as I stood before two enormous
> clasped hands, on paper, pinned in place over the charcoal outline on
> the wall, I was touched with the same feeling I had when I was 12 years
> old and saw for the first time the "Praying Hands" of Dürer. I felt like
> weeping with pity for struggling, suffering, human life.

Porter seems to suggest that Rivera was repentant for indulging in cubism,
which he did not found, although he exhibited cubist works in his Paris exhibition of 1914. The mural she admired is a mestizaje version of creation,
housed in the National Preparatory School. Rivera described it as a "racial history of Mexico" through figures representing all types that "had entered the
Mexican bloodstream."[21] The clasped hands are those of Faith, depicted as an
old Indian woman, reminding Porter of Dürer's hands and "the awful hands of
faith, the credulous and worn hands of believers" that overwhelmed her with
pity at Guadalupe.

In 1931 Porter wrote scornfully of "the legend [Rivera] invented about himself for open mouthed lady scribblers from the north, who worshipped him,"
but in 1922 she was one of them. She first visited his studio with Retinger,
who deposited her there and left. Lying down on a mat, she watched the "magnificent" Guadalupe Marín pose for one of the Creation figures. Eventually
Marín's hands tired, "the right one wandering out into a fading jar of roses,

destructive, wantonly dragging long brown fingers down, petals falling . . . struck crayon out of Diego's hand with a sudden savage humour." Porter adapted this note for her satire of Rivera in "The Martyr": "Isabel, who was tall and thin, with long, keen fingers, would rip her hands through a bouquet of flowers Rubén had brought her and scatter the petals, or she would cry, 'Yah! Yah!' derisively, and flick the tip of his nose with paint" (33). Porter dined with Rivera, Marín, and Nicaraguan poet Salomón de la Selva, dancing later in the glass-littered street of Niño Perdido in front of the old Vizcaínas convent to the music of a "tinny orchestra from the pulqueria around the corner."

In her notes Porter planned to do something with "Diego's stories," for he invented fabulous lies about himself and friends, far outstripping Porter in that capacity. She also described him as an artist after her own heart: "It seems to me he has fulfilled the prime law of creation: bring form out of chaos. Himself tough-fibered and resistant, he will tell you that he rebels by nature from all restraints, all formalisms, all hamperings of natural growth. The chief duty of man is to resist laws imposed from without whenever they come in collision with the laws of the individual being." Although she thought his was a typical anarchist philosophy, it was little different from her own desire for total self-reliance. In 1926 she wrote of instinctively revolting from intolerable associations, "at last [coming] to depend only on the single fine point of reference in her soul."

According to Hank Lopez, David Siqueiros claimed that Porter had affairs with Rivera, Carrillo Puerto, and "that Nicaraguan poet" (63). He was right about Salomón de la Selva, who was educated and taught in universities in the United States, publishing *Tropical Town and Other Poems* in New York in 1918. Entering Mexico sometime in 1921, he became a member of a literary circle that included poets Carlos Pellicer, Jaime Torres Bodet, and José Gorostiza, and published another book of poems, *El soldado desconocido,* in 1922.[22] It is uncertain when Porter met him. According to Doherty, they had an affair ending in an abortion in 1921 when he was living in a little house on Calle Guanajuato. The last detail may explain a mysterious note Porter wrote in Fort Worth in 1922: "That house in Guanajuato was a rook's nest of uncertainties. Why do foreigners behave either like fiends or fools in Mexico? Destroyed her repose and sent her flying out of Mexico." There is also among other jottings in her notes the single word "Abortion."

Whatever their relation in 1921, Porter was frequently in De la Selva's company in 1922. She wrote in the flyleaf of a copy of Emily Dickinson's poetry, "Salomón de la Selva gave me this book in Mexico City in 1922, after reading every poem in it to me." But her notes about him are not as romantic. She recorded with satisfaction that Rivera contemptuously asked him why he must imitate the style of San Juan de la Cruz, a second-rate mystic. With a reputation for erudition among his friends, De la Selva talked of Vidal and Villon to Porter but became silent when he discovered that she knew their work. Perhaps picturing himself as a minstrel-poet, he bragged that women found him irresistible.[23] In her notes Porter accused him of seducing the younger sister of Palma de Guillén, one of Rivera's models. Hyperbolizing his sexual prowess, she wrote that she detested his attitude toward women: "If Salomon met the Virgin Mary, he would introduce himself as the Holy Ghost." She also imagined him at age eleven examining his female baby cousin with a magnifying glass. He became the model for Carlos in "Virgin Violeta," which includes a version of his poem based on their dance in the glass-strewn street. Porter told Lopez that De la Selva had a "sinister fascination that was not easily resisted." His very irresistibility prompted her to label him, along with Hermann Göring, as "totally evil and without scruple" (83, 172).

Before dancing in front of the convent, Porter, with De la Selva, Marín, and Rivera, had spent the evening at Los Monotes. She later described it as "a hole-in-the-wall, decorated by Orozco with Covarrubias caricatures and often filled by the ample presence of Rivera." Returning to the cafe in 1930, she was delighted to find it hadn't changed. She reminisced to Lopez about her inclusion in a select circle of intellectuals and artists who used to gather in night spots like Los Monotes and the Cafe Flores (82). The circle included not only Best Maugard, Rivera, De la Selva, and Guerrero, but the precocious caricaturist Miguel Covarrubias.

Covarrubias's caricatures had already appeared in Mexican and U.S. publications in 1920 when he was fifteen years old. José Juan Tablada discovered him at work in Los Monotes, "an impish-looking child, seated alone, pencil in hand, at one end of the room, regarding him with a malicious eye." In 1923 Covarrubias became an overnight success in *Vanity Fair* after Tablada's friend, Carl Van Vechten, introduced him to Frank Crowninshield,[24] although Porter told Lopez that she had made the introduction (97). Indeed she had taken some of his work to New York in 1922, but he wrote her that he himself was on his way to the States because of Tablada's arrangements. More important, the strong Mexican tradition of caricature that sustained Covarrubias also influenced a distinctive aspect of Porter's art.

It was fitting that Covarrubias chose Los Monotes to practice his art. Opened by Orozco's brother in 1916, it has long since disappeared, but Tablada gives us a good idea of what it was like:

> In the evenings when the neighboring theatres close, one is sure to meet there noted painters such as Rivera, Rodriguez Lozano, Charlot, and Angel, mixing with writers of the most modern kind. Along the four walls of the hall . . . runs a frieze in which the personages of Orozco act and dance in a frenzy of movement and expression—"Follies" girls flirting with old beaus, couples adventuring in old-fashioned hackney coaches, policemen as passive as time-keepers at prize-fights, and, as a *leit motif,* the reckless and alluring girl of the city's middle or popular class with make-up and elaborate headdress. . . . Their creator is positive about the mediocrity of the wonderful figures—painted on board, cut out and

pasted on the wall—notwithstanding that the throngs go there to admire these joyous pictures of city life even more than for the foamy chocolate, the snappy tamales, and other appetizing "firecrackers" of the vernacular kitchen.[25]

Although Los Monotes could mean "The Big Monkeys"—Porter changed it to "The Little Monkeys" in "The Martyr"—Tablada's translation, "big puppets," is more accurate. More accurate still is "big caricatures." Orozco's caricatures in Los Monotes were examples of an art form particularly Mexican. Tablada speculated that it had its roots in "the grotesques of pre-conquest sculpture,"[26] but it was certainly popular in political satire throughout the nineteenth century. For example, *El Hijo del Ahuizote* made Porfirio Díaz its target, caricaturing him in 1900 as the Aztec god of war, to whom General Bernardo Reyes sacrifices Yaqui Indians.[27] During the Porfiriato, offending cartoonists were often imprisoned, but, despite the dangers, contributed to the revolutionary climate because they were able to reach the large illiterate population with their picture-messages. Orozco began his career as cartoonist in *El Hijo* in 1911–1912. His Preparatory School murals of 1923 contain the most caustic caricatures of all the muralists. "The Reactionary Forces" depicts heavy-bosomed sneering dowagers disgustedly picking their way through prostrate beggars. Porter noted that his "mean caricatures of the Mexican middle class" are "much too near the bone to please them."

Political satire also flourished in Mexico's music halls. Diego Rivera fell victim to Roberto Soto, pot-bellied comic at the Lírico. In one of his acts, entitled "Diego Rivera and Land Distribution," Soto carried onstage a large bag of dirt and then proceeded to throw handfuls of it at his assistants dressed in peasant garb. When the equally rotund Morones rose to prominence as the third most powerful man in Mexico, Soto ridiculed his ostentatious life-style,[28] and Porter recorded one of his performances for later use in "Flowering Judas." Lampoons in poem and song as well as street jokes that spread like wildfire display the same satirical spirit. When Felix Palavicini, self-seeking editor of *El Universal,* failed in his attempt to receive an honorary degree from the National University, De la Selva privately published a song, "La Colita del Chango" ("The Ape's Little Tail"), to commemorate the occasion. It is the Mexican political method, Porter noted, to "attack a man through his sexual vanity."

If Porter didn't learn the art of caricature in Mexico, then she sharpened her satiric skills there in several art forms. Covarrubias drew her caricature in 1922 and, in her 1927 book review of *The Making of Americans,* she included a wicked pen and ink caricature of Gertrude Stein. In 1928 she wrote a song that parodied De la Selva's "style, his rhyme scheme, and philosophy": "Lady trailing your gown / Hiding your li-i-i-ttahl fee-eet / Let me sing you a roun-de-laaaaaaaaaay / In the dust of the street! / Let me sell you a rhy-hime / For-or-or a bright penny! / Now is as good a ti-hiiime / To love, to love, to love, as

GOOOOOOOOD / A time, to love as any!"[29] In " Virgin Violeta" she created a cruel literary caricature of De la Selva himself.

There is always an element of revenge in satire—the desire of the satirist to expose or punish with pen or brush the morally reprehensible. In this regard, her fictional note about hatred is instructive: "Little Lino—the child wonder— thin as a finger—'I'm getting fat,' he said, 'Whatever shall I do about it? I'm getting frightfully fat.' 'Oh,' said KA, 'Hate everybody as I do, and that will keep you thin.' 'But KA, you know that I *do* hate everybody, and am getting fat on it!'" Lino is, of course, based on Miguel Covarrubias, whose caricatures could channel his hatred, if they didn't control his weight. Porter's hatred was hardly the only source of her art, but it was a key element in her caricatures. If he ever read "The Leaning Tower," Retinger would have found there Porter's revenge against him. Her main character is Charles Upton, an artist who thought he should have gone to Mexico, "a good place for painters" (440), but instead ends up in Germany, whose inhabitants "resembled the most unkind carica- tures of themselves . . . the very kind of people that Holbein and Dürer and Urs Graf had drawn, too" (443). He too draws the people, among them Ta- deusz Mey, the Retinger character, "sitting over the piano, bird head, little stiff wrinkles at the corners of his mouth, fingers like bird claws"—and thinks, "Hell, maybe I'm a caricaturist" (471). He is because Porter was.[30] Her descrip- tion of Mey as predatory bird contains a malicious implication Covarrubias might have envied. Her belated revenge must have had some cathartic effect if it matched Upton's revenge against his landlady: "With concentrated malice he drew Rosa, first as kitchen sloven, then as a withered old whore, finally with- out any clothes on. Studying these, he decided he had paid off a large install- ment of his irritation with her, and tore them all into minute bits" (470).

"Where Presidents Have No Friends"

Porter published her second political essay, "Where Presidents Have No Friends," a month after her return from Mexico. Like "The Mexican Trin- ity," it gloomily speculated on Mexico's political future, especially since the United States continued to refuse recognition even though Mexico had met requirements concerning the export tax and foreign debt.[31] The essay's theme that the president of Mexico can trust no one is a conclusion drawn from an account of the last fateful days of Venustiano Carranza's life and serves as in- troduction to Alvaro Obregón's own problems as outlined in "The Mexican Trinity" in 1921. It implies that the revolutionary idealism of her friends like Vasconcelos and Gamio will count little over against Mexico's enemies, within and without the country. Like the first essay, it is pessimistic about the lot of the Indian, who still yearns for land and liberty, its tone in marked contrast to the warm enthusiasm with which she viewed the Indian's art in *Outline*.

Porter derived the theme, tone, and form of the essay from Blasco Ibáñez's *Mexico in Revolution,* the book she damned in her 1920 review. His gleeful condemnation of Mexicans based on jokes they told on themselves and his patronizing and sometimes racist comments—he refers to the Mexican's "half-breed appetites"—merited her scorn, but his skepticism about Mexico's future resembled her own; he called the Mexican the "eternal victim of a tragicomedy that never ends, the poor slave whom all pretend to redeem and whose lot has remained unchanged for centuries, the everlasting dupe whom the redeemers shower with fine phrases, never telling him the truth because the truth is frequently cruel" (3).

Ibáñez's anecdotal method also attracted Porter. Referring to his alleged offer to sell his services to the Mexican government, she noted, "For fifty thousand pesos he might have been persuaded to write the truth," and then added a conversation in which a "paid publicity" writer plans to write an indignant story about how federal soldiers deserted to a rebel general for ten centavos more a day, to which his companion replies, "But you know, Pablo Gonzalez gets the money which enables him to pay more, from certain interested gentlemen in the United States—from very well known and respectable gentlemen too—so in a way they're deserting Obregón in favor of the United States—how can you object to that?"

In the same "nicely ironic tone of amusement" (CE 404), a supposed follower of Carranza tells the narrator of "Where Presidents Have No Friends" about his chief's flight and death, the details of his story resembling those that appeared in Mexican newspapers shortly after Carranza's death. Undoubtedly Porter pretended that the storyteller was real to give authenticity to what she considered a peculiarly Mexican attitude toward life: "If for a moment, madame, we thought escape possible, put it down, please, to that persistent naïveté of faith in the incredible which is in the heart of every Mexican. *La Suerte* will not fail forever! And still *la Suerte* betrays us, and still we are faithful to her. It is our happiest fidelity" (CE 405). Luck soon fails when someone disconnects the airbrakes of Carranza's train that was to carry him safely to Veracruz—"the first treachery . . . trivial and potent, anonymous and certain" (CE 405). When rebels force him to abandon the train in the mountains, he releases all his followers from their "loyalty" to him, as if granting them permission to betray him. Then the soldiers "spread flat over the earth behind cactus and hillock, firing at one another, no man knowing whether the other was friend or enemy" (CE 406), their actions implying that in Mexico one can't tell the difference between friend and enemy. Apparently there isn't any because maybe "a friend" killed Carranza in his bed and reported his own escape to "the newest chief," who "would believe him, maybe not. A President of Mexico can trust no one." Her informant's conclusion gives Porter license to elaborate: "That final corroding phrase is the point of a cynical truth: a hundred years of revolutions have taught the President of Mexico that he can trust

no one except his enemies. They may be depended upon to hate h
they will be faithful in contriving for his downfall" (CE 407).

Porter derived her "cynical truth" from Blasco Ibáñez, who ;
story of Carranza's death at the hands of "men trusted to guard
observing elsewhere, "No one knows with certainty on whom h
You never know whether a friend on embracing you will not stab you in the
back" (119–120). Porter restricted Blasco's sweeping generalization to the
"friends" of the president, ominously placing Obregón's problems in the unhappy context of Carranza's death. If he attempts to placate Doheny and the oil
interests in order to gain recognition from the United States, he runs the risk
of savage criticism from his followers. If he helps Mexican labor establish links
with international labor unionism, he will commit "rankest treason" in the
eyes of high finance. Since there are few "faithful sons" (CE 415) among all the
contending factions, his "faith is in himself" (CE 409), just as Porter's faith is
in herself, for she, like Carranza's follower, believes that *la Suerte* rules the
world, although not in her favor. "Redemption" may be a "hopeful, responsible" word when spoken by men like Manuel Gamio, but memories of 1921
overrode her hope in Mexico's future. Blasco Ibáñez's ironic "redeemers" match
the "shrieking Messiahs" in her 1920 review of George's novel. Eight years
later she entitled a novel on Mexico *False Redeemers*.

On July 10, 1922, Retinger wrote Porter, "Your article in the Century from
the literary point of view is certainly very nice, but good heavens how nasty
and really how untrue. After all one [of] the greatest qualities of the Mexicans
is loyalty and idealism." Despite the doubtful sincerity of the last sentence, he
had a point. Even though Porter praised Obregón and attacked Doheny, Mexican officials must have been displeased with her article. At a time when
Obregón had to live down false charges of complicity in Carranza's death,
Porter overly sympathizes with Carranza, even crediting him with redrafting
the Mexican Constitution when in fact he circumvented its provisions on land
reform and labor rights. When Obregón had gone to great lengths to convince
the world of the stability of his government, Porter described Mexico as "a
hotbed of petty plotting" (CE 413) and referred to Obregón as the "newest
chief," no less subject to *la Suerte*'s turning wheel than Carranza. Perhaps she
realized her diplomatic blunder, for she informed her father on July 27 that
after her *Century* "story" she was not going to write about politics anymore,
"for it's too delicate a subject." After her work on the exhibition, she was never
hired by the Mexican government again, although she hoped for some kind of
appointment when Luis Morones became secretary of industry and commerce
in 1924.

Porter probably submitted "Where Presidents Have No Friends" for publication before she left Mexico on June 15 and returned to Greenwich Village. On
July 27 she wrote her father that she planned to travel to Los Angeles in a
month to participate in the art exposition, "the very loveliest show you can

imagine." She never made the trip, but was informed of the show's unhappy progress by Xavier Guerrero and Roberto Turnbull, whose photographs illustrate *Outline*. Because Mexican officials hadn't supplied enough money to cover expenses, the show was held up at the border for several days and after the Los Angeles exhibition did not proceed to San Francisco, as planned; instead Guerrero was instructed to sell its objects as best he could. Nevertheless the show, which also included art work of Guerrero, Best Maugard, and Mexican schoolchildren, enjoyed considerable success in Los Angeles. Although Porter told Lopez that the U.S. government never permitted the show to enter the country (95), in November the *Los Angeles Sunday Times* reported a daily attendance of three to four thousand people.[32] Her misinformation does not diminish the significance of her participation in the exhibition. In 1963 anthropologist Alfonso Caso, one of her companions of 1922, appreciated it and sent her a copy of *Outline*. In 1980 Porfirio Martínez Peñaloza devoted a chapter of his book on Mexican folk art to *Outline*, thanking her for her contribution (91–104).

Porter also informed her father she had charge of "a show for Diego Rivera, the greatest living Mexican-Spanish painter, who is known all over Europe but not here. . . . and that will be pure glory only, but SUCH glory, dear dad!" Porter's uppercase enthusiasm for Rivera had obviously not diminished since her letter to the *Christian Science Monitor*. From all indications, she worked hard to arrange an exhibition. Responding to her request, Retinger informed her that Rivera was sending photographs and Palma de Guillén's notes. But eventually she turned the project over to artist-critic Walter Pach, who also failed to arrange an exhibition.

More significant, Porter announced to her father that she was writing stories, adding, "Dad, my life is so very full, I have arrived at such a serene sort of feeling about my work . . . I can do it, and that is settled." On September 19 she published "Two Ancient Mexican Pyramids–the Core of a City Unknown Until a Few Years Ago" in the *Christian Science Monitor* and in December "María Concepción" in the *Century,* both the result of her association with Manuel Gamio in 1921 and 1922. The article, opening with the myth of the creation of the sun and moon and ending with the myth of Quetzalcoatl, describes the pyramids, temples, and terrain of a city that "stands now, partially uncovered and darkly splendid, dominating a wide deep fruitful valley, gracious as of old, wrapped within itself, keeping a curious secret to which we have not yet found the key." About the identity of its builders Porter offers various theories, including William Niven's theory of Chinese influence. She also mentions Gamio's work of restoration, associating him with scholars, "animated by a spirit intensely nationalistic, which seeks to discover in the racial sources the answer to some of their latter day social and ethical problems."

Porter planned to write a three-part essay entitled "Teotihuacán," but among her papers there is only a description, in rough draft, of her visit to five churches in the region, including the early sixteenth-century fortress-church of Acolman, "sunk into the earth for the distance of the height of a man, stained and mildewed, shadowed and stooping with years, bowed in preparation to descend into the grave with its epoch." Once again statues of the saints inspire caustic descriptions of them—St. Ignatius Loyola "with chaste lace trimmed trousers showing beneath his black cassock," St. Catherine, holding "her cruel iron wheel with the pale fingers curved delicately, unrememberingly over the instrument on which she suffered death," and again María la Soledad: "All the sorrows of the world, of the poor, of the desolate, of the terrible believers of the world . . . have been held up to those unseeing eyes turned forever upon her own griefs." This section was most likely written in 1921, Porter later drawing on her description of Soledad for "The Dove of Chapacalco."

Teotihuacán's statues of gory Cristos also fascinated her:

> Everywhere the awful, pallid blood-streaked mask of the dying Man. Note. Study of this preoccupation with the physical torment of Christ and the saints. Saying of the Indians, "El mas sangriento el mas mila-griento." Their belief that a saint has no power unless he is covered with blood. The statues of the Spanish church in Mexico are endowed with peculiar horror. The statues of the Christ, his body a mass of bloody suppurating wounds, raised in great welts upon his back. Streaked with the scourge, dripping from the hands and feet, pouring thickly from a gash over his heart, thin rivulets of blood upon his face.

Porter asserts that the Spaniards accentuated the blood to compete with the Aztecs, who made blood sacrifice upon their altars. Her source was Gamio, who writes in *La población del Valle de Teotihuacán* of the "profuse clots of blood that cover the statues of Christ from head to foot, giving credence to the saying: *Mientras mas sangrientos, mas milagrientos*," arguing that since Indians today do not worship the bloody Aztec god of war, the reason for creating bloody Cristos had disappeared, as should the statues (98).

"María Concepción"

Upon her return from Mexico, Porter, according to a 1965 interview, took a room with breakfast at 61 Washington Square South. Encouraged to set down her stories about Mexico by George Sill Leonard, art editor of *Century*, she worked on "María Concepción" seventeen days and nights. Literary editor Carl Van Doren accepted it, and $600 proved that art could be monetarily rewarding after years of living hand to mouth (I 141–142).

Porter gave Lopez her version of the story's origins. One day while exploring the area around William Niven's excavations, she encountered in the doorway of an adobe hut a beautiful, almond-eyed woman who offered her tortillas. When the same woman appeared at the digs, live chickens draped around her neck, Niven told Porter the woman's story. She was the wife of his foreman, who had run off with his young mistress to join the army. When the couple returned, the wife killed the mistress and adopted their newly born baby as her own (70–71)—in other words, a story pretty much as it appears in "María Concepción." Porter claimed that the murder occurred three months before her visit, but it never occurred at all. Her version completely obscures the complex ways she transformed fact into fiction.

Givens, the archaeologist of the story, was, of course, based on William Niven, whose pursuit of Mexico's ancient culture Porter later described in "The Charmed Life." Even a brief history of Azcapotzalco refers to his "enchanting fantasy" of a Mongolian lost tribe.[33] "María Concepción" also reveals his patronizing attitudes toward his Indian help, for Givens "told comic stories of Juan's escapades, of how often he had saved him, in the past five years, from going to jail, and even from being shot, for his varied and always unexpected misdeeds" (7–8). The comic stories Niven.told Porter in 1920 he later reported in the *Houston Chronicle* on November 10, 1929. There we learn that Porfirio Díaz, "a staunch friend of the explorer," granted him a concession to conduct excavations in a 7,000-square-mile area in the state of Guerrero. On one occasion, Niven's "faithful old servant" was arrested during one of the frequent rebellions and sentenced to be shot the next morning, but Niven obtained a pardon from the government, went to the jail, and "secured his man" with ten pesos.

The story of Niven's servant is the source of Givens's rescue of Juan from the firing squad in "María Concepción." However, the original rescue occurred *before* the revolution in Guerrero, not during it in Azcapotzalco. Nor does Niven's faithful old servant resemble Juan, Givens's unfaithful young servant, except for the matter of the rescue. However, Juan's "small black beard" (5) does resemble the black Vandyke of Eduardo Damian, one of Niven's Guerrero guides, whose photograph the *Houston Chronicle* reproduced. Damian also wears an immense straw sombrero like Juan's hat of "unreasonable dimensions." Most likely Porter created Juan out of that photograph, for, as she reported in "The Charmed Life," Niven showed her "photographs of himself in the early days, always surrounded by Indian guides" (CE 427).

Porter's version of the story's source unravels further with the revelation in a note that she "should like to see again that honey-colored girl dipping her arms shoulder deep in the hives of honey." Porter turned this language into a poem, "In Tepozotlan," in 1924. A later note states that she put the honey-colored girl "in a story once, and called her Maria Rosa, and gave her a very sad fate." Perhaps Porter saw María Rosa's model during her walking tour to Tepotzotlán with Winold Reiss or in Teotihuacán, where Gamio encouraged the making of honey. Porter based María Concepción herself on Vicenta in "The Dove of Chapacalco," who also has "tilted" eyes and triumphs over the man who wronged her.

Apparently Porter decided late in life that her fiction would be more authentic if she labeled it "reportage," as she did "Flowering Judas," adding that she did "something to it" to make it fiction, "but it happened." Thereby she avoided probing questions about its content and forestalled speculation about literary influence that always upset her. However, she did commit petty theft when she turned Blasco Ibáñez's description of "lean and wan" soldaderas "passing over the country like a plague of locusts" (174) into "María Rosa marched ahead with the battalion of experienced women of war, which went over the crops like locusts" (8). When María Rosa returned from war, she was "lean as a wolf" (10).

"María Concepción" is the most ambitious of all Porter's short fiction. As foreigner, she attempted to penetrate the Indian psyche, a mystery to the average middle-class Mexican, and create an authentic Indian world of which her heroine is both typical product and exceptional member. The story deals with realistic depiction of indigenous life in Teotihuacán, romanticized notions of the "primitive," closely in touch with the elemental forces of nature, anticlerical and feminist notions of the victimization of women, and the mysterious ways fate controls the lives of people beyond their power to comprehend it. These strains both coalesce and clash to produce a powerful but not completely successful story.[34]

The setting of "María Concepción" is presumably Azcapotzalco, the site of Niven's excavations, situated close enough to Mexico City for María Concepción to buy medicine "at the drugstore near the city market" and for Juan to be sent to Belén prison, where Givens rescues him. In the early 1920s it, like Teotihuacán, consisted of several haciendas with a large Indian population. Porter remained relatively faithful to the region even though she relied on Manuel Gamio's knowledge of the Teotihuacán region, twenty-five miles to the northeast. In 1920, 7 percent of Teotihuacán's population was white, 26 percent mestizo, like the story's gendarmes, and 67 percent Indian. Like María Concepción, 73 percent of the population was totally illiterate. Since there was no doctor in the region, most people relied on folk remedies, like those Lupe administers. The "alarming" infant mortality rate gave a realistic basis for the death of María Concepción's baby and the poor health of María Rosa's baby, who "had spat blood the moment it was born" (17). Also 75 percent of conjugal unions were blessed by a priest, but 17 percent were natural because even the simplest religious ceremony was too costly, explaining María Concepción's pride in being married in the church. Most of the population was intensely religious and Catholic, like María Concepción, but 42 percent were "pagan" Catholics who clung to such pre-Hispanic practices as witchcraft, like Lupe. The testimony of Indians who had seen the spirits of the dead rise from the disturbed graves of pre-Hispanic excavations helps explain the fear Lupe inspires with her talk of an "evil spirit" that killed María Rosa. Most inhabitants lived in *jacales* of pre-Hispanic construction, often enclosed by organ cactus, like Lupe's. Women tended domestic fowl, gathered wood, washed clothes, ground corn, and carried food to their husbands at work, like María

Concepción; others cultivated bees, like María Rosa. Men were accustomed to drinking too much pulque, like Juan at the Death and Resurrection pulque shop.

Porter's attention to social realism is also reflected in her frequent use of Spanish words in the *Century* version of the story, which were mostly translated into English in the collected version—"*jefe*," for example, becoming "chief," "*cuartel*" "barracks," and "*pulqueria*" "pulque shop." The retained "gendarme" is a Spanish word derived from the French. "Informal," which Givens applies to Juan, has the Spanish meaning of "irresponsible"; while "no more forever," included in Juan's lament that he will not escape María Concepción, is derived from "*nunca jamás.*"

Much of the psychological tension of the story issues from Porter's attempt to make María Concepción both a typical and an exceptional member of the community, knowing her place and striving to rise above it. As a typical female member, she tells the gendarmes she knows "her place" (19), which is to perform all the domestic duties Gamio lists, the principal one being to serve her husband. Thus she "condescendingly" regards Givens, "that diverting white man who had no woman to cook for him, and moreover appeared not to feel any loss of dignity in preparing his own food." But, despite his defects, Givens is "undoubtedly rich, and Juan's chief, therefore to be respected, to be placated" (7). Her "place" is determined by sex, race, and class. Givens also knows his place as white man and chief, as if he were an hacendado. He "liked his Indians best when he could feel a fatherly indulgence for their primitive childish ways" and says of Juan, "Well, he's a good worker, and I know how to manage him" (7–8).

María Concepción also has "a good reputation with the neighbors as an energetic, religious woman" (4). Indeed, she energetically promotes her reputation by earning enough money to buy a license, "the potent bit of stamped paper" that permits her to marry in the church. Other women are content to let their men pay church fees and marry behind the church, but she "was always as proud as if she owned a hacienda" (4). To define pride in terms of race, sex, and class is revealing. She cannot change any of the three, but she can improve her "place" in the community by simulating the power associated with them. The result is that she elevates herself to a position superior to that of other women of her class, but her hard-gained independence isolates her from the community. At the same time, she is prone to superstitions; just as she fears she will "mark" her unborn baby if she doesn't satisfy her craving for honey, so she hopes that her "potent bit of paper" will strengthen her traditional role as wife and servant. If Juan accepts the paper's magical power, he will perform his duty toward her as she does toward him. But both recourses to magic fail. Juan betrays her with María Rosa and marks her child for death, creating in her a sense of loss she once experienced when she found "her jacal burned to a pile of ash and her few silver coins gone" (6). The association of losses makes Juan seem a commodity María Concepción purchased to establish her reputation as "a church-married woman" (21), the self-identity she trades on at the end of the story to escape suspicion of the gendarmes.

María Concepción's reliance on religion to secure Juan is no more effective after his desertion and the death of her child. In her elevated position of church-married woman, she performs rituals of going "regularly to church, lighting candles before the saints, kneeling with her arms spread in the form of a cross for hours at a time, and receiving holy communion every month" (9). "The Fiesta of Guadalupe," "Teotihuacán," and "The Dove of Chapacalco," in which nuns "taught Vicenta to kneel with her arms spread in the form of a cross when she was at mass," stress the inefficacy of such practices. When María tells Lupe to offer prayers "for others who need them. I will ask God for what I want in this world," Lupe responds, "Did you pray for what you have now?" (9). Lupe's question, provoked by María Concepción's rudeness, is intentionally cruel, but implies a truth endorsed by Porter's anticlericalism. María Concepción's prayers are vain and, worse, isolate her from the sympathy of other women, one of whom speaks for Porter: "'She is wrong to take us for enemies,' said old Soledad, who was a thinker and a peace-maker. 'All women have these troubles. Well, we should suffer together'" (9). Soledad's name is ironic. Like the Virgin after whom she is named, she represents suffering womanhood, but, unlike the church image in "Teotihuacán" and "The Dove of Chapacalco," she can humanly express compassion for others. In her suffering María Concepción resembles the image of Soledad in "Teotihuacán," whose "unseeing eyes" are "turned forever upon her own grief." Solipsistically she has so bottled up her "long devouring sorrow" that "for so long squeezed her whole body into a tight dumb knot of suffering" that it "suddenly broke with shocking violence" (13) in the murder of María Rosa.

María Concepción's behavior reveals her sense of superiority over other women in the story, negatively because she isolates herself from them and positively because she is fiercely independent and will not suffer passively as they have. Porter reinforces her heroine's exceptional qualities by making her a descendent of the ancient people whose remains Givens digs from the earth. Although her "black eyes, shaped like almonds, set far apart, and tilted a bit endwise" (3) make her seem walking proof, like Vicenta in "The Dove of Chapacalco," of Niven's theories about Chinese origins of Mexican culture, they are mainly intended as visual evidence of her link to it. Further evidence is her "grand manner" that "sometimes reminded [Givens] of royalty in exile" (7).

María Concepción's royal lineage points to Porter's conflicting responses to the native population. Gamio's analysis confirmed her view of the Indian as "this inert and slow-breathing mass, these lost people who move in the oblivion of sleepwalkers under the incredible burdens; these silent and reproachful figures in rags, bowed face to face with the earth" (CE 401–402). On the other hand, Indian craftsmen convinced her that they had kept alive the traditions of their ancestors and strengthened her view, expressed in "Xochimilco," of Indians who treasured their independence and seemed "a natural and gracious part of the earth they live in such close communion with." Imagining María Concepción as "royalty in exile," Porter more clearly associated her with Indians of the second group, but placed her in a realistic setting inhabited by Indians of the first, whose pottery did not appear in the 1922 folk art exhibition because its quality had deteriorated along with the spiritual quality of their ancient culture. She is, in fact, a kind of exile since, as she tells Givens, she is from Guadalajara. Porter chose the capital of Jalisco because its inhabitants have a reputation for courage, arrogance, and aggressiveness, traits, in the public mind, more Spanish than Indian and typically male. (As we will see later, Porter partly modeled her heroine after Lupe Marín, Rivera's tall, combative Guadalajaran wife.) Guadalajara as place of origin weakens Porter's attempt to make her creation a product of the world through which she moves as extraordinary being, but is intended to modify her traditional role as submissive woman who knows her place.

María Concepción is also extraordinary because she is not "bowed face to the earth," but, at the beginning and ending of the story, is a natural part of it. Porter's romantic notion of nature in the story is more complex than in "Xochimilco" since it encompasses both benign and cruel phases of its cycle with the benign triumphant, but it blurs perceptions of character motivation. The benign is evident in María Concepción's "instinctive serenity" as she walks "with the free, natural, guarded ease of the primitive woman carrying an unborn child. The shape of her body was easy, the swelling life was not a distortion, but the right inevitable proportions of a woman. She was entirely contented" (3). "Primitive" here has a positive meaning in contrast with Givens's view of the Indians' "primitive childish ways" (7), but is inadequate to explain María Concepción's "serenity," which mainly flows from her status as church-married woman. When she discovers Juan's infidelity, she is no longer serene. The death of her baby may be attributed to the poor statistical chances of its survival or to her reaction to her loss of husband and humiliating loss of status that short-circuits her maternal "instinct," resulting in the unconscious rejection of her baby. Porter's description of María Concepción as primitive obscures the complexity of her behavior and is inconsistent with the description of María Rosa, also a primitive, who is not serene but "burdened with a child daily expected" (10).

If nature, reflected in María Concepción's posture, appears benign, it is also cactus-cruel, as the story's opening sentence shows: "María Concepción walked carefully, keeping to the middle of the white dusty road, where the maguey thorns and the treacherous curved spines of organ cactus had not gathered so profusely" (3). Here she is like the pilgrims in "The Fiesta of Guadalupe" with "their clothes dusty and their faces a little streaked with long-borne fatigue" (CE 394). Although she attempts to keep to the middle of life's road, she can't avoid danger, but, in her haste, doesn't stop to draw "cactus needles from her feet." When she does veer from the road to satisfy her taste for honey, her discovery of Juan and María Rosa internalizes her suffering, "as if a layer of tiny fig-cactus bristles, as cruel as spun glass, had crawled under her skin" (6). Wherever one walks, one will bruise one's feet and heart. "Limping with foot soreness, a layer of dust concealing his fine new clothes," Juan enters the barracks and later walks out, his hair "dusty" and his feet "bare, full of stone bruises" (10). The last view of murdered María Rosa is of her feet, "jutting up thinly, the small scarred soles protruding, freshly washed, a mass of crooked, half-healed wounds, thornpricks and cuts of sharp stones" (17).[35]

The cactus María Concepción peeks through in search of María Rosa "sheered up nakedly, like bared knife blades" (4), the cutting image repeated later by "the long sharped streak of light piercing the corn-husk walls from the level disappearing sun" (14). These natural images obviously relate to María Concepción's butchering knife. When she discovers Juan and María Rosa together, her first thought is to slit their throats. Instead, she later slits the throat of a chicken she has brought for Givens's meal. Unaware of the symbolic nature of the act, he is amazed by her "nerve," to which she responds that her "home country" is Guadalajara. Another answer may be that she is the primitive child of cruel nature, instinctively responding to its force. If so, she is related to non-Indian characters in other stories. In "He," "Mrs. Whipple took the pig with her face stiff and sliced its throat with one stroke"—to the horror of her son (52). In "Noon Wine," Mr. Thompson, blindly attempting to protect his hired man, "knew he had the ax out of the log in his own hands, felt his arms go up over his head and bring the ax down on Mr. Hatch's head as if he were stunning a beef" (255–256). These killings occur on Texas farms where people are close to nature and killing instruments. Although the killers are not "primitives" like María Concepción, they have in common the killing instinct. In "St. Augustine and the Bullfight," Porter's fondness for bullfights makes her "face the cold fact that at heart I was just a killer, like any other" (CE 100). Circumstances determine the nature of killing. Butchering chickens is part of María Concepción's trade. After Juan deserts her, "She worked harder than ever, and her butchering knife was scarcely ever out of her hand" (10). The knife becomes an extension of her personality, forecasting the nature of María Rosa's death.

If the murder of María Rosa reveals María Concepción's primitivism, so to an extent does the murder of Hatch reveal Thompson's, for in both stories the main characters act involuntarily and become unwitting accomplices in a fate beyond their comprehension. The essential difference between the two stories is the frequency of involuntary actions in "María Concepción." When María Concepción discovers Juan's infidelity, her emotional reaction is so strong that it obscures her mental processes. Coming "out of the heavy cloud which enwrapped her head and bound her throat," she "found herself walking onward, keeping the road without knowing it," her "careful sense of duty" keeping her moving toward Givens's excavations (6). Unconscious sense of duty never guides the carefree steps of Juan. When Rosa gives birth, "his emotions so twisted him" that he overly celebrates at the Death and Resurrection pulque shop. "Having thus taken leave of his balance," he starts back to María Rosa, but "found himself unaccountably in his own house, attempting to beat María Concepción by way of reestablishing himself in his legal household" (12–13). Without intending it, he begins a process that will reestablish the old order. Now it is María Concepción's turn to carry out her preordained role. She sets out on "the accustomed road" to the market, but begins to run "with a crazy panic" and loses her bearings "until she realized that she was not going towards the market." Then "she came to her senses completely" to recognize "what she wanted." At this point she gives into "her long devouring sorrow": "She jerked with the involuntary recoil of one who received a blow, and the sweat poured from her skin as if the wounds of her whole life were shedding their salt ichor" (13). "Involuntary" is a key word in a long passage describing María Concepción's suffering. She has become suffering incarnate and in that state kills María Rosa, whose multiple wounds give mute testimony of the blind intensity of the suffering that caused them. Porter does not describe the actual killing, but allows the vivid description of María Concepción's suffering to suggest that cause and effect are one, conveying the sense of forces that rule the lives of characters beyond their conscious power to understand them.

After María Rosa's murder, fate clearly works in María Concepción's favor. Upon her return to their *jacal,* she unwittingly effects a change in Juan that potency of license could not. To appreciate that change, we must view his character from Porter's feminist perspective that influences the working of fate throughout the story. In the Feminist League pamphlet Carrillo Puerto gave her in 1921, Porter read the admonition, "Drop the veil from your eyes to see that man is not your lord, but your equal." It was not something she had to learn, but something María Concepción impresses upon Juan. When Givens saves him from the firing-squad, Juan thanks him elaborately, "From this day my life is yours without condition, ten thousand thanks with all my heart!" (11). He has made a pledge as if to his beloved, one never made to his wife. Through it, he reestablishes, after his freedom fling in the revolution, his servitude to his chief, who knows how to "manage" him. At this point, his consolation, he thinks, is his access to two women. He claims he acts properly toward María Concepción; like the centurion in the New Testament, he says to her, "Come here, and she comes straight. I say Go there, and she goes quickly." His male authority to command extends to María Rosa, "a girl," he tells Givens, "with whom I do as I please." In his "masculine triumph," he makes light of Givens's warning, "Some day María Concepción will just take your head off with that carving knife of hers," assuring him, "I will manage them when the time comes" (12). He thinks he will manage them as Givens manages him; for consolation, the servant to the ruling class tries to assert himself as sexual master in his own sphere.

Juan is a caricature of a Mexican type; courting María Rosa early in the story, he "flourished his wide hat back and forth, walking proudly as a game-cock" (6). The image evokes the macho, who is "muy gallo"–very arrogant and proud. Porter humorously elaborates on the image when Juan, after his rescue, walks out of the drum-head court, "a definite air of swagger about him. His hat, of unreasonable dimensions and embroidered with silver thread, hung over one eyebrow, secured at the back by a cord of silver dripping with bright blue tassels" (10). Outside he conducts an "insufferable pantomime" of fare-well to those still in prison, and tells Givens, "Well, it is nothing much to be shot, my chief–certainly you know I was not afraid . . ." (11). Back in the village, he luxuriates in his role as "hero"; as he walks in the sunshine with "the smoke of cigarettes under his nose," his "situation was ineffably perfect, and he swallowed it whole" (12).

In his fool's paradise, Juan has been set up for the fate that befalls him. After his carousal, he wakes up to see María Concepción in the doorway, "looming colossally tall to his betrayed eyes" with knife in hand (14). He first fears for his own life, but she throws the knife away and crawls toward him to confess her crime. Making him "aware of danger," something the revolution failed to do, she forces him to be responsible. He does not fail; he washes the knife, disposes of her blood-stained clothes, and instructs her on how to answer the gendarmes. She has shocked him into an unthinking immediate response as he stares "at her as at a creature unknown to him, who bewildered him utterly, for whom there was no possible explanation" (15), much as the chickens slung over her shoulders in the first scene "twisted their stupefied eyes and peered into her face inquiringly" (3). María Concepción is exceptional indeed in trans-forming this gamecock, now confronted with "the mysterious fortunes of life grown so instantly confused where all had seemed so gay and simple" (15–16).

At the inquest, the women whom María Concepción had spurned come to her defense. Old Soledad had said, "She is wrong to take us for enemies." Now they prove themselves her friends. Lupe could have ruined María Concepción, "but it was even sweeter to make fools of these gendarmes," who are not part of the close-knit community and are male beside. Anita, her baby feeding at her breast, tells the gendarmes that it was the loss of María Concepción's "child and not of her husband that changed her so" (19), while Soledad "boldly" states that she had told María Concepción that "this is a happy day for you." It is indeed:

> María Concepción suddenly felt herself guarded, surrounded, upborne
> by her faithful friends. They were around her, speaking for her, defend-
> ing her, the forces of life were ranged invincibly with her against the
> beaten dead. María Rosa had thrown away her share of strength in them,
> she lay forfeited among them. María Concepción looked from one to the
> other of the circling, intent faces. Their eyes gave back reassurance,
> understanding, a secret and mighty sympathy. (20)

This climactic passage blends the points of view of María Concepción and of Porter herself. Through her murder of María Rosa, María Concepción has unwittingly mobilized other women who identify with her suffering because, as Soledad says, "All women have these troubles. Well, we should suffer together" (9). If there is solidarity in suffering, there is also a circle of "secret and mighty sympathy" which María Concepción recognizes for the first time, moving her to adopt María Rosa's baby as her own. This act is the last of a series of actions that began with Juan's infidelity. On one level, everything has a psychological explanation, but on another, "the forces of life," identified with the female, triumph over the cactus-cruel forces of suffering and death. *La Suerte* is another name for these forces.

Porter's fascination with *la Suerte* in her just-published "Where Presidents Have No Friends" extends into "María Concepción." In the former, where Carranza's fall begins in "a wide desert, harsh with cactus" (CE 404), *la Suerte* betrays all who trust it, but in "María Concepción" it is more discriminating. When Juan walks past the prison, those inside wave to "the lucky departing one," but he considers his marriage in the church "a great misfortune for a man" (11). When he discovers that María Concepción has killed María Rosa, he "could not fathom . . . the mysterious fortunes of life," (15) and later contemplates his loss: "Oh, Jesus! what bad luck overtakes a man!" (20) Lupe interprets the blood María Rosa's baby spat at birth as a "bad sign" that "bad luck would come to the house" (17). But old Soledad tells the gendarmes, "When I saw María Concepción in the market today, I said, 'Good luck to you, María Concepción, this is a happy day for you!'" (19–20). Luck is in the eye of the beholder; at the end of the story, the faithful woman, content with child in arms, is lucky while the faithless man feels unlucky because his days of faithlessness are apparently over. Givens, the other man in the story, completely absorbed in his fanatic pursuits and without any meaningful relation to another, has already become the Old Man of "The Charmed Life." In the *Century* version of "María Concepción," he is "*jefe*," linking him to Carranza, who is also called "the old man" and "chief" since he himself took the title of Jefe Maximo, or First Chief. In "Where Presidents Have No Friends," *la Suerte* betrayed Carranza, but in "María Concepción" it does not touch Givens at all and positively rewards the faithful woman.

On the mythic level, the "forces of life" relate to the female principle that encompasses both death and resurrection in the natural life cycle.[36] María Concepción, "royalty in exile" to Givens and "looming colossally tall" to Juan, is then the avatar of the earth goddess. In that light, her murder of María Rosa appears even more clearly preordained, María Rosa becoming the necessary sacrificial victim, her life "forfeited" and her body resembling that of the lacerated Cristo that Porter saw in a Teotihuacán church. Males in the story fail to appreciate the woman's mythic qualities and to realize their own manhood. Givens, on a class level, is the authority figure, the *jefe*, but on a human level he is childish as "his young enthusiast's eyes" in "his old-man face" (7) suggest. Juan, a biological father, treats women as if they were children he can "manage," physically molesting them to assert his male authority, but, in the face of

María Concepción's suffering, he wishes "to repent openly, not as a man, but as a very small child." He "stares at her as at a creature unknown to him" because in this story women are creatures men are constitutionally incapable of knowing, except sexually. The only other male authority figures in the story are the gendarmes, whom it pleases Lupe "to make fools of."

The brief last section of the story celebrates those "forces of life" which the circle of María Concepción's "faithful friends" represents. As she and Juan enter their *jacal,* it is clear he does not reside in that circle:

> Juan's exaltation had burned out. There was not an ember of excitement left in him. He was tired. The perilous adventure was over. María Rosa had vanished to come no more forever. Their days of marching, of eating, of quarreling and making love between battles, were all over. Tomorrow he would go back to dull and endless labor, he must descend into the trenches of the buried city as María Rosa must go into the grave. He felt his veins fill up with bitterness, with black unendurable melancholy. Oh, Jesus! what bad luck overtakes a man! (20)

Metaphorically Juan's life is over. María Concepción had enkindled his small reserve of sympathy for her which he exhausted in his effort to save her, but now only the dying embers remain and he doesn't even "know why he had fought to save her" (21). Uncomprehending, he plays the role la Suerte assigned him. María Rosa has vanished into her grave to come "no more forever," and he must enter the symbolic grave he himself has dug at Givens's archaeological site, much as deserters during the revolution were forced to dig their own graves before being shot. Like the people of Teotihuacán, he faces a joyless living death of meaningless drudgery. He feels nothing "except a vast blind hurt like a covered wound," a wound to his manhood signified by the act of stripping "his body of its heavy finery" that had identified him as proud gamecock. Then he falls asleep, "his arms flung up and outward" in childlike exhaustion and surrender.[37] Porter wastes little pity on him, the cause of María Concepción's suffering. She spared his life that he may suffer in the endless torment to which he resigns himself: "Well, there was no way out of it now. For the moment he craved only to sleep" (20–21). If the passage could be forced to mean that after a good night's sleep he will think of some way out, it would make him truer to type. As long as the revolution lasts, he must stay with Givens to escape a drum-head court, but once the revolution is over, nothing would prevent him from still another desertion. Making his defeat absolute, Porter unconvincingly denies Juan the opportunity to continue his irresponsible behavior.

In contrast to Juan, María Concepción is perfectly fulfilled: "The child, fed and asleep, was cradled in the hollow of her crossed legs. The silence overfilled the world, the skies flowed down evenly to the rim of the valley, the stealthy moon crept slantwise to the shelter of the mountains. She felt soft and warm all over; she dreamed that the newly born child was her own, and she was resting deliciously." The evocation of total contentment after a year of torment extends for another last paragraph. As if she had not sufficiently united her heroine with the silence of the world and with the moon nestled in the mountains, as if she wished to prolong her own identification with the primitive, elemental forces of life, Porter added another, longer coda, ending with these four sentences: "The night, the earth under her, seemed to swell and recede together with a limitless, unhurried, benign breathing. She drooped and closed her eyes, feeling the slow rise and fall within her own body. She did not know what it was, but it eased her all through. Even as she was falling asleep, head bowed over the child, she was still aware of a strange, wakeful happiness" (21). No other story in Porter's canon ends so lyrically, so hopefully. It opened with María Concepción's "instinctive serenity" as she carried the "swelling life" of her unborn child. "She was entirely contented" then as she is now, "head bowed over the child." Reading only the first and last pages, one might assume that mother and child in both scenes are the same. And in a sense they are, for they merge into the transcendent figure of the female who nourishes and sustains life.

María Concepción and María Rosa are one, probably because they began as one. The original of both was, most likely, the honey-colored girl tending her hives. In her note, Porter explains why she had given her a "sad fate" as María Rosa: "But it was only because I felt the fatefulness of all beautiful creatures clung about her. And yet her face was very calm and lovely as she stood there and reached her hand in the hive for a comb of honey." She must have seemed like the girl in "The Children of Xochitl," who "should live for a century," almost immortal like the goddess. Porter's desire to see the girl again is an attempt to sustain the illusion of her immortality: "She was there; I felt as if she had always been there." And yet it is an illusion. She will not always be there, nor will her girlhood beauty, even more ephemeral than her being. To kill her in a story is to cruelly shatter the illusion, to rush her to inevitable death. In the context of the story, María Rosa, like a flower, is too sweet, too fragile to last the season. She is also too pliable, too subject to the abuse of Juan, who does with her what he wills. Better to construct out of her beauty another beauty, but, through a kind of natural selection, one more resilient, more durable, more capable of self-defense.[38] Juan beat María Rosa as he pleased, but when he attempts to beat María Concepción, she amazes him by striking back and lives to triumph over him. In the story he is the spermatozoic link between the two women and nothing more. He impregnates women and then flees from them. He will not sustain life, but María Concepción will. She has survived her suffering to become the ideal mother, at one with the cosmos. She is not the Edenic figure in "The Children of Xochitl," but a close relation made more real by her suffering, because all women suffer.

Among Porter's papers is a photograph apparently of a beautiful Indian woman standing in profile by a stone wall, a rebozo over her head and around her shoulders, but, on closer inspection, it turns out to be Katherine Anne Porter posing as an Indian. In one sense, María Concepción is Porter dressed in Indian garb. When her father sank into depression and proved ineffectual after the death of his wife, his talented daughter wondered if she weren't a changeling to have such a feckless man as a father—that is, she imagined herself as exceptional. She married just after turning sixteen, approximately the same age as Vicenta in "The Dove of Chapacalco" when the archbishop took her and as María Rosa when Juan took her. She had violent arguments with her husband over women's rights and eventually divorced him. In Vicenta and María Concepción she projected her own desire to triumph in a man's world, to rise above her lot and fulfill the promise of her nature. But María Concepción is more than Porter in disguise. She is an illiterate, church-going woman with a view of her place in society totally different from the author's. Porter attempted to get inside her skin and feel the suffering of the Indian that she only witnessed from the outside in "The Fiesta of Guadalupe." Although her mythic feminist vision at times conflicts with her attempt to be faithful to the psychological realism of Indian life, "María Concepción" is still a remarkable work. Until Juan Rulfo, few Mexican writers had even attempted what she did.

Two Legends

Shortly before the publication of "María Concepción," Porter and actress-friend Liza Anderson[39] rented an apartment at 15 Gay Street in the Village. On January 30, 1923, she mentioned to Retinger, then in Europe, the "melancholy story" of the Los Angeles exhibition, but was "very thankful" not to be concerned with it nor with any Mexican nor any Mexican plans. She informed him that *Century* turned down an essay she had translated for him because Rivera's illustrations for it were too modern. She thanked him for the invitation to visit Europe, but declined because she planned to go to Asia or Africa. Liza, reading over her shoulder, thanked him, too. Because of the flurry of postcards he had sent, both wondered whether he was celebrating National Post Card week. In answer to his complaint of her "severe" reply to another letter, she told him he had to have everything explained and still didn't understand anything.

Porter also informed Retinger that she was writing short stories and a novel. Begun in the early twenties, the novel was called *Thieves' Market,* alluding to the Lagunilla market in downtown Mexico City. The few surviving notes of the earliest version are based on Porter's 1921 experiences, including her profession of a secret love of Paul Hanna, her "jagged" love affair with Retinger, and her departure from Mexico, Retinger and Doherty seeing her off at the train station. In two scenes the Porter character is called Laura while in others she is Miranda and Doherty is Laura. Porter later dated some Miranda scenes 1921 and 1922, which conflicts with her statement that she adopted the name in 1924.[40] The character of Laura in "Flowering Judas" evolved from some of these scenes.

The stories Porter mentioned to Retinger were probably "The Martyr" and "The Lovely Legend." "The Martyr" was published by *Century* in July 1923 during her third visit to Mexico. It is a light satire about Rubén, a famous rotund muralist who eats himself to death when his mistress-model Isabel runs off with a rival artist. Porter, of course, based her characters on Diego Rivera and Lupe Marín, incorporating her 1922 description of Marín in the story. Her notes also describe "Lupe the Savage" in a "a black dress with jagged bits of shiny green satin sewed on; her enormous high heeled satin shoes, her black satin bonnet shaped like a jockey's cap, her riding crop, more than six feet tall, powerful." Rivera's biographer, Bertram Wolfe, calls her "the wildest and most tempestuous beauty in Jalisco." Before Porter left Mexico in 1922, Marín, who hated Mexico City, returned to Guadalajara. Rivera was heartbroken, couldn't finish his murals, and hardly ate, wasting away "though not exactly to a shadow." He soon journeyed to Guadalajara, married Marín in June, and returned with her to Mexico City. But their marriage didn't alter their turbulent relation; provoked by Rivera's philandering, she would become vengeful, slashing his artwork and once threatening to shoot off his right arm to prevent him from ever painting again.[41]

Marín's escape to Guadalajara inspired Porter's plot in "The Martyr" except that in the story no reconciliation takes place and the legendary Rubén does just the opposite of waste away, his gluttonous demise absurdly implausible in light of the Rivera-Marín relation. Porter believed that Rivera provoked and tolerated Marín's outrageous behavior because he loved the ideal her beauty represented more than he loved her. Ignoring the fact that he won Marín back, she comically explored, not what might have happened, but what should have happened had he not: remove this artist's inspiration and kill the artist as punishment for his exploitation of his beloved as art-sex object. Porter's legend deflates the real legend of Diego, her story becoming an inside joke for readers who know its source. Part of the joke is that the proprietor of the Little Monkeys hopes his cafe will become "a shrine" where the legendary muralist died eating "tamales and pepper gravy" whereas Los Monotes was already famous for that mouth-watering dish and, of course, for the caricatures of Orozco, who despised Rivera.

Beyond the inside joke, "The Martyr" burlesques the male pose, celebrated in popular songs, of suffering untold torment of unrequited love because of his beloved's cruelty. Rubén, the courtly lover, accuses Isabel of being "his executioner," thereby making him "a martyr to love," his death the fitting proof of his devotion. His cynical friends, in control of their appetites, want to tell him "the true cause of his pain," but fearful of bringing up the "indelicate" subject, call in a physician who recommends a sensible diet to control one appetite and vigorous exercise and "ice showers" to control another. Rubén's friends themselves are satirized for their sexist bias. Ramón, who did "heads of pretty girls for magazines," knows "how women can spoil a man's work" (35). They also exploit Rubén's death, hypocritically perpetuating a romantic fiction for profit, the proprietor for his tamales and Ramón for the sentimental biography he intends to write for the gullible public who used to make "pilgrimages" to the Martyr's studio and will now visit the "shrine" of the Little Monkeys.

Ramón, also performing as caricaturist, visually accents the story's genre. Displaying "his new caricature" of the Martyr, he tells his friends he "could as well have drawn it with a compass" (35). The narrator gives another witty version of the Martyr: "He hung in all directions over his painting-stool, like a mound of kneaded dough" (36). Through these images Porter pitted her skill as caricaturist against that of Rivera. Since men make art objects of women, women can turn the tables. Rubén-Rivera can claim he has been murdered, not by Isabel, but by Porter's satirical revenge. However, "The Martyr" is playful enough that Rivera would have appreciated it if he ever read it. After all, several years after their divorce, he illustrated *La Unica,* Lupe Marín's fictionalized biography that exposes her many grievances against him. When "The Martyr" appeared, Porter was busy collaborating with him on an article about the Mexican artists' guild.

"The Martyr" was to be the last of a group of stories told around the central figure of Rubén. So Porter wrote Freda Kirchwey of the *Nation* about "The Enchanting Legend of Rosita," another story in the group. Although she told Kirchwey she loved it very much, it remained among her papers under the title of "The Lovely Legend." The presence of Ramón the caricaturist in the story is our clue that it, like "The Martyr," is genre conscious, but it also raises serious questions about the responsibilities of the artist. Ramón is "a caricaturist who daily distilled synthetic venom in a daily newspaper. It was his duty to be malicious, and so he found it easy to take a harmless rabbit-faced politician, and give him the features of a pig or a tiger, and make the reader say: 'How mistaken I was in this man! See how Ramón has uncovered his true character!'" The duty of the caricaturist is to uncover true character, but Ramón's duty is to destroy it. He is a caricature of the caricaturist as corrupt artist or yellow journalist.

Amado, the story's main character, is also an immoral artist, who closely resembles Salomón de la Selva. Also a native of Nicaragua, he gives a more decadent version of the poem De la Selva wrote after he and Porter danced on broken glass in front of the ex-convent: "She danced for me on broken glass with her white feet bleeding. I knelt and kissed the wounds through the cold iron grill of the gate. I wiped away her blood with my handkerchief." Porter dedicated "this story to the characters in it," freely acknowledging her "debt to one of them for some of the more intimate details here related." Although unnamed, De la Selva is both subject and source of passages in "The Lovely Legend." Her seemingly grateful acknowledgement of debt is license to create a devastating portrait of the person to whom she is indebted.

The story opens with Amado, into his twentieth drink, beginning "one of his endless tales of erotic personal experience in the sub-cellar stratum of romance." He and Porter do not spare us details. We not only learn of the nun with bleeding feet, but of "an innocent little thing" from Amecameca, like "a softly modelled clay jar, the reddish sort with the thin glaze from Tonala," who "could have taught tricks to a Viennese," the jar image borrowed from the archbishop's description of Vicenta in "The Dove of Chapacalco." The bored Rubén notes that Amado remembers all the women "with their color schemes," but Amado insists on their importance, for "they are mixed with my memories of cities; I have seen them on walls and on fruits. The women . . . share these tints with indestructible or recurring things; it is . . . a thousandth reincarnation for them in my memory when they, the least fortunate of living creatures, are vanished out of youth." When Rubén asks whether "these creatures" had faces, Amado replies that faces are "over praised": "I remember them in the tips of my fingers, in my nostrils." The point is obvious. Faces express human individuality which Amado ignores or even fears. On the artistic level, they are, like fruit, colorful objects to be arranged and preserved in a poem after their beauty has fled. Since sex and art object are one, Amado doubly violates human nature.

Amado and Porter as artists are similar in that both are preoccupied with beautiful young girls. In "The Children of Xochitl" Porter describes them as "lovely creatures, the color of polished brown stone." In "In Tepozotlan" she remembers the "honey-colored girl" dipping her arms into the hives of honey. In Oaxtepec in 1930 she saw another girl "with the innocent grace of first youth." This "beauty" was "the first entirely flawless human being I had ever seen, and it occurred to me that she might also be the last. I had the curious sense which comes over me at certain sights or events of uniqueness . . . which fixes suddenly the wandering attention and brings it down to focus." Both Amado and Porter reincarnate girls in their memory since they are sorrowfully aware of their fleeting beauty and youth. But Porter wished to preserve their Edenic innocence in her memory whereas Amado, representing Porter's view of the male artist, wishes to corrupt their innocence and immortalize "the least fortunate of living creatures," as if they had no value outside his art.

Rubén also reveals his egotism as artist. Deploring Amado's taste for soft women, he specifies the kind of beauty he seeks as model for his Maya fresco: "A lean tall woman" with "long hard hands and feet, and a nose with a hooked bridge" and "her hair must be black"—a precise description of Lupe Marín. Amado knows just such a woman, a tubercular prostitute in a nearby brothel. He finds nothing beautiful in this tall "ghost," but Rubén, when he sees Rosita, is attracted by her "ferocity" and the "truly noble arrangement" of her bones and invites her to his home, where she models for him and recovers her health. Beginning to doubt his own taste in women, Amado seeks for "signs of beauty" in her, looking at her "through Rubén's eyes." His fascination grows, but when he witnesses the "virago" hurling Guadalajara pots at Rubén with deadly aim, Rubén, his eyes "male and ruthless," explains: "This violent empty creature, useless as a human being, has for me the value of a work of art. If I make love to her, it is a mere matter of etiquette. I permit her to satisfy her grosser impulses by smashing water jugs on my head. These things have no relation to my Maya fresco." Amado then returns to Nicaragua, where he attempts to rewrite his poetry, all the time remembering Rosita "as he had last seen her magnified portraits on the walls," "her likeness raised to the stature of a goddess." Having fallen in love with Rubén's projection of her, he returns to Mexico only to hear that Rosita's violence and refusal to pose forced Rubén to dismiss her. "Imagine!" Rubén exclaims, "She regarded those gorgeous bones as her own property." He later reports that a woman, "moved by a monstrous jealousy, took Rosita by surprise and stabbed her to death"–exactly the fate suffered by her namesake, María Rosa, in "María Concepción."

Amado then rushes home and weeps profusely that he never told Rosita he loved her and now will never know how she might have replied. In this Edgar Allan Poe mood he dries his tears and in a frenzy composes a long poem to Rosita that he later reads at "the Cafe de los Monotes" to Rubén, Ramón, and Pancho Guerra (Xavier Guerrero), "an Indian sculptor with a face like a sacred tiger in greenish stone." The poem is a ballad "in a hurrying medieval style, relating the sorrowful life, the tragic death, and the triumphal entry into a waiting heaven of Rosita. [Rubén's] superhuman charity to her, and her angelic gratitude, were the two balancing themes." His audience explodes in laughter at this insincere effort and Rubén informs the offended Amado that Rosita, whom he dismissed because his mural was finished, was alive and had returned to the brothel. The "hardhearted" Rubén reassures him: "You have your poem, I have my fresco. They are the ends, what else is in the least important? Rosita? pah, dead or alive, how does she figure in this now?"

But Amado is unwilling to accept such brutal honesty because he has always deceived himself into thinking his art somehow uplifted the woman it exploited. When he returns to the brothel to find Rosita "more hideous than he remembered her the night [Rubén] came to take her away," he realizes that only her death had value to him: "She had shared none of that bath of tears, no honourable burial, no tremendous resurrection in Eternity." Sickened by all the "beautiful thoughts he had had about her," he now realizes that "he did not love her, he had not loved her, again he had been tricked by his own invented emotions. He was ashamed of his ballad, she would have laughed with the rest, and she would have been right." But Porter undercuts his Joycean epiphany since "his feeling toward her persisted with terrible gentleness, as if she were really dead." He last sees her from Rubén's point of view: "Limp, full of angles, the wrist protruded from the white sleeve that muffled up the noble arrangement of shoulder and neckbones." Amado leaves, knowing it would make no difference whether she saw him or not.

Rosita, then, is prostituted in both the brothel and Rubén's studio, her body a property she has no right to claim as her own. Rubén and Amado are moral monsters, the difference between them being that Amado is a self-deceived inferior artist whereas Rubén is intelligent, with no illusions about the demands of his art. Porter names him Rubén after Rubens and in an earlier version Rafael to suggest he is a master. His power to bring the ghostly Rosita back to life and turn her into a goddess in his art speaks to his talent, but he abuses that power by dismissing her and thereby turning her back into a ghost. Like Hawthorne's Aylmer of "The Birthmark," he has sacrificed a woman to his obsession.

Biographically, the story reveals Porter's contempt for De la Selva, who moved her to create a type of male with limitless power of self-deception, limited power of self-recognition, and no power of self-redemption. Her caricature of Rivera as god-artist and devil-man pinpoints the source of her ambivalence toward him. She was right about his obsessiveness as artist; often working on the scaffold seventeen hours straight, he covered walls of public buildings with his art. She was also right that Marín represented to him an ideal of beauty that outlasted their five-year marriage, but she underestimated the staying power of their attachment. Her two legends suggest it was completely utilitarian and would or at least should soon end.

Although Porter, in her notes, called Marín "savage," she employed that quality to counter male aggression in both "María Concepción" and "The Lovely Legend." Both Marín and María Concepción are from Guadalajara, symbolic land of courage and violence. In "The Lovely Legend," Rubén is delighted with Rosita's "ferocity": "There is a menace on [sic] her very clutch on the wine glass. She could cut one's throat with the rim." In "María Concepción" Givens fears that menace when María Concepción slits the chicken's throat. Juan also fears her when she stands "in the doorway, looming colossally tall to his betrayed eyes" (14), her height inspired by the six-foot-tall Marín. Juan's fear contrasts with Rubén's delight at the woman's menace.

The theme of death and resurrection is contrasted in the two stories. The movement of "The Lovely Legend" is from Rosita's ghostliness to her resurrection as goddess and back again to her ghostliness, prefigured by Rubén's false story of her death by stabbing. The movement in "María Concepción" is from life (María Concepción's unborn child) to death (her child and María Rosa) to resurrection and life (María Concepción united with her newly adopted child). In the shifting configurations, even María Concepción's husband, whose full first name is Juan de Dios, is related to sexist De la Selva, whose imitation of Juan de la Cruz is changed to Amado's imitation of Juan de Dios in "The Lovely Legend." Rosita's aggressiveness and vulnerability, both derived from Lupe Marín, also make clear the splitting of Marín's character into the two Marías in "María Concepción." Lupe, María Rosa's godmother, inherits Marín's name as she protects both Marías in turn. Porter shares in María Concepción's triumph over life and revenge against Juan, but in "The Lovely Legend" avenges Rosita's victimization through her damning portraits of Rubén and Amado.

Mexico 1923

Appointed art editor of *Survey Graphic*'s special issue on Mexico, Porter returned to her second country around May of 1923, her visit coinciding with the Bucareli Conferences, which resulted in the resolution of land and oil disputes and in U.S. diplomatic recognition of Mexico on August 31. She did not mention the conferences, but five pages of notes, dated August 30, carefully described Mexico's various political parties and their leaders, among them Porter's acquaintances. She mentioned among Calles's supporters Carrillo Puerto, "anarcho-syndicalist with communist leanings," and reported that everything was being smoothed for the election of Calles to the presidency, which would be rotated in succeeding years among the Sonoran group of Obregón, Calles, and De la Huerta, wisely adding "maybe." Familiar names got special mention concerning Mexico and Russia. Her "Private Opinion" is that "*Morones was under influence of Retinger, who declared a year ago that Morones should not visit Russia*" and was "now taking much counsel with Haberman, who is determined there shall be no alliance with Russia." She found "Haberman grown really powerful," as "right hand man" of Calles and "best friend of Morones." A "great number of people" told her that Mexico's indifference to Russia was not a ploy to hasten U.S. recognition, but was "founded on a very real political antagonism." These notes, written with a view to publication, reveal a journalistic interest in Mexican politics that would diminish after the De la Huerta revolt.

While Porter was still in Mexico, the assassination of Pancho Villa occurred on July 20. In 1920 he had been permitted to retire to his ranch in Chihuahua on condition he keep out of politics, but in ensuing press interviews had criticized Calles, who at least condoned the assassination to remove a still-dangerous political enemy.[42] In a long note, Porter wrote that Villa was "on the point of beginning a campaign of disturbances calculated to harm the case of Calles." She objected to the newsboys' habit of "thrusting pictures of the death mask, made after the face was unrecognizably swollen, under one's eyes as one sat eating peacefully in a cafe, trying to forget politics." Although she considered him a treacherous bandit, she objected to the Mexicans' "discouraging" failure "of form, of technique" since they should have tried him for sedition. She predicted that the instigator of the plot would soon be released. He was.

On August 12, Porter visited Cuernavaca and the pre-Columbian ruins of Xochicalco with Haberman, his secretary, and her sister, "two plump and rosy little feminists, wearing trousers." The purpose of the trip was to attend an official observance of agricultural progress in the region. She dashed off two hasty pages of impressions—of ruined houses and scarred and bullet-battered walls, of Zapata's story, of very eloquent and beautiful speeches of Indian campesinos, of the Yaqui military brass band rehearsing a new waltz, ending her notes: "I sat under a blooming bougainvillea and plucked me a bouquet of sweet blowing grass. I should have been discussing the sugar and rice crops with the Governor. But do I not already know that only community ejidos are being worked . . . and 600 million pounds of rice have been produced?"

Porter was able to trade political impressions with fellow writers from the States. One was Bertram Wolfe, who came to Mexico with his wife Ella to teach English under Vasconcelos's education program and to help unify the Mexican Communist party.[43] Porter later praised him as "the only man in Mexico I ever trusted to tell me a straight story about political and social situations as they came." She also met Wolfe's friend, journalist Carleton Beals, who had taught English to Carranza's officers in 1920 and after his overthrow went to Europe on a passport arranged by Robert Haberman. Again reporting on Mexican politics and culture, he visited the Preparatory School with Porter to view Rivera's murals.[44] She later made a story, "That Tree," out of his account of his marital difficulties.

Porter also began an essay on the Mexican muralists who had become more directly political. The Syndicate of Mexican Painters, Sculptors, and Engravers was formed shortly after David Siqueiros's return to Mexico in September 1922. Their manifesto explained why they had to affiliate with "the revolutionary proletariat" and create "revolutionary art" at a time of "exasperated class struggle," of "imperialism oppressing our people, our native races and peasants."[45] Among the officers were Rivera and Guerrero, both of whom soon joined the tiny Communist party and served on its Executive Committee. Porter doubted Rivera's political acumen: "Romance of the Party. Mad illogical schemes presented to the conferences with such persuasiveness, such irrational fervor, the Committee adopts most of them offhand, discovers later that the move will bring disaster, and reverses it amid clamors."

In his *Survey Graphic* article, "The Guild Spirit in Mexican Art," "as told to Katherine Anne Porter," Rivera explains the artists' identification with the worker. The guild concept nurtured "the community of labor" that "Indian artists have never departed from," for when "art becomes a cult of individual eccentricity," created for the "exclusive, the aristocratic pleasure of the few, it is a dead thing."[46] While translating his ideas into English, Porter wrote that Rivera "was moved by some high romantic dream of reviving the ancient guild spirit, of a group of artists moved by common creative impulses working together in the building up of a generous art spirit," but this dream would fail because the "group of youthful mediocrities" collected around him have neither his "faith" nor his "genius." Her own individualism as artist made the guild idea suspect.

In 1923 she had ample opportunity to survey recently completed murals. She dismissed Dr. Atl's "superficial notions of design over the walls of what was one of the most beautiful buildings of Mexico—the patio of San Pablo and San Pedro, where a series of impossible ocean waves collide with each other," while Roberto Montenegro "has festooned those austere arches with pretty conventionalized flowers." She liked Jean Charlot's "scandalously clever and humorous" art and thought Guerrero came closest to the work of Rivera, but reserved her highest praise for Rivera himself:

> Diego Rivera, with his spacious and human concept of art: who shall touch those walls where he has so faithfully recorded the long-endured and laborious agonies of men buried in mines and bound to looms, bowed face to the earth under wheat and sugar and corn, their garments stained to the colour of clay; the portentous and calm fecundity of the women, the dark eternal menace of a land saturated with the memories of human struggle and suffering. He has set it all down with a dreadful simplicity, with Indian fatalism and a delicate Gachupin sadism; being half Spanish, he understands by nature the value of moral cruelty, and twists the screw at precisely that moment when it is most unendurable.

The murals Porter referred to in her essay are among those on the first floor of the Court of Labor in the Ministry of Education building, six of which she chose for the *Survey Graphic* issue. Viewing this work for the first time in 1923, she was deeply moved by "the dark eternal menace of a land saturated with the memories of human struggle and suffering," the same deathly landscape she saw during her walking tour with Winold Reiss while her image of men "bowed face to the earth" recalls Indians "bowed face to face with the earth" in "The Mexican Trinity." Although the mural "Leaving the Mine," which Porter reproduced, depicts the oppression of the worker, other murals of men at labor were intended to depict "redemptive actions,"[47] but Porter saw only the portrayal of suffering.

Porter never completed her work on Mexican artists. In 1923 she met two women who did complete theirs. Back in the land of her birth, Anita Brenner recorded in her journal, "There is also here a Katherine Anne Porter of *Century*–that is the way they introduce them all except me."[48] Her *Idols Behind Altars* (1929) gave Porter, when she reviewed it, the opportunity to return to her 1923 notes. Alma Reed was another writer interested in Mexican art, as *Orozco* and *The Mexican Muralists* attest. Porter met her briefly in 1923, but came to know a good deal about her because the careers of these two beautiful, socially conscious journalists paralleled each other in uncanny ways. Invited by President Obregón to visit Mexico in November 1921 because of her defense of a Mexican national in California, Reed met Manuel Gamio, whose study of Teotihuacán was the source for her *The Ancient Past of Mexico*. While visiting archaeological sites in Yucatán in February 1923, she met and fell in love with Felipe Carrillo Puerto. On the occasion of their engagement in September, Ricardo Palmerín, at Carrillo's request, composed in her honor the haunting "La Peregrina," which became one of Mexico's most famous popular songs.[49] After his death in 1924, Porter turned Carrillo Puerto and Reed into fictional characters in her notes and in "Flowering Judas."

Survey Graphic

Besides the seven Rivera murals, Porter collected for *Survey Graphic* a Rivera drawing of Lupe Marín's hands, modeled for the allegorical figure "Strength" in his Creation mural; ten examples of Mexican children's art; and Winold Reiss's portraits of Indians and a painting of Cuernavaca. (He had also illustrated "Where Presidents Have No Friends" in *Century*.) A portrait of Sor Juana Inés de la Cruz accompanied Porter's translation of her sonnet "To a Portrait of the Poet," while Best Maugard's drawings decorate Porter's article "Corridos."

Porter's tribute to Sor Juana is noteworthy: "She was, in her beauty, her learning and her Catholicism, the perfect flowering of seventeenth century European civilization in the New World" and "was, like most great spirits, at once the glory and the victim of her age" (182). By "victim" Porter meant that Sor Juana was a double victim as woman and free-thinking intellectual in a tradition-bound age that respected neither. She died of a plague and thereafter her "own pure and candid legend persists and grows, a thing beloved for its unique beauty." Porter did not die in the plague of 1918, but her identification with the beautiful, talented Sor Juana is clear. Porter paid tribute to other legendary heroines over the years. In her foreword to Regine Pernoud's book on Joan of Arc, she was reassured that "every one of the witnesses who spoke of the matter at all had one word for her: she was beautiful."[50] In the thirties she discovered in the Paris Museum the mummy of Thaïs, a heroine from a far more distant past: "All my life I had loved Thais. She was to me the symbol of all loveliness hastening to decay. . . . call it by a name—whatever name is your symbol for the eternal beauty. And Thais was my symbol. . . . Here was my dream, here was my gathered and stored beauty."

The paradox of eternal beauty hastening to decay applies to Porter's honey-colored girl, the young girl from Oaxtepec, and Sor Juana. Following is Porter's literal translation of Sor Juana's "To a Portrait of the Poet":

> This which you see is merely a painted shadow / Wrought by the boastful pride of art, / With falsely reasoned arguments of colours, / A wary, sweet deception of the senses. / This picture, where flattery has endeavored / To mitigate the terrors of the years, / To defeat the rigorous assaults of Time, / And triumph over oblivion and decay— / Is only a subtle careful artifice, / A fragile flower of the wind, / A useless shield against my destiny. / It is an anxious diligence to preserve / A perishable thing: and clearly seen / It is a corpse, a whirl of dust, a shadow, / nothing.

Sor Juana's sonnet is itself a portrait of her portrait, a work of art denying the validity of another that has frozen her in time, as portraits will, in its attempt to preserve a perishable thing. She insists on her mortality, her body "hastening to decay," but her living voice in her sonnet has not perished nor has Miguel Cabrera's portrait, reproduced above her poem, of a beautiful Carmelite nun looking out at us from her desk. Cabrera's portrait was indeed "a painted shadow" since it was painted years after Sor Juana's death, evidence that her "pure and candid legend persists and grows." Porter had Sor Juana's portrait and poem in mind when she began "Old Mortality" with a description of Aunt Amy, "forever in the pose of being photographed" (173), whose legend is embellished by her husband's tombstone poem, "She lives again who suffered life, / Then suffered death, and now set free / A singing angel, she forgets / The griefs of old mortality" (181).

Porter's third contribution to *Survey Graphic* is "Corridos," a remarkably fine essay on the Mexican folk ballad. She read Dr. Atl's treatment of corridos in *Las artes populares en México* and a volume of corridos borrowed from Bertram Wolfe. But most of all she delighted in the songs she heard sung in the streets and marketplaces while their composers sold printed versions "on spongy, luridly dyed strips of paper" for less than a centavo. The very setting in which the song was sung had much to do with its appeal:

> Popular singers vend their wares during early mornings when the citizens crowd to the narrow cobbled streets of the markets. Among the open booths hung with streamers of bright muslins and thin silks, mounds of pottery and colored glass, the heaped melting fragrance of figs, apricots, mangoes and peaches, birds in wicker cages (those sweet-throated doomed creatures whose modest colors have been disguised with brilliant lead paints, which will shortly bring them to death), withies and mats of palm fiber, fowls whose legs have been broken to keep them from wandering, intricate foods simmering over charcoal *braziers,* soft-eyed, self-possessed Indian girls with small stands of brass and silver jewelry, a huddle of beggars and dogs: there, in some accessible corner, the singers squat, strum their guitars, and sing.(157)

Porter excels in this evocation of a Mexican market with its overwhelming jumble of activities, smells, and colors.

And there, amid the teeming life, are the artists, an integral part of the world they capture in song. The birds in wicker cages (later used in "Virgin Violeta") and the broken-legged fowl reflect life's cruelties, subject matter typical of their ballads. Since the ballad's "stories are always concerned with immediate fundamental things; death, love, acts of vengeance, the appalling malignities of Fate," of all Mexican folk arts, it came closest to her own. She closes "Corridos" with a tribute to Mexican singers: "A race of singing people . . . used to sorrowful beginnings and tragic endings, in love with life, fiercely independent, a little desperate, but afraid of nothing. They see life as a flash of flame against a wall of darkness. Conscious players of vivid roles, they live and die well, and as they live and die, they sing" (159). The passage expresses Porter's view of the artistic ideal. No wonder that Mexican songs and ballads have thematic significance in such Mexican works as "Xochimilco," "In a Mexican Patio," and "Flowering Judas." In "Hacienda" Carlos Montaña renders a ballad, "imitating the voice and gestures of a singer peddling broadsides in the market" (160). Porter's poems "In Tepozotlan" and "Fiesta de Santiago" were published in 1924 under the title "Two Songs from Mexico." Of her non-Mexican fiction, the titles of "Noon Wine" and "Pale Horse, Pale Rider" allude to songs that point to the stories' meaning. Miranda identifies "Pale Horse, Pale Rider" as an old spiritual about Death taking away the singer's lover and whole family one after another:

> "But not the singer, not yet," said Miranda. "Death always leaves one singer to mourn. 'Death,'" she sang, "'oh, leave one singer to mourn–'" (304)

Porter first sounded that motif in "Corridos": "Ah, the weeping women of the *corridos*. No man can be so utterly brought down but there will always be left one devoted, steadfast woman to come, weeping, bringing what consolation her love can devise" (158).

The list of *Survey Graphic*'s contributors, among them Calles, Beals, Carrillo Puerto, Gamio, Haberman, Dr. Atl, and Vasconcelos, reads like a who's who of Porter's acquaintances in Mexico. In his introduction, "Mexico–A Promise," Frank Tannenbaum admits that "dream and hope and plan and program" absorb the writers of the issue (132). The essays are filled with such phrases as "common dreams and hopes," "full economic, political and social equality," "Indian liberation and social regeneration," "dreamers of a Social Utopia," and "redemption of the race." Carrillo Puerto, in "The New Yucatán," writes: "The revolution in Yucatan has one main objective–to give the Maya Indian his status as a free man, to save him from the evil consequences of physical slavery and from the cultural and spiritual stagnation which slavery had gradually imposed upon him," adding that in the past the state had to import all it ate but in four years now raised enough to feed itself (138–139). Porter might have taken heart from such accomplishments to alter her pessimistic predictions about Mexico's future except that the De la Huerta uprising that occurred between her departure from Mexico early in September 1923 and the publication of the *Survey Graphic* issue in May 1924 took an estimated toll of 7,000 lives, including those of Carrillo Puerto and three of his brothers, executed by rebel commanders on January 3. It would have mattered little to Porter that Carleton Beals, who finished his *Survey Graphic* article just before publication, credited Obregón's victory to the support of agrarian and labor leaders, including Samuel Yúdico, and of U.S. labor leaders, led by Samuel Gompers (137). The occasion of the uprising was presidential succession, but avaricious generals joined it for their own gain, proving Blasco Ibáñez's estimate of Mexican militarism in 1920 accurate.

4. Thinking of Mexico, 1924–1930

1924–1926

Porter left Mexico in September 1923 and didn't return until April 1930, but in the years between she discussed it in book reviews and depicted it in fiction and poetry. "Two Songs from Mexico" appeared in the January 1924 issue of the *Measure,* one of whose editors was Genevieve Taggard. The subject of both poems, "In Tepozotlan," about the honey-colored girl, and "Fiesta de Santiago," is death. Porter based the second poem on dances she witnessed at the feast of July 25, 1923, noting how successfully the dancer representing Santiago gave "the complete illusion of a man riding a living horse." Her poem, however, describes the dancer moving as if in a "trance," "a smile of death" masking his face and the "odour of silence" on his breath. Like a ghost from the ancient past, he imitates gestures "scrawled upon tombs" of "the indifferent dead" (CE 486). Porter wondered how good her poems were, but after a few rejections decided she was not a poet. Taggard rejected "This Transfusion," one of four "witch" poems Porter said (April 3, 1925) she wrote in Mexico. In it the persona tells a former lover that her hatred is a "distilled Vial of torment" to fill his veins with her "enduring pains" until his "sole desire" will be for death and "the ease of hell." This is an early expression of the theme of hatred.

Back in New York, Porter continued her editorial work for *Survey Graphic.* On April 5, less than a week before the issue was to go to press, she urgently requested Francisco Aguilera, her "Hijito adorado," to help her translate two songs in one of the articles. Porter and Aguilera, a Chilean doctoral student at Yale University, met soon after her return from Mexico, pursued their romance on weekends in New Haven and New York City, and ended it by the summer of 1924, but not before he christened her Miranda. Years later, she wrote that "from that far-off episode I took my alter-ego name which I can never abandon—and there is no reason why I should since it is, in meaning and origin, exactly appropriate to that character!"[1] Swayed by her emotions, Porter deceived herself into thinking she and Aguilera had fallen deeply in love, but in her assigned role as Miranda she had unconsciously entered into a fictional relation. After the affair was over, she wrote her sister Gay that she "had suffered a great deal from love, or rather, the impossibility of finding an adequate substitute for illusion."

If love was an illusion, death was not. Porter returned to her favorite subject in "Requiescat" (later renamed "Little Requiem"), which appeared in the *Measure* in April. Since the "She" should have been the daughter of a king or had a lover instead of only a song, "She has well hidden herself / With the beaten dead. / Since for lack of these things / She knew herself lost, / She has well chosen silence / With her hands crossed" (CE 487). She recalls María Concepción, "royalty in exile," while "the beaten dead" exactly describes María Rosa (20), but she most closely resembles Sor Juana, who had no lover but a song instead, and who was "hidden" in the convent and chose "silence" after the bishop of Puebla suggested she give up her scholarly pursuits. Choosing "silence" also suggests suicide, which Porter contemplated in 1921.

Her affair with Aguilera over, Porter, welcoming the opportunity to escape New York City's summer heat, accepted the invitation of friends John and Liza Dallett to visit them in North Windham, Connecticut. When they returned to New York, Porter stayed on. On November 14 she wrote Taggard that she had finished "Holiday" "in a bath of bloody sweat" *and* was expecting a baby in January, causing Taggard to exclaim to Josephine Herbst, "Good God, Katherine Anne is pregnant." On November 28 Porter wrote that the baby's "name [Miranda] and sex have been definitely chosen for several months at least," but on December 18 reported that the baby, a boy, was stillborn. Porter's letters to Taggard are the only contemporary record of her experience. According to Givner, a friend who saw her daily during that period never noticed signs of pregnancy (171). Apparently in competition with Taggard, whose recently born baby Porter had called "an undeniable success" (July 23), she "chose" pregnancy as she chose the baby's name and sex, consciously toying with the birth of her alter ego. With the publication of "Virgin Violeta" in the same month, Porter gave fictional birth to Miranda under a Mexican name.

"Virgin Violeta" is set in an upper-middle-class Mexican home, a world far removed from that of "María Concepción." Whereas fifteen-year-old María Rosa is taken by Juan Villegas and bears his child a year later, the almost fifteen-year-old Violeta is an innocent, very confused "because she could not understand why the things that happen outside of people were so different from what she felt inside of her" (23). (Adolescent confusion is the source of a formulaic statement Porter made about others—Mary Doherty and Mae Franking, for example—and about herself: whatever the cause at the time, they did not know what was happening to them.) Violeta has a crush on her poet-cousin Carlos who comes to read poetry with her older sister Blanca while her mother dozily chaperons. She grieves that Carlos doesn't notice her, but stares instead at a religious painting on the wall over her head. To attract his attention, she volunteers to retrieve a book of his poetry. Proving he had noticed her all the while, Carlos follows her, but when he attempts to kiss her, she becomes terrified and repels his advances. She threatens him—"I will tell my mother! Shame on you for kissing me!"—but he claims he only gave "a little brotherly kiss" and makes her feel guilty—"Shame on you, Violeta!" (29). Totally confused, she returns with him to the living room, but when he tries to kiss her good-night upon his departure, she "heard herself screaming uncontrollably" (31).

Apparently puritanical Catholicism of the Mexican middle-class reminded Porter of her own strict Methodist upbringing. Violeta, described as "a little newborn calf," has a natural inclination to learn about herself and her body, but the male-dominated system conspires against her, attempting to deny or suppress all signs of her intellectual and sexual maturation. Her father prescribes punishment he expects her mother, herself a victim of the system, to carry out when Violeta supposedly misbehaves. Like Carlos, he fills Violeta with guilt, warning her, "It is your fault without exception when Mamacita is annoyed with you. So be careful" (26). Her mother admonishes her to "consider the feelings of others . . . and control your moods," (25) later repeating her advice: "You are quite a young lady now, and you must learn to control your nerves" (31). "Control" is the key word, understood by the convent nuns who teach male-determined female virtues, "modesty, chastity, silence, obedience, with a little French and music and some arithmetic" (23).

At home Violeta feels like a parrot stuffed in a cage, "gasping and panting, waiting for someone to rescue" it, like the "birds in wicker cages" in "Corridos." Church also is "a terrible, huge cage, but it seemed too small" (26). While the girls in veiled rows tell their beads, Violeta dreams of her love for Carlos, but afraid others may discover her "secret," she "would begin praying frantically, 'Oh, Mary! Oh Mary! Queen Mother of mercy!'" (26) as if her love of Carlos were shameful. But Porter's anticlericalism has indicated the futility of such prayers.

The point is confirmed by the painting Carlos stares at. The metal plate on its frame reads, "Pious Interview between the Most Holy Virgin Queen of Heaven and Her Faithful Servant St. Ignatius Loyola," but in the picture, "The Virgin, with enameled face set in a detached simper, forehead bald of eyebrows, extended one hand remotely over the tonsured head of the saint, who groveled in a wooden posture of ecstasy" (22–23). Violeta thinks it "a perfectly proper picture," but not the narrator. "Detached" relates the Virgin Queen to the "dim and remote" Guadalupe with a sexual dimension added as Ignatius grovels in a "posture" of ecstasy before a simpering enamel doll. Beneath the simulated piety is a suggestion of hidden sexuality repeated in the posturing behavior of Blanca and Carlos. In one scene Blanca "posed ridiculously" with Carlos as she leaned over the table while in another Carlos "would resume his pose" and gaze at the painting above Violeta's head. In a tableau imitative of the painting, he assumes Ignatius's posture: "St. Anthony himself could not have exceeded in respect the pose of Carlos' head toward his aunt" (23), as if she were the Queen of Heaven. In fact, all three women become the object of feigned religious veneration. The aptly named, pale-faced Blanca "blooms like a lily" and is expected by the father to conduct herself like one (23), just as Violeta as "Virgin" is expected to emulate the chaste Queen of Heaven to whom she desperately prays.

To control their women, men insist that they behave like bodiless saints while they remain sex objects. Taught that sex and love are vile secrets, Papacito's daughters respond in unhealthy, confused ways. Blanca "really didn't think of anything but the way she had her hair fixed or whether people thought she was pretty" (27). Treated as object, she behaves like one, self-absorbed and uncaring. Violeta's response takes a different turn when she imagines herself a participant in one of Carlos's poems "about the ghosts of nuns returning to the old square before their ruined convent, dancing in the moonlight with the shades of lovers forbidden them in life, treading with bared feet on broken glass as a penance for their loves" (24). Although the poem is thrillingly romantic to Violeta, it depicts female repression of normal desires for which women must masochistically punish themselves. She cannot distinguish between love and sex or know their proper relation because society, the story tells us, is responsible for her confusion and the guilt Carlos makes her feel after imposing himself on her.

Carlos's poem is a close version of the one Salomón de la Selva composed after dancing with Porter in front of the old Vizcaínas former convent in downtown Mexico and less lurid than the one in "The Lovely Legend." In "Virgin Violeta" Porter projected herself both as Blanca, to whom Carlos reads poetry just as De la Selva read Dickinson's poetry to her, and also as Violeta, whose models are Palma de Guillén's younger sister, whom De la Selva allegedly seduced, and Porter herself if it is true she had become pregnant because of him. In the story, Porter depicts Carlos's transgression, not as a seduction but a rape. When his mouth touches Violeta's lips, she "felt herself wrench and twist away as if a hand pushed her violently. And in that second his hand was over her mouth, soft and warm, and his eyes were staring at her fearfully close. . . . Something was terribly wrong. Her heart pounded until she seemed about to smother" (28–29). His forced kiss permanently changes Violeta. At the end of the story she "amused herself making ugly caricatures of Carlos" (32), just as Porter made ugly caricatures of De la Selva in the story and in "The Lovely Legend." De la Selva was Porter's main model for the predatory male, who, she wrote, "would introduce himself as the Holy Ghost" if "he ever met the Virgin Mary." The remark further reveals the hidden meaning in the religious painting: the male falsely venerates the female with violation in mind. "Virgin Violeta" means virgin violated.

Porter's caricatures of De la Selva are acts of revenge possibly because she conceived his violation of Palma de Guillén's sister as a reenactment of a violation she herself once suffered. She wrote her father (May 22, 1933) that she was so "criminally wronged" in her first marriage with John Koontz and that it took her "years to recover from the shock," while in "Old Mortality" Miranda, Porter's alter ego, refers to her early marriage only as "an illness that she might some day hope to recover from" (213). Porter, married at an age slightly greater than Violeta's, does not specify how she was criminally wronged; perhaps she obliquely recreates in "Virgin Violeta" her early trauma. Not as protected as Violeta but, like her, romantically inclined and sexually ignorant, she may have responded to her husband's sexual advances as if they were a violation from which she never recovered. Significantly, she portrayed loss of virginity at age fifteen in "The Dove of Chapacalco" and in "María Concepción," in which Juan's seduction of María Rosa appears as a rape: "When he seized her, he clenched so hard her chemise gave way and ripped from her shoulder. She stopped laughing at this, pushed him away and stood silent, trying to pull up the torn sleeve with one hand" (5).

It is also significant that Porter complained about her first husband to her father, for Violeta's hysterical reaction to Carlos's advances may reflect, not only Porter's memories of De la Selva and of her first husband, but also her own unresolved Oedipus complex. Karen Horney writes, "The first mate stands in a quite peculiar way for the father": "To the unconscious mind, defloration is the repetition of the fantasied sexual act performed with the father" and with it are reproduced "all those affects belonging to the fantasied act"—"strong feelings of attachment combined with the abhorrence of incest" and "revenge" (52).

Certainly Porter had conscious reasons enough for unhappiness with her father. His own desolation and guilt over his wife's death led him to accuse himself and his children as the cause. This in turn led to Porter's fear of pregnancy and childbirth, as an analysis of "Flowering Judas" and "The Grave" will demonstrate. His rejection of his children also led to her need for affection and approval. The limited attention he did give them was based on physical beauty. Givner points out that his early preference of Mary Alice, whom he considered the prettiest of his daughters, caused Porter's preoccupation with her own beauty for the rest of her life (50). For instance, she wrote Josephine Herbst (August 3, 1934), "Do you remember Virginia Moore? . . . She is really, seriously beautiful, and is more beautiful than when I saw her two or three years ago. She is positively a treat to the eye, the lucky devil. I should like to look exactly like her." Such a desire of the seriously beautiful Porter explains the anxiety of Violeta and Miranda in "Old Mortality" about not being as beautiful as their sisters and their need to be admired by others.

Porter, according to Givner, suffered from frigidity (92), a condition specified in "The Evening," in which the Porter character is called a "gringa fria," and in "Flowering Judas," in which Braggioni calls Laura "cold." Horney states that the condition, defined as the woman's "incapacity" for a full and lasting love relationship (74), is "always an expression of rejection of the male" (128).

Among the causes are the woman's disappointment in the father (79), dread of rape (155), rejection of pregnancy (73), and/or fear of dying in childbirth (104), all of which appear in Porter's fiction.

Horney speculates that a girl's upbringing in which she is segregated from males could cause her to view them unrealistically as "heroes or monsters" (128), precisely Violeta's antipodal views of Carlos and often Porter's views of men before and after marriages or affairs. Even more pertinent to Violeta's character is Horney's description of an adolescent personality type who "feels utterly unattractive despite evidence to the contrary," but, paradoxically, "becomes depressed or apprehensive as soon as there is no man to admire her" (236). If, in her "insatiable thirst for admiration," she enters into sexual relations, she "proves to be frigid" (242). Violeta resembles this type in that she dreams she would some day become "miraculously lovely—Blanca would look perfectly dull beside her—and she would dance with fascinating young men" and "would appear on the balcony above, wearing a blue dress, and everyone would ask who that enchanting girl could be" (24–25). Violeta, in her thirst for admiration, imagines herself "wearing a long veil, and it would trail and flutter over [this] carpet as she came out of church" with "six flower girls and two pages, the way there had been at Cousin Sancha's wedding," adding quickly, "Of course she didn't mean a wedding"(24). Possibly she means her *quinceañera* debut, soon to be celebrated on her fifteenth birthday, but the wedding setting without the groom is significant. She dreams of Carlos as an alternative to her dull, stifling routine, who would pay her court by reading his unreal poetry to her, but when he tries to become physically real, he is a threat and shatters her romantic fantasies.

On one level, Violeta is Porter's early version of Miranda in "Old Mortality," published fourteen years later. In both stories, each girl is sexually innocent, each has an emotionally remote father, each is jealous of an older sister, each dreams of becoming a raving beauty like a glamorous older cousin but fears her dreams won't come true, each attends a convent school where she feels trapped, each undergoes unhappy experiences with a man, and each becomes disillusioned and estranged from her family. "Virgin Violeta" is a story about the sexual confusion of a young, overprotected girl, but when read in the context of its biographical sources, it is a much richer story, more revealing of Porter's personality than "Old Mortality."

"Holiday" is the second story Porter finished in the fall of 1924, a shorter version of that published in 1960,[2] meshing biographically with "Virgin Violeta" and "Old Mortality." Violeta's wish to escape from her convent school anticipates Miranda's escape from her convent school into marriage, a fictionalized version of Porter's own escape from her family into marriage with John Koontz in 1906. "Holiday" is based on her escape from Koontz around 1912 to take temporary refuge at the farm of the Hillendahls, relatives of Jules Hillendahl, who later married Porter's sister, Mary Alice.[3] The story opens with the narrator's declaration that since she was "too young" to cope with her problems, she decided to "run away from them" (407).

Porter's first story set in Texas, "Holiday" is thematically linked to her Mexican works. The constantly recurring theme of estrangement appears in it and in "The Evening," also begun in 1924. In the Mexican story, a "gringa" very much like Porter listens to the chatter of artist friends in a cafe. She speaks "childish Spanish," but when her companions speak rapidly, "the language became a blur." Unable to understand the words, "she leaned back and closed her eyes, and the sounds translated themselves to her in terms of emotion." But later when her friends ignore her, she "felt herself again a foreigner, and the men at her table were strangers." The language barrier in Mexico deepened Porter's sense of alienation, triggering her memory of an earlier experience in Texas.

In "Holiday" the narrator lives with the German-speaking Müllers, themselves aliens, living in "a house of perpetual exile." At first the language barrier is a pleasant relief, as it is in "The Evening": "I liked the thick warm voices, and it was good not to have to understand what they were saying. I had made a journey to find silence, that word having a special meaning for me of remoteness from the urgency of external experience, and this muted unknown language was silence with life in it, one could not be troubled by it, as by the crying of frogs or the wind." As in Porter's note on Amecameca, "Fiesta de Santiago," and "Requiescat," "silence" connotes a deathly withdrawal. In this passage "silence with life in it" suggests a happy mid-state between life and death, implicit in all of Porter's Edenic experiences. The experience appears at midpoint of the seasonal movement in the story, its title indicating a brief escape from the reality of suffering (421). The story is about her failure to sustain her vision of an Edenic world.[4]

When the narrator first views "the desolate mud-colored shapeless scene" (409), she fails to discover the "paradise" (408) her friend (who recommended the Müller farm) had promised, but with the warming days it begins to emerge: "At the edge of the woods there had sprung a reticent blooming of small white and pale-colored flowers. The peach trees were each a separate nosegay of shell-rose and white." And then it is full upon her, caught in one of the most remarkable responses to nature in Porter's fiction:

> When I came up through the orchard the trees were all abloom with
> fireflies. I walked slowly here, and finally stopped and waited, for it
> seemed I must not miss this beautiful thing that I might never chance to
> see again. The trees were freshly budded out with pale bloom, the
> branches were immobile in the thin darkness, but the flower-clusters
> shivered in a soundless dance of delicately woven light, whirling as airily
> as leaves in a breeze, as rhythmically as water in a fountain. Every tree
> was budded with this living light, tiny whirling rings of fragile and airy

designs of cool fire. I came to the gate and ascended the hill. When I
looked back, they were still there. It was no dream.

Out of the unformed slime of the universe nature has formed "this beautiful
thing." Unlike Miranda's vision of the heavenly meadow in "Pale Horse, Pale
Rider," this was "no dream" and far more magical.

The Müller family seems at first a natural part of this Eden: "They were
land-holding German peasants, who stuck into the earth and held fast because
to them life and land were one thing." The relation between the women, children, and farm animals is so close that the narrator blurs distinctions between
the species. Gretchen, "expecting another baby, wore the contented air of a
lazy young animal." In their games little children "miraculously metamorphosed into horses . . . and galloped home. They came at call to be fed and put
to sleep with the docility of their own toys or animal playmates. Their mothers
handled them with an instinctive, constant gentleness." Annetje "cared for the
newly-born kittens, the freshly hatched chicks with her special care," caressing
the weanling calves when she set the milk before them. Her child seemed as
much a part of her "as if it were not yet born," while Gretchen's newly born
baby "bawled and suckled like a young calf."

The narrator herself soon succumbs to the natural rhythms of farm life:
"But their repose, the almost mystical inertia of their minds in the midst of this
muscular life, communicated itself to me little by little, and I absorbed it gratefully, and felt the hidden knotted places in my mind to loosen a little. It was
easier to breathe, and I might weep, if I pleased." The narrator's "knotted"
mental processes are loosened by the Müllers' ties to the earth, "instinctive"
responses, and "mystical inertia" of mind, making them kin to the Indians of
Xochimilco who live in close harmony with nature and seem ageless because
they do not suffer from mind-knotting neuroses. The Müllers' "peasant skepticism" and "peasant fatalism" also seem Indian. Even their "slanted" or "tip-
tilted" eyes are reminiscent of the eyes, "tilted a bit endwise," of María Concepción. And Father Müller, who reads *Das Kapital* as if it were "a very bible,"
shares the skeptical anticlericalism of Porter and her Mexican friends since he
is sure his money and not his atheism will determine whether or not the
Lutheran minister will baptize his grandchild.

But the world of "Holiday" does not remain Edenic, despite the narrator's
attempt to create the illusion. Ottilie, brain-damaged and mute because of a
childhood illness, proves the existence of a fallen world. She is always referred
to as "servant," cooking at all hours for the large extended family and hobbling
about in constant nervous motion—like the woman servants in "In a Mexican
Patio," who work from before dawn until after dusk. With her deep wrinkles
she is, like them, "born old" in service to others. Her face, "so bowed over it
was almost hidden," recalls the Mexican Indians, "bowed face to face with the
earth." And her face, "a brown smudge of anxiety"—"anxiety" appears three

times in the first draft—pointedly relates her to the narrator, whose own anx-
ieties had begun to dissipate under the soothing Müller routine.

Ottilie senses the narrator's concern, drawing her "for some mysterious purpose" to her room where she shows her a photograph of herself at age five, "a
pretty German baby, looking curiously like an elder sister of Annetje's two-
year-old." At that point the narrator recognizes Ottilie as her double:

> For a moment some filament lighter than cobweb spun itself out between
> that conscious cell in her brain and my own mind. The filament came
> from some center that held us all bound to an unescapable common
> source, and so her life became akin to mine . . . and the painfulness of
> her suddenly vanished. She knew that she had been Ottilie, with those
> steady legs and watching eyes, she was still Ottilie within herself. For a
> moment, being alive, she knew she suffered, for she stood and shook
> with silent crying and smeared away her tears with the open palm of
> her hand.

The filament stronger than fate does not permit the narrator to dismiss Ottilie as the Müllers have. She "could do nothing but promise" herself "to forget
her, and therefore to remember her for the rest of [her] life," for Ottilie is a
magnified symbol of the human condition, of all loveliness hastening to decay.
She is Porter's young niece, Mary Alice, who died in 1919,[5] as well as the
honey-colored girl, María Rosa, Rosita, Joan of Arc, and Thais. Her photograph, like that of Aunt Amy or the portrait of Sor Juana, tells us what once
was and is now no more. Even her muteness signifies the near impossibility of
communicating with or finding solace from others, reflecting Porter's own feeling of her family's indifference to her. But Ottilie's suffering individuates her,
making her superior to the rest of the family who share a communal identity.
Since she knows she suffers, therefore she is. At first the narrator wishes to
deny her that existence and put her out of her misery: "Let it be now, let it be
now. Not tomorrow even, but now. Let her sit down quietly in her chair by the
stove and fold those hands." Folded hands recall the woman in "Requiescat"
who has chosen "silence" with "her hands crossed." But Ottilie will not fold her
hands. The narrator's wish is selfish, as if all suffering would disappear at Ottilie's death. The wish is also suicidal since Ottilie represents the core of the
narrator's suffering being. To escape her is to escape life. But, "stripped of
everything but her mere being," she clings to life, teaching the narrator en-
durance, the capacity to go back to her own center, to the creature that rules
her "who will one day say, 'Now I am all you have—take me'" (413).

The narrator's Edenic world disappears once she identifies with Ottilie's suffering. Shortly thereafter a sudden flooding rain kills livestock, levels fields,
and causes the death of Mother Müller. As the grief-stricken Müllers conduct
her coffin to the country burial ground, the narrator "realized for the first time,

not death, but the terror of dying. I went to my room and lay down, an awful foreboding certainly closed over me like a vast impersonal hand. Life was squeezed away drop by drop, a cell at a time I was dying as I lay there." This passage, modified in the final version, reveals the narrator's terrified fear of her own mortality, or her own loveliness hastening to decay, as if a time-lapse X-ray machine were recording the rapid deterioration of each cell of her body. As she slips into a disturbed sleep, a simulated death born of fear of dying, Ottilie ironically brings her back to life. Awakened by a howling, which she dreamed was that of the German shepherd caught in a trap, the narrator hastens to the kitchen to find Ottilie howling "with a great wrench of her body" and pointing in the direction of her mother's funeral procession. Thinking that Ottilie wants to join it, the narrator places her in a wagon and sets off after the Müllers. Then she realizes her mistake, for Ottilie, temporarily freed from her kitchen trap, "suddenly, shockingly . . . clapped her hands with joy" at the "feel of the hot sun, the bright air, the jolly staggering of the wagon, the peacock green of the sun." The "knotted wrinkles of her face" change just as "the hidden knotted places" of the narrator's mind began to loosen on the Müller farm. But such release of the mind is short-lived. The narrator realizes, "There was nothing I could do at all, then, to ease my heart of Ottilie. Well, we were both equally the fools of life, equally fellow fugitives from death. We had escaped for one day more. We would celebrate our good luck. We would make a holiday." Porter often tricked herself into thinking she had escaped into Edenic states. Although they were only brief holidays from suffering, they justified her willingness to endure it.

While completing "Holiday," Porter began her career as reviewer for the *New York Herald Tribune* with her review (November 2, 1924) of two books that don't deserve rescue from "the growing rubbish heap which is the literature about Mexico in the English language." At this time Porter was also polishing her translation of Diego Rivera's "From a Mexican Painter's Notebooks" that appeared in *Arts* in January 1925. Rivera defined aesthetic theories in keeping with Porter's own. He praised the "Indian aesthetic" for its "profound and direct expression of a pure art in relation to the life which produced it" and stressed the need to feel "the presence of the divine mysterious core hidden within the visible spectacle of the world." Those who express the inner world are true artists, but those who merely copy are "optical" painters. Porter applies the term to *A Gringo in Mañana land,* calling it an "optical record of a touring newspaperman in Mexico" to indicate that he has failed to give any inner meaning to his experiences.

At this time Porter was also in contact with various Mexicans shuttling between Mexico City and New York. In January 1925 she returned Rivera's drawings for the exhibit she attempted to arrange for him in 1923.[6] On July 3 Retinger informed her that Morones, "still one of the foremost statesmen in Mexico," was going to visit Washington and New York in August. Since Mexico was planning another art exhibition for which Porter was to do propaganda in the United States, Retinger suggested that she arrange to see Morones. She apparently did meet him, for she told Carleton Beals (January 16, 1926) she tended negotiations "for months," but they "wilted on the stem."

During this period Porter was busy editing Best Maugard's *A Method for Creative Design,* the 1926 English edition of his book on art theory. In letters of September and October, Best mentioned Miguel Covarrubias's return to New York after a long visit in Mexico, where he had told Retinger "lots of stories" about Porter and her work. On December 23, 1925, she reviewed Covarrubias's *The Prince of Wales and Other Famous Americans* in the *New Republic.* Her review begins, "In Mexico there is a well seasoned tradition of fine caricature: almost every one of the younger painters possesses this lacerating gift." In his works he has "exposed the very outer appearance of a sitter that is the clue to an inner quality the sitter has spent most of his life trying to hide, or disguise. If that isn't murder, what is it?" Here Porter, who developed her "lacerating gift" in Mexico, gives a perfect definition of her own satiric method. Her murders began with her caricature of Rivera in "The Martyr."

On January 16, 1926, Porter wrote Carleton Beals that she and Ernestine Evans had formed "a permanent Committee of Discussion on Ways and Means to Get Me to Mexico." She asked him about the possibilities of teaching English in a rural school, teaching dancing in technical schools, as in 1921, or lecturing on American poets, any simple job that would keep her in Mexico "at least two years." She also suggested becoming his "assistant on Tass,"[7] reminding him that she was "a demon newspaper person." She preferred "association with human beings rather than with the bourgeoisie" and would "willingly live in poverty for the mere sake of being" in Mexico. She was convinced that finishing three books she had "planned, outlined, and partially written" depended on being in Mexico "several years more." In closing, she asked Beals to tell Xavier Guerrero that "it is I who can complain now of neglect. He definitely owes me a letter, and I am a harsh creditor."

Since nothing came of her meeting with Morones or letter to Beals, Porter had to settle for more reviews of books on Mexico. The first two reviews of 1926, of D. H. Lawrence's *The Plumed Serpent* (March 7) and *The Rosalie Evans Letters from Mexico* (April 11), were strangely coincidental. Porter called the first "Quetzalcoatl" and her second "La Conquistadora," not totally contrasting titles since the Aztecs mistook Cortés for the fair-faced god. Porter intended "Quetzalcoatl" to refer, not to the English translation of the god's name, but to the fair-faced Lawrence himself, come to Mexico as self-appointed avatar of the ancient. Both Lawrence and Evans were repelled by and drawn to the country and bent on imposing their own order on it, he mythically and she economically. Both failed.

Porter generously praises Lawrence's main strength: "All of Mexico that can be *seen* is here, evoked clearly with the fervor of things remembered out of impressions that filled the mind to bursting. . . . He makes you a radiant gift of the place [and] provides the framework for a picture that does not omit a leaf, a hanging fruit, an animal, a cloud, a mood of the visible Mexico" (CE 421). Lawrence's ocular painting is excellent, but has he, in Rivera's terms, discovered the "mysterious core hidden within the visible"? Is his "inner world" in "harmony with the forces surrounding him"? Porter's answer is unequivocal: Lawrence is pretentious "in having invaded a mystery that remained a mystery to him, and in having set down his own personal reactions to a whole race as if they were the inspired truth. His Indians are merely what the Indians might be if they were all D. H. Lawrences." Like Blasco Ibáñez, he has given us his "mental autobiography."

Because Lawrence attempted to force on his material the "debased" myth of an "expert tribal Messiah," he has written a "catastrophe," yet his consuming fear of death must have responded to Porter's own. His main character, Kate Leslie, listens "to the silence and the strange grisly fear that so often creeps out on to the darkness of Mexico City," while "on the bright sunshine . . . the flowers seemed to have their roots in spilt blood," making her wonder why she had come "to this high plateau of death." For Porter and Lawrence, America itself became "the great death-continent."[8]

Porter might have had more reason to sympathize with Rosalie Evans, a native Texan whom she described as "beautiful, daring and attractive." After her English husband's death, Evans returned to Mexico in 1917 to reclaim his hacienda. She was aware of the dangerous adventure on which she embarked, comparing herself to "the heroines in Fielding's and Richardson's novels who fell into the hands of one villain after another and were always saved by their miraculous trust in God." Since the villains were men, she wrote about one exception, Carranza's secretary of the interior, "I have made men out such brutes that I am glad to record something in their favor."[9] But Evans's struggle against a corrupt male world, ending with her murder in August 1924, did not win Porter's admiration because in her "grotesque" cause she "cast her individual weight against the march of an enormous social movement." Certain her entitlement to the hacienda, contracted by her husband during the Díaz regime, was valid, Evans refused to recognize the 1917 constitution or accept a cash settlement. Although her fight was "admirable as a mere exhibition of daring, energy and spirit," Porter rejected her as a martyr: "She was out for blood, and she had a glorious time while the fight lasted" (CE 417).

Porter traced with fascination the psychological process that inevitably led to Evans's death. At first she would not listen to her friends and then, driven by her obsession, could not: "She loved the romantic danger of her situation, she admired herself in the role of heroine. Her appetite for excitement increased; she confessed herself jaded, and sought greater danger." Porter had Evans in mind when she later defined adventure, in "St. Augustine and the Bullfight," as "something you seek for pleasure, or even for profit, like a gold rush or invading a country; for the illusion of being more alive than ordinarily, the thing you will to occur" (CE 92). In her attempt to sustain the illusion of being alive, Evans became "jaded," but her solution was an even more dangerous adventure, "a deep-lying hysteria" leading to "self-hypnosis": "Toward the last she had almost lost her natural reactions. Anger, fear, delight, hope—no more of these. She was Will." Porter called her letters, published after her death, "a swift-moving account of a life as full of thrills and action as any novel of adventure you may find," but "not a line" in them showed that "she had any grasp of the inward situation" even though "her keen eye and ready wit missed no surface play of event." That is, her account, in Rivera's terms, is ocular; like Lawrence, she could not discover any inner meaning in her world. Her "adventures outran [her] capacity for experience" and "the faculty for understanding what has happened to [her]" (CE 91–92) failed, as Porter feared it had failed her in 1921.

1927–1929

Early in 1927 the Whitney Studio Club's exhibition of children's art from Mexico and the United States, arranged by Ernestine Evans, stirred Porter's pleasant memories of Mexico: "I saw the very beginning of this work in Mexico, which amounted there to a revolution in educational methods; I saw their first exhibitions, and I know the type of tiny rural school they came from. I have seen the children." But she pointed out that the "delightful, perfectly irresponsible records of what a child sees and thinks" are not art because they are "unvexed by aesthetic problems." She could "hardly blame certain grown-up artists for struggling to regain this paradise. They call it being primitive, and name it a virtue," but the artist "does not throw away a developed technique in order to be simple once more."[10] Porter never abandoned her craft, but did use it to recreate the way children see and feel and to imagine a paradise she could not regain.

Porter had not published a story in two years. Encouraged by the expanded circle of friends in New York, she completed seven stories and most of a biography of Cotton Mather before the decade was over. Josephine Herbst, Helen Black, Genevieve Taggard, Kenneth Durant, and Ernestine Evans, friends from the early twenties, still lived in New York. Taggard, Black, and Miguel Covarrubias were now associated with the *New Masses,* which published Porter's next short story. Her new friends in the Village included Caroline Gordon and Allen Tate, Hart Crane, Malcolm Cowley, and Dorothy and Delafield Day.

Porter, always an omnivorous reader, must have enjoyed discussing with friends the latest literary stars. According to Josephine Herbst's account of the period, Hemingway's short stories, *Ulysses,* issues of *transition,* and "The Waste Land" were among the literary topics of discussion. Tate, an early enthusiast of Eliot, also carried on long conversations about the Civil War with Robert Penn Warren, Andrew Lytle, or some other newly arrived "ambassador from the South" joining in.[11] Such discussions reinforced Porter's inclination to explore her own Southern past; she soon began to urge her father, who claimed descent from Daniel Boone, to tell her all he could remember about the Porter family past. While her Southern Agrarian friends talked of recreating a paradise lost, her socialist friends talked of a paradise yet to be won, their arguments uneasily coexisting in separate compartments of Porter's mind as the years passed; except for the prose, her letters in the thirties to the conservative Caroline Gordon and the radical Josephine Herbst seem to have been written by two different persons.

But on March 27, 1927, Porter still sounded like a radical in her review of essays by Moisés Sáenz, Herbert I. Priestly, and two old acquaintances, José Vasconcelos and Manuel Gamio. Probably provoked by Priestly's reassuring comment that the American Federation of Labor is "the most potent agency for teaching liberal rather than radical tendencies in Mexican labor circles,"[12] Porter defined the liberal as one who can present the "quite horrifying facts" and then smooth them over so as to upset no one: "Earth hath no sorrows that a firm mild course of popular education cannot cure . . . Even oil magnates may be taught international good manners by suggestion."[13] Priestly's report of "police wagons rounding up the dregs of society and forcing them into public baths" (133) to combat contagion and infection caused her to consider the "cult of machinery and the bathtub" in this country:

> We have our bread lines, true, and miners' strikes, and the garment
> workers of this superlatively clothed nation have a permanent griev-
> ance. . . . In the South we persist in the aristocratic old tradition of
> Negro peonage, and there is a discouraging percentage of poor whites
> whose insides are riddled with the hookworm. We are exceedingly rude
> to multitudes of our foreign population, and what with our modern effi-
> cient methods of banditry, somebody should hold a round-table discus-
> sion about us.

Porter suspected Moisés Sáenz of "radical tendencies," probably because he complained that Mexico "was getting less income from Mexican oil than the United States government was getting through the income tax from the same oil" (27), but she found his "optimism scarcely warranted by the facts he has managed to expose." She complimented Gamio for coming "nearer to the real life of his own country" than "the liberal-minded Mr. Priestly," but thought the remedies proposed unequal to the problems they attempted to redress: "Cleaning up is dirty work, this is a mere project for washing face and hands. The thundering racket you hear outside is Mexico getting her pockets picked by her foreign investors."

This review could have been written for *New Masses,* where William Gropper, like Porter, scoffed at the liberal who "voted for Al Smith, but when any fundamental social change is suggested, he whispers, 'But oh dear, the facts are not all in yet.'" In a decade of relative prosperity when the middle class was apathetic to social issues, the dwindling minority of intellectuals of the left, still attempting to pick up the pieces of the progressive movement smashed during World War I, were, like Porter, busy defining their social positions. Liberal theory, as advanced by the *New Republic,* "assumed that man was slowly, but surely and without violence, progressing toward a safe and rational world."[14] Porter obviously doubted the sincerity of such gradualism. Her review of *Some Mexican Problems* reflected what she had learned in Mexico about foreign exploitation and the depressing conditions of worker and peasant. She also had not forgotten the Mexican radical view of the American Federation of Labor, calling it, in a letter to her father (July 28, 1928) "a gang of thugs if I ever saw one."

But all stripes of liberals and radicals rallied to the cause of Nicola Sacco and Bartolomeo Vanzetti, sentenced to die on July 14, 1921, for the murder of two men in a robbery in South Braintree, Massachusetts. When the last appeal for a new trial was denied, hundreds, including Edna St. Vincent Millay, John Dos Passos, and Porter, picketed in the streets of Boston, were conducted to jail, bailed out, and appeared the next day to repeat the process until the executions on August 22, 1927. In *The Never-Ending Wrong,* published on the fiftieth anniversary of the executions, Porter's frequent mention of Mike Gold, William Gropper, and Paxten Hibben, all editors of the *New Masses,* and a photograph of her and Hibben with their picket signs indicate the companions of her committee, although, in her revision of the past, she professed not to know how she got mixed up with the likes of them, criticized the Russian sympathies of her old friend Bessie Beatty, and claimed she was in 1927 a "liberal idealist" who had learned of the dangers of anarchism in Mexico.[15]

After the executions, Porter rejoined Luis Hidalgo, whom she had fallen in love with earlier in the year. He was a Mexican artist whose wax caricatures were exhibited in New York in 1927 and sold to art museums in Boston and Brooklyn.[16] Porter wrote her sister Gay (March 5, 1928) that she "almost married Hidalgo, the famous Mexican caricaturist, about six months ago. He is a love, and a charming person: but I 'scaped out of that. . . ."

During her affair with Hidalgo, Porter wrote "He," her first published fiction in three years, set in the Texas of her poverty-stricken childhood. The struggle of the Whipples to scratch a living from their farm interested her radical friends of the *New Masses,* where it appeared in October 1927. The story begins, "Life was very hard for the Whipples. It was hard to feed all the hungry mouths, it was hard to keep the children in flannels during the winter, short as it was . . ." (49). "It was a hard winter. . . . The crops were about half of what they had a right to expect; after the cotton was in it didn't do much more than cover the grocery bill" (54). The Whipples' constant fear of going under is essential to understanding them, but the focus of the story is Mrs. Whipple. Porter, her interest in caricature renewed by Hidalgo,[17] exposes "the very outer appearance" of her main character "that is the clue to an inner quality [she] has spent most of [her] life trying to hide, or disguise," thereby meeting the standard she set in her Covarrubias review.

Mrs. Whipple's "simple-minded" son is referred to only by the third-person masculine pronoun throughout the story. That is the point: although He is constantly on her mind, He has little human identity in her eyes. She constantly says she cares for Him, but she protests too much, her main preoccupation being her fear that her neighbors might think she neglects Him, and she does. When He dirties His clothes, she orders Him, "Get off that shirt and put on another, people will say I don't half dress you!" (52). Her whole life is filled with two pronouns, "He," whom she does not love, and "they," whom she fears. When the Whipples are forced to place Him in the Country Home, only then does she have a glimmer of His feelings. She feels He is "accusing her of something" and accurately remembers various times she neglected him, but prefaces them with "maybe"—"Maybe He remembered that time she boxed his ears . . . maybe He had slept cold and couldn't tell her about it." But she concludes that "she had loved Him as much as she possibly could . . . there was nothing she could do to make up to Him for His life. Oh, what a mortal pity He was ever born" (58). The brilliance of the story lies not only in the way Mrs. Whipple inadvertently convicts herself through her own speech, but also in the way the narrator's voice adopts Mrs. Whipple's idiom, insinuating ridicule into her point of view; for instance, "Mrs. Whipple loved her second son, the simple-minded one, better than she loved the other two children put together. She was forever saying so, and when she talked with certain of her neighbors, she would even throw in her husband and her mother for good measure" (49). The last clause effectively undermines the sincerity of her claim. Porter later used the technique with equal brilliance in "Rope," "Hacienda," "That Tree," and "Noon Wine."

"He" is also the most poignant example of child victimization, first initiated in the portrait of the young servant girl in "In a Mexican Patio" and pursued in "The Dove of Chapacalco" and "Holiday." Both He and Ottilie are exploited and mute, their defect symbolizing a more serious one in their parents, who cannot hear, understand, or love them. Porter projected onto these mutes her childhood resentment at not being appreciated or loved. Mrs. Whipple's wish that He had never been born echoes the dark thoughts of Porter's father about his children. Porter returned to the subject of aggrieved childhood in the Miranda stories and "The Downward Path to Wisdom." Few writers have been more preoccupied with childhood trauma than Porter.

In 1927 Porter decided to exercise her skill as caricaturist on Puritan divine Cotton Mather; with a $300 advance from Boni and Liveright, she researched her subject in New York and then at the Essex Institute in Salem, Massachusetts, from January to March of 1928. Her choice of subject may seem odd, but from Van Wyck Brooks's *The Wine of the Puritans* (1908) to Matthew Josephson's *Portrait of the Artist as American* (1930), book after book convicted the Puritans as source of America's moral ills.[18] D. H. Lawrence (1923), William Carlos Williams (1925), and Vernon L. Parrington (1927) were among their most ardent detractors. Williams accused them of "producing a race incapable of flower," their religious zeal leading to "the confinements of a tomb." [19] Reprinting Mather's defense of "witchcraft persecutions," he let the Puritan divine damn himself. Porter must have admired Williams's account of her "kinsman," Daniel Boone, "a great wild voluptuary against the niggardliness of the damming puritanical tradition; one who . . . destroyed at its spring that spiritually withering plague" (130).

In a letter (September 11, 1927) to the *Nation* critic Isidor Schneider, Porter wrote about the Puritans in the same vein. But first she had to begin with Mexico: "I prefer to live in the country in Mexico; my true interest is there." She mentioned that she "helped to organize the first exhibition of Mexican peasant art ever brought to this country," wrote a booklet on Mexican arts, "brought the first set of Diego Rivera's drawings to New York," and attempted to peddle Covarrubias's caricatures. She also gave a fanciful version of her family history, admitting that this information had nothing "that even remotely has to do with Cotton Mather. But we are approaching." She remembered reading about Cotton Mather and the "Witchcraft Delusion" as a child and later "snooped around" voodoo doctors in Louisiana and Indian witches in Mexico, but when she visited New England for the first time three years ago,

> it had all the strangeness of a foreign country. Mexico seems a simple
> natural place to me, I can live there almost without adjustment, but the
> air of New England put the fear of God in me. It seems to me that the
> dry rot of America began there, it is a dead body that breathes out a
> plague on all life in this country. I hold that this Massachusetts Bay was
> settled not by a fresh and ingenuous people, but by a people already sick
> to death. They brought their decadence with them, these Puritans, and
> though fresh life came afterward, they had the first strangle hold, and
> they have never been shaken off.

The first fathers, "rapacious, cruel, ambitious and unscrupulous," had no illusions about themselves, but it was Cotton Mather who "began the legend of their conscious godliness and high aim." Porter hoped her biography of Mather "shall sell enormously, for then I shall go to Mexico and live in an Indian house near Lake Pascuaro [*sic*], and write my two novels."

Setting the history of Puritan New England against her own romanticized autobiography, from her Southern ancestry up through her adventures in Mexico, Porter struggled with the problem of evil. Influenced by works such as Williams's, she depicted the first generation of Puritans as land-grabbing conquistadors and the next generation as hypocritical creators of a legend of Puritan piety that masked their brutality. Thus she applied her anticlericalism, developed in Mexico, to Massachusetts, which seemed more foreign to her than Mexico ever did. And, substituting Lake Pátzcuaro for Xochimilco and Amecameca, she once more envisioned Mexico, which she was anxious to revisit, as an Edenic refuge free of evil. Southern history became another refuge,

its early settlers having escaped the Puritan blight, as Williams points out. Reinforced by his favorable view of Daniel Boone, Porter remembered her father's
claim of being a descendant of Boone and made the same claim herself in her
review of *Daniel Boone: Wilderness Scout* in 1926.[20] While researching the Puritans, she kept an eye peeled for any mention of Porters in colonial history
and questioned her father (February 16, 1928) when she came across one.

In Porter's view, Calvinistic doctrine itself also contributed to America's
moral decline. In an undated letter from Salem to Gay, Porter, upholding
"eighteenth century rationalism," which she and her brother "soaked up" from
her father, attempted to explain Gay's "religious temperament" by supposing
"any faith will serve in a crisis." She added, "I should like to see one child in
the family brought up free from original sin. I guess it's up to me to adopt one,
and carry out my theory." (In the same letter, she again contemplated Mexico's
Edenic possibilities: "I mean to have a quinta in Mexico, with fruit and flowers,
and a baby burro, and a great gay-colored monster parrot called a Guaca-
maya—try that on your ocarina—and God help me to get it before I am 71.")
Porter attacked Calvinistic doctrine in "He," written during her initial investigation of Mather in New York. The Whipples' neighbors hypocritically veil
their meanness in religious platitude: "'A Lord's pure mercy if He should die,'
they said. 'It's the sins of the fathers,' they agreed among themselves. 'There's
bad blood and bad doings somewhere, you can bet on that.' This behind the
Whipples' backs. To their faces everybody said, 'He's not bad off. He'll be all
right yet. Look how He grows!'" (49–50). The neighbors are, in Porter's view,
latter-day Mathers, inheritors of doctrines that spread like a "plague" into the
South. But those doctrines also infected Porter, as the imagery of corruption in
her letter to Schneider proves. However much she subscribed to her father's
"eighteenth century rationalism" or to Mexican socialistic theories that encouraged her to reject religious experience, she retained the belief in the per-
vasiveness of evil, even though in 1927 she made little distinction between
doctrine and the reprehensible behavior of those who spread it.

The sins of the fathers. Original sin. On February 27, 1928, Porter composed a remarkable soul-searching examination of conscience not unlike those
practiced by the Puritans, except that God did not enter into it. Intended as
self-exhortation to force her to "buckle down" to the drudgery of research, it
attempted to account for the causes of her perceived moral weakness. The earliest explicit analysis of her depression, it is an important key to understanding
her personality and such stories as "Theft."

> The bad habits of my father and the grown ups that brought me [up]
> have corrupted me and are about to spoil my life because . . . I failed to
> criticize with discrimination or rebel against the really damaging condi-
> tions. I was romantic and egoistic, and took naturally to the examples of
> laziness, inefficiency and arrogance I saw about me. Now let me take
> myself in hand . . . and do my work to the limit of my capacity, without

the preoccupations of vanity and fear. I am corrupted also with the ego-
tistic desire to be right always and the fear of criticism. I have thought
too much about my career ever to buckle down and make one. Root of
this trouble, a false point of view in those who influenced me in my
childhood, my own romantic acceptance of those views, and failure to
train myself in habits of concentration and of finishing one job before I
undertook another. This has destroyed my health, my nervous system,
and almost destroyed my vital contacts with reality.

She also blamed her "sexual impulses" that led her into situations she could
not "control," but worse she "allowed all sorts of persons to trespass on [her]
human rights" because she was too timid, too lazy, and indifferent "to put up a
battle" necessary to hold her "proper ground." Thus she "harmed" others by
"allowing them to trespass on me, by my weakness encouraging them to quite
predatory acts against me." She admitted she was "neurotic almost to a patho-
logical degree" apparently because she allowed the "natural instincts" of others
"to exploit their knowledge" of her. She complained she had "suffered a good
deal" because others "have been able to make some use" of what she gave them,
"whereas my disorderliness and lack of self-discipline have made my material,
got from others, almost useless to me." The result was inability "to believe in
anything," her "doubt" of the "motives" of others "founded in a fear of their
power over" her, although she called the state she let herself "drift into" "absurd and childish." Finally she accused herself of "drifting again to a condition
of inertia and apathy, a desire to give up," but promised to "put again in working order" what was left of her will.

Although Porter had praised her father for his enlightened rationalism, in
this confession she accused him of corrupting her with his sins: inertia, apathy, laziness, and lack of ambition that dragged his family into poverty. But she
did not exactly equate the sins of the father with original sin. Distinguishing
between the corrupt and the corrupted, she depicted herself as victim of the
instinctive predatory nature of others. She was only at fault in apathetically
letting them "trespass," a twice-used word, when she should have resisted
them by an exercise of will, standing her "own ground"—also a twice-used
phrase. That is, by sheer exercise of will, she might have escaped corruption,
but her willpower, weakened by apathy, itself a sin of her father, made the
prospect of success extremely doubtful. Her self-description of "neurotic"
seems correct, but she was unable to diagnose her paranoid symptoms, evident
in constant blame-shifting and fear of the power of others over her. Although
she accused herself of wanting always to be right, she, in her defense, appears
self-righteous, essentially different from others: they corrupt while she is only
weak in allowing herself to be corrupted by them.

While in Salem, Porter began "The Jilting of Granny Weatherall." In search
of her family's past, she centered, not on the mythical time of the Old South,
but on the hard times of a character similar to her grandmother. Porter

projected onto Granny all those qualities she confessed she lacked in her self-analysis: courage, self-discipline, energy to finish tasks, and "pride in human achievement." As Granny lies dying, she can take great satisfaction in successfully raising her family and managing a farm after the early death of her husband. However, her persistent memory of her true love who had jilted her at the altar long ago proves that she never recovered from the humiliation, just as Porter never recovered from her father's rejection of his children after the death of his wife. That painful episode from Porter's past is also marked by Granny's memory of her daughter Hapsy, who died in childbirth. As death draws near, Granny finds her lifelong devotion to her religious faith unavailing. When God fails to appear at the moment of her death, she suffers another jilting and blows "out the light" (89) of her existence. God is a man like any other and her faith is as futile as that of the Indians in "The Fiesta of Guadalupe."

"Magic" was the second story of the Salem period. In her letter to Isidor Schneider, Porter associated snooping around voodoo doctors in Louisiana with the Puritan witchcraft delusion. "Magic," set in New Orleans, concerns Ninette—a name derived from the Spanish *niña*—who works in a "fancy house." When she accuses the madam of cheating her, the madam begins "to lift her knee and kick this girl most terribly in the stomach, and even in her most secret place" so that when she got up from the bed she had fallen into "there was blood everywhere she had sat" (40). The suggestion of rape (and/or miscarriage) intensifies the brutality of the beating, associating Ninette with Porter's young female victims in "The Dove of Chapacalco," "Virgin Violeta," and "María Concepción." When she flees the house, the madam's cook concocts a charm to make her "come back to you believing you are [her] friend" (41). In seven days Ninette returns. Mather would have called the madam and cook witches. Porter would have agreed they deserved hanging, not for their ineffectual charm, but for reducing Ninette to such a state that she preferred sexual slavery over death by starvation.

In another note from the Salem period, Porter expressed the same hopelessness she felt for Ninette. If she "were really liberated," she "would stand [her] ground, and make [her] own terms," but "in a world of second best choices," she had chosen her present work, although to her "unending chagrin" she "can lay hold of nothing in the world worth living for, or dying for." But then she turned slightly hopeful, countering corrupt reality with an Edenic dream: "But it does add to my gusto for life, that I share a sort of joy in casting the roots of my sensations in a common earth with trees and [flowers and] animals and birds. I do have a robust, pure, untainted joy in simple living" that "compensates for everything else." She "cannot spend [her] life in prison," but wishes to find "some quiet place where this tide rises and flows" with "less corruption," for it now flows "along muddy channels and city gutters and the unclean minds of people," among whom she feels "an alien."

In her letter to Gay of March 5, six days after her self-analysis, Porter's thoughts turned to aging. Almost marrying Luis Hidalgo, ten years her junior, forced her to admit that although she didn't "feel more than twenty-five," "the dread disease of age" had attacked her in the teeth. Earlier in the letter, she referred to Gay's former husband as "a sort of mortal disease to you, and until you were cured of him you couldn't possibly be cured of anything else"— much the same language Miranda in "Old Mortality" uses to describe her marriage. In her fear of aging, Porter thought of marriage as something that hastened the process. To remain single was to keep the illusion of girlhood. Her weight also sustained the illusion. Telling Gay that "Pop says you are fat and efficient," she bragged, "I weigh about 108 in my galoshes." (Weight was a constant preoccupation. In 1920 she had written her family, "And now I am tipping the scales steadily a mighty tip at 127, which is about ten pounds too much for estheticism. Picture me taking vapor baths and doing without my accustomed stint of food in order not to be fat," for she was determined "to drop those objectionable superfluous pounds." On November 8, 1931, she proudly informed her family she was "thin as a lathe." In *Ship of Fools,* Jenny and David, modeled after Porter and her third husband, Eugene Pressly, "were agreed that to grow fat was the unpardonable sin against all the good in life, from morals to esthetics and back again."[21] The humor notwithstanding, growing fat revealed a concern not explained by vanity alone, as "Flowering Judas" proves.)

Shortly after her return from Salem in March, Porter spent the summer in Erwinna, Pennsylvania, where Josephine Herbst and John Hermann had settled, "a soft warm, green country, very sweet, with many running streams and little hills," as she described it to her father (July 28, 1928). In the same letter she expressed her dismay at the recent news from Mexico. Much had happened in Porter's four-year absence. Enmity between church and state erupted in the bloody Cristero rebellion in 1926 and was still smoldering in 1928. After congress amended the constitution in 1926 to permit nonconsecutive reelections, Obregón, thwarting Luis Morones's presidential aspirations, won the election unopposed (since the two rival candidates were executed for plotting to overthrow the government), but on July 17, 1928, he was assassinated by a young Cristero fanatic. In the turmoil that followed, Morones, accused of being implicated in the assassination, resigned from Calles's cabinet and never regained power. Samuel Yúdico was also implicated, but had mysteriously died in April.[22]

In her letter to her father, Porter lamented, "One by one I see all my friends there die before the firing squad, or driven out of the country. My friend Felipe Carrillo [Puerto] . . . was killed with all of his cabinet during the de la Huerta counter-revolution. And men that I thought good revolutionaries turn against the government and try to get into power, and are executed over night." She surmised that her "friend" Luis Morones could have been implicated in the assassination of Obregón, although Calles had more to gain from it. Morones "had done badly" by "selling out" to the American Federation of Labor (a charge made against him by radical labor leaders back in 1921). She hoped "the Jingoes in this country" wouldn't try "to intervene in the Mexican affairs," since she preferred Mexico "to any other place" and hoped "to spend several years there at least."

In reaction to these events, Porter created a scene for her novel *Thieves' Market.* In it an unidentified Mexican discovers Anna, just returned to Mexico after a four-year absence, wandering about the stalls of the market. He tells her that "the great bust" Cardenas (Bardas) made of her the summer she tried to get José (Retinger) out of jail can still be seen through the window of her former apartment. She considers staying in Mexico to help Felipe with his book, but when she hears he is dead, "her eyes blazed with pure shock: without grief or regret, without comprehension." She speaks with "nothing personal in her voice or manner": "In all my life in the United States, even from my childhood, I have lost only three friends by death. But here in Mexico, whenever I come back, even if it has been only a year, I find two or three gone for all sorts of causes." There had been a "bond" between her and Felipe, "but nothing had come of it. Felipe being dead did not really interrupt anything." As Anna drifts away, the man contemplates her face, "now greenish pale with the reflection from the washed stones of the market floor. He remembered her when she was alive, slowly the life had been sapped from her, she was not related to anything that he knew or cared for any longer." Porter's projection of herself as a ghost, apathetically returning to Mexico to find her friends dead, seems totally inconsistent with her desire to live there more than anywhere else.

Upon her return to the Village in the fall, Porter became copy editor at Macaulay and Company and rented an apartment on Charles Street owned by Thorberg Haberman. At this time she met and fell in love with Matthew Josephson, who had just published his biography of Zola. Although he soon extricated himself from the affair, he continued as friend and helpful critic, accepting "The Jilting of Granny Weatherall" in *transition.*[23] When Porter came down with a serious, apparently psychosomatic, ailment during the winter, Becky and John Crawford arranged, with the help of Josephson, Andrew Lytle, and others, to send her to Bermuda to recuperate.

In Bermuda she rented a spacious country home called Hilgrove, overlooking the sea. In letters to her family, Becky Crawford, Delafield Day, and Josephine Herbst, she expressed her delight in the lush beauty of the island, and in Hilgrove itself with its well-stocked library, rose gardens, and banana groves. Bermuda wasn't Lake Pátzcuaro, which she hoped to visit the year before, but, she wrote her sister Gay (March 5, 1929), it came closest to "a lazy woman's notion of Paradise." She later repeated the same idea to Robert McAlmon (November 12, 1932): "I spent eight months of self-elected hermit life in Bermuda . . . and it is really my kind of Paradise, all brilliant color and tropical sun and fruitfulness."

A letter of July 7 from her father intruded into her paradise to remind her of her childhood past:

If there is such a thing as bad luck groping its way among the atoms . . .
it never fails to track me up and run me down. I had a fortune in my
grasp in Mexico when only 22 yrs old, when a revolution I didn't make
ruined me. Three disastrous drouths set me flat in the West with an in-
valid wife and four children. When your mother was gone I had to give
the place I intended for a home away . . . was forced out of farming
cotton. . . . This last catasstrofee . . . is nothing new in my young life. If
it was raining soup I should be in high luck if I could get hold of a salad
fork to scoop up my share.

If paranoid tendencies and writing talent are a matter of genes, then Porter
is daughter of this self-described Jonah. She replied, "Chance [*la Suerte*] is a
very good name for that mysterious element which goes such a very complicated road from cause to effect, there is very little use in making your calculations by any mathematical rules, either moral or physical," but in her "hopeless
optimism," she stressed the family's "grand gift of tenacity to life" and claimed
that she got her philosophy and "literary bent" from him. Writing him two
years later (June 26, 1931) in another mood, she wondered "if we would any
of us ever recover from our peculiar despair of poverty."

In Bermuda Porter's solution to her remembered past was to replace it with
a mythical past, supplemented by details of Hilgrove's affluence.[24] In the Miranda stories, she visualized her family as descendants of the old slaveholding
aristocracy, in economic decline since the Civil War, but able to preserve the
social amenities through the years. In keeping with her developing aristocratic
view, she asked Delafield Day in an undated letter, "What in hell is a Bour-
geiouse: I never know how to spell it, so I give you a good selection, and you
can fix it up yourself. It appears to be something that everybody else is except
oneself." In 1926 she had no problem with spelling when she wrote Carleton
Beals that she preferred "association with human beings rather than with the
bourgeoisie."

Inspired by the Hilgrove setting, Porter revised "The Fig Tree," "about an
episode of [her own] childhood" which she had completed in Salem. In it she
carefully establishes the social status of Miranda's family as it moves from
town to farm with a small retinue of black servants, but the story, like "Virgin
Violeta" and the other Miranda stories, expresses Porter's resentment of adult
authority that curbs the child's freedom to investigate and understand the
world around her. In the first paragraph, Aunt Nannie, acting on orders, grips
Miranda with her knees to fasten her bonnet on. "When Miranda wriggled,
Aunt Nannie squeezed still harder, and Miranda wriggled more" (352), marking the child's determined struggle to be free of societal restraints. In imitation
of the parental act, she attempts to impose her will on kittens, dressing them in
doll clothes, but they quickly free themselves. "Kittens had sense" (357), an
instinct for freedom of movement. The grandmother, the authoritarian en-

forcer of restrictive codes of behavior, is the cause of Miranda's fear of engulf-ment, asking her, "Where are you going, child? What are you doing? What is that you're carrying? Where did you get it? Who gave you permission?" (355), questions an older Miranda dreams of fleeing from in "Pale Horse, Pale Rider."

The editors of *Gyroscope* turned down "The Fig Tree,"[25] (which appeared thirty years later in *Harper's*), but accepted "Theft," another Bermuda story prompted by the upsetting news from Becky Crawford (April 7, 1929) that in March a young man Porter had lent her apartment to attempted suicide there and was ejected by Thorberg Haberman. Porter had brooded over her own mental state while living in that apartment and in Salem, writing Gay from Bermuda (March 5, 1929) that she had been "on the edge of just going into a complete melancholia." "Theft," recreating that state, is about an unnamed woman (Porter) who has lost her lover (Josephson) and whose "empty purse" she cannot fill until the arrival of "a check for her latest review" (62). Critics have offered conflicting explanations of the cause of the unnamed woman's discontent,[26] their fascination with the story reflecting Porter's attempt in her Salem confession to explain her "inertia and apathy." This non-Mexican story sheds light on Porter's personality and gives a context for viewing "Flowering Judas" that six months later dealt more effectively with the same psychological issues, especially the principle of rejection.

As the story opens, the unnamed woman surveys "the immediate past" to account for her missing purse. Her three remembered encounters with differ-ent male friends from the night before, all struggling artists like her, give in-sight into her personality. Camilo (Hidalgo?) "by a series of compromises had managed to make effective a fairly complete set of smaller courtesies, ignoring the larger and more troubling ones" (59), like the woman herself. Roger, who bumps into her at the subway entrance and takes her home in a cab, plans "to do something definite" about Stella and to "hold out" concerning a play he has written. Holding out is equivalent to "standing my own ground" in Porter's Salem confession, but in both cases the promise belies a basic indecisiveness. The woman does not hold out in her encounter with Bill, who hails her as she passes his apartment. When he claims he can't afford to pay her the fifty dollars he owes her for helping write his play, even though he received seven hundred dollars, she says, "Let it go, then," although "she had meant to be quite firm about it" (63). Thus, like Porter, the woman has "allowed all sorts of persons to trespass on [her] human rights because [she] was too timid to fight for them, and too lazy and indifferent to put up a battle that [she] knew was necessary to hold [her] proper ground."

After recalling the events of the night before, the woman realizes that the janitress had stolen her purse while she was bathing. Her first response is to "let it go," as with Bill, but with this decision "there rose coincidentally in her blood a deep almost murderous anger" that prompts her to walk down three flights of stairs and confront the janitress. Her anger is disproportionate to its immediate cause, as is her vision of the janitress as diabolic with "face streaked with coal dust" and "hot flickering eyes" (63–64). It is really self-anger for giving in to Bill who has robbed her, the janitress becoming a monstrous objectification of all the Bills in her life whom she has harmed "by allowing them to trespass on [her], by [her] weakness encouraging them to quite predatory acts against [her]." When the janitress protests her innocence, the woman reverts to type and once more gives in, telling her to keep the purse if she wants it so much. As she walks away, she remembers "how she had never locked a door in her life, on some principle of rejection in her that made her uncomfortable in the ownership of things" and her "paradoxical boast" that "she had never lost a penny by theft," her boast "designed to illustrate and justify a certain fixed, otherwise baseless and general faith which ordered the movements of her life without regard to her will in the matter" (64). Here the woman sounds like a self-deceived Puritan who has surrendered her will to God, who in turn will justify her faith and reward her antimaterialism by making her theft-proof. But she now admits her faith is "otherwise baseless," exposing her lack of will, her inability to put her life in order.

Around the time she was working on "Theft," Porter wrote Delafield Day (letter undated) that her "prejudice against [Floyd Dell] is really founded, I love to flatter myself, on a certain principle of rejection in my mind," based on a few fatuous remarks she overheard him make. "Certainly it can't be personal," she added, "for I never saw him but twice." The principle was a built-in defense mechanism to avoid those she considered unpleasant or threatening. But in "Theft" she altered the principle from rejection of people to things. If the two are interchangeable, then the principle has not worked as happily for the woman, who now questions its value as she contemplates various thefts, "material" and "intangible," she has suffered. They include "things lost or broken by her own fault," "books borrowed from her and not returned" (another's fault), "journeys she had planned and had not made" (her fault), and "words she had waited to hear spoken to her and had not heard" (another's fault). Her list ends with "bitter alternatives and intolerable substitutes . . . yet inescapable: the long patient suffering of dying friendships and the dark inexplicable death of love . . ." (64). The piling up of negatives—"intolerable," "inescapable," and "inexplicable"—indicates a hopeless state the woman does not comprehend any more than Porter comprehended her melancholia in Salem. Is the woman responsible for the death of love? Earlier she read snatches from her lover's letter, one of which asked her "why were you so anxious to destroy" (63). His possibly just accusation does not deter her from thinking the death of love "inexplicable."

When the janitress follows her upstairs and confesses she stole the purse for her niece who is "young and needs pretty things," the narrator attempts to return it to her, disowning it once again, but then the janitress manages to make the woman feel she had stolen her own purse: "I don't want it either now. My niece is young and pretty, she don't need fixin' up to be pretty, she's young and pretty anyhow! I guess you need it worse than she does!" The story ends with the woman's self-accusation: "I was right not to be afraid of any thief but my-self, who will end by leaving me nothing" (65). It is difficult to know whether the woman accuses herself of not standing her ground against the janitress and all those out to take advantage of her or of letting love die. It is certain, how-ever, that the thief is time itself that has stolen the woman's youth, leaving her at middle age in a melancholic state, spiritually drifting and not totally aware of what has happened to her as Porter was unaware in Salem.

In Bermuda Porter also completed eleven chapters of *The Devil and Cotton Mather*. Advertised to appear in the fall, it never appeared at all except for three chapters published in 1934, 1940, and 1942. Givner speculates (188–190) that Porter may have had trouble making the facts of Mather's life conform to her preconceived notions of him since she had made, according to David Levin, numerous factual errors concerning Mather's boyhood. Other biog-raphers were also guilty of what Levin calls "The Hazing of Cotton Mather," among them Ralph and Louise Boas.[27] Ironically Porter, in her 1928 review, found their book, *Cotton Mather: Keeper of the Puritan Conscience,* "sympathet-ically softened wherever possible": "Cotton Mather has never lacked for apolo-gists, and he still has friends at court after two hundred years," although "all the elements of civilization were lacking in that life, and the religious practices were as little humane, and considerably less imaginative, than those of the early Aztecs."[28] Levin, with Porter in mind, warned against cheapening "his-torical art or human reality with caricature" (57), but when he concedes that Mather's *Diary* "reveals at times an immense vanity and an almost shattering discrepancy between the motive we can see and the motive he claims" (37) he inadvertently points to Porter's method of caricature, for her portrait drama-tizes that discrepancy, at times heightening it by distorting facts. Facts should be a biographer's concern, but Porter wrote of the Boases, "Scrupulous fairness in biography seems to mean a gentle leaning toward the side of their hero, a careful building up of the elements of his defense." She was not out to defend Mather, but to expose him, even if it meant leaning in the other direction to tell her truth about him.

Bored with her Bermuda paradise, Porter wrote Herbst, "This island is so rotten ripe it simply wears me down. It simply sprawls and festers in the heat."[29] She left at the end of summer, rented a room in the Crawford home in Brooklyn, and wrote seven book reviews in the next six months to help earn her keep. The first was of *Idols Behind Altars* by Anita Brenner, then an editor of the *Nation,* with whom Porter was corresponding about an article on Sor Juana and Gabriela Mistral.[30] Porter's long review of *Idols* became the occasion of her own brief history of the Mexican muralists. In her diaries Brenner noted that Porter's review was "full of little pin-pricks and just as reluctant as pos-sible, but nevertheless intelligent. Jean [Charlot] says that she resents not having written it herself." However, in December Porter listed *Idols* along with Hemingway's *A Farewell to Arms* in the "Recent Books I Have Liked" section of the *New York Herald Tribune.*

Also in December Porter reviewed Ernestine Evans's *The Frescoes of Diego Rivera*, calling Rivera "the most important living painter," who, despite his "philosophic anarchy," "selected a difficult, uncompromising medium and proceeded to inclose his intractable material within the confines of a formal beauty."[31] These words could have described the work Porter finished in late November. She told an interviewer in 1975 that, after declining Becky Crawford's invitation to bridge, she produced in the space of six hours "Flowering Judas" (I 180). Her account is not true since she mentioned the story to Matthew Josephson almost a year before (March 19, 1929), but it is true that the story simmered in her mind ever since her early Mexican experiences on which it is based and took final shape after her soul-searching in Salem and in "Theft."

The Making of "Flowering Judas"

"Flowering Judas" is about Laura, a beautiful young American who betrays the conflicting principles of her Catholic and revolutionary faiths, her companions, and herself. The setting is, except for one scene, her apartment in Mexico City, where the powerful revolutionist Braggioni entertains her with his guitar and attempts to seduce her. As he plays, Laura's mind wanders to other activities of her life in Mexico: haunting the markets, slipping into a church to pray, teaching Indian children in Xochimilco, attending labor meetings, visiting prisoners, smuggling letters to men in hiding, and resisting courtship of two admirers, a Zapatista captain and an organizer of the Typographers Union. In the second part of the story, Braggioni talks of revolution and women and Laura tells him of the suicide in prison of Eugenio, who took an overdose of tablets she gave him. Failing to overcome Laura's resistance to him, Braggioni returns to his wife, who forgives him for his infidelity. Laura retires and dreams of Eugenio, who accuses her of betraying him and tempts her to join him in death. A third-person narrator modulates the whole story so that the reader is both inside and outside Laura's mind at the same time. Since many events in the story, including Braggioni's visit, depict Laura's routine in Mexico, they blend and seem suspended in the emulsion of her mind. The effect is reinforced by narration in the present tense so that "time may be caught immovably in this hour, with [Laura] transfixed, Braggioni singing on forever" (99).

In 1942 Porter first discussed the autobiographical source of "Flowering Judas," stating that all its characters and episodes were based on "real persons and events," but as time passed, "all assumed different shapes and colors, formed gradually around a central idea, that of self-delusion, the order and meaning of the episodes changed, and became in a word fiction." The idea came to her when through the open living-room window of the woman she called Laura in the story, she "had a brief glimpse of her sitting with an open book in her lap, but not reading, with a fixed look of pained melancholy and confusion in her face. The fat man I call Braggioni was playing the guitar and singing to her." Porter "thought" she understood "the desperate complications" of the woman's mind and feelings, but if she did not know "her true story," she did know a story "that seemed symbolic truth."[32] In subsequent interviews she expanded on the "small seed" from which her story grew. In 1963 she added the Judas tree and identified the woman as her friend "Mary," who was teaching in an Indian school and was not "able to take care of herself, because she was not able to face her own nature and was afraid of everything" (I 90). In 1965 she added the fountain and insisted that the small apartment where "Mary Doherty" lived alone was exactly as it appears in the story. Doherty, whom a young Zapatista captain attempted to help from her horse, was a "virtuous, intact, straitlaced Irish Catholic . . . born with the fear of sex," who had asked Porter to sit with her because she wasn't sure of the man coming to sing to her. This Porter did, outwaiting him until he left in frustration. She rolled "four or five objectionable characters into one" to create Braggioni. She told Lopez that she, like Laura, took "messages to people living in dark alleys" (I 123) and that she visited political prisoners in their cells, two of whom she named (119–120). In a lecture taped at the University of Maryland in 1972, Porter gave the fullest and least reliable account of her story's genesis, stating that both she and Doherty brought food and sleeping pills to political prisoners, one of whom persuaded Doherty to give him fifty pills with which he killed himself. When Doherty reported the man's death to "Braggioni," he told her they were well rid of him. Later she dreamed that when she refused "Eugenio's" attempt to lead her to death, "he gave her the flowering Judas buds." "That is her dream," Porter claimed, adding, "You see, my fiction is reportage, only I do something to it; I arrange it and it is fiction, but it happened." In a film made at the University of Maryland in 1976, she stated that Doherty should have known better than to give pills to the prisoner, and, for the first time, gave Yúdico as Braggioni's model. As Porter added details about "Flowering Judas" over the years, "reality" more and more resembled what grew out of it, the story becoming "reportage," mainly of the actions and motives of Mary Doherty, about whom Porter could only speculate in her most accurate statement of 1942. Porter did indeed "arrange" reality to make it fiction, both in the creation of her story and in her evolving versions of that creation. Her story is "based on real persons and events," but not as in her versions. The distinctions between the "real persons and events" and the "different shapes and colors" they assumed reveal the motives of the writer when she created her story and when she looked back on it many years later.

"Flowering Judas" is not historical fiction that fixes on a specific time in Mexican history, but intentionally obscures and rewrites history to make it conform to fictional needs. Nevertheless historical events underlying the transformations can be reconstructed. For instance, when Braggioni states, "Once I dreamed of destroying this city, in case it offered resistance to General

Ortiz, but it fell into his hands like an over-ripe pear" (100), he gives a skewed version of May 1920, when Obregón entered Mexico City after Carranza had fled. The army of Pablo González was already camped around Mexico City, while one of his generals, Sidronio Méndez, was in command of the plaza and in position to blow up the city. Nobody could have resisted Obregón's entry except González, who had discreetly joined forces with him. So in this garbled history, Porter, as in "The Evening," resurrected the fated Sidronio Méndez, for whose death she felt responsible.

Braggioni's report of "May-day disturbances coming on in Morelia" when "two independent processions" of Catholics and Socialists "will march until they meet" (99) derives from the Morelia clash of May 8, 1921, that resulted in the death of Isaac Arriaga. Porter's note about Yúdico and Haberman polishing their pistols in anticipation of trouble is the source of Braggioni's request that Laura oil and load his pistols. Thus the story recreates her fearful response to the events of mid-1921, including the sudden deportations, described in "The Mexican Trinity." At this time she visited Haberman in hiding and described him sitting on a tumbled bed and going over a long piece he had composed about how Americans "crack the whip" over Mexico. Later she turned this incident into a fictional note about "a certain Roumanian Jew agitator" who recites "romantic yarns of personal treason." He is finally transformed into the "prisoners of [Laura's] own political faith in their cells, where they entertain themselves with counting cockroaches, repenting of their indiscretions, composing their memoirs, writing out manifestoes and plans for their comrades" (94). The passage also reflects Porter's visit to the imprisoned Retinger in Laredo.

When Porter learned she herself was on the deportation list, she wrote, "I should like to deny that I am terrified but I am." Her "uneasiness" about violence and death in "The Mexican Trinity" echoed her uneasiness over her personal crisis. So in "Flowering Judas" "the sight and sound of Braggioni singing threaten to identify themselves with all [Laura's] remembered afflictions and add their weight to her uneasy premonitions of the future" (91). Like Porter, Laura feels engulfed by the presence of death, "a slow chill, a purely physical sense of danger, a warning in her blood that violence, mutilation, a shocking death, wait for her with lessening patience" (93). Out of her own remembered fears of 1921 Porter created the deathly atmosphere of "Flowering Judas."

With Laura's "warning in her blood" Porter gave full expression to her all-consuming theme. Influenced by memories of past dangers and by her states of depression, she frequently depicted death as a terrifying physical presence. In a fragment from *Thieves' Market* a woman complains, "There is something altogether horrible here . . . I am frightened of all sort of things. I have terrible dreams," and her companion replies that he is "influenced by some indefinite thing in the air, a hovering and sinister presence." In "Hacienda" the narrator speaks of "the almost ecstatic death-expectancy which is in the air of Mexico. . . . strangers feel the acid of death in their bones whether or not any real danger is near them" (143). Here Mexico is tangibly a place of death, symbolized by the "sour" odor of pulque. In "Pale Horse, Pale Rider" the air is contaminated with influenza, infecting Miranda, who smells "the stench of corruption" (312) in her own wasted body. Although this story is based on Porter's near-death struggle with influenza in 1918, she wrote in her journal that she felt "the terror of death" stronger in 1921 than in 1918. The terror expressed in "Pale Horse, Pale Rider" in 1938 had been magnified by her Mexican experience. Death is the firm link between Porter's Mexican and Miranda stories. A novel she outlined in 1931 began with "Book I: Introduction to Death," which was to include Miranda's childhood. "The Grave" (1935) gives that introduction and tellingly ends with odors in Mexico triggering Miranda's childhood memories: "It was a very hot day and the smell in the market, with its piles of raw flesh and wilting flowers, was like the mingled sweetness and corruption she had smelled that other day in the empty cemetery at home" (367).

Not only the atmosphere of Mexico but also Porter's acquaintances contributed to the making of "Flowering Judas." Both Haberman, whom she caricatured in "The Dove of Chapacalco," and Retinger appear in the story as indistinguishable Tweedledum and Tweedledee:

> She borrows money from the Roumanian agitator to give to his bitter enemy the Polish agitator. The favor of Braggioni is their disputed territory, and Braggioni holds the balance nicely, for he can use them both. The Polish agitator talks love to her over café tables, hoping to exploit what he believes is her secret sentimental preference for him, and he gives her misinformation which he begs her to repeat as the solemn truth to certain persons. The Roumanian is more adroit. He is generous with his money in all good causes, and lies to her with an air of ingenuous candor, as if he were her good friend and confidant. (94–95)

This passage gives a precise description of the relation of Retinger and Haberman to each other, to Morones, and to Porter. Behind the love talk of the Polish agitator is that of Retinger to Porter in the Café Colón on the Paseo. In the story, Laura is not deceived as Porter at first was by Retinger. Reading the story, he would know she had taken revenge, as she did again in "The Leaning Tower."

Retinger also contributed to "Flowering Judas" through his *Morones of Mexico,* which appeared in 1925. His adulation of Morones and Yúdico in this book ironically turns into Porter's condemnation of them in the person of Braggioni. Retinger wrote that "Yúdico, a tall, fair man, is a regular jack of all trades . . . he knows every corner of the Republic, and understands the sufferings of the workers. Frank and outspoken, his equanimity is appreciated by his companions and his goodheartedness makes him a friend of everybody."[33] Porter reserved Retinger's hollow rhetoric for Braggioni's followers, who "say to each other: 'He has a real nobility, a love of humanity raised above mere personal affections'" (91).

Although Porter did indeed roll "four or five objectionable characters" into one to create Braggioni, Yúdico was the prototype, as a 1921 note confirms: "Yúdico came in tonight bringing his guitar, and spent the evening singing for Mary." The Yúdico who entertained Doherty was a tall, rather stout man with fair complexion, light brown hair, and deep green eyes, sedately dressed with no pistols in evidence. His father, like Braggioni's, was Italian. Braggioni's "tight little mouth that turns down at the corners" (99), giving him a "surly" (90) expression, perfectly describes Yúdico. Porter turned Yúdico's green eyes into "yellow cat's eyes" (93) and increased his stoutness into the "gluttonous bulk of Braggioni" which "has become a symbol of [Laura's] many disillusions" about how revolutionists should look and act (91). Porter's Yúdico was not the man who visited Mary Doherty or the one Retinger idealized in his biography of Morones. If they overlooked whatever defects he had, Porter, in her notes, exaggerated them.

Porter was fascinated with Yúdico from the start. On September 8, 1921, she wrote of doing four portraits of revolutionaries, with his portrait almost complete. A fictional fragment of 1921 describes him as "a completely savage and uneducated Indian revolutionist, a man with the eyes of a cat and the paunch of a pig," who agrees with Retinger "that a woman was good for one thing," while another note begins, "Yúdico and his wife—went home to wash feet, wife came home sobbing" and then continues, "Third Wife, fiftieth concubine—not faithful to anything. Study of Mexican revolutionary . . . Given charge of blowing up and destroying Mexico City" if it falls into the hands of the enemy. In these passages the sexual and political mesh in a completely fictionalized Yúdico, who has already become Braggioni. In "Flowering Judas" Braggioni revenges himself on a thousand women for the humiliation one woman caused him in his youth, just as he would brutally revenge himself against his political enemies if the need arose. His psychology, according to another note, is typical of revolutionaries who escape "from bondage to themselves. Their desire to rule, their will to power, is sort of revenge" to compensate for "their own insignificance." Braggioni's will to power is symbolized in his pointed use of Jockey Club perfume, an allusion to Yúdico's role in obtaining the Jockey Club for the Casa del Obrero Mundial. Braggioni has betrayed the revolution, whose principles included just treatment of the worker and woman's equality.

When Yúdico mysteriously died in 1928, Porter shifted her attention to her old friend Luis Morones, explicitly identifying him with Braggioni in her notes. As leader of CROM and Minister of Industry, Commerce, and Labor, he enjoyed the prominence and power Porter attributes to Braggioni, with Retinger and Haberman contending for his favor. Porter's 1920 note about Morones speaking at a labor meeting she attended with Thorberg Haberman is clearly the source of Braggioni "speaking in the hypnotic voice he uses when talking in small rooms to a listening, close-gathered crowd" (100).

Porter must have known Morones's reputation as a corrupt politician long before she wrote her father in 1928 that Morones had done badly. Her acquaintance Carleton Beals ridiculed him, in *Glass Houses,* as "a big pig-like man . . . always meticulously dressed and perfumed, his hands glittering with diamonds" (58). In the same vein Porter described Roberto Soto's caricature of him as a "swollen labor leader . . . [who] removes inordinate silk scarf, and flashes his diamonds like spotlights," adding, he has "no higher idea than simple comforts and cheap elegancies. The direct forthright grabbing of whatever he could get." This description fits Braggioni with his diamond hoop and "elegant refinements" of silk handkerchief and perfume (93). She used the occasion of Morones's fall from power in 1928 to prophesy that Braggioni "will live to see himself kicked out from his feeding trough by other hungry world saviors" (98). In 1922 she had written in her journal, "If Morones is next president, salvation of Mexico is assured." In "Flowering Judas" words like "salvation" and "savior" became bitterly ironic.

Angel Gómez and Felipe Carrillo Puerto, whose portraits Porter planned along with Yúdico's, also contributed to Braggioni's portrait. Gómez's role as anarchistic "bomb thrower" or "dynamiter" in notes and in "The Dove of Chapacalco" accounts for Braggioni's pinning his "faith to good dynamite" (100), envisioning everything "hurled skyward" so that nothing the poor has made for the rich shall remain (100). He is typical of the revolutionaries of Porter's notes, "busily making over a world to their own desires," but, unlike Gómez, he doesn't really believe his apocalyptic rhetoric since he enjoys the luxuries of the rich he would exterminate. Carrillo Puerto didn't live long enough to disillusion Porter, but her notes reveal her ambivalence toward him. He is the "beautiful bandit from Yucatan," "a dreamer of violent and gorgeous dreams," and "a complete dictator." His rhetoric, like Braggioni's, was radical while his claim of direct descent from Mayan nobility explains why Braggioni's Mayan mother was "a woman of race, an aristocrat" (98). Porter's fictional name for Carrillo in *Thieves' Market* is Vicente, Braggioni's first name (94).

Carrillo and other socialists contribute to the ironic Christian imagery that helps unify Braggioni's portrait, first suggested to Porter in Blasco Ibáñez's book. The photograph Carrillo dedicated to Porter appeared in *Redención,* a publication of the Feminist League of Mérida. Socialists, opposed to a Catholic Church that in their opinion promised redemption to the poor in another life while collaborating with their oppressors in this one, reinterpreted Christian language imbibed in childhood and offered political and economic redemption here and now. Porter, in "Where Presidents Have No Friends," calls "redemption" a "hopeful, responsible word one often hears among these men" (CE 415). But when her own hope vanished, Braggioni emerged as a perverse savior who, like Morones, only talks of "sacrificing himself for the worker."

Porter planned his reappearance in her never-completed novel *Many Redeemers,* which "is all about how men go on saving the world by starving, robbing, and killing each other—lying, meanwhile, to themselves and each other about their motives."

Porter's portrait of Braggioni as the corrupt revolutionary is more complex than that of Angel Gomez in "The Dove of Chapacalco," but she strains credibility when she has him plan to participate in a street brawl between Catholics and Socialists, as Angel Gómez probably did, while suggesting that he is a ruthless general capable of destroying Mexico City. Braggioni's portrait is mainly a composite of laborites Porter knew, but there is a world of difference between the radical Gómez, with his own private agenda, and Morones, leader of the labor establishment. Braggioni, in his corpulence, vanity, and cynicism, is more successful as "the symbol of [Laura's] many disillusions" and of other facets of her troubled personality she does not fully comprehend.

Laura herself is a complex blend of Mary Doherty, Alma Reed, and, principally, Katherine Anne Porter. The seed of Laura's character is contained in a portrait Porter did of Doherty in 1921. She pictures her at a table, "a little preoccupied, infallibly and kindly attentive" to Yúdico as he entertains her with his guitar. She is "a modern secular nun. Her mind is chaste and wise, she knows a great deal about life at twenty three, and is a virgin but faintly interested in love. She wears a rigid little uniform of dark blue cloth, with immaculate collar and cuffs of narrow lace made by hand." Her lace is her "one extravagance" since she thinks there is something "dishonest" in machine-made lace. Her "romantic sense of adventure has guided her to the lower strata of revolution. Backed by a course of economics at the Rand School, she keeps her head cool in the midst of opera bouffe plots, the submerged international intrigue of her melodramatic associates." She intended to organize working women into labor unions, but doesn't comprehend that those who thwart her efforts are not as "clear and straight minded" as she. Although she has developed "a little pucker of trouble between her wide set grey eyes," she still "has the look of one who expects shortly to find a simple and honest solution of a very complicated problem. She is never to find it."

Retinger's inquiry of December 1921 and thereafter about Porter's "nun" story proves that the composition of "Flowering Judas" began with this portrait. In it Porter saw Doherty as she saw Yúdico, pictorially, associating her "rigid little uniform" with her nunlike virginity, a uniform Doherty was still wearing in 1926, as Edward Weston's photograph shows. That uniform will eventually symbolize Laura's fearful rejection of love in contrast to Doherty's dawning interest in it. Doherty's lace, like Laura's, is her one extravagance, but what she "thinks" about the dishonesty of machine-made lace was already a fiction in the sketch since Doherty told me she bought her lace at Altman's in New York, unaware whether it was handmade or not. In "Flowering Judas" Laura feels guilty about wearing handmade lace when the machine is "sacred" to revolutionists (92). In the sketch Doherty and her dress had already begun to evolve into Laura with her "uniform of an idea," but the meaning of the uniform changed in the story.

Doherty's Irish Catholic background also reinforces the image of "secular nun," but her attendance at the Socialist Rand school hints at the ideological clash between Catholic and Socialist in the story. In *Thieves' Market* Porter placed Laura in church, but gave her nothing to pray for: "Let me set my heart on something, I don't care how poor it is . . . the legless woman in the Alameda has a perfectly faithful lover—oh God, out of your charity send me something." Porter, who told me that she often saw the legless woman on a park bench sharing money with her lover, assigned Laura's lines about the woman's lover to Braggioni and created another prayer scene for Laura:

> She was born Roman Catholic, and in spite of her fear of being seen by someone who might make a scandal of it, she slips now and again into some crumbling little church, kneels on the chilly stone, and says a Hail Mary on the gold rosary she bought in Tehuantepec. It is no good and she ends by examining the altar with its tinsel flowers and ragged brocades, and feels tender about the battered doll-shape of some male saint whose white, lace-trimmed drawers hang limply around his ankles below the hieratic dignity of his velvet robe. (92)

The saint originally appeared in "Teotihuacán" as "St. Ignatius Loyola with chaste lace trimmed trousers showing beneath his black cassock," the transformation of "trousers" into "drawers" denigrating him further. Porter's anticlericalism combined with her view of men to deny Laura the consolation of her lost faith even though she still clings to its precepts.

Doherty contributed other details from her life to the creation of Laura. She taught Indian children in Xochimilco, although she never planned to organize women into labor unions as Porter's portrait claimed. Her horse once ran away from a former Zapatista, Genaro Amuezcua, who was head of the agrarian bureau in Cuernavaca, where she first met him.[34] Porter also knew him, describing him as "the only intelligent pro-feminist in Mexico," an ironic footnote to Laura's rejection of him and all other men in the story. However, such details do not account for Laura's personality. Doherty's honesty and genuine devotion to revolutionary reform, however naive they seemed to Porter in her 1921 portrait, bear little resemblance to Laura's alienation and mechanical performance of duties in "Flowering Judas."

Porter's claim of responding to Doherty's request to protect her from Yúdico is a fiction. At that time Doherty was not living alone, but with the Habermans. She categorically denied that she was ever afraid of Yúdico, whom she described in a postcard in 1925 as "one of my good friends." Why then Porter's fabrication? Apparently she placed herself outside and inside the scene with Doherty and Yúdico. Outside, she imagined herself coming to the rescue of Doherty, who should have been afraid instead of sitting "infallibly and kindly

attentive." Porter's later account of outwaiting and frustrating Yúdico is another posthumous revenge on him, supplementing Laura's ability to resist and
frustrate Braggioni in the text. Inside the scene, Porter identified with Doherty/
Laura's threatened virginity. She detested what she interpreted as Yúdico's
advances on the Virgin Mary Doherty and fictionalized her detestation in
"Flowering Judas."

After depicting endangered virginity in "The Dove of Chapacalco," "María
Concepción," "Virgin Violeta," and "The Lovely Legend," Porter gave us her
most thorough and complex treatment of the subject in "Flowering Judas." To
her admirers, Laura's "notorious virginity" (97) is a puzzle, but to Laura it
symbolizes her resistance to the world's corruption. As in "Virgin Violeta," it
relates to Porter's fear of pregnancy and childbirth as well as to her seemingly
conflicting desires to avenge herself against the male and at the same time seek
his admiration. They are at the root of Porter's recurring states of depression.
When she wrote in 1942 about Doherty's "fixed look of pained melancholy and
confusion," she really projected her own melancholy, remembered from 1921
and reexperienced in 1928 and 1929, just before the completion of "Flowering
Judas." Two Mexican songs hidden in the story's text help us explore her
concerns.

Braggioni's "gluttonous bulk" contradicts Laura's notion that "a revolutionist should be lean, animated by heroic faith, a vessel of abstract virtues,"
causing her to feel "betrayed irreparably by the disunion between her way of
living and her feeling of what life should be" (91). Braggioni is symbol of the
disunion but not its cause. If he were thin and heroic, the disunion would still
have existed because reality, including Braggioni's and her own corporeality,
has betrayed ideals associated with childhood innocence. Laura looks at Braggioni "like a good child who understands the rules of behavior" (92) and attempts to behave like a child whose innocence she refuses to admit she has
lost. Her "uniform" is like the one Violeta in "Virgin Violeta" might have worn
in her convent school, but whereas Violeta feels like a caged bird, Laura is "en-
cased" in her own uniform. Violeta is distraught by Carlos's advances because
she has been kept innocent, but Laura tries to preserve her innocence as if she
were a child, clinging to her virginity not simply out of fear of Braggioni's
sexuality but of her own. She does not wish to admit her adulthood or accept
her womanhood.

One of the songs Braggioni sings reveals the cause of Laura's fear:

> Braggioni catches her glance solidly as if he had been waiting for it, leans
> forward, balancing his *paunch* between *spread knees,* and sings with tre-
> mendous emphasis, weighing his words. He has, the song relates, no
> father and no mother, nor even a friend to console him; lonely as a wave
> of the sea he comes and goes, lonely as a wave. His mouth *opens round*
> and yearns sideways, his *balloon cheeks* grow oily with the *labor* of song.
> He *bulges marvelously* in his expensive garments. Over his lavender col-

lar, crushed upon a purple necktie, held by a diamond hoop; over the
ammunition belt of tooled leather worked in silver, buckled cruelly
around his *gasping middle;* over the tops of his glossy shoes Braggioni
swells with *ominous ripeness,* his mauve silk hose *stretched taut,* his ankles
bound with the stout leather thongs of his shoes. (92–93; italics mine)

Porter accurately translated Braggioni's song from the ballad "A la Orilla de
un Palmar" ("By the Shore of a Palm-grove"). In it the singer relates that when
he asked a beautiful young woman he happened upon whether anyone was
with her, she replied in tears, "I am alone by the palm-grove. I am a little orphan, alas. I have no father and no mother, not even a friend [*amigo*] who
comes, alas, to console me. I pass my life by the shore of the palm-grove and all
alone come and go like the waves of the sea." Since the male singer in the song
directly quotes the woman's lament with which the song ends, Braggioni can
assume the roles of singer and orphan, of potential protector and protected or
of predator and victim since the song is an obvious male fantasy with sexual
conquest lurking just below its sentimental surface. By catching Laura's glance
and weighing every word, Braggioni focuses her attention on the meaning of
the song and encourages her to identify with the woman in it, but his insinua-
tion only increases her resistance to his intentions.

Braggioni's song is made more sinister through the fearful description of his
body. Critics have likened it to "a kind of overripe plum as dangerous as a
grenade," "a grotesque Easter egg," and "a huge tumescent phallus."[35] His body
is phallic, but the words italicized in the passage also suggest a repugnant picture of a woman in labor. Braggioni's song and body work subliminally on
Laura as a before-and-after object lesson of what could happen to her if she
relaxed her vigilance. The pregnancy his body suggests does not give promise
of new life, but only evidence of shameful, misshapen violation and danger of
death in childbirth. It helps explain Laura's contrastingly defensive posture
and dress: "Her knees cling together under sound blue serge, and her round
white collar is not purposely nun-like" (92). Laura's closed knees, like her
"firmly closed" underlip (95), communicate her resistance to Braggioni's
"spread knees." While her posture defends against his sexuality, her dress attempts to repress her own, for she "covers her great round breasts with thick
dark cloth" and "hides long, invaluably beautiful legs under a heavy skirt. She
is almost thin except for the incomprehensible fullness of her breasts, like a
nursing mother's," but Braggioni "is not put off by that blue serge" as his "cat's
eyes waver in a separate glance for the two points of light marking the opposite
ends of a smoothly drawn path between the swollen curve of her breasts" (97).

While Laura's blue serge has the opposite of its intended effect, it fails to
hide her body that seems in conflict with itself. Reflecting Porter's own determination to remain thin, Laura's anorectic thinness is consistent with her notion that the ideal "revolutionist should be thin" and with her desire to remain
immaturely childlike, but her "nursing mother's" breasts betray her ideals. She

won't accept her woman's body as a living organism subject to the laws of growth and maturation because association with Braggioni threatens "a shocking death" (93). She rejects him as evil, but along with him "all external events." Garbed in her self-protective childlike "uniform of an idea," she rejects "knowledge and kinship in one monotonous word. No. No. No. She draws her strength from this one holy talismanic word which does not suffer her to be led into evil" (97).

Porter bestowed on Laura her own "principle of rejection" with a vengeance. Six months before completing "Flowering Judas," she had proudly claimed the principle's success against Floyd Dell, but in the story she dramatizes its tragic consequences. A self-protective principle, it measures the degree of self-love that makes it operative. Although Laura accuses Braggioni of an "excess" of "self-love" that has "flowed out, inconveniently," over her (91), she opposes it with her own love of idealized self that extends far beyond him, forcing her to take extreme measures against anybody who threatens it. And everyone does. Laura could have thought what Porter wrote in her Salem confession: "Now I seem unable to believe in anything, and certainly my doubts of human beings and their motives are founded in a fear of their power over me." But fear of another's power makes love as dangerous as Braggioni's lust. Laura wisely rejects his advances, but also rejects the proffered love of the "gentle" Zapatista captain and the young union organizer, even the love of the children she teaches, "who remain strangers to her" (97). Drawing from her memories of her first year in Mexico, later expressed in "The Evening," Porter turned geographical alienation into a metaphysical state; unable to imagine living in "another country" (93), Laura, ultimately, is "not at home in the world" (97).

Several times in the story Laura contemplates escape, as Porter escaped Mexico in 1921 and, in her revision of "Holiday," recommended as a solution against "troubles and dangers" not "truly ours" (407). But escape from Braggioni, "symbol of [Laura's] many disillusions," is also escape from self, from the impossible demands of the ego ideal, and, like escape from the world where she is not at home, is tantamount to suicide, the option already taken by Eugenio, who in a dream tempts her to "a new country" (102). Suicide lies behind Laura's contemplated escape from Braggioni: "Sometimes she wishes to run away, but she stays. Now she longs to fly out of the room, down the narrow stairs, and into the street where the houses lean together like conspirators under a single mottled lamp, and leave Braggioni singing to himself" (92). Porter developed this passage from a 1921 journal entry in which she complained she would "like exceedingly to die," not having "that sense of urgency" she had when she nearly died of influenza. Then she wrote, "The streets are bowl shaped, and the houses lean inward. . . . I have continually the sensation of stepping into space, and the side walk seems to curve downward from the outer edges," predicting, "In a week probably I shall be dead." The surreally leaning houses, viewed as if through a fish-eye lens, imply escape into another world no better than the real one. The suicidal urge Porter felt in

1921 recurred in her attacks of melancholia during the twenties. She later wrote her father (June 26, 1931) that she had struggled a long time "against the very strong temptation just to . . . quit the whole devilish nuisance of life."

Eugenio's suicide is a decisive act in a story filled with apathetic routine. It is a frightening example of the evil in Laura's own rejection principle that could lead to her own death. Hiding her "nursing mother's" breasts, she has rejected her role as nourishing life-giver and instead has become the mother of death by administering narcotics to Eugenio. Although she doesn't fully comprehend the inefficacy of her idealistic principles, her guilt-ridden dream awakens her to their consequences. It tells her she has betrayed Eugenio and others by betraying herself.

Porter gave conflicting versions about the basis of Eugenio's suicide. She accused Mary Doherty of supplying pills to a prisoner and of dreaming about his death, but Doherty told me she had never set foot in prison until she visited photographer Tina Modotti in 1930. Porter's description of Doherty as "virgin office wife" and "hanger on" confirms her friend's staid activities in Mexico. A few years before her death, Porter, in tears, told me she herself had given sleeping pills to a prisoner who hoarded them until he had enough with which to kill himself, adding that only the death of the man who caught influenza from her in Denver had affected her as much. However, it is more likely that she created Eugenio out of her guilt over the death of Sidronio Méndez, just as she later created Adam Barclay in "Pale Horse, Pale Rider" out of her guilt over the death of the man in Denver. Porter's claim of visiting prisoners in their cells is based on her visits to Haberman in hiding and to Retinger in his cell. Her claim of smuggling letters is based on her copying William Niven's letters about Sidronio Méndez and his co-conspirators; in 1921 she described Doherty as keeping "her head cool in the midst of opera bouffe plots, the submerged international intrigue of her melodramatic associates," but also described her own melodramatic exposure of Méndez's plot as "an act of opera bouffe treachery." His death clearly contributes to the atmosphere of death, betrayal, and guilt that permeates "Flowering Judas."

Through "A la Orilla de un Palmar" we can grasp Laura's psychological preoccupations. By projecting her own melancholia onto Mary Doherty, both in the story and in her later comments on it, Porter was able to analyze its dangerous consequences in Laura's rejection of love, something she was unable to do satisfactorily in "Theft." Through the other song Braggioni sings, Porter gives a more positive view of Laura's struggle in a corrupt world.

In an unpublished poem, written in 1921, Porter describes a blind boy playing on his flute a "song about the girl from the north, with green eyes," the last line of which includes a direct quotation from "La Norteña": "Linda no llores. Pretty thing, don't cry." In "Flowering Judas" Laura remembers hearing "the blind boy playing his reed-flute" (90), his music a sharp contrast to Braggioni's "painful squeal," but Porter assigns the song the boy plays in the poem to Braggioni, making him its creator: "'O girl with the dark eyes,' he sings, and reconsiders. 'But yours are not dark. I can change all that. O girl with the green eyes, you have stolen my heart away!'" (97). Porter, through Braggioni, insists on green eyes even though the narrator earlier tells us that "all praise [Laura's] gray eyes" (95). Unless we assume Braggioni is color-blind, a look outside the text helps explain the apparent discrepancy. Glenway Wescott reported in 1964, "One of the revolutionaries wrote a song about her, 'La Norteña,' which, I have heard tell, has become a folk song . . . I understand that another lady lays claim to it."[36] Obviously Wescott heard tell from Porter herself, although "La Norteña," mentioned in "Xochimilco," was written before her arrival in Mexico. Wescott's revolutionary, then, turns out to be the fictional Braggioni. Porter began to create a legend about herself even before she wrote "Flowering Judas" and embellished it thereafter.

Porter modeled her legend after that of Alma Reed, the other "lady" Wescott alludes to, countering "Peregrina," the song that immortalized Reed's romance with Carrillo Puerto, with "La Norteña." Porter was both envious and contemptuous of Reed's notoriety. In fragments of *Historical Present,* a novel she was working on in 1930, she planned to begin with Reed's "cashing in on Felipe's death" and go on to her "gradual building up the legend" to become "patroness of all Mexico." Porter probably heard the seamy side of the legend from Carleton Beals, who wrote Anita Brenner in 1924 that Reed was "staying at the Waldorf Astoria on Felipe's money." In 1929 Reed, recently returned to New York from Greece, entertained Brenner, Luis Hidalgo, and other Mexican artists in her apartment. Porter was well aware of the patroness's presence as she began "Flowering Judas."

Porter blended her impression of Mary Doherty as virgin in 1921 with Reed's and her own desire for the limelight to create the mysterious legend of Laura: "Nobody touches her, but all praise her gray eyes, and the soft, round under lip which promises gayety, yet it is always grave, nearly firmly closed: and they cannot understand why she is in Mexico. . . . No dancer dances more beautifully than Laura walks, and she inspires some amusing, unexpected ardors, which cause little gossip, because nothing comes of them" (95). Braggioni "wishes to impress this simple girl" with "her great round breasts" and "invaluably beautiful legs" and puzzles over her "notorious virginity." Because of her inaccessible beauty, Laura is a challenge to him, who, like a courtly lover, composes a song to celebrate her, especially her green eyes that, according to the lyrics of "La Norteña," "sparkle like precious stones" and "killed . . . with a glance." He hopes his song will melt her heart, but instead it commemorates her mysterious inaccessibility. If his song were to become popular, as "La Norteña" had, it would be an ironic record of Laura's victory over him. Laura's legend reflects Porter's own need for admiration as well as her fear of its consequences.

Although seemingly unaware of it, Laura owes her public image and "her comfortable situation and her salary" (91) to Braggioni, who has compromised her high ideals, symbolized by her dedicated virginity. She also compromises herself by oiling and loading his pistol for an enterprise she scorns. The phallic symbolism of the act also suggests unconscious sexual compromise, but her refusal to answer his question about love while she "peers down the pistol barrel" (100) expresses her unflinching resistance to it. Her virginity is "notorious," not just because it resists would-be seducers, but because it attracts to repel. The frustrated Braggioni gets his just deserts, but Laura's similar treatment of the young union organizer to whom she throws a flower betrays his love, as the presence of the Judas tree in the patio where he sang to her suggests.

What Laura does unconsciously to men, Miranda, in a fragment from *Thieves' Market,* does consciously, setting herself "perversely" against Jerome when he was "passionate," refusing to "respond" and feeling "happy in having spoiled his plan for her." Other times she was "really cold, as inaccessible as a virgin." Jerome would then call her "a Russian nun," telling her that she expected "to be taken as if [she] were the Holy Wafer." In "The Evening" the young American woman, enjoying the speculation about her by her companions in a cafe, is sized up by one as a "cold woman with an experienced glance. He knew them well, these visiting gringas frias. They let you make love to them as if they thought you meant to pick their pocket." Laura resembles Miranda and the woman in "The Evening," both of whom resemble Porter herself, as Braggioni's comments prove: "You think you are so cold, *gringita* [sic]! Wait and see. You will surprise yourself some day! May I be there to advise you!" (97). His hope that she is not cold is vain. In Laura, Porter created a character whose notorious inaccessibility is meant to frustrate the predatory male who rightly suspects her frigidity. She is unwitting femme fatale, victorious in her resistance to him.

"Flowering Judas" originated with Porter's portrait of Doherty with its lyrical mode. In the same mode is the closely related 1921 sketch, "In a Mexican Patio." Pleased with this sketch, Porter wrote of doing other things in the "Patio" manner. Like "Flowering Judas," it is narrated in the present tense and tightly observes unity of time and place. The expression of the lonely narrator's concern about love inspired several scenes in "Flowering Judas." In both works, a young man enters the patio with its fountain at night to express his love for his enamored, watching from the balcony. In the patio is a "bougainvillaea vine, whose fronds rise to my balcony, thrusting their purple branches now flowering lavishly through hospitable windows," which Porter transformed into the "dull purple" of the Judas tree. In "In a Mexican Patio" a man with a guitar sings a song about "love, how it is cruel, because life devours us, a day at a time, and a dream at a time, until we are ended utterly," a song expressive of Laura's mood. Like "Flowering Judas," "In a Mexican Patio" ends ominously at night: "In the sunlight one may laugh, and sniff the winds, but the night is crowded with thoughts darker than the sunless world."

On November 29, 1929, Porter wrote R. P. Blackmur that she owed the title of "Flowering Judas" to T. S. Eliot's "Gerontion," a few lines of which she wished to use as an epigraph to her story.[37] The poem is the source of Porter's title and of Laura's dream in which she greedily eats the "warm, bleeding" Judas flowers as Eugenio accuses her, "Murderer! . . . Cannibal! This is my body and my blood!" (102), helping Porter focus symbolically on the self-betrayal she experienced in 1921 and struggled with in "Theft." But the story's brilliance comes from her ability to give voice to all the complex and contra-dictory emotions and attitudes within her, each of which subtly shades and qualifies another. Even the character of Braggioni is qualified. Although he is a symbol of all Laura's fears, he is partially based on the character of Luis Morones, whom she worked for, praised in articles, and, if Colonel Miller is correct, was intimate with. At least Braggioni has the capacity to function, however corruptly, in the real world, to recognize that he and Laura "are more alike" than she realizes (93) and to benefit from "the solemn, endless rain of [his wife's] tears" (101). Laura's principle of rejection is also qualified. Her "No" to everything she considers evil changes to a "No" to suicide. She lives in a limbo between life and death. Although she wants to flee Braggioni, "Still she quietly sits, she does not run" (93). When he leaves, she thinks, "I must run while there is time. But she does not go" (101). She exists on the edge of two unacceptable alternatives, the corrupt life of the real world where love also exists or the sterile idealism of an unreal world where love dies. Porter sympa-thetically invested Laura with all her own unresolved psychological problems but admires her ability just to survive.[38] For that Laura deserves her legendary status, as the allusion to "La Norteña" suggests.

In 1943 Porter wrote Doherty, "Mexico was new to us, and beautiful, the very place to be at that moment. We believed a great deal—though I remember well that my childhood faith in the Revolution was well over in about six months." By May 1921, the time of the deportation crisis, the models for Brag-gioni had convinced her that Mexico as potential paradise could be nothing but a dream. But out of the dreamer's failure came the artist's success. If Mex-ico could not assuage her troubled psyche, it helped her contemplate the entwined betrayals of revolution and self, and transform her disillusion and spiritual isolation into Laura's. By donning, as it were, Mary Doherty's nunlike uniform, Porter was able to give voice to all her conflicting emotions and view them with dispassionate objectivity as if they were not her own. In her com-ments about the creation of her story, she persisted in her disguise, claiming that her friend was the model for Laura. "Flowering Judas" was not "repor-tage," as she claimed in 1972, but it did contain "symbolic truth" of her Mexi-can experience. Her transformation of the purple bougainvillaea in her Mexi-can patio into the flowering Judas tree is example of the process that brought art out of life.

5. Mexico Once More, 1930–1931

Ernesto Pugibet

Porter stayed with the Crawfords for about eight months. When she developed a bronchial ailment and a doctor recommended a warmer climate, they again came to the rescue and persuaded an unnamed benefactor to contribute ninety dollars a month for a year in Mexico. In the meantime Harcourt Brace, at the urging of Matthew Josephson, agreed to publish *Flowering Judas* and also *Thieves' Market* upon its anticipated completion at the end of 1930, contracts of March 1 and 3, 1930, calling for an advance of six hundred dollars. Now there was money enough to finish the Mexican novel in the country Porter had wanted to revisit for the last six years. Readers of "Flowering Judas" may wonder why, as Porter herself soon did. In her sixteen-month stay in Mexico, she hardly wrote a word of the novel she contracted to finish. Instead she wrote frequent lengthy letters to her friends in New York, complaining about everything, from corrupt homosexual politicians to American entrepreneurs who were ruining Indian folk art—even the conducting of composer Carlos Chávez did not escape her scorn. Frequent states of depression influenced her negative view of the country. Her attempted cure was bursts of social activity, which, in the aftermath, caused her to complain all the more, guiltily blaming others for her failure to write and making her epistolary record of her months in Mexico appear more dismal than they actually were.

On April 29, 1930, the day of her arrival in Mexico City, Porter sent a note to Carleton Beals, asking him to visit her at Dorothy Day's house where she planned to stay while house-hunting. At the time, Day, a recently converted Catholic who had come to Mexico in December to live among the poor, was living with her young daughter in a thatched hut in Xochimilco. Porter celebrated her birthday there in her Eden of nine years ago.[1]

Porter also explored the possibility of living in Taxco, a colonial town in Guerrero "which hangs like a nest in the hollow of a mountain side." On "that terrible and beautiful road" to the town, she witnessed from the bus "an Indian man and woman beside the dusty way, engaged in killing each other with knives and stones . . . his shaven head was gashed round and the blood streamed down in his face which looked like the Indian Christ's in the country churches; he was done for, his face showed it, but she was still screaming and wild and furious . . . we rattled and bounded by in a whirl of dust and gasoline fumes." In Taxco William Spratling, collector of Indian antiquities and later proprietor of a booming silver jewelry business, gave her the use of his house as he rushed off to Mexico City. That night she woke up "to the strains of a country orchestra on its way home from a three days' fiesta" and to "ten thousand bedbugs" beginning "guerilla warfare" on her "martyred remains." Unable to sleep, she "sat in the window and watched two cats fight in the steep cobbled street, mending their quarrel in haste when a dog came along." At daylight she "cravenly" crept away, resolving never to return, but saved her "Notes from letter to Caroline" for eventual use in *Ship of Fools*.

When Day returned to Mexico City, Porter found an apartment for forty dollars a month at Calle Ernesto Pugibet 78, six blocks east of the Alameda. It had four rooms running around a balcony she "filled with potted plants and little trees and ferns." She hired a servant, bought second-hand furniture, and kept busy making "pajamas" for her chairs. Her prize possession was a small decrepit antique rosewood piano she bought for fifty dollars and hoped to learn to play. She told Gay (May 30, 1930) it "was an extravagance, the kind I mean to commit every time I have the slightest opportunity." She meant it then and whenever she had money to spend. Recalling "all the damned houses and apartments" she had painted, decorated, and furnished only to give them up in two months, she also meant to settle down and write and "if anything blasts me out of it in under two years, I am a wretch who deserves no sympathy" (L 21–23). She stayed in the apartment eight months.

On June 7 Porter wrote Delafield Day that she had planned a going-away party for Dorothy, who was leaving in a few days, but when Dorothy decided to have the party at her house, Porter pleaded illness and did not go. She believed they didn't want her, but she didn't mind; "Is this not symbolic of some great change in my life?" she wondered. It may have been symbolic of Porter's principle of rejection. She claimed, however, that her "first feeling of melancholy, as if it had been a mistake to come back here where so much had happened" to her, had passed and now she felt she could manage her life and live by herself. In the same letter she mentioned that "Gene the youth" had presented her with a small flask of very fine cognac. The youth, fourteen years her junior, was Eugene Pressly, an employee of the Crane Foundation who later became her husband and the model for David Scott in *Ship of Fools*. Porter had met him on May 5 while still living in Day's house and on June 21, their first date, accompanied him to an Indian village to witness a fire festival where they "were badly rained on instead."[2] He soon fell in love and started courting her seriously, but neither he nor his cognac seemed to dispel her loneliness and discontent.

Porter also wrote Delafield about "epidemics of typhoid and small pox," "leprosy in Tlalpan, a few miles away, and a terrible scourge of some eye disease in a near-by state, and everybody warns me I must watch out for bedbugs." Her precaution was antityphoid shots, which sent her to bed. She complained to Caroline Gordon of being "wearier and wearier" and hoped that in a month she would "spring out full of vigor." She had written "sobbing little scenes on *Thieves' Market*," but destroyed them when she left her bed. Her spirits revived with the arrival of Liza Dallett (her Village roommate in 1924), in Mexico to celebrate her separation from her husband with Porter's help. Both attended a party Mary Doherty gave in honor of René d'Harnoncourt (organizer of the Carnegie Mexican Art Exhibition) and then made a two-day visit to Oaxtepec, a warm-spring resort in Morelos; Porter's notes of August 13 record, "We left Mexico at seven o'clock in the morning, and drove through such a landscape as can be only in Mexico during the rainy season: so washed, so fresh and dustless, tempered by sunlight, you lose your sense of corporeality, you walk melted into the air around you." Oaxtepec also gave Porter her vision, mentioned above, of the young girl, "the first entirely flawless human being [she] had ever seen." Another fleeting glimpse of Eden.

But when Dallett left for Acapulco with Mary and Peggy Doherty "and a choice handful of Mexico's politicians, artists, and homosexuals," Porter's dark mood returned: "My inertia, my day by day feeling that today I must rest, and tonight sleep, and tomorrow I shall not be so tired, but may really work. It's a devilish state, and hell will be like that, without the sun and hopefulness." She wrote Allen Tate (September 30) that Liza's one-month stay gave her "the sensation of sitting in on a running performance of rather talented amateur theatricals," but left her with tonsillitis and a high fever which she suspected was "a self-defensive measure." Free of Liza, she inconsistently looked forward to the Cowleys' arrival since there was no talk, swimming, dancing, "and really no one even to drink with a little [not even Pressly apparently], for nearly all the artists walk with a lisp and are kept by the politicians, most of the good ones are gone, to New York or Paris [Covarrubias, Orozco, Guerrero]; and a few are in prison [Siqueiros]" and "some are dead [Abraham Angel]," but she concluded that "the things I loved in this country I still love . . . and I have a kind of happiness here."

In "Notes from a letter to Ernestine [Evans]" (October 3), Porter gave an even more jaundiced survey of "show-Mexico." She accused Diego Rivera of accepting $22,000 from Ambassador Dwight Morrow "to spoil Cortes palace with his dummies" while paying his assistant five pesos a day. After drinks with Rivera at a party, she renewed her friendship with him "after a fashion," despite all he had done. He invited her to Cuernavaca to watch him work and talk about old times, but she didn't go. She also deplored the degeneration of Mexican folk crafts, sold in "Arty Shoppes" at inflated prices at no benefit to the Indian craftsman. Spratling urged the lacquerware industry to produce "crude and frightful objects," and in Tonalá an American woman—she forgot "the animal's name"—had shown traditional potters how to bastardize their craft to make it more marketable. There were no funds for the Fresh Air schools, while one of the Fine Art schools got its main revenue by imitating Aztec statues for "one of our more homosexual politicians." Foreigners were everywhere. Frank Tannenbaum (editor of the *Survey Graphic* Mexican issue of 1924) was busy "writing up" the country, but "can't move a leg without a thesis as a crutch," the representative of the Crane Foundation (Eyler Simpson) was taking surveys with the "dream of gaining moral power by boring into the country, like a worm," and René d'Harnoncourt was "the belle of the ball here among innocent ladies who think he is just too sweet." Even her old friend Adolfo Best Maugard had degraded himself as "one of the main springs of the Tourists Board." She added that "desiccated females looking for romance" attached themselves to "charming inverts," while a prominent politician kept inviting her to his country house so that he could come up on weekends with "limp haired boys," but she was not going to play "gooseberry to a homosexual honeymoon." After "the Carleton Bealses and all the other God-Awful mediocrities who swarm over the place eating the heart out of it like white ants," she looked forward to the arrival of the Cowleys.

This information, beside implying Porter's extensive contact with the world outside Ernesto Pugibet 78 and explaining why her novel was not moving forward, contains a carefully orchestrated thesis about various forms of corruption and decadence. Even in the same notes in which she exulted in the "heavenly" skies of Oaxtepec, she lamented that "there in the midst of the warmth and loveliness were the same listless, ragged hungry people, and the same starving dogs and emaciated burros and inanimate babies and blind pock-marked beggars, and the same overpowering sense of death-in-life which only death itself can cure. I am wounded to the bone by it . . . ." Her constant dark mood was ready-made for a story she did not discover until her visit to the Hacienda Tetlapayac nine months later.

Some of Porter's facts in her Evans notes are unreliable. Morrow paid Rivera not $22,000 but $12,000 for five months' work, out of which he had to purchase materials and pay all his workmen. Five pesos a day was the going rate for assistants.[3] Porter was misinformed, possibly by Pablo O'Higgins (Paul Higgins), who came to Mexico as an assistant to Rivera in 1924, joined the Mexican Communist party in 1927, and in the fall of 1930 gave Porter piano lessons for six weeks. Rivera had been drummed out of the party in 1929 because he objected to its confrontational attitude toward the government with which he compromised by becoming director of the Academy of San Carlos. O'Higgins reported that Siqueiros had called Rivera an opportunist and collaborationist,[4] pretty much what Porter implied in her letter. Shortly thereafter, she became well acquainted with Siqueiros, who had been imprisoned until December because he participated in May Day disturbances in 1930. She promised to translate the poetry of his wife, Blanca Luz, and to arrange publication of his essay "The Syndicate of Painters and Sculptors of Mexico and Its Importance as a Revolutionary Factor" in Europe in 1931. She sided with him against Rivera, whose "dummies" she had not seen in Cuernavaca—a slight that could not have pleased Evans, who had published her book on his murals in 1929.

Porter's preoccupation with homosexuality in the Evans notes continued in other letters and notes. She wrote Genevieve Taggard of "gentlemen, making love to one another 'over my head and across my lap,'" adding, "How pleasant it will be to see again men who love women, even if they don't like them, and like them even if they can't love them."[5] In "Note for novel . . . From letter to Raymond [Everitt]," she declared, "All the men are homosexuals. . . . I speak of the party in power, the politicians, artists, musicians, educators." Porter gave the impression of a serious decline in Mexico's heterosexual population in sharp contrast to the early twenties when she viewed the Yúdicos and De la Selvas as menaces to womanhood. Another fiction note may explain her pique: "The men all suspect homosexual. . . Carlos confirmed. Men and women alike attracted to the warm brown healthy senseless young animal. Mir[anda] challenged by the situation, sets out deliberately to make Carlos jealous. . Does it. . Trouble and bitterness and suffering in the surface gay party. She is happy [to have] the center of the stage, feels the whole affair revolving around her . . ." At the bottom of the page Porter penciled in "Liza Dallett," but the desire of Miranda, her alter ego, to be center stage, like the gringa in "The Evening," suggests that Porter resented playing second fiddle. She never explained why she chose the company she kept. Evans, in an undated letter to Beals, wrote, "A gossip came in the other day who described Katherine Anne as now horrendous in her hate of homosexuals, her court for so long."

Porter had Liza Dallett in mind when she complained to Gay on October 10, "I lack nervous vitality and must be careful not to waste my strength on any thing but what is essential to my own plan. I think mostly that people like to see you destroying yourself, and will help you that way if they can." Responding to Gay's mention of their sister Mary Alice, Porter remembered her as "a beautiful thing" who in her youth "had the same suicidal mania that you and I had" because of "our horrible hopeless childhood, which I cannot remember now without a sinking of the heart." She rejected the philosophy that "all pains are necessary," but "there is such a thing as good and bad fortune," and the former did not reward virtue and the latter evil. Although one cannot say how much "inner character" and "outward pressure" play a part in one's life, "good character can survive and even give meaning to the horrors of life, but that does not make the horrors good, nor even necessary. And the suffering of children is not their fault." She took responsibility for everything that "happened" to her, but if she "had had a decent, civilized childhood," she "might have been better equipped for the ungodly struggle [she] had to make." Her attempt to grapple with the mysterious relation between "inner character" and "outward pressure" was as inconclusive as it was in Salem. In her May letter to Gay, she had speculated that her father enjoyed having "a specially venomous Voodoo on his trail," but like him she felt victimized by *la Suerte*. As in Salem, she wished to rely on "inner character" and take responsibility for her life, but she could never hold firmly to that point, for "outward pressure" in the form of her victimized childhood, of a Liza Dallett, who would like to see her destroy herself, or of the "horrors of life" in Mexico, including the threat of typhoid fever, ultimately accounted for her melancholic view of her condition.

The arrival of Malcolm and Peggy Cowley on October 17 became a welcome distraction. On the twenty-third they all attended a saint's day party Moisés Sáenz gave for Frances Toor, editor of *Mexican Folkways,* at the Regis.[6] Later, on their way to visit Sáenz in Taxco, their car almost went off the winding mountain road, prompting them, upon their arrival, to have an ex-voto painted to hang in the church in thanksgiving for their deliverance.[7] They also went, Porter for the third time, to a performance of Pastora Imperio, the "great gypsy dancer, really the last of her kind."[8] Porter in a note: "Remember the strut, the ferocious orgiastic female pride as she came across the stage for the first time. Her audience responded, shouting, and all over the house men groaned in a suffering voice as at a long delayed enormous orgasm." Imperio stage center. Porter must have envied her and did remember her in *Ship of Fools.* Also, at a party Helen Augur gave, Porter kicked Carleton Beals on the shins, "something I have been longing to do for eight years, and I wish I had done it on first impulse."[9] (In 1934 she gave him a literary kick on the shins in "That Tree.") At the invitation of Sáenz, Porter went to Acapulco in company with Leopold Stokowski, who, she felt, transformed the Mexican Symphony Orchestra after the "abominable" conducting of Carlos Chávez.

Porter was the dubious beneficiary of the lavish entertaining of Sáenz, who had served as director of the National Preparatory School under Carranza and was presently director of Beneficencia Publica.[10] His brother, General Aarón Sáenz, held cabinet posts under Obregón and Calles and was governor of Nuevo León in 1930. Porter told Lopez that Sáenz met her at the train in 1920 and took her to Calle Eliseo. She also claimed that he, one of "her closest friends and confidants," introduced her to marijuana in Cuernavaca. In a hallucinatory state, she thought she could walk out into space, but her host stopped her from climbing over the railing and plunging into a ravine one hundred feet below (61–67). However, Sáenz's name first appears in Porter's notes of 1930–1931 with no indication there or in her letters that she ever knew him before. She also told Lopez that among the party in Cuernavaca was "Rogelio," probably Rogerio de la Selva, Salomón's brother. Perhaps she confused Sáenz and De la Selva. Her dramatic reaction to marijuana is suspect since in 1931 she wrote that "some one who knows tells me" that the music of Julián Carrillo "is like music heard in the mind under the influence of Marihuana, when, it is a popular saying, the leaves on the trees sing"—unless the "some one who knows" is Porter.

Even though she accepted his hospitality, Porter identified Sáenz as the most convenient example of official corruption. In a fictionalized note entitled "Moisés," Porter wrote, "The new order. President of Public charities . . . the best graft in Mexico. Airplane. Country house two weeks after appointment.

Town car, country car, gradually hacienda and fruit ranches." The "utter arrogance, the contempt" of the bureaucratic type is caught in her description of Sáenz "roaring for the road in his high-powered speed car," furious with anyone who will not pull to the side and let him pass. When a policeman stops him for going three times over the speed limit, he identifies himself, at which the policeman gives up and tells him to go as fast as he wants. Arrogance and love of speed also distinguish don Genaro in "Hacienda."

Porter's note on Sáenz concluded, "What wouldn't they do if they hadn't to keep up a little longer their pretense of being friends of the workers?" The "they" included anybody in the administration of Plutarco Elías Calles, who had consolidated his power before Porter arrived in Mexico. Some of her radical friends felt the effect of that power as early as 1925. Retinger informed Bertram Wolfe that if he insisted on aiding autonomous labor unions, he would be tossed out of Mexico since Retinger, Haberman, and Morones recommended expulsion of all Communists. Wolfe and his wife were soon expelled.[11] After his term of office, Calles as Jefe Maximo hand-picked Mexico's presidents. Pascual Ortiz Rubio, Calles's complete puppet, became president in November 1929 in a rigged election while José Vasconcelos, the opposing candidate, fled the country. After an attempted assassination of Ortiz Rubio, the government used the occasion to punish its perceived enemies. Porter's friend, photographer Tina Modotti, was jailed and then deported. Even Carleton Beals was seized and briefly held incommunicado, an incident Porter refers to in her review of his novel, *The Stones Awake.*[12] Although Calles as president had repartitioned more land in two years than Obregón in four, his reforms fell far short of expectations. Historian Lesley Byrd Simpson writes of the "revolutionary plutocrats" Calles represented, similar to the "old hacendado-clergy-foreigner complex" of the Díaz dictatorship. Like Díaz, Calles was the policeman of the New Order and "the principal beneficiary."[13] Simpson's view confirmed Porter's prediction in "The Mexican Trinity." Nine years after her essay, she noted that "the agrarian question is now settled, with every general and politico in Mexico beautifully provided with a great hacienda" and that Calles's "immense hacienda" supplied milk to public hospitals, orphanages, schools, and homes for the aged at a price higher than the private consumer pays to ordinary dairies, while the poor remained as she saw them in "The Fiesta of Guadalupe." These notes led to her conclusion in "Hacienda" that the revolution had changed nothing.

Yet "Leaving the Petate," accepted by Malcolm Cowley for the November 5 issue of the *New Republic,* deals with changes "so gradual" it is impossible to say when they began. Porter uses the *petate,* the Indian's sleeping mat of woven straw, as her central symbol, perhaps remembering Anita Brenner's treatment of it in *Idols Behind Altars* since both quote the saying "Whoever was born on a *petate* will always smell of the straw" (CE 388).[14] Porter's thesis is that the Indian, at the first chance, "leaves his *petate* and takes as naturally as any other human being to the delights of kinder living," for "you can never convince me he is really comfortable, or likes his way of sleeping" on it (CE 389). Since the *petate* is symbol of Indian ways, Porter implicitly approves of acculturation in her contrast of her modern servant Eufemia and Eufemia's traditional aunt Hilaria, although she had Eufemia pose for a photograph in a traditional Tehuana costume. Hilaria wears braids, a *rebozo,* is a curandera who "sticks firmly to her native herbs," and plans to return to her village (her *petate*), but the younger Eufemia has had her hair bobbed, now wears a scarf and high-heeled pumps, uses bicarbonate of soda, is leaving the *petate* for a brass bed, and "will never go back to her village" (CE 393), just as Porter, except in memory, never went back to her symbolic *petate* in Texas. Eufemia's children may turn out to be "good little right-minded dull people" or, with her "fighting spirit," become "*mestizo* revolutionaries, and keep up the work of saving the Indian" (CE 393). Porter's observations of Eufemia and of Consuelo, Mary Doherty's maid, are sharp and good-humored, but made from the patronizing point of view of mistress of the household who knows that Hilaria, "a born intriguer," spends hours in her kitchen advising Eufemia "about how best to get around" her (CE 389). She later wrote Herbst (February 11, 1931) that she disliked Aztecs (like Eufemia), and hoped her new maid, an Otomi, and Doherty's maid, a Totonac, would not kill each other because of the traditional animosity between the two "tribes" (L 31).

Porter's new maid was Teodora, whose adventures as soldadera in the revolution Porter began to set down. At Christmastime they both watched from the roof posada singers going from door to door. Porter set up a creche of painted clay figures and celebrated Christmas Day with Teodora by setting off roman candles. In separate letters to Delafield Day and Caroline Gordon on January 6, she gave a detailed description of Christmas customs in Mexico, the posadas, the breaking of the piñata, midnight mass, and the feast of the Three Kings— exchanging gifts and eating *rosca,* "a dry sweet bread made in a ring, full of fruit, and a tiny porcelain Christ-Baby concealed in it for you to break a tooth on." She also mentioned her progress with Chopin preludes—perhaps in imitation of the lonely woman of "In a Mexican Patio." The end of the year had come and gone and with it the deadline for the novel she was to have finished but had hardly begun.

In her letter to Delafield, Porter congratulated her on her pregnancy: "Even now, I have an insane idea to marry and have a baby of my own. But I never shall, it would be worse than insanity." (Reasons for that conclusion appear in "Flowering Judas" and "The Grave.") She also complained that "Dorothy dislikes me very much and towards the end was so unfriendly I couldn't approach her about anything." She found it "mysterious," as Dorothy herself might have since she had let Porter use her apartment, invited her for a weekend in Xochimilco, and after returning to the States, told John Crawford that the Cotton Mather manuscript Porter had shown her was a "masterpiece, the last word on a most interesting subject."[15] Perhaps religion caused the problem. Porter, in 1929, had asked Delafield, "Does Dorothy keep her ingenuous convert fanaticism? Such a strange end for her! But religion is necessary at certain crises to certain temperaments. . . . But never for me. And I am always amazed when I see a grown person deliberately embrace a religious life." But Dorothy, taking seriously Porter's claim that she was a born Catholic, must have tried to bring her back into the fold, for she had asked her to see Father McKenna, although "you don't have to go to confession."[16]

In her January letter to Gordon, Porter also praised *I'll Take My Stand* (although it wasn't "belligerent" enough) and contemplated buying a cabin close to the Tates in Tennessee. But then she remembered why she had left the South, where she was "smothered in the atmosphere of traditionalism and formalism," adding, "Only in New York do I feel as though it doesn't greatly matter how I live. . . ." The Tates were a strong pull on her, but her wavering showed that she wasn't ready to take her stand. It was better to think and write about the South from a distance.

Four days later Porter wrote Gay that she had written forty-two letters, two to six pages long, "a perfect debauch of communication" to friends scattered all over the globe. The only two (unidentified) persons in Mexico she "can bear the sight of" do not come round for fear she "might be writing a masterpiece—ha, little they know!" Instead of her novel, she wrote to those who gave her "human companionship . . . in little envelopes," as if companionship required aesthetic distance to survive. She also noted that friends were writing her about the results of the stock-market crash: "In New York unemployed men are selling apples on every street corner, but here . . . thousands of men and women make all their living selling peanuts and sugar cane in tiny dusty little piles. They are very well off if they eat enough once a day."

Porter kept up her debauch of communication, writing two more letters to the Tates, one to Allen on the twenty-seventh and the other to Caroline on the twenty-eighth. She made the most elaborate plans about the cabin, planning to send Caroline seventy-five dollars as down payment and shipping her furniture up, rosewood piano and all—that is, if she didn't get the Guggenheim which would take her to Europe. To Allen, Porter described the earthquake of January 16 that devastated Oaxaca and toppled over fifty buildings in Mexico City: "The floor began to heave gently under our feet like an anchored ship, and through the open kitchen door I saw my Teodora . . . holding the kitten, with a look of blind terror in her face." They reached the street, which was dark "except for a curious greenish, reddish light." Nearby a family knelt together "crying 'Jesus, Mary, and Joseph' in a long monotone, and Teodora was murmuring 'Jesus Mary and Joseph' under her breath, kneeling and holding my hand." When the earth rocked again, Porter became dizzy and held on to a lamp post. Rumors came of plagues and mountains heaving lava, "but all apocalypses take place elsewhere." She also reported that Sergei Eisenstein, in the process of making *Que Viva Mexico!*, flew to Oaxaca to film the earthquake (L 28–29). She had met him at a supper given in his honor and sent a caricature she had done of him to Josephine Herbst (February 11, 1931).

Tate's report that Donald Davidson had given up poetry for political and social reasons launched Porter into a passionate defense of the artist's role: "If they are artists, they are cheating themselves and the race by reneging on the task they took up. . . . The artist who comprehends his time and the movement of the world in which he lives brings something better to it than mere agitations and controversy. He may join in these, but there is something beyond, and his value lies exactly in his sense of beyondness" (L 29). Porter probably felt she had been both revolutionist and artist when she lent her pen to various causes in the early twenties, complaining in "The Mexican Trinity" that in Mexico "there is no conscience crying through the literature of the country" (CE 401). In her notes she also condemned Pablo O'Higgins, who had "decided that all art was mere childishness in the face of the great oncoming wave of world change." In that case, he should become a worker in Russia and "so lose that individuality which he insists is the curse of human nature."

Porter's defense of the artist may have been a self-administered pep talk, for she had hardly practiced her own art since coming to Mexico. She told Gordon she admired Josephine Herbst's "ability to sit down and write a story straight through in spite of everything," whereas she was "tied up in knots and can't write a line," adding, "The whole trouble with me is that I have no plot. Everything is happening at once, everybody is so tangled up with each other and with circumstances they can't move, and there is no solution and no end." She was referring to her life as much as her art. Her "new idea of Hell" was to see her life "unrolled like a scroll, and at every turning point you could then see clearly precisely where your mistakes were made" and know they could have been avoided.

If Porter didn't have a plot, she had a theme, the corruption of Mexico. She wrote Delafield Day (February 17) about the "sink this country has become," what with its rotten politics and "every dumb, second-rate human being in the world" in Mexico to study the Indian and his art while "the Indian is in as bad a fix as ever, and I hope with all my heart to have looked my last on the place by September." Ironically, she also blamed Mexico for her inability to write about it: it was "very hard" to work on her novel, for "I find myself constantly choked by my own gall rising in my throat." Using her favorite metaphor to register mood, she blamed art dealers and dabblers for "poisoning the air" for her. Using another favorite metaphor, she complained of living "among hostile strangers who come to see me and invite me out from just sheer curiosity. . . . The atmosphere is pretty thick unless I just keep out of the way." In her "misanthropic" mood she couldn't imagine living among "such beastly unfriendly people," but might improve if she could go to Tennessee, which sounded like "Utopia," or at least "to a house in the country nearby" where there would be "more sun and air" or if she could make headway on her novel.

The next day she wrote Malcolm Cowley, connecting her inability to finish a review of Kay Boyle's short stories with her feeling, after a supper with Moisés Sáenz and Roberto Montenegro, that she was "not really loved here."

As with Dorothy Day, she probably imagined their animosity to justify her rejection of them. Rejection is the point of what she wrote Peggy Cowley on the same day she wrote Malcolm. It was a little parable about Ixcuintla, her cat who had brought a boyfriend into the house: "She was charming to him for about a week, seizing him around the neck and washing his face, sharing her bowl of milk and making little purring noises at him. Then suddenly one day she turned and beat him over the head with both front paws as if she were playing a drum, and he took the hint and left." Aware of the Cowleys' impending divorce, Porter projected her own principle of rejection onto Peggy, adding, "I have always said that when women learn to follow more surely these natural impulses, the world, Miss Peggy, will be a happier and a saner place."

Porter also told Peggy that she was writing all day long and had found "the leading thread" of her book called *Historical Present:* "Nothing to do but get four hundred pages of book into marching order. Oh, I do love life with all my heart. I wonder why I sometimes am so gloomy and useless." On February 20 she was still in a manic mood, writing to Herbst and John Hermann that she "must have written one hundred thousand million words" and giving an idea of the novel's structure:

> The first part has the story of seven men, all beginning from the period
> of the so-called revolution ten years back, and the story of each man
> picks up somewhere the story or stories of the men following him, with
> the women involved in each story coming in for just the share of the life
> of each man. Then the second book takes the women in succession, and
> tells the story from their angle, and the rest of their lives too. . . . I
> suppose you couldn't call it a novel . . . but I found that way I could
> make a full history of a period as seen by certain people that moved
> through it . . . and trick or no trick, I'm doing it.

The men Porter named are Carrillo Puerto, Morones, Retinger, Rivera, Sáenz, Siqueiros, and John Fulano de Tal, the last name meaning anybody or nobody. The women are Alma Reed, Mary Doherty, Lupe Marín, Frances (Paca) Toor, and Porter's servants, Eufemia and Teodora. Porter also mentioned "The women who came to worship Diego: Paca, Tina [Modotti], Ione [Robinson], keeping friendly with Lupe while sleeping with her husband. His marriage—legal—with Frida [Kahlo]." (Toor, founding editor of *Mexican Folkways,* to which Porter contributed a translation of a folk song,[17] was a special object of scorn, a "study in greed and envy and low ambition." Robinson, a Guggenheim fellow, was an assistant to Rivera.)

Porter's note on Siqueiros is typical of the writing she did: "Siqueiros, the Communist (combine with Angel Gomez the dynamiter). See notes for story of how he left his wife who told tales that he had a vile disease and was now living with a spy. Gachita a loose-lipped woman. . . . Party demanded that Siqueiros give up Blanca Luz. . . . How S[iqueiros], agent provocateur, betrayed the party, was himself betrayed by the government and jailed for a time . . . released, and very badly fed by the various sympathizers—Moisés, for one." She wrote "little scribbles on the story of Felipe which leads off the first chapter" and planned to use the story he told her in 1921. She also mentioned Alma Reed's "dramatic account of how she was standing by what chance she never explained in the hotel lobby, in full white satin with veil and orange blossoms rehearsing her wedding dress, when the news came" of Felipe's death, and noted the story of Retinger and Niven's letters.

Porter wrote her father (February 24) that she planned to write twelve or so interconnected short stories "in the style of 'Flowering Judas.'" Competing with Gordon and Herbst, who were then publishing their novels, she conceived a large, overly schematic novel which she never completed. Having created in that story Braggioni, *the* revolutionary, it was unlikely that she could now create two more, using two of the models who contributed to the first. She had already written all she wanted to say about that topic. Although she sent Malcolm Cowley a "scrap" on the Juana chapter, which she was almost entirely "lifting from the eloquent lips of Teodora," her papers contain no finished scenes from the novel, only short summaries of scenes she intended to create. She probably wrote nothing but those notes. Her plan was like a promissory note on which she began to borrow, writing her rival Herbst about the hundreds of pages she produced as if she had already produced them. In that same letter she described her drinking habits; she would remain sober until six o'clock and then "break down" with "a little cocktail or a sloe-gin rickey or a Black Strap Rum punch, and then with supper" had "three or four modest glasses of red wine, and then a little cognac to top it off and there is the evening, all ablaze!" Not the regimen of one intent on finishing a long novel before leaving Mexico.

On February 24 Porter used her novel as an excuse to discourage her father from visiting her. Recounting the enthusiastic reception her last four stories had received, she wrote that she didn't expect to be a popular writer but wanted "to be free to say what I feel and think as exactly as I am able." She reminded him that except for Bermuda she "never before had a day's freedom or leisure without worry and torment" about how she "was even to eat." She hoped to forget how her experiences had "scarred" her "rather badly," but would "never forget enough not to know how other people feel when they are in such a situation." Although it was part of her education, "it can go on too long, and destroy one, almost." By implicitly blaming her father for her past poverty, she proved how deeply scarred she was, so deeply that she couldn't easily cope with the leisure she now had to write her novel, although she couldn't forget "how other people feel" in such a situation, especially in Mexico. She fled the country each time she came, but returned, not just because it promised an elusive Eden, but because, on some opposing unconscious level, it opened old wounds. As a land of death, it held a "desperate attraction" for her, as it did for D. H. Lawrence.[18]

Mixcoac

Porter wrote her father (February 24) that since the ninety-dollar stipend from her "philanthropist friend" in New York had ended, she decided to move on March 1 to "a nice big old house in Mixcoac with a garden and a tank where you can swim round and round, like a goldfish" and where rents were cheap, but she didn't mention that Eugene Pressly, with whom she had already been living, would support her and share the house along with Mary Doherty. Years later Lopez found Porter unclear about why she moved in with Pressly, but accurately guessed that economic security was a factor (148). Certainly no one would guess from her letters of the period that she was in love. And she seldom mentioned Doherty, who then worked for Moisés Sáenz. Doherty's younger brother John fondly remembered Porter when she was still living on Ernesto Pugibet. He told me Eugene Pressly met him at the railroad station since Doherty had not returned from a long trip on horseback with Porter and Sáenz. Porter later invited him over for drinks; when reminded that he didn't drink, she declared it was about time he learned.

Today Mixcoac is part of Mexico City, about six miles from the center and easily accessible by metro, but in 1931 it was in the country, where Porter lived in a ten-room house with "a great sunny room for me, a big roof to romp on, a long front garden full of fruit trees and rose bushes," a swimming tank, a menagerie of dogs, cats, turkeys, hens, and "a little Greek goat with golden eyes who loved roses." She gave Josephine Herbst (June 1) a long detailed inventory of flowers and fruit trees and described her morning routine: "We take a dip in a tank of ice water about eleven o'clock, bake in the sun, put the kittens out in their baskets, pick up the alligator pears that have fallen during the night, explore for ripening figs, walk around to see how much the plants have grown during the night." By the time she wrote her father in June, there were ten more turkeys and three ducks. She described how "the sun comes up warm from the very edge of the morning, and the colors and smells and feel of the washed air are as near Paradise as I ever hope to come."

But in April Hart Crane had made his serpentine entrance into Paradise. Arriving in Mexico City on a Guggenheim on the eleventh, he planned to stay a week with his "old and wonderful friend, Katherine Anne Porter."[19] On May 13 Porter wrote to Susan Jenkins Brown, Crane's close friend, that he stayed an excruciating two weeks, becoming "madly" drunk every night and bringing policemen and youths back to the house. She "would" hear people prowling around the house all night and the next day "would" discover that money had disappeared. On one occasion, Crane became very insulting to her when she refused to invite to dinner her carpenter's fourteen-year-old son, whom she said he was trying to seduce. A few days later he found a house around the corner that "all agreed amiably" would be perfect for him. However, on April 30 he "came shouting under my window the most abominable things I have ever heard," howling that "he hated me worse than anybody on earth." When a policeman came, Pressly bribed him with three pesos not to arrest Crane, who accepted money Pressly lent him, took a taxi into town, and ran up a huge bill at the Hotel Mancera. After Porter accepted his notes of apology, "things have been very amiable," but she admitted she did not like him, for he had shown "a spirit so incredibly brutal and mean." What Porter claimed Crane "would" habitually do he had at most done once, but she consistently exaggerated his outrageous behavior in letters to their mutual friends.

At this time Porter made Pressly's presence known to her friends, pretending to Brown that Crane had chosen her as victim because he and Pressly hated each other on sight. She naturally supported Pressly, who had loved her "for nearly a year" with an "amplitude of feeling," in which she could "move with perfect freedom." In a letter to Herbst (June 1, 1931) she expanded on her praise of Pressly, who was completely loyal to her and "has worn through" her "fits of depressions," although she still had the "deep feeling" that she would do better living alone—a feeling deeper than her love for him.

On May 15 Porter celebrated her birthday by inviting to dinner her friends, among them Moisés Sáenz, who presented her with silver rosary beads and later helped her extend her visa until September. She also entertained Sergei Eisenstein and his assistants, who invited her to visit their filming site in Hidalgo. In early June Eugene Jolas, editor of *transition,* became her guest. She wrote Cowley (June 17) that Hart came over "and we were all most dismally drunk." Crane reported to friend Lorna Dietz that everything had been going smoothly with Porter, who frequently dropped by his house for chats and beer. She even photographed him wearing an ancient silver bridle he purchased with the help of Moisés Sáenz, who had invited him to Taxco for several days.[20]

But the fatal break came when Porter and Pressly did not appear at an afternoon dinner he had carefully prepared for them. While trying to keep food warm, he nipped tequila and finished his drinking downtown. Once more he ended up at Porter's gate uttering what he couldn't remember later. He wrote another note of apology, but said that Porter never explained why she hadn't come to dinner and had not communicated with him since. He wrote Dietz his version of that night after his return to the States because he knew Porter was broadcasting word of his escapade to their friends, the reason he kept away from them.[21]

Crane had indeed written Porter a note informing her that he had spent that night in jail, but "if it hadn't been for waiting for you—hour on hour, and trying to keep food warm, cream sweet, and my damnable disposition—don't suppose I'd have yelled out at you so horribly en route to doom!" In an unsent letter, she explained that she waited most of the day for her passport at the Consulate and, the day spoiled anyway, finished other errands, returning in time to hear him at the gate—an unsatisfactory explanation since she had undertaken a task that guaranteed a late return. She also reminded him that he had called her a whore and deplored those who "hide behind liquor" to utter what they don't have the courage to say when sober and, since a drunken mood mirrors the truth, concluded that "you bear a fixed dislike to me, of a very nasty kind." She was "beginning to believe that a sanitarium for the mentally defective is the proper place for you" and urged him to grow up and stop behaving "like a very degenerate adolescent," for his tantrums "take away my last shadow of a wish to ever see you again. . . . Let me alone. This disgusting episode has already gone too far" (L 45–46). Porter's hostile language explains why she never sent the letter. Instead she chose silence. In her version of that night, given six years later to Crane's first biographer, she never explained what caused Crane's outburst, but concentrated on his madness. He had cursed her and everything under the moon and stars in "words so foul there is no question of repeating them."[22] She concluded that he did not hate her or Pressly but himself, for he talked "every day" of committing suicide and approved of suicides he read about in newspapers. Porter never spoke to Crane again, although she continued to write about him. She told her father on June 26 that he was "mad as a hatter," and "half a dozen times" she had to bribe policemen with three pesos to keep him out of jail, but the last two times let them take him away. She refused to see him even though he "takes it very hard." These wild exaggerations cast more doubt on the reliability of her report to Susan Brown.

Porter also reminded her father once more of her unhappy past, wondering "if we would any of us recover from our peculiar despair of poverty, that chained feeling we have that we have no money, can never by any chance get any, and can't move hand or foot until we do get some." Yet, despite everything, she had accomplished "quite a lot of things in the face of actual starvation," although she had long struggled against the "strong temptation" to "quit the whole devilish nuisance of life," an urge she had now overcome. Crane's obsession with suicide had reminded her of her own. On some level of her mind she saw him as a monstrous object lesson of the artist in mental torment, drinking too much, turning against his friends, unable to concentrate on his writing, and fearful he had dissipated his talent. In "About Hart Crane," written in 1940 "For MY Own Use When I Begin to Write the Mixcoac Story," Porter compared Crane with other "paranoiacs" who worked in the arts, including Liza Dallett, and concluded that they all

> had the same delusions of grandeur, of persecution . . . they suffered the same horrible sense of insecurity in the world which made them perpetually worried about money. . . . they all had unsatisfactory sex experiences in one way or another, which obsessed them, and took very ugly channels of satisfaction, they were all dully and repetitiously obscene in their talk when their fits were on them. . . . All of them wept a great deal, and talked about themselves constantly. They all clung desperately to any other human beings who showed them sympathy, and always mistreated and betrayed brutally such persons.

Except for mention of obscenity and brutality, Porter might have been drawing her own negative self-portrait. Crane fascinated her precisely because, in light of her own depression, she sensed terrifying connections between her plight and his. She claimed that since he had lost the capacity to write, he was interfering with her work, but, in his letter to Dietz, he vehemently denied the charge since Porter had been in Mexico a full year before his arrival and hadn't written "one paragraph" of the book she planned to write, and if she wanted to encumber herself with turkeys, geese, chickens, and "a regular stock farm," that was her business.

In her letter to Susan Brown, Porter also used Crane as an example of those who come to Mexico and "promptly go off their heads and display a strange being": "Mexico is getting to be for me a kind of touchstone of character: evidently no one can hide himself here." She did not go off her head, but, given the opportunity to live in comparative affluence, she indulged herself in an attempt to compensate for the poverty and deprivation of her youth. As Crane observed, she never accomplished what she set out to do. On July 8 she wrote Andrew Lytle that she wanted to escape Mexico, for the scenery "is not enough and the things I love in this country are being so spoiled so fast I do not want to stay for the end," and "the Indian life is so hopelessly sad and deprived it weighs on your spirits like the memory of some mysterious sickness in another life. It is like a race memory—somewhere before I have seen the desolation, I have had it on my conscience." Her conscience would soon cry out over what, ironically, she was trying to escape, the poverty that painfully reminded her of her past.

Hart Crane left Mexico on July 6 because of the death of his father. Peggy Cowley, whom he had looked forward to seeing, arrived shortly thereafter to arrange her divorce from Malcolm Cowley with the help of Robert Haberman. Her arrival was an event:

> On the boat coming up she fraternized with two elegant and distinguished gempmun from New Orleans . . . they came out for supper one evening, and after that it was a continual round of gayerty, with the gempmun taking us to the grandest restaurants and feeding us on New Orleans style food, and selecting wines New Orleans taste, and burning Cafe Bruleau for us, and paying us stately compliments New Orleans manner, and of course it was too good to last, as they had come down for only a week.

Porter wrote this account to Malcolm Cowley on July 22, presumably to inform him in what spirit his wife was arranging her divorce. She did not mention what Eugene Pressly thought of the gentlemen from New Orleans, but indirectly revealed why she was making little progress on her novel. She enjoyed an "all-night riot" with a group of friends, among them Eugene Jolas, recently back from Taxco. After he left, Achilles Holt and Lallah Rogers arrived: "Yesterday we flew around with first one gang and then another, breakfast with one, lunch with another, tea with a third, dinner with a fourth . . ." She also wrote she was in the best of health and the "dog, the cats, the turkeys, the ducks, the chickens are all well, and send their respects." She promised to return quickly her review of Stuart Chase's *Mexico: A Study of Two Americas* and mentioned her visit to the Hacienda Tetlapayac and her plan to leave Mexico on August 26.

"Hacienda"

The last piece Porter completed in Mexico was her review of Stuart Chase's *Mexico,* a work principally valued today for its sixteen drawings by Diego Rivera. Although Porter picketed with Margaret Hatfield Chase against the execution of Sacco and Vanzetti,[23] past friendship did not temper her vitriolic review, putting Malcolm Cowley in an awkward position since the *New Republic* had already published portions of the book. He, of course, turned the review down, accusing her of making Chase the victim of her bitterness toward others in Mexico. She conceded his point, but defended her evaluation and was obviously displeased with his rejection. Thirty-four years later, she informed him that she hoped he would be glad to know that she still had the review and their correspondence about it "for the record."[24]

Porter's review, one of the last records of Porter's attitude toward Mexico in 1931, created a symmetry with her first review in 1920, for Chase had committed Blasco Ibáñez's error of gathering information on Mexico "to stuff it all down in a hurry and rush back with a book while the racket is still good." But whereas Blasco Ibáñez had written, in Porter's view, a harshly unfair evaluation of Mexico's revolution to appeal to U.S. prejudices, Chase wrote "a cautious bread-and-butter letter to a friendly host," taking "a passing whack at grafting politicians" but "careful not really to tell anything," praising "all the things the professional propagandists have been paid for praising all these years." She correctly criticized him for attempting "to be historian, explorer, critic and apologist of a way of life strange to him," but betrayed her own mood in her chilling first sentence: "Mexico is not really a place to visit any more, or to live in." That sentence captures the tone of "Hacienda," clearly not a bread-and-butter note to a friendly host.

On July 22 Porter wrote Cowley about her three-day visit to Tetlapayac, where Eisenstein was working, but he had a fever and "one of the lads on the place killed his sister by accident or mistake [on July 15], and was in jail."[25] She found film assistants Alexandrov and Tissé attentive and promised to bring silk stockings and perfume to their friends in Moscow. Ernestine Evans reported to Genevieve Taggard (September 28, 1931) that Porter "has some sort of compact with Eisenstein" and planned to go to Russia via Paris in October, but she never went; Eduard Tissé's undelivered letter to his sister about the silk stockings lies among Porter's papers.

Porter also mentioned doing "a piece on Tetlapayac, but with names and such disguised." What she described as "only an article" appeared in the *Virginia Quarterly Review* in October 1931. On November 5 she informed Cowley that she decided to submit her piece, which "unrolled itself" into a 4,500-word story, to *Scribner's*. Over two years later, it was "still growing, expanding," and finally appeared in 1934 in a separate volume, over three times longer than the first version. Porter wrote her family that the "line about it being all fiction simply represents the publisher's terror of a libel suit. . . . The characters are all real, and most of the story too."[26] She was right; of all her stories, "Hacienda" is closest to fact. After more than a year in Mexico, she had received a going-away present from the country, the story that had hitherto eluded her and perfectly reflected her despairing mood.

It is difficult to summarize "Hacienda" since at the beginning of the story "Nothing had happened . . . nothing could happen" (142), and again at the end, "Nothing had happened" (167). What does happen happens offstage and is reported to the narrator by different characters. As the story opens, Kennerly, Andreyev, and the writer-narrator board a train to the pulque hacienda. On the train Kennerly complains bitterly about everything in Mexico, from crooked officials he has had to bribe to food and climate: "'God,' he said to me, 'you don't know. But I'm going to write a book about it'" (141), clearly not the same book the narrator writes. After he falls asleep, Andreyev tells his story through photographs of the hacienda, giving the narrator a preview of "this unchanged world" whose inhabitants live "under a doom imposed by the landscape" (142). Andreyev also tells another "story about Lolita and don Genaro" (143) and about Genaro's jealous wife, doña Julia, who became close friends with Lolita while he was in Mexico City. After boarding the train at the next station, the young leading actor in the film tells the next story: Justino, another Indian actor, accidentally killed his sister, fled, was captured by his friend Vicente, and is now in prison. At the hacienda, Betancourt, the film's Mexican adviser, and doña Julia express their insincere pity at the death of Rosalita. Then don Genaro bursts in on the scene with his story that the judge refused to release Justino. Later Betancourt confides to the narrator that composer Carlos Montaña is a failure, while Carlos sings a corrido about Justino's love for his sister Rosalita. The narrator then retires to her room directly above the vat room and falls to sleep in the pulque-saturated air. The next day Kennerly laments that they did not film Rosalita's death since the same participants enacted exactly the same event in the film. The narrator then tours the hacienda, including the vat room, while Stepanov, Uspensky's other assistant, takes photographs. Don Genaro returns from a second visit to the judge, but refuses to pay two thousand pesos for Justino's release. Later Doctor Volk comes to treat Uspensky's flu and stays to play billiards with Stepanov. The narrator retires for the night and leaves the next day. Since Justino is still in prison, filming is still suspended. All the characters seem caught in a doomed landscape where nothing reaches conclusion.

The events on which "Hacienda" is based are as follows. Upton Sinclair financed the filming of *Que Viva Mexico!* and appointed his brother-in-law, Hunter Kimbrough (Kennerly), as business manager. Although the Mexican government had approved the project, Kimbrough, Eisenstein (Uspensky), and his assistants, G. V. Alexandrov (Andreyev) and Eduard Tissé (Stepanov), were arrested on December 21, 1930, by one set of government officials and released with apologies by another. On January 17 the Russians took excellent footage of the Oaxaca earthquake, but officials prevented its timely distribution. Kimbrough, at Eisenstein's urging, hired government censor Adolfo Best Maugard (Betancourt) as film consultant along with composer Manuel Castro Padilla (Carlos Montaña) and artist Gabriel Fernández Ledesma, the "thin dark youth who was some sort of assistant to Betancourt" (168). After filming in Tehuantepec, the company moved.to Tetlapayac, a pulque hacienda in the state of Hidalgo owned by Alejandro Saldivar, whose grandson was Julio Saldivar (don Genaro). The old hacienda, at the time defended against agrarian raids by soldiers supplied by Calles (Velarde), was perfect for Eisenstein's story, set in the days of Porfirio Díaz.

All the above information, contained in Hunter Kimbrough's letters to Upton Sinclair, appears in "Hacienda." One of his most remarkable letters concerns Felix Balderas (Justino):

> Yesterday one of our three bandits, the boy who always laughed in the picture when he was being pursued, stole Tisse's Pistol and accidentally killed his sister. He tried to escape through the maguey fields, in the same way he did in the picture you saw, over the same ground, for the same reason. Saldivar sent off the horseman after him, the same horseman who chased him in the picture. After shooting over his head several times the horseman rode alongside of him and hit him over the head with his pistol. Exactly the same way he is captured in the picture. He is in jail now charged with manslaughter. He will probably get a sentence, but Saldivar is going to try to get him released for a few days under police guard in order to finish his part in the picture, which consists of being chased and captured by the same man who actually captured him. It is very strange. They have been working on the scene, then it happens in reality. Now they will complete it for the picture.[27]

Porter makes the killing the focal event of "Hacienda," including even the detail of Felix Balderas's laughter: ". . . Justino thought everything was a joke. In the death scenes, he smiled all over his face and ruined a great deal of film. Now they are saying that when Justino comes back no one will ever have to say to him again, 'Don't laugh, Justino, this is death, this is not funny'" (169).

Truth is stranger than fiction, especially in Mexico. After showing the narrator photographs of "picturesque" peons, Andreyev tells her that they "shall be accused of dressing them up" (143), just as Porter might be accused of inventing a preposterous story in which reality copies art which in turn copies reality.[28] She explored the surreal possibilities of that reality, making it seem as if the lives of Justino and his sister were predetermined by some supernatural filmmaker. Hoping to witness the making of a film, she discovered that everything had stopped, as if life itself were in suspended animation. Nothing will happen until the cameras roll. In the meantime everybody on the hacienda waits, like the overseer on a bench, "hoping that something, anything may happen" (164) until the director gives him a role to play. Seizing upon the temporary lull in the filming, Porter gave it a metaphysical dimension.

Porter shaped the given facts of her visit in other ways. The story hints that the death of Rosalita was not accidental; Porter told me, "Everybody knew it wasn't an accident. The man who got him back was the man he was jealous of." She may not have known the name of Felix Balderas's sister, but Rosalita's fate is like that of María Rosa in "María Concepción" and of Rosita in "The Lovely Legend." Porter also stated she took liberties with doña Julia, who was not modeled after the younger Saldivar's wife but his mistress. In the story Genaro's grandfather is disturbed by the "sudden, astonishing marriage of his grandson" to a woman who in his day "would have had at best a career in the theatre" (153). The model for Julia, with her Hollywood Chinese clothes, really was what Julia only seemed to be in the story. Ione Robinson, who also visited Tetlapayac, was met at the station by Saldivar and "Lupe," an actress in the film who was wearing "silk pajamas,"[29] Julia's costume in "Hacienda."

The love affair between Julia and Lolita, along with the suggested homosexual relation between the effeminate Betancourt and his "very sleek and slim-waisted" (168) assistant, is in keeping with Porter's frequent complaints in her letters about homosexual artists and politicians, but it mainly serves to confound the sexist hacendados. The grandfather "had always known how to judge, grade, and separate women into their proper categories at a glance" (153). Genaro "had borne his wife's scenes" because it was a "wife's first right" to be "jealous and threaten to kill her husband's mistress," but when he returned to find the two women "affectionately entwined," he "could not get them separated"—that is, returned to their conventional roles—for the women are "oblivious to the summons from the embattled males." When Lolita finally returns to the set, "she forgot her role, and swung her leg over the saddle in a gesture unknown to ladies of 1898" (144). Don Genaro, "who had no precedent whatever for a husband's conduct in such a situation, made a terrible scene, and pretended he was jealous of Betancourt" (145) of all people. In this amusing interlude, making scenes and playing roles in and out of the film blur the distinction between appearance and reality. By refusing to play their prescribed roles, Lolita and Julia have temporarily avenged themselves against the male order. Nevertheless woman remains in her place in the unchanging mind of don Genaro, who likes things to move fast, "whether a horse, a dog, a woman or something with metal machinery in it" (155).

Porter brilliantly transformed Saldivar, Kimbrough, and Best Maugard into Genaro, Kennerly, and Betancourt. Ione Robinson's report of the Saldivar family as "one of the last feudal clans of Mexico" confirms Porter's view of them. Kennerly resembles Kimbrough, who "frankly" told Robinson what he thought of Mexico and the Mexicans—he was fed up with "the food and the climate, and, above all things, having to stay with the Russians." While on the train to the hacienda, he "emptied bottle after bottle" of beer (170).

Betancourt's name is French enough to remind insiders of Best Maugard and René d'Harnoncourt. "Mexican by birth, French-Spanish by blood," Betancourt "was completely at the mercy of an ideal of elegance and detachment perpetually at war with a kind of Mexican nationalism which afflicted him like an inherited weakness of the nervous system" (152), a description Porter lifted almost verbatim from her art notes on Best. She also precisely caught his physical appearance: "He had burning fanatic eyes and a small tremulous mouth. His bones were like reeds" (152). As the "neat light figure" of Betancourt "posed gracefully upon its slender spine, the too-beautiful slender hands" waving "rhythmically upon insubstantial wrists," the narrator remembers all that Carlos Montaña had done for him "in other days" (159)—specifically, in 1918 when Manuel Castro Padilla wrote the musical score for "Ballet Mexicano," for which Best created the sets.[30] But since Montaña "piled on" Betancourt's "thin shoulders a greater burden of gratitude than they could support," Betancourt "had set in motion all the machinery of the laws of Universal Harmony he could command to help him revenge himself on Carlos" and to declare him a "Failure" (159).

> [He] had spent his youth unlocking the stubborn secrets of Universal Harmony by means of numerology, astronomy, astrology, a formula of thought transference and deep breathing, the practice of will-to-power combined with the latest American theories of personality development; certain complicated magical ceremonies; and a careful choice of doctrines from the several schools of Oriental philosophies which are, from time to time, so successfully introduced into California. From this material he had constructed a Way of Life which could be taught to anyone, and once learned led the initiate quietly and surely toward Success . . . (158)

This gleeful compilation might have been a review of Best's *The New Knowledge of the Three Principles of Nature,* which "will enable man to surpass himself." Best modestly claimed that "by imbibing the teachings of the new knowledge," he had "succeeded in excelling and in becoming the fulfillment of the Ultimate Purpose of Life," for he possesses "the knowledge of that *Truth*" which gives him "the Wisdom for adequate guidance of [his] actions and for imparting that knowledge to others."[31] (Best's book was influenced by the concept of a higher race in *Tertium Organum* by P. D. Ouspensky, whose name Porter slightly altered to Uspensky and gave to Eisenstein.) She turned on Best to pay him back for his "revenge" against Castro Padilla and to condemn him for violating artistic freedom as censor of Eisenstein's work.[32] Significantly, the narrator gives no indication that Betancourt, like his model, is an artist, but identifies as artists Andreyev and Montaña, who are distinguished by their sense of humor, their disapproval of Kennerly and Betancourt, and their sympathy with the peons.

In the portraits of Genaro, Kennerly, and Betancourt, Porter gives a virtuoso performance in the deadly art of caricature and at the same time thematically integrates all three. Although they speak in completely distinct voices, they unite to form the Mexican Trinity that Porter, in 1921, feared would survive the Mexican Revolution. The political connection between her essay and the *Virginia Quarterly* version of "Hacienda" is pointed. The hacienda had survived and with it the traditional hacendado, represented by don Genaro, "a blue-eyed Spaniard, formed and hardened by inherited authority, smoothed over and speeded up by life in Europe and the capital; a rich young hacendado having his fling before settling down to lord it over serfs on the family estates. . . . If you opened his skull you would find there, neatly ticketed and labelled, a set of ideas unchanged in essentials since 1650" (562). In the final version, Genaro reveals in his own words his 1650 mind: "I told [the judge], Justino is my peon, his family have lived for three hundred years on our hacienda, this is MY business" (155). Genaro's immense ego reduces the tragedy of Rosalita and Justino to a simple matter of property rights. Doña Julia, who had earlier challenged his male assumptions, now becomes a mere extension of them when she tells the narrator that Justino will soon forget his sister, for "They are animals. Nothing means anything to them" (169). In both stories Genaro is called a blue-eyed Spaniard, "Spanish" in all Porter's writings on Mexico being a code word for white. The point in "Hacienda" is that Genaro, like Hernán Cortés in the sixteenth century, is a pure conquistador of the brown-skinned natives he exploits; in Mexico nothing has changed, especially racist imperialism.

Kennerly as business manager of the film company represents the second group of the Mexican Trinity, the "splendid horde of invaders" who enter Mexico to exploit it. Back from "'God's country,' meaning to say California" (138), he takes "possession of the railway train among a dark inferior people" (135). He builds a "nest" in the first-class car where "there were no natives to speak of" (136), his womblike isolation signaling his fear of all kinds of contamination. When they board the wagon that will take them to the hacienda, he tucks the narrator's skirts around her "knees with officious hands, to keep a thread of [her] garments from touching the no doubt foreign things facing us" (149); since he thinks of the narrator as a "lady," his solicitude betrays sexual fears.

When he hears of Rosalita, he is afraid of a lawsuit until he discovers to his relief that her death did not occur on the set. Later he laments that the camera didn't capture Justino's flight since it was part of the film's scenario. His response to the tragedy, like Genaro's, measures his egotism and inhumanity.[33]

The church, the third member of the Mexican trinity to thwart revolutionary change, is represented by Betancourt, an ersatz mystic who preaches the superiority of the self-appointed elite. His "Way of Life" adheres to "Eternal Laws" that lead to "Wealth" and "Success" (158–159). "Beggars, the poor, the deformed, the old and ugly, trust [him] to wave them away," his response perversely echoing Christ's compassion. Concerning the death of Rosalita, he laments, "'I am sorry for everything' . . . lifting a narrow, pontifical hand, waving away vulgar human pity which always threatened, buzzing like a fly at the edges of his mind." He hypocritically offers conventional consolation: "'But when you consider . . . what her life would have been like in this place, it is much better that she is dead. . . .' With his easy words the girl was dead indeed, anonymously entombed" (152). Betancourt's religious pontifications are, of course, free-lance, but his easy identification with privilege and power is, in Porter's view, worthy of any Mexican churchman of the old school.

Despite differences of national origin and occupation, Genaro, Kennerly, and Betancourt are essentially alike. They are all white, foreign, and "superior," their responses exclusively determined by their own well-being and never by the humanity of the peon whom they disdain. Ironically, they all pride themselves in being "modern" in their love of fast machines—Genaro's wealth allows "him to be at least twice as modern as Betancourt" (154)—and in their devotion to Hollywood. Kennerly is accustomed to the "four-square business methods of God's own Hollywood" (145), Genaro's wife loves "Chinese dress made by a Hollywood costumer" (144), and Betancourt wears "well-cut riding trousers and puttees," for "he had learned in California, in 1921, that this was the correct costume for a moving-picture director" (154). But their tastes render them ridiculous and fail to mask their closed minds.[34]

The political meaning of Porter's eyewitness account is reenforced by the story's mythical structure. Her early sketch, "The Children of Xochitl," is the positive of her hope for Mexico out of which she developed "Hacienda" as despairing negative. Both are united by the presence of Xochitl, who, according to one legend, discovered pulque. In *Outline* Porter wrote that the ancient Mexicans left their images for us "to wonder at, and to make our own legends about them" (9). She follows that suggestion by transforming Xochitl from goddess of life in her sketch to goddess of death in her story.

In "The Children of Xochitl" the fictitious village patriarch proclaims, "Xochitl sends rain. Xochitl makes the crops grow—the maguey and the maize and the sweet fruits and the pumpkins. Xochitl feeds us!" The narrator adds, "Xochitl is the legendary Aztec goddess of the earth, of fruit, of abundance, who discovered pulque—especially the strawberry flavored kind!—and also made known the many other uses of the maguey plant, by which the Indians can live almost entirely," and concludes, "Of all the great women deities from Mary to Diana, Dana of the Druids to Kwanyin, this Xochitl has been endowed with . . . the most beneficent attributes."[35] Porter's creation of Xochitl proves her familiarity with Mexican mythology. In *Outline*, where she describes several Mexican myths, she lists among her reading Vicente Riva Palacio's *México a Través de los Siglos,* the first volume of which includes scholarly discussions of Xochitl and Mayahuel. Mayahuel, not Xochitl, was the authentic Aztec goddess of pulque. Porter chose Xochitl's name because of its linguistic connection to Xochimilco, but derived her goddess's attributes from Mayahuel. Aztec codices picture Mayahuel emerging from the maguey or enthroned in front of it, holding a cup of pulque or suckling a child. The Vatican Codex describes her as having innumerable breasts, like Artemis-Diana, with whom she is compared.[36] Like all Mexican moon goddesses, she developed into a goddess of fertility and generation and a patroness of women's arts. In precisely these terms Porter describes Xochitl. Relating her to Diana, Dana, and Kuan Yin, Porter evokes a deity whose "clearest expression" of "giving-outward is the breasts, which typify woman as giver of nourishment."[37] Of all earth goddesses the goddess of pulque is the most obvious since her juice is sucked from her plant and in its fermented state has a milky color.

Although unnamed, Xochitl also appears in "Hacienda." The narrator and her companion discover in the vat room of the hacienda "a faded fresco relating the legend of pulque; how a young Indian girl discovered this divine liquor, and brought it to the emperor, who rewarded her well, and after her death she became a half-goddess." In a visit to the Hacienda Tetlapayac, I discovered in the same vat room the mural to which the narrator refers. Copied from "The Discovery of Pulque," an oil painting of José Obregón (1832–1902), it depicts Xochitl, flanked by her parents, presenting her gift of pulque to the Toltec king Tecpancaltzín.[38] Porter, seizing upon the mural she chanced to see in the vat room, reshaped its legend to express her deep disillusion with what she witnessed at Tetlapayac.

The worlds of the two works in which Xochitl appears are diametrically opposed, one prelapsarian, the other fallen. In "The Children of Xochitl," the narrator is enchanted by "benign air" and the perpetually blooming chinampas which amply supply the Indians with food and livelihood. But in "Hacienda" she is repelled by "deathly air" and the cruel, monotonous landscape of "spiked" magueys which "doom" the peons (142), forcing them to wait for the corn to grow before "there will be enough to eat again" (170). The Indians of Xochimilco can express their individuality because "they have maintained an almost unbroken independence of passing governments." The Indians of the hacienda also live in an "unchanged world," but one of brutalizing peonage: their "closed dark faces were full of instinctive suffering, without individual memory, or only the kind of memory animals may have, who when they feel the whip know they suffer but do not know why and cannot imagine a remedy" (142). Rosalita might have escaped this condition because of her role in

Uspensky's film, but she is killed by her brother and "anonymously entombed" (152) by Betancourt's callous words.

Porter consciously created one world in direct antithesis to the other. In her first version of "Hacienda" she distinguishes between "peons" of the hacienda and "fighting Indians of free villages" (565). She had Xochimilco in mind, for two paragraphs later she writes, "But I have drunk pulque cold, freshened with strawberry juice, and remember yet the good taste in my mouth," echoing a passage from "The Children of Xochitl": "My memory of Xochimilco is always a drowsy confusion of wet flowers on the chinampas, the taste of cold sweetened pulque flavored with strawberries." In her final version she deleted allusions to Xochimilco, thereby universalizing her experience at Tetlapayac to represent all of Mexico.

In the contrasting worlds of Xochitl the conjunction of landscape and social system affects the Indians in totally opposite ways. In "The Children of Xochitl" it seems happily circumstantial, enabling Porter to idealize her experience. In "Hacienda" unhappy circumstances conspire to dehumanize the peons, the doomed landscape objectifying her bitter response to their oppression and to the political ironies involved in it. Bitter is the irony that Velarde, "the most powerful and successful revolutionist in Mexico," owns "two pulque haciendas which had fallen to his share when the great repartition of land had taken place. He operated also the largest dairy farm in the country, furnishing milk . . . to every charitable institution" in the country at twice the price that others asked (156). Porter took this information from her notes on Calles, who contributed an idealistic article on land reform to *Survey Graphic's* 1924 Mexican issue. His behavior justified her view that the revolution had totally failed.

It is not surprising, then, that Porter would reinterpret the legend of Xochitl depicted in the vat room. As an earlier note proves, she was aware that earth goddesses had two manifestations: "O earth, my tender, soberly smiling mother, Oh fruitful nourisher, Oh demonic fury, Oh drinker of blood, insatiable devourer of rotting flesh!" The goddess in the vat room is no longer "fruitful nourisher," but has "something to do with man's confused veneration for, and terror of, women and vegetation" (165). Passages dealing with pulque confirm the sinister metamorphosis she has undergone.

As soon as her train reaches maguey country, the narrator hears cries of "Fresh pulque!" from Indian women, "mournfully" urging passengers to buy the "thick gray-white liquor," but the pausing train only raises "false hopes," and the women are "left clustered together, a little knot of faded blue skirts and shawls, in the indifferent rain" (138). Here the milky pulque, derived from the "cactus whose heart bleeds the honey water," contributes to the tragic tone of suffering and despair. The same passage opens the first version of the story and is the source of her contemplated title, "False Hopes." The desolate pulque vendors were intended to set the mood of the story; they retain that function even though the revised version opens with the despised Kennerly. The narrator later describes an Indian drawing "with his mouth the juice from the heart of the maguey." The act could suggest the drawing of milk from the life-giving plant, but the metaphor, "heart of the maguey," recalling "the cactus whose heart bleeds the honey water" of the earlier passage, personifies the plant as sacrificial victim, uniting it with the drawer of its juice. This meaning is reinforced a few lines later by the Indian "leaning between the horns of the maguey, his mouth to the gourd," who has a "formal traditional tragedy, beautiful and hollow" (142).

At the hacienda the odor of pulque overwhelms the narrator: "The smell had not been out of my nostrils since I came, but here it rose in a thick vapor through the heavy drone of flies, sour, stale, like rotting milk and blood . . ." (161). The rotting milk conveys, not nourishment, but a sickening corruption, with sexual overtones, that emanates from the vat room, where the next day the narrator watches "flies drowning in the stinking liquor," and observes that the legend of the goddess involves man's terror of woman's fertility. The stench seems as much cause as symbol of "the almost ecstatic death-expectancy which is in the air of Mexico. . . . strangers feel the acid of death in their bones whether or not any real danger is near them. It was this terror that Kennerly had translated into fear of food, water, and air around him" (143). In such a pervasive atmosphere all terror has a common source, whether it is Kennerly's terror of the elements or man's terror of woman's fertility which has the smell of death in it.

Pulque connotes hopelessness, suffering, and corruption because it is at the heart of the oppressive social system of the hacienda. The endless rows of maguey rob the peons of sufficient land on which to grow corn. Producing and drinking the liquor, they are doubly victimized by the hacendado's greed:

> The white flood of pulque flowed without pause; all over Mexico the Indians would drink the corpse-white liquor, swallow forgetfulness and ease by the riverful, and the money would flow silver-white into the government treasury; don Genaro and his fellow-hacendados would fret and curse, the Agrarians would raid, and ambitious politicians in the capital would be stealing right and left enough to buy such haciendas for themselves. It was all arranged. (168)

Here the "white flood" is not milk but a universal drug transformed into the flow of "silver-white" money to create still more corruption.

Although the above passage appears almost three pages after the vat room scene, a strong identification exists between the goddess and her "corpse-white liquor." In the first version the identification is explicit:

> The Indians drink pulque. . . . They account for its discovery in one of their most familiar legends. Even now, each vat room is decorated with a fresco, as unvarying as the Stations of the Cross in the chapels, relating how a young woman made this divine refreshment from the honey water

> of maguey, and was rewarded with semi-deification. Her apotheosis co-
> incides with that of Maria Santísima, who stands always in a painted
> niche with a shrine lamp and paper flowers. Maria Santísima enjoys a
> formal preëminence, but the two live side by side in harmonious confu-
> sion. Both are anodynes: pulque and the merciful goodness of Maria
> Santísima. The Indians drink pulque and call upon the Mother of
> God. . . . The Indians drink the corpse-white liquor, swallow forget-
> fulness by the riverful. Pesos pour by the hundreds of thousands into the
> government treasury . . . (565)

In both versions Xochitl rules over a doomed landscape rather than an
Aztec paradise, offering her children her defiled milk to induce a deathlike
trance. Ironically they "swallow forgetfulness" of their "instinctive suffering"
with the very product that caused it in the first place.

The goddess's partner, María Santísima, has also undergone an alteration.
In "The Children of Xochitl" the "alien" Mary is tolerated in the company of
"the great women deities," but in both versions of "Hacienda" she suffers a decline paralleling Xochitl's. The first version makes the decline obvious while
the second suggests it by juxtaposition with the goddess: "María Santísima
stood primly in her blue painted niche in a frame of fly-blown paper flowers,
with a perpetual light at her feet. The walls were covered with a faded fresco
relating the legend of pulque . . ." Her importance in the vat room is now
muted, yet the "frame of fly-blown paper flowers" effectively discredits her and
reveals once more Porter's anti-Christian bias. Religion, pagan and Christian,
contributes to the Indians' demoralization as they drown like flies in the stinking pulque. The most corrupt of all is Velarde, who has perverted the ideals of
the revolution for personal gain while fighting "political corruption" in his
newspapers. Like Xochitl, he undergoes an apotheosis into the Terrible Mother,
"furnishing milk" to every charitable institution at twice the regular price.

Porter's changing goddess and the contrary worlds over which she presides
perfectly fit Erich Neumann's description of the Good and Terrible Mother:
"Just as world, life, nature, and soul have been experienced as a generative and
nourishing, protective and warming Femininity, so their opposites are also
perceived in the image of the Feminine; death and destruction, danger and dis-
tress, hunger and nakedness, appear as helplessness in the presence of the
Dark and Terrible Mother" (149). The drink associated with the Good Mother
is nourishing, but the same drink associated with the Terrible Mother becomes
a "negative toxicant and poison," leading "to stupor, enchantment, helplessness, and dissolution" (174). Xochitl's presence as goddess of death dictates
the emotional state of her subjects. Her "corpse-white" liquor permeates the
"deathly air," demoralizing the peons who begin their morning work in the
fields with "another day's weariness" (143). The contagious atmosphere also
infects the non-Indians. Kennerly reacts in hypochondriac terror to all unclean-
liness, Betancourt preaches "You must fail" to Montaña (159), while Genaro

indulges in violent outbursts against the judge only to give up "in a voice gone suddenly flat, as if he despaired or was too bored with the topic to keep it up any longer" (156). In fact, all the guests at the hacienda are infected with "the vast incurable boredom which hung in the air of the place and settled around our heads clustered there" (151), recalling the hopeless pulque vendors "clustered together . . . in the indifferent rain." The overseer is the quintessential figure of moral paralysis: "There he sat nearly all day, as he had sat for years and might sit for years more. His long wry North-Spanish face was dead with boredom" (164). This state perfectly fits Neumann's description of the "psychic depression" resulting in the "irruption" of the "Terrible Devouring Mother"; the symptoms are "lack of enthusiasm and initiative, weakness of will, fatigue, incapacity of concentration and work" and "thoughts of death and failure" and "weariness of life" (27).

Escape seems the only remedy for the universal depression and paralysis of will; just as Uspensky abruptly leaves the dining room "as if he were seeking another climate" (157), so the narrator cannot "wait for tomorrow in the deathly air" to leave the hacienda. But as she leaves, the Indian driver promises her that in ten days "the green corn will be ready, and ah, there will be enough to eat again!" (170). With his words the story ends. They contain the only spark of hope in "Hacienda"; the Terrible Mother will release her grip on the land and the Good Mother will renew it once more. But the enslaved peons will again feel hunger when their meager supply of corn gives out.

The narrator's escape from the hacienda coincides with Porter's escape from Mexico. She blamed the country and various individuals in it, including Hart Crane, for her need to escape to a different climate even though she was trying to escape from herself.[39] The symptoms of her "psychic depression," inadvertently described by Neumann, existed long before her visit to the hacienda. In creating her story, she unconsciously projected her depression onto those she had met there or discovered in their condition symptoms that matched her own. The situation at Tetlapayac justified the despair she felt but could not understand; in her February letter to Delafield Day, she complained that art dealers were "poisoning the air" for her, but the stench of pulque gave her an appropriate objective correlative of her feelings. The "almost ecstatic death-expectancy of Mexico" exacerbated, as it did in 1921, her abiding fear of death, a fear the narrator shares with Kennerly.[40]

Porter, however, was not alone in her reaction to the political-social conditions of the hacienda. In *Idols Behind Altars,* Eisenstein's source concerning the Mexican fascination with death, Anita Brenner notes that pulque haciendas after the conquest "became a source of gold and double-exploitation of the peasants. . . . 'Peons are machines that run on pulque,' hacendados have often said; contemptuously, but not regretfully. To the peons it is still a boon; at least the boon of escape in stupor" (173). When the Russians chose to film at a pulque hacienda, they were as aware as Porter of the ironies involved. In "Hacienda" the narrator's first response to the tragic suffering of the peons is through the photographs of Andreyev. Ione Robinson's perceptions were similar to theirs: "The only form of amusement [the peons] have on Sunday is to pray and get drunk. Their religion is practiced in an abnormal emotional stupor. . . . There seemed to be no hope for them" (175).

In Porter's literary development, "The Children of Xochitl" was the first expression of her yearning for paradise whose lost promise she expressed in "Hacienda." Together the works form a paradigm for her later works, in which characters attempt to recover from a sense of betrayal as reality shatters their dreams. In "Pale Horse, Pale Rider," for example, Miranda has a "child's dream of the heavenly meadow" just before her recovery from influenza, but "the bright landscape" gives way to "the colorless sunlight slanting on the snow, under a sky drained of its blue" and to "the stench of corruption," not of pulque, but of her own wasted body. The dim light of reality is unbearable because it must always be compared with "the light she had seen beside the blue sea that lay so tranquilly along the shore of her paradise" (313–314). The landscapes of Xochimilco and Miranda's dream both deepen the response to the worlds of corruption and death. The image of Eden is a constant in Porter's fiction. The "inner repose" of the girl washing clothes in "The Children of Xochitl" and Miranda's dream of "confident tranquility" have a common source in the author's psyche. However, over the years the significance of the image shrank. In 1921 it appeared as real, but in 1938, as a shattered dream. Xochitl helps us trace Porter's lost hope of happiness.

6. Becoming Miranda

The Thirties

In the thirties Porter published two Mexican stories, "Hacienda" and "That Tree," and all her Miranda stories except "The Fig Tree." In the forties, as her thoughts again turned to Mexico, she published "The Charmed Life" and a translation of Lizardi's *The Itching Parrot*. In 1955 one more Mexican work appeared, "St. Augustine and the Bullfight." This chapter explores how her "time in Mexico and Europe," as she put it in "'Noon Wine': The Sources," gave her back her past (CE 470), and traces in the process the fictional ways in which she responded to her depression.

Porter left Mexico a month after her visit to Tetlapayac. After finding homes for her menagerie and peddling her furniture, she threw a farewell party that lasted until four in the morning. After two hours of sleep, she and Pressly left Mixcoac and boarded a train for Veracruz in hope of viewing for the last time Mexico's famous mountains, but they were enshrouded in fog. As if the country were determined to leave her with no pleasant memories, a bolt of lightning hit an elevator shaft twenty feet from her hotel room in Veracruz, almost deafening her, "the last straw." They left Mexico on August 22 aboard the German ship, the *Werra*.

So Porter wrote Caroline Gordon on August 28, her letter turning into "a kind of log" of her voyage (L 46–60). In it a short story was "working around"— eventually becoming *Ship of Fools* thirty years later. She pitied the 876 Spanish third-class passengers expelled from Cuba when its economy failed; they moved from "misery through misery to more misery." When an oculist from Texas commented that it wasn't as if they were "dirty Bolsheviks," he startled Porter, who had thought he represented "whatever of enlightenment that place has to offer." He became the bigoted William Denny in *Ship of Fools,* but "a nice young electrical engineer from Kennedy [Kenedy] Texas" never found his way into the novel. She also mentioned a Zarzuela troupe returning to Spain after their "failure of hopes" in Mexico, country of "false hopes" as "Hacienda" reveals. Except for the ship's doctor, "with the kindest, most serviceable pair of tan eyes" (Dr. Schumann), she depicted the Germans as "Herr Doktors and

Herr Professors . . . with such typically German Frauen—vast, bulky, inert, with handsome heads and elephant legs, who drink beer all day long, swallowing a steinful in two drinks, smacking their lips and saying 'Ja, Ja!' quite as the colored postcards had taught me to expect." After World War II, she darkened this stereotype considerably.

Porter was fascinated by a Cuban woman exiled to Tenerife for helping revolutionary students. The woman claimed that her husband was killed in the revolution and her sons were fugitives, but she had never married and in her unhinged mind, "Cuba is her murdered husband and the students are her children." Taken up by an obnoxious group of Cuban students who mocked her behind her back and elected her to their club that involved singing verse after verse of the Mexican revolutionary song "La Cucaracha," she was ready-made as La Condesa in *Ship of Fools.* Porter also mentioned "a huge fat man with a purple face and watermelon pink shirt" with "a voice like seven foghorns" who roared and guzzled beer, but when his wife and child came on in Havana, he became mute, unlike the novel's political agitator in the cherry-color shirt. The ship's company also included Porter's cabinmate, "a hefty Swiss girl" (Elsa Lutz), "a little dying man" who "sits curled up on his pillows and coughs all day" (Wilibald Graf), a hunchback who wears flashy ties (Karl Glocken), and "a beautiful Spanish bride with her devoted bridegroom": "If ever I saw two persons walking in Eden, it is now." In the novel they remain unnamed and serve as romantic contrast to the rest of the ship's passengers.

Porter also mentioned sighting whales, taking photographs with a camera once used by Tina Modotti, tasting wines and viewing the agile milk carriers of Tenerife, and attending parties where "All of us put on our hats and grin vaguely at the others, who grin back, every body orders wine, the band strikes up 'Wiener Blut' . . . and for the moment every one is acquainted with everyone else. But nothing has changed, really half of us do not salute the other half on deck the next morning, and not from rancor but from indifference." This description comes closest to the mood of *Ship of Fools,* prompting an idea for a short story entitled "Wiener Blut," but Porter's overall impression of her voyage was favorable: "It seems to me now I am having the loveliest time of my life," enjoying a "community existence" after the "anarchic freedom" of Mixcoac, where she did not want to share her garden with anybody else. Even the Asturians in steerage, well fed and dancing on the lower decks, "are all looking better, and smoother, and happier, as does every face on board" (L 45–48). The mood of her letter is light-miles from that of her novel.

The *Werra* deposited Porter and Pressly, not in France, as they had planned, but in Bremerhaven. For the next five years, Porter lived in Berlin, Basel, but mostly in her beloved Paris. In 1933 she finally married Pressly, whose financial support gave her the opportunity to write, although for a good deal of the time she managed to be in one place while he was in another, preferring to communicate with him through long letters.

When Pressly took a job at the U.S. Embassy in Spain, she remained in Germany, where she wrote him in November 1931 about her depression, wondering about his casual mention of "that poor neurotic person in the Embassy," when he knew that she was "the most nerve-wracked, queasy animal in the world":

> What has all the difficulty been, but that I really cannot endure jars and jostles, hardly a touch sometimes, it is as if I had lost at least one layer of skin. Only with you am I really at home, and yet these weeks in Berlin were simply horrible—and why? . . . I never thought I was a fearful, timid one, but I am frightened of something now, and I don't quite know what . . . horrified would be a better word. It is more like horror than fear. It goes beyond fear. It is like a substance in the air here.

Six months earlier she had complained to Josephine Herbst about her "deep, incurable . . . painful melancholy" that she had suffered from "for years, without any alleviation." She had hoped that sitting in the Mexican sun or her planned trip to Europe would cure her, although "journeys don't change the traveller much" (L 44). Her prediction was, unfortunately, correct. She also probed her depression in her daybook:

> Berlin 1931—I really suffer from a feeling of personal danger, I have no faith in tomorrow in this place, and surely this communicated to me from the awful climate of painful insecurity—nobody around me is in the least happy, or hopeful, the young seem reckless and cynical, the elders disheartened.
>
> It is true that I am used to anxiety, to insecurity, but it was my own, I believed, not communicated and not shared by those around me. . . . As a child I lived in an anxious house where there was very little love, and this seemed the natural explanation for my incurable disturbance of the mind and desolation of my heart. But in this place the oppressive constant threat of disaster comes from without. I seemingly absorb it and cannot reject it again, it is an insidious gas settling in the air.

The second passage seems to explain or simply justify her nameless horror in the first. In the blurred relation between internal stress and external circumstances, her chronic state of depression, originating in childhood, became a sensitive instrument that registered something out there, something in the air in Berlin in 1931, just before Hitler took power. So, in a 1932 daybook entry, it detected in Faulkner's stories "an overtone, something ominous, terrible in the very air, something dreadful and sub-human that scares you to the heart, and yet you do not quite know where it comes from. I don't know if any but a southerner would feel this. Something deathly in the air that has been breathed off from the long and painful relations between the black and white, a dreadful memory between them that poisons the very daylight." "Something deathly in the air" in the South is directly linked to "the almost ecstatic death-expectancy which is in the air of Mexico."

Yet her fear of death, first noted in Mexico in 1921, felt once more in Berlin, and expressed in her revision of "Hacienda," had its root in her childhood relation to her father, when she lived in a loveless "anxious house." She wrote Gay (January 30, 1932) that he "literally let us go to rags and almost to death without making one reasonable attempt to pull us out of the hole we were in after Grandmother's death. I shall go to my grave mystified by his whole attitude toward us, towards life—so deathlike and despairing and inert and will-less. I too have these seeds of despair and lack of will, and I know the signs when they come. . . . we are all equipped to be hopeless failures." As in Salem in 1928, Porter felt victimized by the sins of the father. In a letter to Gay (October 11, 1933) she included the whole family in her indictment: "As for being a family to me, when were you ever? I should have been dead in a ditch years ago if I had depended on my family to exhibit any of the old-timey characteristics."

Porter had reason to lash out against her father, but when she felt particularly threatened, she was capable of making others the scapegoat for her psychological problems. So it was with Hart Crane, who seemed to follow her from Mixcoac to Europe. She wrote Malcolm Cowley (November 5, 1931) that she was just getting over "the atrocious attack of the Hart Crane episode, which made me sick and fairly took my skin off" and "had finally driven me to the point where I wished to repay brutality with brutality." She wrote Pressly (November 23) about her "nostalgia" for Mixcoac, where, she admitted, she stood in her own way and in his too because she could not "overcome the nervous irritations and the intrusions of people," especially of Crane, who "was simply murderous in his determination to cause me trouble if he could, as much as he could. My blood be on his head!" Crane, it should be remembered, arrived in Mexico a year after Porter, saw her for only a few months, and refused to be blamed for her inability to write her novel, although she claimed to friends that she had written thousands of words. His exposure of her pretense threatened her self-image and caused her hatred of him. When Peggy Cowley asked her to forgive him, she refused (February 20, 1932) because "he did to me the most unpardonable thing one human being can do to another; he behaved with beastliness and obscenity toward two people who had never harmed him. . . ." She concluded, "Every afternoon when my fever runs up and my chest aches, I remember well who broke into my small store of health and peace at Mixcoac and destroyed them both . . . as if we had taken a human being into our lives and found it metamorphosed into a hyena." When she received news of his suicide, her opinion of him became, if anything, more hostile. She wrote Caroline Gordon (June 16, 1932) that he had "revealed himself . . . as so indescribably swinish that I was utterly sickened and alienated." She regretted his "beastly exhibition of malice" toward her, but did not regret his death: "I think it was well done." However, she did not express the same sentiment to Mary Doherty, who had written a letter expressing her grief at Crane's death. Between October 21 and 25, Porter composed three versions of an answering letter, the final one including a long update of her adventures in Europe, but really written to discover whether Crane's friends, "bent on creating a perfect legend," were telling "lies" about her "to complete their thesis." She asked Doherty to keep her well informed and closed her "indiscreet" letter by requesting its return since she might need it "in reference to what I have written about Hart." No evidence exists that Crane's friends threatened her reputation, but she had apprehensively armed herself just in case.

Because "Hacienda" channeled and objectified her depression, it renewed her confidence in her creative powers, enabling her to undertake several other projects. She published "The Cracked Looking-Glass" in 1932 and shortly thereafter began "That Tree," which eventually appeared in the *Virginia Quarterly Review* in 1934 after several other magazines had rejected it. She later commented on the story:

> That Tree has for its hero something like ten thousand wistful American boys who have been brought up in dull ways and dull surroundings, and are infected with the notion that romance and glory lie in other places, and in a different occupation. To be a poet is the most romantic thing he can imagine. So he decides to be one, in a strange, fascinating country where he can forget his provincial beginnings. I didn't give this boy a name, because it should justly have been Legion. He is defeated, of course, he has a grudge, he blames it on all sorts of things, but mostly he blames it on his wife, who is the same kind of person he is, socially and economically, but who has stuck by her own training and her own beliefs. She is his Nemesis, the instrument of his defeat, but the defeat was in him from the beginning. I laid the scene in Mexico because I felt at home there, and because so many persons of this sort were there then.

"That Tree" begins, "He had really wanted to be a cheerful bum lying under a tree in a good climate, writing poetry." The tree symbolizes the unnamed hero's idea of Edenic life: "no respectability, no responsibility, no money to speak of, wearing worn-out sandals" (66), and having carefree sex with an Indian girl who "divided her time cheerfully between the painters, the cooking pot, and his bed" (72). Without realizing it, he already had what "he had really wanted," or thought he wanted, before proposing marriage to his former sweetheart, a schoolteacher from Minneapolis. His invitation to Miriam released his disapproving superego in her form to act as "avenging fury" against him. He thought he wanted to convert her to his Bohemian ways, washing "a lot of gayly colored Indian crockery outdoors in the sunshine, with the bougainvillea climbing up the wall and the heaven tree in full bloom. Not Miriam" (75), who told him "she had no intention of wasting her life flattering his male vanity" (71). Only when she left him did the "shock" bring him to himself, "as if he had been surprised out of a long sleep." Like Rip Van Winkle, "he got up stiff in every joint from sitting so long," but, unlike Rip, he was still young enough to make amends: "He had started out, you might almost say that very day, to make a career for himself in journalism" (67) and succeeded as a best-selling "authority on Latin-American revolutions" (66).

The journalist recounts his life to a third-person narrator ten years after Miriam left him. It is an ongoing "confession" of discoveries about himself, made "to any friends and acquaintances who would listen to him." He readily admits that "the day Miriam kicked him out was the luckiest day of his life" (66). He now knows he was a "lousy poet" and that his artist friends weren't devoted to "holy Poverty," but "were looking for the main chance" (76), as Miriam knew then. He had to admit she was right in everything: "His old-fashioned respectable middle-class hard-working American ancestry and training rose up in him and fought on Miriam's side. He felt he had broken about every bone in him to get away from them and live them down, and here he had been overtaken at last and beaten into resignation that had nothing to do with his mind or heart" (77). He is even perceptive enough to realize that "he was always making marvelous discoveries that other people had known all along" (67), but he always lags behind the reader's discoveries about him.

Since "That Tree" is narrated in the third person, it consists of two simultaneous stories. The first is the journalist's "confession," the joke he tells on himself in his secure perch as best-seller, and the second is the narrator's story that knocks him off that perch. His story could almost have been a monologue, narrated in the first person, but in Porter's caricaturist method, perfected in "He," the narrator constantly mocks him through his own speech. For instance, "He thought there was something to be said for living with one person day and night the year round. It brings out the worst, but it brings out the best, too, and Miriam's best was pretty damn swell. He couldn't describe it" (67–68). His "pretty damn swell" catches the quality of his expression, humorously undercutting his claim that he "could really write, too: if he did say so, he had a prose style of his own" (78).

Third-person narration also gives us an outside view of the journalist. On this occasion of retelling his story, he has picked a bar he usually frequents. When another foreign newsman, deep in his cups, makes a feeble joke about the revolution, he ridicules him, provoking the other to call him a "banjo-eyed chinless wonder" (68–69), a caricature very similar to one Miguel Covarrubias drew of Carleton Beals. After the resulting commotion evaporates, the journalist tells his companion, "If there was one brand of bum on earth he despised, it was a newspaper bum. Or anyhow the drunken illiterates the United Press and Associated Press seemed to think were good enough for Mexico and South America" (69–70). But since his beat is also Latin America and since he orders drinks four different times while narrating his story, he seems little different from the drunken bums he claims to despise. He really wanted to be a "cheerful bum" and write poetry under a tree, but Miriam deromanticized the word for him. Now that he is successful, he applies her meaning to others, but the narrator subtly reapplies it to him.

The journalist, proud of his story-telling technique, tells his companion, "I've been working up to the climax all this time. You know, good old surprise technique. Now then get ready" (78). The surprise is that since he now has become what Miriam has always wanted him to be—a success—she has asked him to take her back and he plans to do so, but this time exactly on *his* terms, which include his refusal to remarry her, but his "guest wished to say, 'Don't forget to invite me to your wedding,' but thought better of it." After finishing his last drink, the journalist finishes his story: "'I don't know what's happening this time,' he said, 'don't deceive yourself. This time, I know.' He seemed to be admonishing himself before a mirror" (79). The story's climax is not the one the journalist imagines. What he sees in the mirror is the man Miriam wanted him to become. He has made peace with his superego but does not know the extent of his capitulation.

Although Porter states that the hero of "That Tree" could be "ten thousand American boys," he is partly based on Pablo O'Higgins, who romanticized his name, went Indian, wearing serape and huaraches, and, like the poverty-stricken artists the journalist idealized, was barely eking out a living as a muralist when Porter engaged him to give her piano lessons. His visit on his way to Russia in December 1931 may have inspired Porter to begin her story. Her principal model, however, was the weak-chinned Carleton Beals, whom she first met in 1923 when he was still married to his first wife Lillian. Like Porter's hero, he was a schoolteacher in Mexico in 1920. In 1924 Lillian broke with him in Italy, causing him to undergo a mental crisis from which he recovered to become an authority on Latin America and a best-seller. Although Porter asked Beals for a journalistic job in 1926 and immediately contacted him when she arrived in Mexico in 1930, she wrote Ford Maddox Ford in 1934 that Carleton is "very sweet and friendly and I have nothing against him," but he's "a rotten writer." She later referred to him as "a cheap journalist" with "no talent whatever." However, her view of him as writer in "That Tree" is more humorous than malicious except for the comment that the journalist's "sympathies happened to fall in exactly right with the high-priced magazines of a liberal humanitarian slant which paid him well for telling the world about the oppressed peoples" (78). Shades of Blasco Ibáñez, whom she accused of working the other side of the political street for personal gain.

The most humorous part of the story and the least reflective of Beals's situation is the journalist's sexual encounter with Miriam:

> He had believed that all virgins . . . were palpitating to learn about life, were you might say hanging on by an eyelash until they arrived safely at initiation within the secure yet libertine advantages of marriage. Miriam upset this theory as in time she upset most of his theories. . . . In their most intimate hours her mind seemed elsewhere, gone into some

darkness of its own, as if a prior and greater shock of knowledge had
forestalled her attention. . . . She let him know also that she believed
their mutual sacrifice of virginity was the most important act of their
marriage, and this sacred rite once achieved, the whole affair had de-
scended to a pretty low plane. (73)

Although Beals probably thanked Lillian for doing him a favor by leaving
him, he didn't contemplate remarrying her. A womanizer, he numbered among
his conquests Tina Modotti's sister, Mercedes. On November 18, 1931, he married Betty Daniels, whom Porter, in a December letter to Peggy Cowley, remembered dropping in with Beals at "our party" at Silvain's restaurant in Mexico City. The marriage ended in divorce in 1934, at which time he married the
third of his four wives. Perhaps Porter wished to rewrite history and make
Beals pay for his cavalier treatment of women, as Salomón de la Selva in "Virgin Violeta" and Samuel Yúdico in "Flowering Judas" paid.

Like "Virgin Violeta" and "Flowering Judas," "That Tree" is also a story of
the avenging virgin. The journalist "had something of a notion he was freeing a
sweet bird from a cage. Once freed, she would perch gratefully on his hand. He
wrote a poem about a caged bird set free, dedicated it to her and sent her a
copy. She forgot to mention it in her next letter" (74). The image recalls Virgin
Violeta's feeling like parrots "stuffed into tiny wicker cages," but Carlos fails to
set her free, for Porter's young women, whether compared to parrots or doves,
wish to escape their cage, not exchange it for another. If Violeta's horrified
response to Carlos reflects Porter's first sexual encounter at age sixteen, the
same source may account for Miriam's view of the "sacrifice" of her virginity
and her frigid disinterest in her husband's lovemaking, "as if a prior and
greater shock of knowledge had forestalled her attention."

Porter also resembles the journalist as well as Miriam. Like him, she had
"longed to live in a beautiful dangerous place among interesting people who
painted and wrote poetry" (73–74). But sometimes Mexico could become too
dangerous. The journalist accuses others of "always getting mixed up in affairs
that were none of their business, and they spent their time trying to work up
trouble somewhere so they could get a story out of it. They were always having
to be thrown out on their ears by the government" (70). There is hidden irony
in this passage since in 1930 Beals himself was almost thrown out of Mexico
by the Calles government, as Porter notes in her 1936 review of his *The Stones
Awake*: "They took him away very quietly and popped him into jail and kept
him incommunicado for an uncomfortable length of time. Mr. Beals, who
rarely confuses himself with the hero of his own works, was bored and angry
and nervous all at once, being uncertain whether they meant to shoot him."
Porter is amused by Beals's experience, but the passage in "That Tree" could as
well refer to her intrigue in connection with Niven's letters and the threat of
her own deportation, something that did not amuse her at the time.

Porter's most ambitious project, begun at the end of 1931, was *Many Re-*

deemers. [1] Book I, *Introduction to Death,* would trace the "History of the rise and break-up of an American family up to the Great War." Book II, *Midway of This Mortal Life,* would deal with an "uprooted, disrupted People," including the "Mexican interval which is a tangent for Miranda" and "the complete negation of all she has known, a derailment up to 1928 or 30." She wrote Pressly (January 1932) that the title alluded to Dante's pilgrimage through hell, but her book would be a "pilgrimage through this world." Book III, *"Beginning Again: the End,"* would deal with the "present, the rich and crumbling society, with some of the cures offered by diverse Saviours." She wrote William Harlan Hale (September 13, 1932) that her novel "is all about how men go on saving the world by starving, robbing, and killing each other. Lying, meanwhile, to themselves and each other about their motives." Since this idea was inspired by her Mexican experience and realized in "Flowering Judas" and "Hacienda," she soon dropped it and gave the title *Legend and Memory* to the story of Miranda and her Southern past. She explained to her father in 1934: "I am trying to reconstruct the whole history of an American family (ours, more or less) from the beginning by means of just those two things—legend and memory." She asked him to write down "all the stories you know, with all the details you never had time to write . . . all your memories, do you see, with what the old people told you when you were a child, and thus I hope to build a bridge back." She had made the same request on January 21, 1933, trying to jog her father's memory about her ancestors: "You know, I have very little patience with people who try to live on their ancestors, and southerners here wear me out talking about their families. But I do have a little private interest of my own in family history, and I wish you would write down for me everything you remember about all branches—for example, you never say a word about the Porters" (L 88).

Since her father contributed little to her reconstruction of family history, Porter relied on her own memory of her childhood and on her grandmother's memories, fictionalizing them to create six short interconnected works: "The Source," "The Old Order," "The Witness," "The Circus," "The Last Leaf," and "The Grave." Calling them fragments of a novel, she attempted but failed to publish them as a unit in the *Atlantic Monthly* in 1934. "Old Mortality," also begun in the early thirties and tapping family legend, was as close as she came to Book I of her projected opus. With its publication she had exhausted the possibilities of her fictionalized Southern past.

In the *Legend and Memory* stories, Porter did not so much draw from a family past as she constructed one she felt she should have had. It was crucial to the public self she was attempting to consolidate, especially after meeting the Tates. In praise of Caroline Gordon's novels of the Old South, she wrote that "places, spots of earth, only have meaning and dignity to us when the people who live there love these places, and their lives are wrapped up in them and . . . human experience was as deep and full of meaning as it has been anywhere." In another letter she regretted not buying a cabin in Tennessee: "I suddenly realized I am frightfully homesick for clear bright steady heat, south country sounds, niggers shouting at mules . . . . When, when ever again?" When Gordon's *Aleck Maury, Sportsman* appeared, she praised its "fine masculine prose" since "[you are] writing with the sound of your father's voice, all the voices of your fore-fathers, in your ears. It's odd in a way how our development runs along neck to neck."[2]

Porter, feeling the need to identify with Gordon's genteel South, most prominently created it in "Old Mortality," but her attitude, as in "The Fig Tree," was ambivalent because she could not forget the injuries done her in the poverty-stricken South of her youth. While urging her father to explore his memories of his past, she continued to nurse her grudge against him for his indolence. On November 8, 1931, she answered his charge of being extravagant: "But ah, we have all been so poor and wretched, it is natural for us to enjoy what we have when we have it, for we were never the kind of people who should have been poor and worried about money all the time," but "none of us could realize the hard fact that money has to be attracted by some means or another." The first person plural barely disguises the accusation aimed at him. Identifying with the kind of people who should never have been poor, she made Miranda's shadowy father prosperous enough to send her and her sister to a convent school whereas her own father let them support him, but, however cultivated and prosperous Porter painted her family in her fiction, she could not suppress her grievance against their lovelessness and neglect.

Since her family gave her neither money nor love, Porter came to think of herself as a self-made woman, born with an extraordinary talent she nurtured against all odds to become a famous writer of fiction. That self-perception is evident in her projection of Miranda in her early notes to *Many Redeemers*:

> History of how all her life she would tolerate the things she hated and
> was instinctively right to hate. Born as she was with a set of antennae
> that could sense at a distance—natural sympathies and hostilities—de-
> liberately she distrusted or ignored them, on principle. Drove herself
> mercilessly into experiences, associations, from which she revolted in-
> stinctively, and from which her natural impulses were powerful and—all
> the miserable people she tolerated, helped, and was victimized by—at
> last comes to depend on the single fine point of reference in her soul.

Although earlier versions of Miranda had appeared in fragments of *Thieves' Market* and in "The Fig Tree," here Porter constructed the Miranda who would soon appear in the *Legend and Memory* stories and in *Pale Horse, Pale Rider*. In "The Grave" she repeated the antennae image to describe Miranda's "powerful social sense, which was like a fine set of antennae radiating from every pore of her skin" (365), while "the single fine point of reference in her soul" became in "Pale Horse, Pale Rider" "a minute fiercely burning particle of being that knew itself alone, that relied on nothing beyond itself for its strength; not susceptible to any appeal or inducement, being itself composed entirely of one single motive, the stubborn will to live" (310–311).

Porter created in Miranda an idealized version of herself. Her alter ego is an exceptional human being, born with extraordinary powers of perception (antennae) that enable her "instinctively" (twice used) to pass judgment on the evil beings in the world with whom she is forced to associate. She "drove herself mercilessly into experiences" (in Mexico), perhaps to test the world, but escaped with her "natural impulses" intact. Although she tolerated some and helped others, they victimized her and taught her that she could trust no one but herself. Powerless to change the world, she relies on her own strength, like Granny Weatherall and the grandmother in "The Source." Since nature itself has not rewarded her, as it rewards María Concepción, she can only suffer life's indignities, withdrawn protectively into the fortress of self. Porter's self-portrait is idealized because she eliminated from it all references to her own confessed weaknesses in Salem. Her tendency to blame others for her depression now resulted in a Miranda who, from the author's point of view, is a relatively faultless victim of her world, unlike Laura in "Flowering Judas." Porter viewed her idealized alter ego as someone who "tolerated, helped, and was victimized by others" when, in fact, others—for example, Kitty Crawford, Becky Crawford, Matthew Josephson, her unnamed benefactor, the Tates, and Eugene Pressly—helped advance her career. She resented her family for not supporting her, but, at the same time, seemed to take secret pleasure in their neglect because it bolstered her view of herself as self-made artist. For that same reason she was loathe to admit that others had supported her, as if her need for support were an admission of weakness.

In her November 1931 letter to Pressly in which she called herself neurotic, Porter explored her expanding sense of individualism as "a way of living, an attitude not necessarily visible to the casual passing eye": "More and more I look upon life as something for my personal use and contentment, I feel very little call to explain myself or conform in any way to anybody else's set of rules. Less and less I am disposed to keep open house in my heart and mind. . . . I like fewer and fewer persons . . . I need less and less human society." This statement is an elaboration of her attitude in Mexico when she imagined that others disliked her to justify her rejection of them. Having escaped the South's smothering set of rules, she now wished to be a rule unto herself, isolated from others who might thwart her desire for absolute freedom. Her egotism is tied to her view of herself as artist. She wrote her brother Paul (March 8, 1932), "I do not have to explain anything or listen to explanation, and I do not have that feeling of being at odds with society because I am an artist" (L 79). Relying on her role as divine right, she declared her independence of others, ironically declaring it to Pressly, whose economic and psychological support she needed in Mixcoac and in Europe, but since she could not realize it in her own life, she fictionalized it through Miranda, whose survival in a chaotic world justified the author's view of herself as artist.

The Miranda stories record the terrors of the world, resembling, in their origins, those in "Virgin Violeta." "The Circus" views a very young Miranda whom her family, after some debate, allows to attend her first circus. A triumph of point of view, the story allows the reader to share Miranda's experiences and even to assume that she, in her innocence, misinterprets them, but it really reveals her instinctive reaction to the evil world the circus represents, just as Virgin Violeta reveals her instinctive reaction to the sexual evil Carlos represents. Miranda, who has the fatal power of seeing what others do not, first discovers two urchins huddled under the stands, causing the servant Dicey to draw her knees together when Miranda informs her of their presence. The urchins' sexual threat is amplified by the circus's "sound and color and smell" that "rushed together and poured through her skin and hair and beat in her head and hands and feet and pit of her stomach" (344), recalling the "sick thumping" in "the pit of [Violeta's] stomach" when Carlos forces his kiss on her. This overwhelming assault is immediately followed by the description of a clown on the high wire with his "bone-white skull and chalk-white face," who "blew sneering kisses with his cruel mouth." When she realizes the clown is human and flirts with death on the wire, she is terrified. She penetrates his disguise to see his "perpetual grimace of pain" while the unseeing crowd roars "with savage delight, shrieks of laughter like devils in delicious torment." When she screams and covers her eyes, her unsympathetic father, the laughter "not wiped from his face," orders the servant Dicey to take her home at once. As she leaves, a dwarf makes "a horrid grimace at her, imitating her own face." At first thinking him a child, she then discovers his "haughty, remote . . . grown-up look" (345), a look that turns him into an exaggerated version of her remote father. Later her older cousins taunt her with what she missed at the circus, "their malicious eyes watching Miranda squirm" (346). Like the crowd, they are diabolic, too much of this world to recognize its hellishness as Miranda does: "She fell asleep, and her invented memories gave way before the real ones, the bitter terrified face of the man in blowsy white falling to his death—ah, the cruel joke! . . . She screamed in her sleep and sat up crying for deliverance from her torments" (347). Her experience of reality as nightmare is like Violeta's "nightmare that went on and on and no one heard you calling to be waked up" (30). Neither father nor grandmother hears Miranda calling— only Dicey, who responds merely out of duty. Afraid to sleep again, she desperately clings to her unsatisfactory mother substitute, but she must bear her "torments" alone, for no one understands or loves her—like Violeta, whose mother's breast "had become a cold, strange place" (31). The experiences of Miranda and Violeta reflect Porter's own terror of sex and death, but none reflects that terror more directly than "The Grave."

Porter wrote Pressly (May 28, 1932) that "it came to me suddenly that from the first breath all creatures are aware of [death]: to be alive even for an instant is to know death," an idea she repeated years later in "'Noon Wine': The Sources": "We are born knowing death" (474). The statement could serve as epigraph to "The Grave," a story paradigmatic of the way Porter's Mexican experiences triggered fearful memories of her early childhood. At the end of the story an adult Miranda

> was picking her path among the puddles and crushed refuse of a market street in a strange city of a strange country, when without warning, plain and clear in its true colors as if she looked through a frame upon a scene that had not stirred nor changed since the moment it happened, the episode of that far off day leaped from its burial place before her mind's eye. She was so reasonlessly horrified she halted suddenly staring, the scene before her eyes dimmed by the vision back of them. An Indian vendor held up before her a tray of dyed sugar sweets, in the shapes of all kinds of small creatures: birds, baby chicks, baby rabbits, lambs, baby pigs. They were in gay colors and smelled of vanilla, maybe. . . . It was a very hot day and the smell in the market, with its piles of raw flesh and wilting flowers, was like the mingled sweetness and corruption she had smelled that other day in the empty cemetery at home [when] she and her brother had found the treasure in the opened graves (367).

Porter wrote Daniel Curley (April 6, 1958) that the final episode is set in Mexico, but couldn't explain why she "ended it that way except it had its true meaning in my blood somewhere." She may have been disingenuous about the story's meaning since its fearful coupling of life and death plays out her guilt over her mother's death.

The story's Edenic images are almost as insistent as those in Hawthorne's "Rappacini's Daughter." It opens with a lost Eden of a "neglected garden of tangled rose bushes and ragged cedar trees and cypress" whose recent sale makes Miranda and her brother Paul feel "like trespassers" (362–363). At the same time, the children wear "the same outfit" of shirt, overalls, and sandals (364) that preserves their innocence by obscuring their sexual identities until "bad-tempered old crones" make Miranda "ashamed" (365) of her boy's clothes. Up to this point Miranda had "faith in her father's judgment" in dressing them in such a practical (or innocent) manner, but only after the women speak does the gold ring found in the family grave turn Miranda's "feelings against her overalls" and toward "the thinnest, most becoming dress she owned" (365). But her feminine yearning quickly vanishes when she discovers dead baby rabbits in the womb of the mother rabbit Paul has just killed and opened; then the "very memory of her former ignorance" (366) fades. After hiding the rabbit's body in the sagebrush, Paul, the male instigator in this version of the Fall, warns Miranda to keep their knowledge secret: "Don't tell Dad because I'll get into trouble. He'll say I'm leading you into things you ought not to do" (367). Without needing to be told, Miranda buries her knowledge in the grave of memory until it is dislodged twenty years later.

Miranda's father, attempting to preserve her innocence, has left her vulnerable to the criticism of the old crones and unprepared to understand her sexuality. So Porter's own father had created in her the desperate need to cling to the innocence he ironically denied her by plunging her into early guilt over her mother's death. That twinning of innocence and guilt is caught in the name "Baby," as Miranda is called in "The Circus" and "The Fig Tree." Porter appropriated it from her younger sister, Mary Alice, whose birth led to their mother's death a few months later. Thus "Baby" signifies both Miranda-Porter's desire to remain innocent and her father's desire to baby her, thereby leaving her unprepared to face the terrors of the fallen world. It also carries a guilt-laden reminder that a baby can cause its mother's death. Porter's memory explains why Miranda suppresses her memory of the rabbits. When "the episode" leaps from "its burial place" (367) twenty years later, she buries it again, replacing it with her memory of her brother Paul "standing again in the blazing sunshine, again twelve years old," fondling the silver dove found in the family grave (368). She evokes his innocence before she and he fell into their fatal knowledge of the rabbits, the significance of which she as adult still cannot face.[3] "The Grave" also explains why Laura, clinging to her lost innocence, fears love, pregnancy, and death.

All three stories of *Pale Horse, Pale Rider,* also begun in the early thirties, are death-ridden. The iconographic unity of the three derives from Albrecht Dürer, whose work Porter studied in Basel in 1932. In notes of 1935, she wrote about looking again at Dürer's scenes representing St. John's revelations: "But I have his view of the Apocalypse, and it is mine: I was there." In "Old Mortality" Miranda and her sister view "pictures in the old Holbein and Dürer books" and never doubt "either Death or the Devil riding at the stirrups of the grim knight" (178), referring to Dürer's "Knight, Death and Devil" and anticipating in "Pale Horse, Pale Rider" an older Miranda's dream in which she attempts to "outrun Death and the Devil" (270). In "Noon Wine," Mr. Helton, a walking dead man, resembles the figure of Death riding with pitchfork on his pale horse in Dürer's "The Four Horsemen." When Mrs. Thompson asks him if he would like to accompany them to church, he rudely rebuffs her while leaning on a pitchfork, the same instrument he had shoved "right square through his brother" (251), according to Hatch's report to Thompson. Porter stated that she wrote the scene between Hatch and Thompson "in Basel, Switzerland, in the summer of 1932" (CE 469).

All three stories indirectly reflect Porter's Mexican experiences as well as her psychological state in the thirties. As we have seen, Virgin Violeta is an early version of Miranda of "Old Mortality," who at the end of the story is in a more advanced stage of alienation from her family, hating "loving and being loved" (221). Her determination not "to stay in any place, with anyone, that . . . said 'No' to her" (220) sounds petulant, but is in the spirit of Porter's declaration of independence to Eugene Pressly. Miranda's aunt Amy, seen through a "romantic haze" (212), is a projection of Porter's worst fears about herself; she is cold to Gabriel, her suitor, can't "imagine wanting to love anybody" (183), is "sick of this world" (188), and apparently escapes from it through suicide. Trapped in her role as Southern Belle—Gabriel even sends her a "cage full of small green lovebirds" (181), recalling the caged birds in "Corridos," "Virgin Violeta," and "That Tree"—she displays all the symptoms of Porter's self-confessed "melancholy," a word that appears in the text three times (175, 201, 210). The youthful Miranda, hoping to escape the condition, thinks she won't have "false hopes" (Porter's projected title for "Hacienda"), but, in "her hopefulness, her ignorance" (221), she is wrong.

In "'Noon Wine': The Sources" Porter wrote of the South's "underlying perpetual ominous presence of violence; violence that broke through the smooth surface almost without warning . . ." (CE 472). Mexico reminded Porter of that South; Laura, in "Flowering Judas," "feels a slow chill, a purely physical sense of danger, a warning in her blood that violence, mutilation, a shocking death, wait for her with lessening patience" (93). In "Noon Wine," violence erupts nine years after Mr. Thompson hired Mr. Helton. In that period the taciturn Helton made Thompson's farm prosper, an accomplishment that "seemed like a miracle" (259) to Mrs. Thompson. But one day Mr. Hatch, a bounty hunter, enters the farm to inform Thompson that Helton is an escaped lunatic who had killed his brother in Minnesota. When Helton suddenly appears, Hatch moves toward him, knife in hand. Thompson, thinking that Hatch, to whom he had taken an instant dislike, has wounded Helton, fells him with an ax. Although a jury accepts Thompson's plea of self-defense, he cannot convince himself he is not a murderer and when his own family implicitly agrees, he kills himself with a shotgun.

If character is fate, then Porter created in "Noon Wine" her only tragedy of Faustian dimensions, in which Thompson's flaws lead to his downfall:

> Head erect, a prompt payer of taxes, a yearly subscriber to the preacher's salary, land owner and father of a family, employer, a hearty good fellow among men, Mr. Thompson knew, without putting it into words, that he had been going steadily down hill. God amighty, it did look like somebody around the place might take a rake in hand now and then and clear up the clutter around the barn and the kitchen steps. . . . He would sometimes in the slack season sit for hours worrying about it, squirting tobacco on the ragweeds growing in a thicket against the wood pile, wondering what a fellow could do, handicapped as he was. (234)

Here Porter, employing her caricaturist method, has Mr. Thompson unconsciously convict himself through his own thoughts and language. He considers himself handicapped by a sickly wife not strong enough to do the chores he thinks she should do, but he is really handicapped by his own pride, laziness, and self-ignorance. However, unlike Porter's other caricatures, he is not the object of ridicule. He is, like the man she claimed was his model, "absurd, fatuous, but with some final undeniable human claim on respect and not to be laughed at, except in passing, for all his simple vanity" (CE 481).

Thompson is also like Porter's father,[4] who complained to her in 1929, "If there is such a thing as bad luck groping its way among the atoms . . . it never fails to track me up and run me down." *La Suerte,* capitalizing on Thompson's flaws, does indeed run him down. His self-esteem bolstered by the farm's prosperity, for which Helton is responsible, he defends Helton as if he were defending himself and kills the hated Hatch, a distorted version of himself, with an ax Helton had left in the chopping block a short while before. Porter called "Noon Wine" "a story of the most painful moral and emotional confusions, in which everyone concerned, yes, in his crooked way, even Mr. Hatch, is trying to do right" (CE 479). But everyone fails, partly because each, knowing better, relies on others, who unintentionally betray that trust. Mrs. Thompson "wanted to believe in her husband, and there were too many times when she couldn't" (226). She also finds "it was no use putting dependence on a man," like Helton, "who won't set down and make out his dinner" (232). Thompson laments "how short-sighted it had been of him to expect much from Mrs. Thompson" (234) while her children "had no faith in her good will. She had betrayed them in the first place. There was no trusting her" (240). Hatch makes the fatal mistake of expecting Thompson to cooperate in capturing Helton, who had made the equally fatal mistake of trusting his mother not to advertise his whereabouts upon receiving a check from him. Behind such miscalculations is Porter's conviction, frequently expressed to her sister Gay, that she never could depend on her family. In "Pale Horse, Pale Rider" Miranda learns to trust only herself.

"Pale Horse, Pale Rider," the last Miranda story, reveals more than any other Porter's interrelated political, aesthetic, and psychological attitudes in the thirties. Probed in Chapter 1 for evidence of her radicalism in 1918–1920 before entering Mexico, it suggests that after she left the "grafting politicians" of Mexico, she had no hope of finding a better world elsewhere. She wrote her father aboard the *Werra,* "I leave a troubled world and go to one more troubled. Mexico is in ferment," Cuba is "under martial law" and Germany is "on the verge of Famine," while in the United States, "the rich and the upper middle class are quite content to see millions starving around them and do nothing, and I have very little hope that the starving ones will really do anything by way of protest." In a daybook entry of 1932 she reviewed America's past wars, calling the Spanish-American War "a disgraceful episode," lamenting the "general waste incurred in the pursuit of conscientious objectors, Bolsheviks, slackers, and pacifists and German sympathizers" during World War I, and fearing that "there is no reason why they should not fight again" because of the country's "screaming eagleism" that stampedes its people to war: "Self Help is our motto. Help yourself to what you can grab and devil take the hindmost. That is the grand Old American Tradition of finance." She asked Peggy Cowley (December 9, 1931), "What are you going to do in the next great war? Me, I says, I'm going to get up on a soap box and tell everybody how sick it makes me and what tommyrot it is until they get so irritated they lock me up." "Pale Horse, Pale Rider" was as much inspired by fears of a new war as by memories of the old one.

Porter's radicalism offered no political solutions. Although she believed "more nearly the things [the Communists] believe than any other creeds floating around," she asked Eugene Pressly (November 1931), "Yet, how can you give yourself over, bound like a chicken for the market to the Communists as we know them? Why exchange one kind of slavery for another?" Nevertheless, she went out of her way to meet Johannes Becker, editor of the Communist newspaper *Röte Fahne,* for which she planned to write articles on the United States, and in 1932 attended the meeting of the thirteenth annual celebration of the Communist party.[5] In 1935 she subscribed to the sessions of the Congress of International Writers to hear such leftist speakers as André Malraux and Louis Aragon.

Porter's political position fluctuated according to her correspondent. She wrote Josephine Herbst (March 11, 1933) that the farmers in the United States should turn and fight, for they have been too long "patient and long suffering and heavy burdened" (like the Mexican Indian), but in reply (March 21, 1935) to Caroline Gordon, who had wondered whatever happened to the revolution, she claimed she had infuriated Mike Gold way back in 1921 by asking the same question. On May 3, 1937, she wrote her family, whom she apparently liked to shock with her left leaning, "Saturday being May Day, I got right out and marched with my old friends the proletariat," just as in Paris the year before, although that march was "a prettier sight, for the whole street was one live mass of floating banners as far as you could see in either direction. I spoke of this to my crowd, and we agreed that next year we'd have to put on a prettier show, with more music and flags." Politics reduced to the aesthetics of May Day marches.

Aesthetics greatly influenced Porter's politics after her activism in Mexico a decade before. Having decided that as artist she was independent and answerable to no one but herself, least of all would she be answerable to a government which, her Mexican experience taught her, was never to be trusted. In notes to a 1931 letter to Pablo O'Higgins, she wrote, "I look forward to a world in which the artist has his true place as a useful being, not for political purposes, but in his true function, which is that of a finder, a bringer, a giver of new forms of expression based on life, but seen with imagination and creativeness." She added, "Art must grow out of some profound belief, and the strange thing about beliefs is, it does not matter much what they are, or have been, the artist gives them beauty and meaning by his own vision of them." She hoped the Soviet government would preserve "the true works of art," as we preserve those of ancient Greeks and Egyptians whose gods "no one any longer believes in" (L 66, 67). With no faith in politics and religion, Porter made art her absolute value, thereby solidifying her own importance as an artist who would express her own suffering and despair in a meaningless world. That is the meaning of "Pale Horse, Pale Rider," whose title not only alludes to Dürer but to "an old spiritual" in which the rider takes in death a whole family: "'But not the singer, not yet,' said Miranda. 'Death always leaves one singer to mourn. "Death,"' she sang, '"oh, leave one singer to mourn—"'" (304). Like Miranda, Porter conceived herself as the courageous survivor, the one singer left to mourn.

In creating "Pale Horse, Pale Rider," Porter had as a model "Flowering Judas," for Miranda and Laura are remarkably similar. Both fear death in a dangerous world, inadvertently cause the death of a man, resist the temptation to escape the world, and end isolated and despairing but determined to survive. The apparent difference between them is that Laura must face the consequences of her rejection of love, symbolized in the death of Eugenio, whereas Miranda falls in love with Adam and survives influenza only to discover that he has died from the disease contracted from her. Laura is victim of her own character whereas Miranda *seems* the blameless victim of circumstances beyond her control. Porter views Laura more dispassionately, later making explicit her flaws as if they were those of Mary Doherty, but she identifies sympathetically with Miranda, her idealized self. Yet the overriding fact remains that both women are carriers of death to their potential lovers, created out of Porter's guilt over the death of Sidronio Méndez and of the man in Denver in 1918.

Porter wrote her father (January 21, 1933) about the man from Denver when she began work on "Pale Horse, Pale Rider":

> When I was so desperately sick in Denver, in 1918, a young boy twenty one years old, whom I did not know at all, who happened to be living in the same house with me, took care of me for the three days before a doctor or bed in the hospital could be found for me. Nursed me and gave me my medicine and came in three times every night to see how I was. Ten days later, while I was unconscious in the hospital, he died of influenza. I cannot forget this, it is terrible that he should have saved my life and lost his own. In this case, I feel directly responsible, for he was a big healthy fellow who lived out of doors, and need never have come in contact with the epidemic at all. (L 90)

The unknown man became Adam, whose courting of Miranda Porter had to invent, as she invented the relation between Laura and Eugenio in "Flowering Judas."

Since the deaths of Eugenio and Adam are linked to the psychology of both heroines, Porter's mental states at the period established in the story and at the period of composition are important. In 1921, the time frame of "Flowering Judas," Porter wrote that she was more terrified of death than she was in Denver in 1918 and had "the same overpowering sense of death in life which only death itself can cure." In 1927 she wrote, "Sometimes I have been simply worn out and embittered . . . and have hovered perilously near the poison bottle or the loaded pistol. But I never do more then hover: I like to live, and I bought my life dearly enough in 1918, so I think the balance owes me a quick and easy death." As already noted, her depression pursued her from Mixcoac to Europe. She wrote Pressly (January 5, 1932), "Part of my suicidal depression has been the accumulated nervous fatigue of suspense and uncertainty, I think after I made up my mind not to expect anything unusual, my nerves relaxed, for I have been sleeping better—since I just let go and openly expressed my complete despair! What is the matter that we find the ordinary routine of existence, such as every human being must make for himself . . . an almost insoluble difficulty." Two days later she wrote Liza Dallett of her "natural melancholy": "I have been suicidally gloomy, and have to shake myself severely from time to time not to drop into the bottomless pit. It has no definite cause except too many desperate memories and a periodic resurgence of any deep conviction that life is a fatality and to be cheerful about it is just so much blah."

In "Pale Horse, Pale Rider" Porter returned to 1918 to assign "definite" causes to her melancholy of 1932, just as she had done with "Hacienda." We can understand the nature of her depression and her reaction to it if we view her alter ego, Miranda, in light of R. D. Laing's "ontologically insecure person," defined as one who "cannot take the realness, aliveness, autonomy, and identity of himself and others for granted"; whereas the secure person can find "relatedness to others potentially gratifying," the insecure person is preoccupied with preserving rather than gratifying himself: the ordinary circumstances of living threaten his *low threshold* of security" (42). When Porter complained to Pressly that "the ordinary routine of existence" was "an almost insoluble difficulty," she herself exhibited a low threshold.

"Pale Horse, Pale Rider" opens with a dream about Miranda's chronic struggle with life and death. She envisions herself in her childhood home, readying for a predawn journey she does not "mean to take": "Daylight will strike a sudden blow on the roof startling them all to their feet; faces will beam asking, Where are you going, What are you doing, What are you thinking, How do you feel, Why do you say such things, What do you mean? . . . How I have loved this house in the morning before we are all awake and tangled together like badly cast fishing lines . . ." She wonders where "that lank greenish stranger" is, as if she were seeking him, and then decides to saddle her horse and outrun "Death and the Devil." The stranger then appears and rides with her, "regarding her without meaning, the blank still stare of mindless malice," but she tells him to ride on, after which she "slowly, unwillingly" awakens, waiting "in a daze for life to begin again." Then "a gong of warning" reminds her of the war which she had "happily" forgotten (269–271).

Not remembering her dream, Miranda thinks sleep a happy escape from war: while bathing, she "wished she might fall asleep there, to wake up only when it was time to sleep again" (274). Later in the day her desire to escape becomes an explicit death wish: "There's too much of everything in this world right now. I'd like to sit down here on the curb . . . and die, and never again see—I wish I could lose my memory and forget my own name . . ." (289). But her dream of the Pale Rider suggests that Miranda's fear and insecurity are ultimately rooted, not in the present circumstance of war, but in her childhood. The young Miranda awakes before her family to escape demands she considers a threat to the self; her escape is from the human condition, conceived in terms of sleepers shocked into an unhappy resurrection by the sun and then, as it runs its course, hopelessly entangled with each other until they can sleep and forget again. Her fluctuating attraction and aversion to the Pale Rider reveal her paradoxical attempt through death to preserve the self from extinction and her determination to live on despite her fears. She rejects the Pale Rider and with him the dream-escape itself as she waits "in a daze for life to begin again," just as the sleepers in her dream would be "startled" to life by a "blow of daylight." Ironically, her forgotten dream of escaping war has played out the hopelessness of escaping anything, as she learns at the end of the story: having been shocked back to life on Armistice Day, "she folded her painful body together and wept silently, shamelessly, in pity for herself and her lost rapture. There was no escape" (314).

Miranda's dream is a paradigm of her unbearable dilemma throughout the story; fearing both life and death, she reluctantly chooses life that threatens death. She fears "engulfment" that is felt, according to Laing, "as a risk in being understood (thus grasped, comprehended), in being loved, or simply in being seen" (44). Her flight from the well-meaning questions of her family is an explicit example of her fear of being understood. Just as she seeks sleep as an escape from war, a temporary death that preserves life, so in the dream she wishes her family temporarily dead because awake they and she become "tangled together like badly cast fishing lines," an image of her fear of losing autonomous identity. In an essay on Willa Cather, Porter quotes approvingly Cather's similar fear: "Yet every individual in that household . . . is clinging passionately to his individual soul, is in terror of losing it in the general family flavor. . . . Always in his mind each member is escaping, running away, trying to break the net which circumstances and his own affections have woven about him" (CE 31–32). The common ingredient in Miranda's dream and Cather's comments is the fear of engulfment, expressed by the fishing line and net images. Cather implies that this fear in some form is common. Laing would agree, pointing out that in the "comprehensible transition" from the sane to the psychotic, "*sanity or psychosis is tested by the degree of conjunction or disjunction between two persons*" (36). The key word is "degree." Miranda's disjunction is remarkable enough to view her symptoms in light of Laing's study, but she is sane whereas the totally alienated Helton in "Noon Wine" is not.

Miranda's distrust of others is reflected in the Pale Rider's "blank still stare of mindless malice," matched by the "really stony, really viciously cold" stare of the Liberty Bond salesman (272) and by the "malign eyes" of the rainbow-colored birds of her second dream (299). The "unfriendly bitter" eyes of the hospitalized soldier (277) anticipate Miranda's own "covertly hostile eyes of an alien" (313) as she too lies in a hospital bed at the end of the story. Her eyes reveal her sense of betrayal, yet the hostility of all the eyes has a common source in her mind; without realizing it, the betrayed are self-betrayed. Her remark that "the worst of the war is the fear and suspicion and the awful expression in all the eyes you meet . . . as if they had pulled down the shutters over their minds and their hearts and were peering out at you, ready to leap if you make one gesture or say one word they do not understand instantly" (294) applies equally to her. The "hard unblinking point of light," identified with the essence of her being in her last dream, has the power of a stare and represents her loveless determination to survive in a hostile world against which she has formed her defense. To Laing's insecure person, "every pair of eyes is in a Medusa's head which he feels has power actually to kill or deaden something precariously vital to him. He tries to forestall his own petrifaction by turning others to stone" (76). Miranda's preoccupation with hostile eyes seems justified by war hysteria, but it reveals an anxiety that predates the war. In "The Circus" a young Miranda witnesses the "bold grinning stare" of one of the boys under the plank seats and is tormented by the "malicious eyes" of her cousins, "watching [her] squirm" (346).

Miranda's dream and painful recollection of the preceding day are partially offset by her love for Adam, who "was in her mind so much, she hardly knew when she was thinking about him directly" (277), although the first nine pages of the text offer no evidence that he was. "Pale Horse, Pale Rider" is a love story with a difference, for Miranda in love is like the engulfed person who "regards his own love and that of others as being as destructive as hatred" to the extent that his need for love is not enough for him to overcome his dread (163). The poignancy of Miranda's story lies not in Adam's death but in her belief that she could have loved him if he had lived.

Miranda's love for Adam is constantly coupled with her pessimism about their future together: ". . . he was not for her nor for any woman, being beyond experience already, committed without any knowledge or act of his own to death" (283–284); she "faced for one instant that was a lifetime the certain, the overwhelming and awful knowledge that there was nothing at all ahead for Adam and for her" (291); "Pure, she thought, all the way through, flawless, complete, as the sacrificial lamb must be" (295). Caroline Gordon complained about such passages: "Adam and Miranda seem a little too omniscient about the war. That is, they are using hindsight they have no right to possess." But Miranda's premonitions have their source, not in unjustified hindsight or in wartime uncertainty, but in her unconscious desire that Adam die, for she fears love: "'I don't want to love,' she would think in spite of herself, 'not Adam, there is no time and we are not ready for it and yet this is all we have—'" (292).

Miranda's ambivalent response to love explains her idealization of Adam as pure and flawless, a prelapsarian Adam who cannot survive in the fallen world of war, disease, and love. She idealizes him out of existence because she fears accepting him as real. Porter indeed created him as unreal—Miranda's double, the projection of the perfect male. He and Miranda are both "twenty-four years old each, alive and on the earth at the same moment" (280), both are Texans, are vain about their appearance, keep "unwholesome" hours, and like to swim, dance, and smoke. The remarkable similarities reveal Miranda's self-absorption. When she tells him she thinks he is "beautiful" (301), he objects to the inappropriate adjective, but she really applies it to herself, seeing her beauty in him. The sentence telling us that Adam's "image was simply always present" in her thoughts is immediately followed by "She examined her face in the mirror . . ." (278).

Miranda projects Adam's "beauty" and perfect health because she desires eternal youth, but the reality of her situation—"I have pains in my chest and my head and my heart and they're real" (296)—causes her to transform him from a god into a time-doomed victim of her fears of old age and death. When Adam first greets her, "She half noticed . . . that his smile faded gradually; that his eyes became fixed and thoughtful as if he were reading in a poor light" (278), as if they were "fixed" in death. The word recurs twice more: his eyes are "fixed in a strained frown" (284); "his face [is] quite fixed and still" (292). At the end of the same day Miranda completes his transformation from god to mortal as he sits in a restaurant "near the dingy big window, face turned to the street, but looking down. It was an extraordinary face, smooth and fine and golden in the shabby light, but now set in a blind melancholy, a look of pained suspense and disillusion. For just one split second she got a glimpse of Adam when he would have been older, the face of the man he would not live to be" (295). Her glimpse gives her a premonition of herself in the same condition. Having created his image out of her desire for immortality and then infected it with fear of aging, she finally denies him the aging process, as if his death were a defense against the ravages of time. Her shifting images of him anticipate her own worst fears at the end of the story. His "blind melancholy" and "look of pained suspense and disillusion" precisely describe her mental state after her recovery from influenza. Even the "dingy" window and "shabby light" of the restaurant foreshadow the "melancholy wonder" of the hospital scene, "where the light seemed filmed over with cobwebs, all the bright surfaces corroded" (314). Her metamorphosis, wrought by disease, embodies all her earlier fears of aging. She is like one of the "old bedridden women down the hall," her trembling hands tinted "yellow . . . like melted wax glimmering between the closed fingers" (313), as if she aged as rapidly as she had imagined Adam aging in the restaurant. She projects Adam as dead or soon to die to protect herself from the engulfment of his love and to express her death wish through him. Identifying with him, she unconsciously wishes him dead because he reminds her of what will happen to her in time. By removing him from time, she can preserve him as god and, at the end of the story, evoke him unchanged as "a ghost but more alive than she was" (317). He becomes her "sacrificial lamb" because he enacts her death wish, allowing her to follow her stronger instinct of self-preservation.

Miranda's sexual fears also express her fears of engulfment and aging, as the symbolic relation between her influenza and love of Adam suggests. Eleven days elapse between the couple's first meeting and the day influenza forces her to bed. Since the incubation period of the disease is from ten days to two weeks, her love and disease develop simultaneously. In her flashback of the first nine days, we see her and Adam frequently together with neither revealing any strong feeling for the other. But on the tenth day she is preoccupied with her love for him and with malaise. She holds hands with him in the theater, apparently for the first time, and goes dancing with him; "They said nothing but smiled continually at each other, odd changing smiles as though they had found a new language" (296). But their budding love is counterpoised by the Wasteland conversation of the girl at the next table who recounts her rejection of a former date's advances. In an abrupt transition we then discover Miranda in bed, gravely ill with influenza. Adam nurses her and finally tells her he loves her, lying beside her, his arm under her shoulder and "his smooth face against hers," whereupon "Almost with no warning at all, she floated into the darkness, holding his hand" (304), only to dream of killing him.

There is a causal relation between their intimacy and the content of her dream. In it Adam is struck in the heart by flights of arrows, but rises each time "in a perpetual death and resurrection," but when Miranda "selfishly" interposes between him and the arrows, they pass through her heart and kill him: ". . . he lay dead, and she still lived, and . . . every branch and leaf and blade of grass had its own terrible accusing voice" (305). The dream expresses Miranda's guilt in exposing Adam to contagion, but also confirms the ambivalence of her love for him, as in her earlier predictions of his death. His "perpetual death and resurrection" again reveal her desire for immortality in her projection of him as god, impervious to the onslaught of war and love, but again the image gives way to Adam's mortality. His death, caused by her interposition, proves her unconscious fear of her destructive love and also her desire to escape his love by killing him.[6] The bowdlerized version of the dream which Miranda gives Adam when she wakes—"There was something about an old-fashioned valentine" with "two hearts carved on a tree, pierced by the same arrow" (305)—directly equates his death with the interlinking of their hearts. The arrows of her dream represent war, pestilence, love, and sexual contact. To Miranda they are equally lethal. As noted earlier, Porter frequently equated love with disease. She wrote Peggy Cowley (December 9, 1931) concerning the divorce of the Dalletts, "I feel a little as if both of them were cured of a long sickness."

When Adam leaves shortly after Miranda's dream, she never sees him again. In the hospital she suffers through the crisis of her disease, represented in a dream in which she "sank easily . . . until she lay like a stone at the farthest bottom of life, knowing herself to be blind, deaf, speechless, no longer aware of the members of her body, entirely withdrawn from all human concerns . . ." At this point, "all ties of blood and the desires of the heart" dissolve except her "stubborn will to live" (310–311). She has escaped into nothingness, shedding her humanity by becoming an inanimate stone—just as the insecure person, once he has successfully destroyed in his mind the image of anyone he loves and reduced all wants to nothing, "descends in a vortex of non-being . . . to preserve being from himself" (93), for "to forgo one's autonomy becomes the means of secretly safeguarding it; to play possum, to feign death, becomes a means of preserving one's aliveness. To turn oneself into a stone becomes a way of not being turned into a stone by someone else" (51). Miranda, of course, does not feign death but literally almost dies, yet the metaphorical meaning of becoming a stone accentuates her desire to withdraw "from all human activity."

Out of Miranda's will to live springs "her paradise," "a child's dream of the heavenly meadow." She does not envision an afterlife, for eternity is "unknowable," but an idealized version of this life, where all the "living" are "transfigured," their "untroubled" eyes without the "awful expression of fear and suspicion" she complained of earlier. They are "pure identities" who cast no shadows in a timeless world where it is "always morning." Miranda, "desiring nothing," "within touch but not touching" anyone, has purified human relationships out of existence in an attempt to render them harmless. But as she begins to gain consciousness, she feels "distrust in her joy," for "something, somebody, was missing. . . . Where are the dead? We have forgotten the dead, oh, the dead, where are they? At once . . . the bright landscape faded" and "pain returned" and she saw the nurse filling a hypodermic needle (311–312). Her vision of paradise is a stage between her desire to protect herself by turning into a stone and her counter-desire to return to life from which she fled. Her paradise fades, as did her vision of Adam as god, because it is unreal and cannot be sustained. Having fled death-threatening life into states of nonlife too similar to death, she returns to life defined by the presence of death. Miranda needs the dead to know she is alive despite the grief it causes her. She does not resist death because she wants to return to Adam, but because "somebody" missing is dead. When she does return, she makes no inquiry about Adam until she reads several days later the letter informing her of his death. Then she complains, ". . . I wish you had come back, what do you think that I came back for, Adam, to be deceived like this?" (317). But his death does not deceive her; knowing he is safely dead, she deceives herself into thinking she returned for him.

After her recovery, she exhibits all her earlier symptoms. Awakening to the smell of death in her body, she thinks, "The body is a curious monster, no place to live in, how could anyone feel at home there? Is it possible I can ever accustom myself to this place?" (313). To her "all objects and beings" are "meaningless, ah, dead and withered things that believed themselves alive!"

She is "not quite dead now . . . one foot in either world," but she reassures herself that she will "cross back and be at home again" (317). "Condemned" to this life by those who have "conspired" to restore "her disordered mind," she views them with the "covertly hostile eyes of an alien who does not like the country in which he finds himself, does not understand the language nor wish to learn it, does not mean to live there and yet is helpless, unable to leave it at his will." Although she knows people will say they love her, "her hardened, indifferent heart shuddered in despair at itself, because before it had been tender and capable of love" (313–315). In Laing's terms, she lives "in despairing aloneness and isolation" and feels "more dead than alive," unable "to experience [herself] 'together with' others or 'at home in' the world" (17), but now she can justify her melancholy by her loss of Adam.

Miranda's alienation resembles that of Laura in "Flowering Judas," who "is not at home in the world" (97). Porter, beginning with "In a Mexican Patio," created in her Mexican works the alienated character, ghostly in her isolation from mankind. In "Old Mortality" Amy complains to her mother, "I'm sick of this world. I don't like anything in it" (188), escaping from it in suicide. Young Miranda "would have no more bonds that smothered her in love and hatred" (220), revealing her fear of engulfment. In "Noon Wine" Helton, by killing his brother, irrevocably removes himself from any place in the world. He is a ghost, a walking dead man, his voice coming "as from the tomb" (224). After his death, Thompson takes on the appearance of Helton, his face "like a dead man's face," his eyes "hollowed out and dead looking" (258). Mrs. Thompson also suffers extreme alienation: "Life was all one dread, the faces of her neighbors, of her boys, of her husband, the face of the whole world. . . . There was no place to go, only one thing to do, bear it somehow—but how? . . . How was she going to keep on living now? Why had she lived at all?" (257).

According to Porter, Mrs. Thompson "lacks the courage and the love to see her sin [lying to protect her husband] through to its final good purpose," adding, "There is nothing in any of these beings tough enough to work the miracle of redemption" (CE 481). Like Porter's other alienated characters, she doesn't understand what has happened to her, but the mature Miranda of "Pale Horse, Pale Rider," tough and resilient, seemingly does. Her vision of paradise confirms her despair of ever finding happiness, but also reinforces her "stubborn will to live." Knowing there is no escape from the world, she is stoically determined to live in it but not be part of it. She will disguise her face with makeup and mask her inward feeling with a smile so as not to "tamper with the courage of the living" (315) who suffer from the illusion that happiness can exist, but her brush with death has given her an insight into the "truth" they are not privileged to share. Thus her secret knowledge, the source of her despair, makes her unique in her own eyes. As she prepares to reenter the world and "face the dead cold light of tomorrow" (317), she almost covets that despair because it implies a courage superior to that of others.

So Miranda sees herself and so, it seems, Porter wanted the reader to see her. Wayne Booth agrees, stressing Miranda's "moral superiority": "She must be accepted at her own estimate from the beginning," for "the slightest suggestion that she is at fault" or "that author and reader are observing [her] from above rather than alongside will destroy, at least in part, the quality of our concern and hence of our final revelation."[7] But our inability to accept Miranda at her own estimate, although it may change the quality of our concern, does not diminish our sympathy for her any more than for Laura, Mr. Thompson, or Porter's other self-deceived characters. Porter wanted us to see Miranda as blameless victim because she wanted to see herself in that light, but she could not put so much of herself into her alter ego without exposing the contradictory aspects of her own character.

In a 1963 interview Porter described herself in terms which identify her with Miranda:

> It took me a long time to go out and live in the world again. I was really "alienated," in the pure sense. It was, I think, the fact that I really had participated in death, that I knew what death was, and had almost experienced it. I had what the Christians call the "beatific vision," and the Greeks called the "happy day," the happy vision just before death. Now if you have had that, and survived it, come back from it, you are no longer like other people . . . (I 85)

Whether or not Porter believed her beatific vision, in the thirties she wanted to think of herself as unique, that her near-death was a sign that she was destined for greatness as an artist. As early as 1920 she wrote her father,

> I wish our lives might run along a bit closer together. But it seems to me that I was predestined to slither off the main stem. You know Dad I had from my cradle the born conviction that I was a person apart, and that life would not do the usual thing to me. . . . All my life has been a hideous blind mad struggle to break my shell and achieve to my destiny, and I am now just beginning to see that I was right, that I was not deceived by that inner conviction. I am an artist, a little deformed by my battle, and a little weakened by a long grinding resistance, but a living creative force, just the same. I was not fooled.

Like Porter, Miranda is "a person apart," who has survived suffering and near-death to become the "one singer to mourn." "Pale Horse, Pale Rider" is Porter's new spiritual, composed to justify her role as artist.

Yet other comments of Porter imply that Miranda deceives herself into thinking she returned from the grave, like Juliet, only to find her beloved had died in her service. Such deception is in the best tradition of romantic love, on which Porter theorized in a letter to her nephew in 1948. In "love at first sight," the lover is "instantly transfigured with a light of such blinding bril-

liance all natural attributes disappear and are replaced by those usually associated with archangels at least. They are beautiful, flawless in temperament"
while the love lasts. "And when I have recovered from the shock" and "put my
mangled life in order, I can then begin to remember what really happened."
Porter concluded that this "silliest kind of love" was all her fault: "If one ever
treats a man as if he were an archangel, he can't ever, possibly, consent to being
treated like a human being again. . . . It begins to look as if I had never wanted
it" (CE 111–112). The language here recalls Miranda's description of Adam,
her dream of paradise, and her subsequent disillusion. In that light, Miranda's
very act of idealizing Adam suggests that she, like Porter, "never wanted" a
lasting love relation at all, although she, unlike Porter, is unaware of it. Porter
claimed she once told a friend in Mexico that the man in Denver was the only
one she could have spent her life with. "And he replied, 'Just think, now he can
never disappoint you.' And I suppose if there is anything at all good about it,
that's it, but it does seem an awfully high price to pay to keep one's illusions,
doesn't it" (I 140). Her sardonic Mexican friend may be an invention since he
simply gives a twist to a brief note she wrote in 1921: "Her love affairs were
always playful or tragic and she always believed them permanent."

If Adam resembles anybody, it is Eugene Pressly, whom Porter put off marrying twice before finally committing herself in 1933. Although she depended on
and confided in him, she could not live without him nor with him for long,
preferring to live apart as much as possible and write him long intimate letters
instead. Brooding and taciturn, he inspired Miranda's view of Adam sitting in
the restaurant, his "extraordinary" face "now set in blind melancholy, a look of
pained suspense and disillusion." Among Porter's papers are photographs that
caught Pressly in that mood. Like Miranda with Adam, she "got a glimpse of
[him] when he would have been older, the face of the man he would not live to
be" still married to her. Below the surface of "Pale Horse, Pale Rider" is another
story of how Porter wrote Pressly out of her life. He went through a perpetual
death of departure and resurrection of return until his divorce-death in 1938.
He hoped to remarry her, but, in a letter to Mary Doherty (November 1, 1943),
Porter made clear why his brief visit was in vain:

> He had got fat, a hard, red, tight sort of fatness, less hair, and his features
> all drawn into a tight little smirking knot due to the strain of keeping his
> important personality all to himself. I let him come to see me, and then
> was sorry. Such a bore. If he got anything out of Russia, I am sure no
> one will ever know. Perhaps not even himself. I said good bye with
> blessed relief, and hope he is gone for good . . . whoever it was I thought
> I knew in Mexico by that name has been gone for a great while now.

He had become Adam, if he had lived, aging *and* fat—a justification of the fear
Porter felt and expressed through Miranda.

"Pale Horse, Pale Rider" might have forewarned Pressly about the hopelessness of his new marriage proposal. Like Miranda, Porter, in Laing's terms, oscillated between the "equally unfeasible" extremes of "complete isolation" and "complete merging of identity" (53). Fearing love, she lamented its loss through Miranda, but secretly exulted in her heroine's courageous isolation, as if dependency were a sign of weakness. Like Miranda, she trusted the "minute fiercely burning particle of being that knew itself alone, that relied upon nothing beyond itself for its own strength . . . the hard unwinking angry point of light . . ." (310–311). A symbol of their solipsism, the light is angry because hatred seemed the best defense against a hostile world. Unable to overcome her chronic depression, Porter fused it with her uniqueness as artist and made it heroic. But glorification of her condition could only aggravate it. Although she continued, in her oscillations, to respond to the need for love, there were times when she viewed the world with Miranda's "covertly hostile eyes" and lashed out at those like Hart Crane, who seemed to threaten her.

Perhaps Porter had Crane in mind when she wrote that "friendships collapse as swiftly as other things in Mexico" in her 1937 review of *Portrait of Mexico,* by two old friends, Diego Rivera and Bertram Wolfe.[8] The other thing that had collapsed was the Mexican Revolution: Wolfe "proves by implication rather clearly that the first step to a stable 'revolutionary' government is to kill off all the real rebels as early in the game as possible. His list of honest murdered men and living crooks is impressive." She praised his history but dismissed his "conventional hope for a new dawn," "so rosy one would like to share it, and so vague one does not know where to begin." With World War II about to erupt, hope indeed was an illusion.

As for Rivera, Porter's adulation of him had cooled considerably since 1922. She now caricatured him as "this big slow-moving man," "broadbeamed" and "ox eyed," accused him of "childish social theories and personal opportunism," and found in his National Palace murals "long dreary stretches of plain hackwork, overcrowded, incoherent, mechanical." Yet she admitted, "No single man in his time has ever had more influence on the eye and mind of the public who know his work than Diego Rivera; for he has made them see his Mexico, to accept his version of it, and often to think it better than their own." She herself felt his influence: "Mexico does not appear to me as it did before I saw Rivera's paintings of it"; now "the mountains, the Indians, the horses, the flowers and children" are all Rivera's.

1940–1950

In October 1936 Porter returned to the United States and completed the three stories of *Pale Horse, Pale Rider,* which appeared in 1939, the capstone of her literary career. That same year she also published "The Downward Path to Wisdom," in 1940 "A Day's Work," and in 1941 "The Source" and "The Leaning Tower"—all interesting but not as brilliant as her earlier stories.

During most of the decade, Porter devoted her energy to *Ship of Fools,* publishing seven sections of it by the end of 1950.

In January 1942 Harrison Porter died after a long illness. Porter had interrupted her stay in Europe to visit him in 1936, but heard about the violent and abusive behavior of his last days from her sisters. Shortly before his death, she wrote Mary Alice (October 3, 1941) that he "hated us all our lives, his indifference to our fates showed it, but not until the end could the truth come out." She hoped that she would "not live so long that news of [her] death will be a relief to everybody": "I have resistance and vitality too, a combination of will and tough tissues that give way very slowly, and it frightens me for fear I shall live too long . . ." After his death, she again wrote Mary Alice (January 24, 1942) that he "fought so hard and hated and feared death so terribly." Identifying with him, she feared that she too would hate death and hate others because of her fear. She confessed to Glenway Wescott (February 5) that she was her father's child by temperament, an observation she had fearfully made several times in the past.

Hatred by this time had already become a key word in her vocabulary. She reflected her own experiences of a loveless childhood in "The Downward Path to Wisdom" (1939), in which young Stephen, after witnessing various forms of adult hatred, especially that between his mother and father, sings, at the end of the story, "his new secret; it was a comfortable sleepy song: 'I hate Papa, I hate Mama, I hate Grandma, I hate Uncle David, I hate Old Janet, I hate Marjory, I hate Papa, I hate Mama . . .'" (387). He is the victim of his environment, learning hatred through horrible example, but the horror of his song is the comfort he takes in his "wisdom," a word the author does not use ironically in the title, for it is his protective strategy against those who hate him, just as the Virgin Violeta's "ugly caricatures" of Carlos are hers.

Porter had both stories in mind when she wrote "Love and Hate" in 1948 (later renaming it "The Necessary Enemy"), in which parents of the typical woman described in the essay tell her to "control" her feelings "in the black times of her hate," but "the real fright came when she discovered that they at times hated each other; it was like standing on the doorsill of a familiar room and seeing in a lightning flash that the floor was gone . . ." She feels guilty because she discovers "she is capable of hating her husband, whom she loves faithfully," and who, "while she is hating him . . . might very well be hating her as much or even more" (CE 182–183). The essay concludes:

> Hatred is natural in a sense that [romantic] love [earlier described as the "moral enemy"] . . . is not natural at all. Yet it did not come by hazard, it is the very imperfect expression of the need of the human imagination to create beauty and harmony out of chaos, no matter how mistaken its notions of these things may be, nor how clumsy its methods. It has conjured love out of the air, and seeks to preserve it by incantations; when she spoke a vow to love and honor her husband until death, she did a

very reckless thing, for it is not possible by an act of the will to fulfill
such an engagement. But it was the necessary act of faith . . . the statement of honorable intention to practice as well as she is able the noble,
acquired faculty of love, that very mysterious overtone to sex which is
the best thing in it. Her hatred is part of it, the necessary enemy and ally.
(CE 186)

The apparent point is that recognition of the existence of "natural" hatred enables one to escape the impossible demands of unnatural romantic love, which
denies hatred's existence, yet in the syntactical maze of the above passage with
the shifting meanings of "it," hatred, the natural necessary enemy, seems to
gain ascendancy over romantic love, the unnatural mortal enemy, just as "the
hard unwinking angry point of light" in "Pale Horse, Pale Rider" sustains Miranda after she escapes the fearful danger of love.

Hatred informed the curious circumstances surrounding the appearance in
1942 of "The Charmed Life," Porter's portrait of William Niven, who had died
four years before. Ten days after divorcing Pressly on April 9, 1938, she married Albert Erskine, business manager of the *Southern Review,* proving that
she, unlike Miranda of "Pale Horse, Pale Rider," could not live in total isolation. The marriage soon broke up, however, and when Erskine later wished to
remarry, he pressed for a quick divorce. After receiving a long letter from Mary
Doherty about the death of Moisés Sáenz, Porter, in reply, fondly remembered
Sáenz and inquired about a Mexican divorce. On March 24, 1942, the always
accommodating Doherty supplied her with all the details and planned a fiesta
in Porter's honor with fifty-three invited guests, adding that Salomón de la
Selva sent his love and that José Vasconcelos remembered the ballet classes
Porter had given in 1921. On April 1 Porter, embroidering on Doherty's letter,
told Monroe Wheeler she planned a Mexican divorce and had heard from old
friends in Mexico "now well placed in government" who seemed "very
friendly" toward her, leading her to speculate on employment there. A few
days later she again wrote Wheeler that she was not going to get a divorce in
Mexico but would still like to go there. Without informing Doherty of her
change of plans, she chose Reno for her divorce instead, staying there the required six weeks in May and June.

In Reno Porter wrote Donald Elder (June 14, 1942) that a young, tall, and
handsome FBI agent had "finally tracked" her down to inquire about "friends,"
who, as far as she knew, had "no political consciousness whatsoever." She realized that the "dirty business" had to be done, but wished they would seek out
those better informed (L 240). However, the FBI report, reproduced in Elinor
Langer's biography of Josephine Herbst, contradicts Porter's version, for in it
she stated that Herbst, then employed by the U.S. government, was a member
of the Communist party and, as a courier for the Soviet Union in the thirties,
had made contact with French Communist Louis Aragon. According to Langer, Porter's story was "a malignant reinterpretation of everything she knew

about Josie's history" since there was "absolutely no way" Herbst could have been traveling as a courier to and from Moscow. Langer wonders whether honest misapprehension, wartime flag-waving, or simple malice accounts for Porter's behavior (251–256). Joan Givner speculates that Porter, in economic difficulty and hounded by publishers with whom she had signed contracts, was in a "dangerously paranoid" state. Recognizing her vulnerability, the FBI agent may have "plied her with liquor and attention," thereby provoking her attack, which she would regret if she remembered it the next day.[9]

Why would Porter feel such venom against Herbst, one of her favorite correspondents over the years? While in Germany, she wrote Delafield Day (September 27, 1931) that she was looking forward to Herbst's visit to Europe, "for we want to be together. Now I am here I realize how very German Josie is. I always liked them, and her best qualities belong to the best of the life here." Her facile classification of Herbst as German would soon prove an ill omen. In Paris in the summer of 1935, Porter found Herbst an ideal guest, but seemed to prefer the fawning attention of Glenway Wescott and Monroe Wheeler, both of whom Herbst considered shallow. Politically Herbst had remained radical, but Porter wavered between her old radicalism and her pose as Southern aristocrat. Although she had written Herbst to praise *Pity Is Not Enough,* she agreed with Caroline Gordon (March 21, 1935) that it was too political, adding, "But you must remember what kind of people [Herbst] writes about, and oh, what hundreds of thousands of them there are in America; the second and third generation of European peasants, hungry, anxious, struggling, gaining a little and getting rapacious and dishonest." She described Herbst to Robert McAlmon (August 28, 1935) as "a seething mass of hatred," "justified by a muddled political notion, Communist theory coming in collision with an old-fashioned human sentimentality." Sounding a bit like Mr. Hatch of "Noon Wine," Porter proclaimed, "I love America, I am of the old stock, that is my country, and I do not need any of them to tell me what to think and feel about it." After visiting Herbst in Pennsylvania, she wrote Pressly (November 28, 1936), " . . . it's no good trying to deny it, [Herbst] has a very underbred nature. . . . one has the feeling of being with a servant girl who has managed by some freak of will and imagination, to lift herself to a plane above herself, but is not always able to stay there." Porter, bolstering her own self-image, had decided that her friend was below her, artistically and socially. Even so, her changing attitude, although it may have fueled her betrayal, does not fully explain the betrayal itself.

Porter must have been reduced to a serious state of panic in Reno in 1942. Perhaps the FBI agent intimidated her by reminding her that only four years before she had described herself as a "fellow traveler" to Archer Winsten of the *New York Post,* thereby encouraging her, in self-defense, to put the worst possible light on Herbst's activities in order to prove her own patriotism in time of war. Whatever the provocation, Porter projected guilt for her own activities onto Herbst, for she herself had planned to visit Moscow and served as a funnel for Pablo O'Higgins, who sent letters from Moscow to his friends in Mexico and the United States, mysteriously signing himself Paul Chapin. Porter informed Herbst (February 20, 1931) that she attended a conference in which Aragon participated. Porter's guilty projection was also compounded by her memory of 1921 when she betrayed Niven by acting as a courier of his letters. "The Charmed Life" appeared in *Vogue* one month before her interview with the FBI agent on May 23, 1942. On that day, she betrayed Herbst, as she had Niven twenty-one years before. When she felt threatened, she acted impulsively, irrationally, but later could not easily admit what she had done. She wrote Herbst (July 20, 1947), "When I read about the Communist hunt in Washington, I remember that you were one of the victims. You know I don't like the Communists, the American brand. But I hate to my bootsoles the Fascists who are doing so successfully just what Hitler did." This guilty statement almost contains an apology.

Porter's hatred of Germans during and after the war also reveals her irrationality. In "Pale Horse, Pale Rider" Miranda, in a delirious state, accuses Dr. Hildesheim of being "a Boche, a spy, a Hun, kill him, kill him before he kills you. . . . She woke howling" and "heard the foul words tumbling from her mouth" (309). Miranda's unconscious reflection of war hysteria uncannily anticipates Porter's own. In "The Leaning Tower" (1941), as in her seven published chapters of *Ship of Fools,* Porter reinterpreted her experiences in Germany in 1931 to reveal its incipient fascism just before the outbreak of war. As if hatred, the necessary enemy, had found its deserving object, she became antifascist with a vengeance, freely identifying those in her own country with fascist tendencies. She wrote Doherty (October 11, 1944) that in her first political speech she hoped "to do Dewey, the Republican party, Ham Fisher and our native fascists great damage." Two days later she again wrote Doherty that "any kind of anti-Fascist is not popular with the State Department or the after-war Commissions. So I'll stay at home, and continue to harry various officials asking them why they don't break off diplomatic relations with Franco-Spain and Argentina." Such comments are consistent with her old-time radicalism, but her description of Germans as the "curse of the human race," who go on "periodic binges of blood-drinking" and "as a people are all Nazis and all hopeless" (April 29 and May 5, 1945) perpetuates war-time hysteria. She made these remarks to Josephine Herbst—well aware of her friend's ethnic background—as if to justify her betrayal of her in 1942. Pressly also suffered her rejection in German terms. In the margin of a letter to her family in which she praised him in 1933, she noted in 1950 that "on his mother's side he was German! *half-German!* and behaved like one at last." On a note in which she had recorded Winold Reiss's admiration for the "beautiful brown people" of Mexico, she scribbled, "Typical German longing to be someone else." Such prejudice weakened her portrayal of Germans in *Ship of Fools.*

Besides "The Charmed Life," the other Mexican work Porter published in 1942 was a translation, with preface, of José Joaquín Fernández de Lizardi's early nineteenth-century novel, *The Itching Parrot (El Periquillo Sarmiento).* In fact, it was Eugene Pressly's translation begun in Mixcoac and finished in Paris. Porter wrote literary agent Raymond Everitt (July 27, 1933) that she thought so well of Pressly's work that she edited it "somewhat" and helped cut its length. However, when publishers showed no interest, she eventually gave her name to the work. (Ernestine Evans wrote Carleton Beals that she was scandalized by the deception.) Deriving information for her preface from Herbert I. Priestly's *The Mexican Nation: A History,* Porter emphasizes aspects of Lizardi's life as artist that particularly appealed to her. Lizardi was a "perpetual dissenter" (CE 360), writing "indignantly against all the causes of misery and the effects of injustice in this maddening world," unafraid "to suffer a long, miserable existence for the sake of his beliefs" (CE 367). In his lifetime, "there was never to be [a government] he could get along with, or accept altogether" (CE 369). He was the artist doing battle with a world he rightly could not trust. His death from tuberculosis, from which Porter herself had suffered, cemented her identity with him.

Mary Doherty did not see Porter in Mexico in 1942. Instead she decided to seek employment in the United States, prompting Porter to write her (November 2, 1943) that her departure broke the last tie with Mexico—"no reason at all I know of for going back there." She then gave her frank opinion of several acquaintances from the old days, exercising the same principle of rejection she used against those identified as German. She was annoyed that Xavier Guerrero had informed Doherty instead of her that she had borrowed one hundred dollars from him in 1922, but promised to pay it back. The subject of borrowing money led her to J. H. Retinger, "my old enemy and parasite." She borrowed four hundred dollars from "the American Charge d'Affaires" (Summerlin) for him (when he was in the Laredo jail), "which got me into very serious trouble" (presumably when Summerlin found out why she had borrowed it). In 1923, "he simply grabbed with both hands as my money was paid me," managing to get more than half of the fifteen hundred dollars (payment for her *Outline* work), but never paying it back as promised. Then she demolished him with her favorite accusation, "I realize now that Retinger is a Fascist, he told me so himself one day, sitting on one of those benches in the Alameda in the sunshine, admired Mussolini . . . and taught Morones his politics, modelled on Mussolini's. But I was too ignorant to understand." If she had known that Retinger was then adviser to Churchill on Polish matters, it would not have mattered: "The whole Polish government in exile is worthless, that rotten, anglophile aristocracy who has no intention towards the people of Poland but to keep them serfs as they have been. And the Fascist set in England will help them." She concluded, "I was indulgent towards his rottenness as a man, a real cad if ever I knew one, but the thing that made me hate him was his unscrupulousness in politics. . . . Somehow political rottenness for me is the basest rottenness there is. Any kind of personal or other immorality smells respectable beside it. Retinger stinks, always did, always will." (Her hatred of him had found literary expression a year before in her portrait of Tadeusz

Mey in "The Leaning Tower.") "Well, let it go," she wrote, "Goodbye, Mexico. Goodbye, Sprat[ling], Paca [Toor], The And[erson—Sherwood's ex-wife], Diego, Ret, Xav. et al. Good bye now, and a thumb at my nose for the lot of you." Her rejection was all-encompassing.

Then she began again,

> Hello Mary . . . . . Here you are, the lone survivor as friend of that incredible time and place. I never thought I would heave a sigh for the good old days, for I remember them as mostly hell, but still, I will say, must say, they had something, mysterious, indefinable, that made them better than the present, in that country and in a good many others. They had hope . . . . . I think that must have been it. Even the young don't have any hope now, it seems. Least of all the young. We were just so certain there was something worth fighting for and things were going to get much better almost at once. . . . Mexico was new to us, and beautiful, the very place to be at that moment, we believed in [it] a great deal—though I do remember well that my childlike faith in the Revolution was well over in about six months. After that it was merely a matter of saving the pieces. Yet I think politically Mexico has done rather better than this country, let's say. . . . But then. Well, that was hope, the feeling that kept us going like mad and making all our odd mistakes.

Porter's early writing in Mexico reveals that her faith and hope were never childlike, but she tried to keep their flickering flames alive up until the deportation crisis, six months after her arrival. When faith and hope totally failed, she expressed the loss in her fiction.

Surprisingly, less than two months after writing Doherty, Porter wrote Herbst (December 28) that she was "to be sent to Mexico on a kind of errand" by the U.S. government from March to June of 1944, but didn't understand the secrecy about the plan since she was to talk to students about writing. She had also written to Morton Zabel (December 19), wondering whether he had anything to do with it. Nothing came of it or of the prospect, mentioned to Mary Doherty on November 2, of being sent on a commission to "one of the South American countries." Her tenuous plans betray an urge to escape from herself once more. A note of 1943 reads,

> I make plans and decisions in my firm, sensible rational states of mind, and then in my irrational states I find myself to my horror trapped in my own decisions, and helpless in a situation I have in cold blood created for myself. Luckily, my rational states are more lasting than the other, and I am always glad to come out of my fits of renunciation or desire for flight and find myself safely anchored and at home with myself and my life and my work.

She probably meant that she made irrational decisions in what she thought was a rational state at the time and was later horrified by the consequences. Whether she could always distinguish one state from the other is a question. Each time Porter left Mexico, she resolved never to return. Tempted once more to return, she found her better judgment overcome by some irrational hope.

By the mid-forties Porter had gained celebrity status, working as a script-writer in Hollywood, attending writers' conferences, lecturing, and teaching in universities. Her essays now appeared in better-paying popular magazines such as *Mademoiselle, Vogue,* and *Flair* and her book reviews in the prestigious *New York Times Book Review.* She continued to jettison old friends. She called Mary Doherty a nuisance even though she had encouraged her to share the Georgetown house she was renting in 1944 just as she had invited her to live in Mixcoac in 1931 for the same economic reason. She wrote in the margin of a letter from Ernestine Evans, "EE has persisted in calling me by this detestable name ([Kath' Anne] for 30 years at least, and still does not know why our friendship has not flourished. I really have stopped liking her on this account. It is only one symptom of her almost complete insensibility to my feelings on this or many other subjects." About Evans's former husband, Kenneth Durant, she wrote in 1953, "I grew to dislike and distrust Kenneth Durant thoroughly after learning his really crooked mind, yet this letter [of March 6, 1936] shows a kind of after-glow of a pleasant old friendship." Porter replaced old friends with new ones. In the thirties she had begun what became a long-lasting friendship with Glenway Wescott and Monroe Wheeler, whose adulation in-flated her ego.[10] Her letters to them have the air of an official record, without the intimacy and spontaneity of her earlier letters to her women friends.

"St. Augustine and the Bullfight"

Capitalizing on her access to wide readership, Porter produced for *Mademoiselle* in 1955 "St. Augustine and the Bullfight," a Mexican work based on her experiences of the early twenties. Classifying it as autobiography, she later included it in her *Collected Essays* rather than in her *Collected Stories,* where it more properly belongs.

In the work Porter writes of falling in with "a most lordly gang of fashion-able international hoodlums," who "stalked pleasure as if it were big game" (CE 94–95), among them, according to her notes, a Spanish marquess who was a champion jai alai player and a Spanish duke "who imported French ladies for great public occasions such as the presidential inauguration." One of the hoodlums introduced her to "Shelley," a wealthy member of the poet's fam-ily, a widower of three years, and "mad about horses," who took her to the-aters, the fronton, street fairs, good restaurants, and strolled with her in the Alameda. Although she claims that their relation was "superficial," it was by her own report time-consuming. She also claims that after he persuaded her against her will to attend a bullfight that revealed to her unacceptable truths about herself, their friendship faded, but thereafter she became an impassioned spectator of over a hundred bullfights, even sitting in cafes with aficionados and going at two o'clock in the morning to see bulls brought into the city.

Porter did indeed know the man she calls Shelley. John Shelley, according to his grandson Jaime, first worked for the British Aguila oil company and later raised thoroughbred horses. He was probably a friend of Colonel Harvey Miller, for in 1923 U.S. Military Intelligence reported that he had been "of considerable assistance to the Government" (MID 2447–255). Undoubtedly, Porter accompanied him to a bullfight, for she describes his friend Hattie Welton, "a fine buxom figure of a woman, a highly colored blonde with a sweet, childish face," whose horsemanship is so expert that "'She makes the bullfight seem like an anticlimax,' said Shelley tenderly" (CE 97). Welton, whom Porter calls Weston in her text, was "formerly a circus performer, [who] now owns a riding school and stables in Mexico City, and is a unique personality in the foreign colony." So Leone Moats introduces her in *Thunder in Their Veins,* repeating the many stories Hattie told of her adventures during the revolution. Since her horses were her livelihood, she had to strive mightily to prevent their requisition from whatever military leader happened to be in the neighborhood at the time, from Zapata's brother, Eufemio, to Obregón himself.[11] Undoubtedly, Shelley informed Porter of Hattie's fabulous adventures. However, the identity of Shelley and Welton does not guarantee the autobiographical authenticity of "St. Augustine and the Bullfight."

In the work Porter gives meaning, not to the adventures of Hattie Welton, but supposedly to her own. As noted earlier, she distinguishes between adventure, "something you seek for pleasure . . . for the illusion of being more alive than ordinarily," and experience, "what really happens to you in the long run; the truth that finally overtakes you" (CE 92). She enjoyed, she tells us, the adventure of climbing a cliff in Colorado, but was overtaken by "muscle poisoning" that put her in bed for nine days, presumably forcing her to question why she had climbed the cliff in the first place. The lesson is that adventure, undertaken as a pleasant escape from reality, ultimately ends in the hangover after the binge, but if art can turn adventure into experience by extracting meaning from it, its product—in this case, "St. Augustine and the Bullfight"— is adequate compensation for the pain of self-discovery it describes.

Porter anticipates the meaning of the bullfight through another incident out of her more distant past. In her youth she attempted to maintain her "purity" by refusing to kill what she ate even though she had an incurable "taste for flesh." When her father forced her to overcome the "cowardice" of her moral inconsistency, she discovered that killing animals did not alter her taste, even though she was still offended by "all forms of cruelty." What she witnesses at the bullfight forces her to confront the "contradictions and paradoxes" of her human nature and begins a process that ends in the loss of the illusion of purity. When she hides her eyes at the sight of a gored horse trampling its own intestines, Shelley, her surrogate father, holding her hands in her lap, forces her to look: "Don't you dare come here and do this! You must face it!" (CE 99). So she watches "under the power" of her own "weakness": "When the time came to kill the splendid black and white bull, I who pitied him when he first came into the ring stood straining on tiptoe to see everything, yet almost blinded with excitement, and crying out when the crowd roared, and kissing Shelley on the cheekbone when he shook my elbow and shouted in the voice of one justified: 'Didn't I tell you? Didn't I?'" (CE 101). Again confronted with "her taste for blood," she hates Shelley for what he has revealed to her about herself, but becomes "drunk" on bullfights in a "wild dream" from which she does not wish to be awakened; she still clings to a view of herself "as a unique case, as a humane, blood-avoiding civilized being, somehow a fallen angel perhaps?" (CE 100). But this self-delusion does not last. When she reads in Augustine's *Confessions* how Alypius, after being forced to witness a gladiatorial combat he had previously condemned as "cruel and criminal," became "more bloodthirsty than any," she has to face the fact that she was not unique, that "at heart" she "was a killer like any other," a realization Laura in "Flowering Judas" comprehends only in a dream.

Porter's autobiographical "essay" is not just about how adventure turns into experience, but about how the artist transforms experience into art. And therein lies another paradox. Whereas "Literary art, at least, is the business of setting human events to rights and giving them meanings the artist feels they should have," she intends to write "notes" "about my life, here and now, and so far as I am able without one touch of fiction, and I hope to keep it as shapeless and unforeseen as the events of life itself" (CE 94). But she fails to keep this work "shapeless," an exercise of art in itself, since she carefully prepares the reader for the bullfight through the story of her muscle-poisoning in Colorado and of her failure to become a vegetarian. Throughout the work she draws our attention to fiction by denying its existence. Thus, she tells us, Shelley's "whole appearance was so remarkably like the typical horsy, landed-gentry sort of Englishman one meets in books" that "if this were fiction I should feel obliged to change his looks altogether, thus falling into one stereotype to avoid falling into another" (CE 96)—a clever way of persuading the reader to accept the stereotype as authentic. (If she wanted to individualize Shelley, she could have mentioned, as her 1955 notes do, that two of his children died of diphtheria and his wife of grief shortly thereafter, but that information would have shifted our attention from her to him.) Later, after telling us that the first bull was "as enormous and brave and handsome as any I saw afterward," she adds parenthetically, "This is not a short story, so I don't have to maintain any suspense" (CE 99), but then saves her reaction to the killing of that "beautiful monster" for the very end of her story. She protests too much over the nonfictional nature of her work.

The reader may wonder about truth when Porter, "looking back nearly thirty-five years on [her] earliest days in Mexico" (1920), insists that this work "will be notes on a fateful thing that happened to me when I was young and did not know much about the world or about myself" (CE 94). But she was then thirty years old and had expressed the weight of those years in her *El Heraldo* review of George's novel. Either she is lying about her age or, like Laura in "Flowering Judas," attempts to cling, at whatever age, to her childlike "purity," later claiming that it was Laura's model, Mary Doherty, who didn't know what was happening to her.

Porter also gets her dates wrong when she claims that the bullfight she witnessed "was the first bullfight of that season; Covadonga Day; April" (CE 96). But the first day of the regular season is in November and Covadonga Day, commemorating the first victory of Christians over Moors, is in September. She may have seen a bullfight in November 1920, but Rodolfo Gaona, one of the bullfighters mentioned in her work, didn't return to Mexico until mid-September 1921,[12] a few weeks after Porter had left the country. She later told Hank Lopez that she met Shelley in 1922 (87), but she wasn't in Mexico in the fall of that year. Moreover, if she had attended bullfights in Mexico City every Sunday both during the regular season, November through March, *and* during the rest of the year when novices performed, she could have witnessed in 1920–1921 only about forty bullfights, not the hundred she claims.

Failure of memory after thirty-five years may account for the confusion of dates, but Porter herself encourages us to question the authenticity of her autobiography when she gives another definition of adventure as "an afterthought, something that happens in the memory with imaginative trimmings if not downright lying, so that one should suppress it entirely, or go the whole way and make honest fiction of it" (CE 93). If we apply this statement to her memories of Mexico in the sixties, we would conclude that she was guilty of downright lying or, at best, recreating adventures in Mexico while suppressing the truth about their eventual outcome. Augustine's *Confessions* inspired her to create an adventure "that happens in the memory with imaginative trimmings." Her work consists of fictional variations, some based on autobiography, that parallel Augustine's theme of Alypius, the crowning and deceptive fiction of all being her insistence that her product is pure autobiography. Even her reaction to the killing of the bull may be fictional since its possible source is *Life in Mexico* by Fanny Calderon de la Barca, who finds "the wounding and tormenting of the bull . . . sickening," but confesses that "though at first I covered my eyes and could not look, little by little I grew so much interested in the scene, that I could not take my eyes off it . . ."[13] Porter had marked this passage in her copy of the book.

Hardly the first writer to set traps for the reader over the distinction between autobiography and fiction, Porter immediately follows her statement about downright lying with a long explanation of how she writes fiction:

> My own habit of writing fiction has provided a wholesome exercise to my natural tendency to try to wangle the sprawling mess of our existence in this bloody world into some kind of shape: almost any shape will do, just so it is recognizably made with human hands, one small proof the more of the validity and reality of the human imagination. . . . Perhaps my soul will be saved after all in spite of myself because now and then I take some unmanageable, indigestible fact and turn it into fiction; cause things to happen with some kind of logic—my own, of course—and everything ends as I think it should end. . . . Otherwise, and except for this safety device, I should be the greatest liar unhung. . . . What is Truth? I often ask myself. Who knows. (CE 93)

This passage undercuts Porter's statement that reading Augustine enabled her to see "in a flash of light" what the bullfight event "really meant" (CE 94), for meaning resides not in reality, but in the art that transforms it. For one who constantly lied about her life, autobiography was always fiction in which everything ended as she thought it should. Fiction was her defense against accusations of lying because its lies create order out of "unmanageable" events in the chaos of "this bloody world." What passes as truth, then, is determined by the success of the work of art. Wallace Stevens might have admired her rage for order.

The ordering power of the imagination explains Porter's inclusion of Hattie Weston in "St. Augustine and the Bullfight." She agrees with Shelley that Hattie "makes the bullfight seem like an anticlimax": "And there she went, the most elegant woman in the saddle I have ever seen, graceful and composed in her perfect style, with her wonderful, lightly dancing, learned horse, black and glossy as shoe polish, perfectly under control—no, not under control at all, you might have thought, but just dancing and showing off his paces by himself for his own pleasure" (CE 97). Weston's horse is a figure for Porter's dancing prose. "You might have thought" she wasn't controlling it, apparently keeping it "shapeless and unforeseen as the events of life itself," but it is "perfectly under control."

Porter devotes a whole paragraph to Hattie but makes scant mention of Rodolfo Gaona and Ignacio Sánchez Mejías, who "each killed a bull that day" (CE 96), whereas Hemingway in *Death in the Afternoon,* which may have prompted Porter to write her own bullfight story, celebrates both bullfighters in his text and photographs.[14] He used the bullfighter as his figure of imaginative control, but perhaps neither Gaona nor Sánchez Mejías had lived such an adventurous life outside the bullring as Hattie Welton.

Pleased by her friends' reception of "St. Augustine," Porter often read from it in lecture engagements. Glenway Wescott praised it as a "new art form,"[15] but Porter placed it under the "Personal" section of her essays, confirming it as an autobiography or deceptively making its place there a fiction. Exploring the intricate interplay between adventure-experience and reality-imagination, it deserves more attention than it has received. As autobiography, it reveals associations Porter never recorded in her early notes, but it tells us more about how she transformed reality than about reality itself. It also serves as metaphor of the way her Mexican adventures, enthusiastically begun but ending in disillusion, were transformed later into the compensating form of art. However, in it Porter confesses her guilt as "fellow-sinner" with Alypius, who, like her, had run with "a gang of clever, wellborn young hoodlums" (CE 101), but his bloodthirstiness concerns the death of men, while hers concerns the death of animals. It would have been much harder for her to confess her guilt over the death of Sidronio Méndez. She did it explicitly in one fiction fragment and obliquely in "Flowering Judas" through Laura's guilt over the death of Eugenio. Running with various gangs of hoodlums in the "bloody world" of Mexico, Porter participated in many adventures. Some she suppressed while others she wangled into the shape of art.

7. *Ship of Fools*

Structure and Content

In 1962 Porter published the story she had first contemplated in 1931 and labored over in the forties. After trying to write a novel for forty years, beginning with *Thieves' Market* in the early twenties, she at last succeeded in getting what she called her albatross off her neck. The best-seller success of *Ship of Fools* brought her the deserved fame and economic security she always dreamed of, but its literary reputation, disputed from the first, fell below that of her brilliant shorter works. Her comment to Glenway Wescott (September 13, 1940)—"Truth is, I am a writer of short stories, and when this novel got simply too much for me, I lightly jumped the track and did something I can do, and a good thing"—reinforces the opinion that the novel was the mediocre work of a writer of short fiction.[1]

Structurally, the novel, like "Hacienda," depicts virtual strangers of several nationalities, gathered in one place. But "Hacienda" has one clear focal incident, the tragedy of Rosalita and Justino, in response to which the main characters reveal themselves and the world of the hacienda. The plight of the peons in general corresponds to that of the Spanish steerage passengers in *Ship of Fools,* but the novel, in its long progress, contains several other focusing incidents—for example, the rescue of the bulldog Bébé and the ostracism of Freytag—but with each new incident character responses become repetitious and predictable. The culminating incident, the fiesta arranged by the Zarzuela dancers, is intended to expose the passengers in all their evil, but they have already suffered from overexposure by that time. One critic, noting Porter's talent at caricature, finds that Genaro and Kennerly of "Hacienda" would not be out of place in *Ship of Fools.*[2] Certainly they are fools, but the brilliance of their caricatures lies partly in the economy of presentation. If subjected to repeat performances aboard ship, they would soon lose their effectiveness. Perhaps Porter's frequent escapes from and returns to the novel over the years reflected her oscillating attraction to and rejection of friends. No wonder short stories with their early closures suited her temperament.

Before turning, then, to the autobiographical character of Jenny Brown, whose experiences in Mexico with David Scott are based on Porter's experiences with Eugene Pressly in 1931, this chapter first explores the novel's overall structure and thematic concerns as well as Porter's partially successful attempts at caricature, developed in Mexico.

Whereas Porter discovered evildoers and the political context in which they operated at the Hacienda Tetlapayac, she had to create them in *Ship of Fools* to illustrate her sense of evil, later reinforced by her views of German fascism, since her long letter to Caroline Gordon did not mention evildoers aboard the *Werra,* only the Cuban expulsion of the Spanish passengers whom the Germans treated well.[3] Grappling head-on with the meaning of evil in the forties Porter wrote Josephine Herbst (January 23, 1946) that her novel, "is about the constant endless collusion about good and evil; I believe that human beings are capable of total evil, but no one has ever been totally good, and this gives the edge to evil." She also wrote Andrew Lytle (July 14, 1947):

> We have a little easy habit of blaming everything on our times. . . . We have no evils now that were not prepared for [in the past], and our evils are no greater except in scope—in mere volume, and man has preponderance of evil because he loves evil and cannot live without it. . . . And it is in *him,* it is no power outside himself. But there are periods when balancing the scales between good and evil is more artful, more just, the contest is more even. But it never lasts for long, the scales crash on the side of darkness inevitably for a time. Did you ever hear of the world falling into a state of Good? If evil is the true God, it is because man prefers it so; he has only to choose. And he does choose. But he will not accept the responsibility of his choice. . . . he simply cannot, cannot— Oh why not? this is to me the riddle of the universe—face his own nature.

In this statement Porter, in her attempt to account for the horrors of World War II, wavered between concepts of freedom of will and natural depravity. She did not explain why man would bother to admit his evil nature if he loves, needs, and prefers it. Instead she restated the riddle through various characters in her novel. For instance, Frau Schmidt "had always believed so deeply that human beings wished only to be quiet and happy . . . but there was a spirit of evil in them that could not let each other be in peace" (SF 152). Frau Hutten is mouthpiece for the novel's main idea:

> I do know full well there are many evil people in this world, many more evil than good ones . . . evil by nature, by choice, by deepest inclination, evil all through; we encourage these monsters by being charitable to them. . . . Too indifferent to be bothered so long as they do not harm *us.* . . . we do evil in letting them do evil without punishment. They

think we are cowards and they are right. At least we are dupes and we
deserve what we get from them. (SF 294–295)

Here the world is divided into the totally evil and the potentially good, a minority who commit evil by acquiescing to the active evil of the majority.

Porter's conclusions about human nature in the abstract were partly based
on her own personal experiences. Her memory of her father's hatred of his
children, communicated to her sister Mary Alice at the time of his death in
1942, found expression in "The Necessary Enemy" in 1947. Her essay, however, did not include what she confided to Andrew Lytle that same year: "That
men and women don't really like each other is a fact that only a fool could
escape noticing in everyday life." Karen Horney explains that distrust between
the sexes springs from "our instinct for self-preservation," for "we all have a
natural fear of losing ourselves in another person" (108)—a fear of engulfment, which Porter expressed in her essay on Willa Cather. It also springs
from "the glitter of sexual overestimation": "We take the magnitude of such
overvaluation for the measure of our love, while in reality it merely expresses
the magnitude of our expectations" (109)—a point Porter makes in "Letters to
a Nephew." But on a deeper level, distrust may spring in some cases from
a woman's fixation on the father, resulting in "a deep-seated desire for revenge . . . to get the better of the man, to cast him aside, to reject him just as
she herself once felt cast aside and rejected" (206–207). Horney's observation
sheds light on the source of Porter's hatred. Her letters to her father are filled
with proclamations of her talent and announcements of her literary successes,
evidence of her need to prove herself to him and to reprove him for his rejection of her. And as Joan Givner points out, regardless of her own age, Porter
formed short-lived relationships with men in their thirties—her father's age
during her childhood years—many of whom resembled him physically (51).

Porter dealt with hatred between the sexes in the context of an Edenic ideal.
Beginning with "Xochimilco," she imagined human beings living in harmony
with nature and each other. In this state, male and female, like innocent
brother and sister, are happy reflections or doubles of each other, but the illusion does not hold. In "The Grave," for example, Miranda and Paul in their
unisexual outfits appear innocent, but after discovering the pregnant rabbit,
they guiltily keep their knowledge secret. In "Holiday" the narrator, after her
friend's description of the Müllers' farm, asks, "Just where is this paradise?"
When she enters it, she sees in every face of the Müllers' extended family "the
pale, tilted eyes, on every head that taffy-colored hair, as though they might be
brothers and sisters, though Annetje's husband and still another daughter's
husband had gone by after greeting me" (411–412). Later one of the daughters
attends the Turnverein "with her suitor, who resembled her brothers enough
to be her brother, though I think nobody ever noticed this except myself . . ."
(421). The narrator's view is exceptional because it is informed by her dream

of paradise, which fades with her growing awareness of Ottilie. In "Pale Horse, Pale Rider" Miranda and her unfallen Adam, both the same age and from the same state, seem at first like twins, but once they speak of love, he dies from the suggestion.

In *Ship of Fools* the newly married Mexican couple, shunning all association with other passengers, seem to have, as Wilhelm Freytag puts it, the look of "Eden just after the Fall. That little interval between the Fall and the driving out by that jealous vengeful old God" (SF 92). David Scott, projecting the ideal marriage, "the kind he believed he wanted for himself," sees them as "charmed visitors from another planet. They did not dance or put on paper hats or drink or play cards or grin at other people. They did not even talk much to each other; but they were paired, that was clear" (SF 126). The pair seem exceptions to the ship's company of fools, but their ideal state is an illusion created by Freytag and Scott and by themselves as their insipid conversation reveals: "'Die young? We'll never die. We're going to live together until the end of the world!' They laughed together for happiness, without a trace of irony . . ." (SF 440). However, the trace of irony in the narrator's voice reveals them as self-deceived. In contrast, Jenny and David, who "in the first days of their love had hoped to be the ideal image of each other" (SF 44), fail in their attempt at Edenic illusion. On one occasion, they are able to recreate their early feelings as Jenny responds in the correct mythic terminology: "David, darling, when you're like this, I could creep back inside and be your rib again!" (SF 488). Her response is the perfect expression of total union or fusion, but one David earlier realized was "not long enough or often enough for any continuous illusion" (SF 54). (Jenny's response is also escapist, as is that of Freytag's wife, who "woke screaming in nightmares and clung to him pressing her face under his arm as if she were trying to hide inside him" [SF 140]. In both cases the female conceives of the male as a protective mother figure into whose womb she wants to return, as Porter seems to have conceived Eugene Pressly for a time.)

Unwilling to give up the illusion of perfect union, Jenny and David resort to sex to attain it. After arguing about their European destination, they "made love fiercely half the night as if in a revengeful rage against whatever it was that kept them apart" (SF 28), but their desperate attempt at union leads only to wider separation. David, viewing himself and Jenny as complementary pieces that should fit together, can't understand why she "refused to become that part of him which was missing, which would have made him whole" (SF 221), but he egotistically defines her as a projection of his felt needs rather than an autonomous being. At the end of the novel he is dimly aware of the problem. Realizing that the person "he thought he had once known . . . had vanished," he "watched her turn into someone else, someone he did not know, maybe would never know, yet this new creature before him was certainly one he had created for himself, as he had created the other, out of stray stuffs of his own desire" (SF 488). Jenny will always be unknowable to him since subjective desire precludes the possibility of knowledge.

Instead of being "the ideal image of the other," the couple "were both ashamed of the evil natures they exposed in each other" (SF 44). Whether or not they view their egotism as evil, their sexuality is. As David remembers his sexual activity in a Mexican mining town, "slowly there poured through all his veins again that deep qualm of loathing and intolerable sexual fury, a poisonous mingling of sickness and deathlike pleasure: it ebbed and left him as it always had before, merely a little sick." Calling his reaction a "Methodist hangover," Jenny hopes he doesn't make himself "sick" on her (SF 281). Porter seems to approve of Jenny's liberation although she had assigned her own Methodist background to David and, as already noted, in letters and stories equated marriage, love, or sex with illness from which she and her characters hoped to recover.

The Spanish troupe conveys the novel's overwhelming sense of evil, sexual and otherwise. They represent the underside of the other passengers' human nature, unadorned by any saving grace. Ric and Rac, the twin offspring of Manolo and Lola, are a distillation of evil. A ship's officer considers them "no worse then their elders," since they illustrate the "dogma of Original Sin" (SF 199), but they are remarkable because of their age and the single-minded symbolic function Porter makes them serve. For example,

> Ric and Rac, outside the traffic of dancers, were doing a dance of their own. Facing each other, as always teeth to teeth, their toes almost touching, they clasped hands, and leaning backwards from each other at the farthest possible stretch, they whirled round and round like planets fiercely, the tips of their toes clattering delicately as castanets. The game was to see which one would be exhausted first, relax his hold and get a good rolling fall. Even better, one would let go of the other, at the same instant throwing himself forward, keeping balance while the other got his head bumped. In fact, however, such triumphs were largely theoretical, since they were evenly balanced in body and soul. . . . So they turned on their axis, shoulders far out, chins tucked in, eyes staring into eyes as balefully as two infant Gorgons intent on turning each other to stone. Neither gave way, but whirled furiously, digging their claws in each other's wrists, stamping carefully on each other's toes, working up to that moment when by perfect unspoken consent they would break and fly apart and see which one got the fall . . . (SF 308)

The twins enact the dance of life all couples must endure while they remain partners. Their mutual infliction of pain persists until the climactic flying apart. Although they will unite to separate again, they remind us that Jenny and David as well as Amparo and Pepe intend to separate for good, and their separation will "leave dents in each other," as Jenny puts it, since she will "be carrying David like a petrified fetus for the rest of [her] life" (SF 169). The simile reverses her former desire to creep into David and become his rib. Petrifaction is a defense against fusion. Like the "two infant Gorgons intent on turning each other to stone" and Miranda in "Pale Horse, Pale Rider," who receives and returns the hostile stony stares of others, Jenny has effectively killed David, although he will remain an unhappy reminder of her former desire for fusion.

The dance of Ric and Rac can be juxtaposed against the macabre dance of death Jenny witnessed on the road to Taxco, based on Porter's memory of 1930:

> As the bus rolled by, Jenny saw a man and a woman . . . locked in a death battle. They swayed and staggered together in a strange embrace, as if they supported each other; but in the man's raised hand was a long knife, and the woman's breast and stomach were pierced. The blood ran down her body and over her thighs, her skirts were sticking to her legs with her own blood. She was beating him on the head with a jagged stone, and his features were veiled in rivulets of blood. They were silent, and their faces had taken on a saintlike patience in suffering, abstract, purified of rage and hatred in their one holy dedicated purpose to kill each other. Their flesh swayed together and clung, their left arms were wound about each other's body as if in love. (SF 144)

In the murderous dance and the choreographed murder, the sexual opponents are mirror images of each other.

Throughout the novel Porter doggedly insists on the twinship of Ric and Rac, making it the heart of her statement about human sexual relations. We learn that "their fierce little faces" are "exactly alike except for the mysterious stigmata of sex" (SF 112). They "were of one mind and spirit, and lived twined together in a state of intense undeclared war with . . . the whole world" (SF 71). The twinning, twining image is repeated when, after a beating by their parents, they "crawled into the upper berth looking for safety; they lay there half naked, entangled like some afflicted, misbegotten little monster in a cave . . ." (SF 360). Earlier they fall into a lifeboat, "all tangled up giggling in the darkness": "Locked in what seemed to be a death grapple, they rolled to the bottom of the boat and fought furiously, knees in ribs, claws in hair; the pain they inflicted on each other had a strong undertow of pleasure. Little by little they fell quiet and then began to giggle again" until they are discovered by a ship's officer whom they "turn to stone" at sight of their unspecified activity (SF 195–196), proving they are Gorgons indeed. Aping adults, they demonstrate the hostile, bestial, and incestuous character of human sexuality as Porter sees it.

The adult members of the Zarzuela troupe serve the same sexual purpose.

The hermaphroditic body type of male and female makes their sexes almost indistinguishable. All the men are "wasp-waisted" and "entirely too graceful" (SF 18) while all the women have "round small hips" (SF 47). Amparo and Pepe stroll the deck, "their narrow, highly specialized behinds swaying gracefully" (SF 166). Most significant is their entrance into the ballroom at the end of the novel: "The Spanish company led the way, paired off and swung into step as their feet touched the deck, stepping out rhythmically pair by pair, matched like slender porcelain figurines alike in their practiced grace, serpent-litheness, thin-boned, smooth narrow heads, fine feet and hands. They seemed to be a beautiful, evil-tempered family of brothers and sisters, their hard eyes and bitter mouths denying their blithe motions" (SF 432). Sharply contrasted with the innocent pairs of brothers and sisters in the Eden imagined in "Holiday," these pairs are fallen children of the serpent. When Pepe and Amparo make love, their "supple dancer's legs writhed together for a moment like a nest of snakes" (SF 224), recalling the monster formed by the entangled bodies of Ric and Rac.

Porter's view of the human condition is close to that of Edgar Allan Poe, whom Miranda's father in "Old Mortality" calls "our greatest living poet" (178), quoting the ninth stanza of "For Annie." He might more fittingly have quoted the first: "Thank heaven! the crisis—/ The danger is past, / And the lingering illness / Is over at last—/ And the fever called 'Living' / Is over at last—/ Is conquered at last." His life as disease metaphor inspired Gabriel's poem about Amy, "who suffered life" but now "forgets / The griefs of old mortality" (181). Poe's preoccupation with incest also sheds light on Porter's use of it in *Ship of Fools*. Allen Tate finds the key to Poe's romantic idealism in the thesis of "Eureka": "In the original unity of the first thing lies the secondary cause of all things, with the germ of their inevitable destruction." The pattern extends to Poe's fiction in which his characters attempt to return to their original unity. The very birth of Roderick Usher and his sister "had violated their unity of being. They must achieve mutual identity in mutual destruction."[4] Because they cannot reenter Eden as one harmonious pair, they attempt to possess and consume each other. In his study of Poe, D. H. Lawrence concludes that man's trouble is his insistence on oneness: "It is easy to see why man kills the thing he loves. To *know* a living thing is to kill it. . . . For this reason, the desirous consciousness, the *SPIRIT*, is a vampire," for "to try to know any living being is to try to suck the life out of that being."[5] Lawrence slightly shifts the metaphor with the idea that too much loving is like too much eating, but cannibalism is part of the vampire legend of man's fear that ghosts or demons would suck his blood or eat his flesh.

Both metaphors apply to Porter's work. She wrote Tennessee Williams (January 25, 1958) in reference to *Suddenly Last Summer*, "That we eat and drink each other, as do all the other creatures, has been no news to me, any more than to you, for a great while. (Did you ever read 'Flowering Judas'?)" In "Marriage Is Belonging" (1951), Porter scorns "that ecstatic reciprocal cannibalism which goes popularly under the name, and which is indeed commonly one of the earliest biological symptoms (Boy Eats Girl and vice versa) . . ." (CE 188). The "art of belonging" should not mean "surrendering gracefully . . . as much of your living self as you can spare without incurring total extinction . . ." (CE 187). Porter is much better at explaining what love is not than what it is. In *Ship of Fools* David discovers he can't paint while Jenny is painting, as if she had temporarily managed to draw all his talent out of him, a talent they mutually possess but cannot share. Lizzi Spökenkieker graphically becomes a vampire as "her thin wide mouth gaped alarmingly and her sharp teeth gleamed" and "now set grimly in [Rieber's] jowl, just under his jawbone" (SF 284). Horney may best explain the source of Lizzi's behavior: when a woman who as a little girl "was badly hurt by her father will transform her innate instinctual wish to receive from the man into a vindictive one of taking him by force," causing her "to harm the male, to exploit him, to suck him dry. She has become a vampire" (111).

In *Ship of Fools* all attempts at love fail, the characters countering hatred with hatred in fear of being devoured by the other, then separating and withdrawing into themselves and viewing those with whom they attempted intimacy as strangers. Even at the very beginning of the novel, we learn that each passenger chooses "to maintain his pride and separateness within himself" (SF 11). Persons "obviously related in whatever way sat mute as if with strangers" (SF 29). Young Hans Baumgartner yearns "for kindness, hoping his beautiful good mother would come back soon. She vanished in this frowning scolding stranger, who blazed out at him when he least expected it, struck him on the hands, threatened him, seemed to hate him" (SF 33). Freytag defines his fellow passengers' impossible choice: either "gnawing curiosity . . . as if you were being eaten alive by fishes" or "total rejection" (SF 133). Since there is no happy middle ground, total rejection is preferable to being cannibalized. At the end of the novel, Jenny, feeling "far from home, in a strange, strange land," laments, "Everybody looks tired. It's just the same as we were in Veracruz, or in Havana. We all remember we're strangers and don't like each other" (SF 400–401). The novel has come full circle, ending as it began. However, its conclusion does not have the force of Mr. Thompson's complaint about Mr. Hatch: "It doesn't pay to be friendly with strangers from another part of the country. They're always up to something, or they'd stay at home where they belong" (250).

Characters and Caricatures

The difference between the masterful "Noon Wine" and *Ship of Fools* does not lie in the themes they share, but in Porter's ability to realize them dramatically through her characters. The novel's satiric title indicates that once more she intended to use caricature as she defined it in her review of the work of Miguel Covarrubias in 1925. But some critics used the term pejoratively in their discussion of *Ship of Fools;* one critic called her portrait of Julius Löwenthal a "caricature of Jewish vulgarity,"[6] implying that Porter had created an anti-Semitic stereotype. She wanted to explore mutual hatred between Jew and (German) Gentile in her novel, a legitimate topic, but in fleshing out her ideas she created stereotypes of both, more worthy of the regional bias of Texan William Denny, himself a crude stereotype. She made Braggioni in "Flowering Judas" a convincing caricature of the failed revolutionary because she based him on several of her acquaintances, but the equally arrogant Captain Thiele is more a cardboard figure, based on nobody she knew and conceived from the start as an ironic allegorical God the Father.

The intention behind Porter's caricaturist method remains constant in *Ship of Fools,* especially since characters themselves use caricature as an act of revenge, like Charles Upton in "The Leaning Tower." The Cuban students mock fellow passengers. For instance, they exchange "critical medical views" on the rail-thin Lizzi Spöckenkieker: "'Chronic skeletonism,' they said of Lizzi, gloating over the instant look of fright in her face. 'No Hope'" (SF 341). In the same way they poke fun at the Huttens' obesity. Later they vent their malice on the bulletin board, writing about Jenny and David, "Look! *The American artists so-called are afraid if they take their noses out of their sketchbooks, someone will discover that they draw caricatures for each other because they can't read,*" to which Jenny responds, "Let's make a few caricatures of them and post them here" (SF 346–347). Jenny had already made a caricature of David, prompted by the "treacherous" thought that all the food and alcohol he consumed "would catch up on him someday":

> Jenny, stealing slant-eyed glimpses at him, began a prophetic portrait of David, say at fifty. She draped forty sagging pounds on David's familiar bony framework, added jowls, thinned his hair back level with his ears, doubled the size of his unbelievably handsome aquiline nose, extended his chin so extravagantly he began to resemble Punch, and as a last satisfying luxury of cruelty, she added a Teutonic roll of fat across the base of his skull. She was so happily absorbed and soothed in the execution of her little murder, her features assumed the sweet serenity and interior warm light that David loved to see . . . (SF 339)

This passage is an important gloss on "Pale Horse, Pale Rider," in which Miranda, depicting Adam grown old, unconsciously wishes him dead. Porter, basing David on Eugene Pressly, had the advantage of hindsight when she remembered how fat he had grown when he visited her in 1943.

The primary practitioners of Jenny's "luxury of cruelty" are the members of the Zarzuela troupe. They are, as Jenny points out, "life-sized dolls moved by strings, going gracefully through a perpetual pantomime of graceless emotions" (SF 108). The author herself moves their strings to make them stark caricatures of evil and the main vehicle for caricaturing others. At the end of the novel they demonstrate their function in their dance: "Pepe and Amparo had become perfect impersonators of Mrs. Treadwell's mincing, arm's length style" while "Manolo and Concha did a wicked imitation of Herr Freytag's somewhat muscular aggressiveness and Jenny's abandoned, swooning manner, head thrown back loosely. Pancho and Pastora had from the first stuck firmly with their parody of Herr Rieber and Lizzi, Pancho bouncing like a rubber ball, Pastora turning on an axis like an animated flagpole" (SF 433). The dance is part of a special entertainment they have arranged to humiliate and victimize the others, their takeover of the captain's table symbolizing a temporary ascendancy of chaos over order, of id over superego. Their dance parody establishes the relation between them and their prey, for, as the evening wears on, the other passengers, unable to repress their antisocial instincts, become versions of the dancers. Thus Mrs. Treadwell, drunkenly masquerading as Amparo, tattoos the face of the equally drunken Denny with the steel-tipped heel of her shoe and Johann as Manolo gratifies his lust with Concha. But the outbreak of violence of Mrs. Treadwell or of Hansen, who breaks a bottle over Herr Rieber's head, has none of the horrifying force of Mr. Thompson's unintentional murder of Mr. Hatch in "Noon Wine." Despite the attempt at climactic revelation, we learn little new about the passengers. Encouraged to despise Denny and Herr Rieber throughout the novel, we are given the dubiously gratifying pleasure of seeing them done in.

Porter's reliance on caricature dovetailed with the growing importance she gave to hatred, the necessary enemy, but she reduced the individuality of several characters to the common denominator of their evil. William Denny, for instance, is a narrow-minded bigot and Arne Hansen is a champion of the downtrodden, but their compulsive sexuality makes their political and social differences seem insignificant; they are brothers under the skin. In contrast, Thompson, Helton, and Hatch of "Noon Wine," in which Porter also employs caricature, are remarkably dissimilar in physical appearance, regional background, speech patterns, and attitudes toward life. Although, as Porter points out, all three are "trying to do right" (CE 479), they converge to destroy each other, evil mysteriously working in them and beyond them to bring about their destruction. *Ship of Fools* does not shock us with the mystery of evil because Porter, in her absorption with its abstract nature, created many characters merely as illustrations of it.

Ric and Rac are a case in point. They are a symbolic center about whom other characters speculate. Dr. Schumann is dismayed at the twins' "blind, unwinking malignance" (SF 112), convinced that their "evil is in the egg of their souls" (SF 198), while Father Garza calls them "devil-possessed children" (SF 318). If Ric and Rac had fallen overboard, as they almost do, nobody would have saved them: "Deeply, deeply not one of them but would have found a sympathetic agreement with all the others that overboard, the deeper the better, would have been a most suitable place for Ric and Rac. Any one of them would have been indignant if accused of lacking any of the higher and more becoming feelings for infancy; but Ric and Rac were outside the human race" (SF 330). That is where Porter puts them, making them, in their defensive hatred of adults, monstrous versions of Stephen in "The Downward Path to Wisdom."[7] Ric and Rac and the adult Zarzuela dancers are intentionally one-dimensional. In league with the author, they highlight the evil in other passengers, leaving us with evil by multiplication. Although Porter successfully creates several complex and sympathetic characters—Jenny Brown, La Condesa, and Dr. Schumann, for example—the novel encourages us to care no more about the fate of others than they do about that of Ric and Rac. Porter's pessimistic view of human nature so predominates that the identifying thumbprint she stressed in "Noon Wine" almost seems an illusion.

Not only Porter's thematic concerns but her creative method drained her characters of individuality. The small cast of characters in her best short stories was based on herself and on keen observation of others. To create a large cast not based on observation, she resorted to stereotype or again mined her own personality which she had to spread too thin. Responses to the Spanish steerage passengers, objects of pity like the peons in "Hacienda," measure the humanity or inhumanity of the first-class passengers but also reveal the varying success of Porter's power to create distinctive characters.

Consider the responses of Jenny Brown and Wilhelm Freytag to the steerage passengers. Although Porter, in her 1931 letter to Caroline Gordon, reported that the conditions of the Spaniards aboard the *Werra* had improved, in her novel she returned to her original impression of people moving from "misery through misery to more misery" because she darkened all the experiences on which the novel was based and because the exiles reminded her of the demoralized Mexican Indians first depicted in "The Fiesta of Guadalupe." We first view them through the eyes of Jenny Brown, who most resembles Porter:

> The air was not air any more, but a hot, clinging vapor of sweat, of dirt, of stale food and befouled litter, of rags and excrement: the reek of poverty. The people were not faceless: they were all Spanish, their heads had shape and meaning and breeding, their eyes looked out of beings who knew they were alive. Their skins were the skins of the starved who are also overworked, a stark dirty pallor, with green copper overtones. . . . Their bare feet were bruised, hardened, cracked, knotted in joints, and their hands were swollen fists. It was plain they were there by no will or plan of their own, and in the helpless humility of complete enslavement they were waiting for whatever would be done to them next. (SF 57)

Jenny's indignation at the passengers' "helpless humility of complete enslavement" is pinpointed in the image of their "bruised" and "cracked" feet, Porter's obsessional image of the Mexican Indian. At the same time, Jenny experiences a physical revulsion to and fear of the "reek of poverty," which dominates in Wilhelm Freytag's unsympathetic response:

> He paused on his way to bed and glanced into the dim pit of the steerage. The deck was covered with huddled figures, their heads resting on bundles, with only the floor under their bones. . . . The rest slept piled upon each other like dirty rags thrown out on a garbage heap. He stood and contemplated the inviolable mystery of poverty that was like a slow-working incurable disease, and there was nothing in his own mind, his history or his temperament that could even imagine a remedy for it. . . . He had a moral aversion to poverty, an instinctive contempt and distrust of the swarming poor spawned like maggots in filth, befouling the air around them. Yet he thought, moving on with a reluctant tinge of pity, they are necessary, they have their place, what would we do without them? And here they are, being sent from a place they are not wanted to a place where they cannot be welcome; they are going from hard labor and hunger to no labor and starvation, from misery to misery—what kind of creature would endure this except a lower order of animal? He shook off his own pity as hateful to him, and went back to his own dilemma. (SF 62–63)

Porter lifted Freytag's thought of the passengers moving "from misery to misery" from her 1931 letter to Caroline Gordon, making her original response the source of his and Jenny's. However, she reversed her dominant emotion to attribute to Freytag just a "tinge" of the pity and used his momentary lapse to stress his super-race mentality. In contrast, Jenny's emotions are more psychologically subtle because they reflect Porter's own. At the same time, Freytag's view of poverty as an "incurable disease" expresses Porter's despair that the plight of the poor was beyond solution. She felt it periodically in Mexico in the twenties, but by the time she wrote *Ship of Fools* she had come closer to the conclusion that human nature itself was beyond redemption.

Porter's mixed emotions also appear in Herr Graff's "sick pity" at the passengers' "misery" as "a strange mingled smell of vegetable and animal rot rose from them" (SF 73) to give one of several predictable instances of the dying man's faith in his healing power. But the response Porter invents for proto-Nazi Captain Thiele sounds like war-film propaganda: he interprets the "savage rhythms" of the music in the steerage in light of "the perpetual resistance of the elemental forces of darkness and disorder against the very spirit of civilization—that great Germanic force of life . . . in which Science and Philosophy moved hand in hand ruled by Christianity," thereby justifying his contempt for "these filthy cattle" (SF 216). Later referring to them as "scum," he attempts to "conceal them as well as we can and keep their plague from spreading" (SF 345), echoing Freytag's image of "incurable disease." Finally, he scorns "all the gutter-stuff of the steerage moving like plague rats from one country to another, swarming and ravening and undermining the hard-won order of the cultures and civilizations of the whole world" (SF 425). Since he is contemptuous of all passengers, including his countrymen, his perch in the "sanctuary of the bridge" somewhat resembles the author's perch in the sanctuary of her art from which she looks down on humankind, although, it should be added, character and author are significantly unlike in the degree of their fear, disgust, and alienation. Porter is more like the caring Dr. Schumann, who, after too much contact with his fellow passengers, "rejected them all, everyone of them, all human kinship with them. . . . He did not in the least care what became of any one of them. Let them live their dirty lives and die their dirty deaths . . . so much carrion to fill graves" (SF 469). But also like Schumann, she guiltily struggles against her disgust-filled principle of rejection.

Arne Hansen's response to the steerage passengers is determined by his politics. In a "booming intolerant voice" he fumes about the way religion makes "dupes of those poor people" (SF 160–161). Porter undermines his position, which resembles her own in 1921, through Freytag, who "discovered about Hansen something he had surmised a good while ago about most persons—that their abstractions and generalizations, their Rage for Justice or Hatred of Tyranny or whatever, too often disguised a bitter personal grudge of some sort far removed from the topic apparently under discussion" (SF 411). Yet the novel's major theme is precisely the passengers' lack of Rage for Justice; Herr Glocken confesses that he and "all the others," who witnessed the thievery of the Spanish troupe in Tenerife, refuse to admit their "guilt and complicity."

Ship of Fools is the product of Porter's attempt, inspired by the horrors of World War II, to account for the nature of evil. In the process, she attributed to humanity her own defensiveness, alienation, and hostility toward others. In "Hacienda" hostility appears in vengeful caricatures of Genaro, Kennerly, and Betancourt, but they are offset by the sympathetic narrator, Andreyev, and Montaña. In *Ship of Fools* hostility outweighs sympathy. Only two characters elicit our total sympathy, the Indian servant Nicolasa and the Basque woodcutter Echegaray, whose names others do not know or easily forget.

Mexico and Jenny Brown

Since most of the *Vera's* first-class passengers lived a number of years in Mexico, the country gets special mention. The first scenes of the novel are set in Veracruz, where Porter embarked for Europe in 1931. She gave no hint in her letter-log to Caroline Gordon of her displeasure with the city, but since it was intended to set the novel's mood, it became a "little purgatory," "a pestilential jumping-off place into the sea," whose inhabitants "carry on their lives . . . with a pleasurable contempt for outside opinion, founded on the charmed notion that their ways and feelings are above and beyond criticism" (SF 3). Porter's view closely resembles that of her favorite chronicler of Mexico, Fanny Calderon de la Barca, who describes Veracruz as "a melancholy, wholly deserted-looking burial ground," whose citizens hold it up "as superior to all other parts of the world" (29). Its citizens in *Ship of Fools* liberally express pleasurable contempt for the straggling disoriented future passengers of the *Vera,* who in the "stony white rage of vengeful sunlight" fear to complain of the "vile" food, "slapped down before their sunken faces by insolent waiters" because "the very smell of violence was in the air" (SF 11), as Porter felt it was in Mexico City in 1921.

Establishing the novel's imagery of cruelty and disgust, Porter invented a kind of animal fable in which a cat stares at "his enemy the parrot, that interloper with human voice who had deceived him again and again with an invitation to come and get food, "while the parrot eyed a chained monkey who "jeered at him all day long in a language he could not understand" (SF 5). When a woman feeds the parrot a rotten banana, the monkey "chattered with greed and fear," while the cat, "who despised them both and feared neither," is roused by the smell of "raw, tainted meat," but before he can reach it, a "mangy dog" chases him up a tree. The dog passes by a sedentary Indian, who plants a kick in its ribs. A little later a group of soldiers come and escort the Indian to jail for some inexplicable reason. Moving up the evolutionary ladder, Porter establishes a pattern that endures throughout the novel; as John Edward Hardy points out, "Man as we see him in this book is chiefly man as animal" (133). The Swiftian pity of it all is that his very humanity that might raise him above his animal nature plunges him below it.

Inhumanity is revealed in a long newspaper editorial and in the reaction of several businessmen to it. They read of a bombing intended for "a rich, unscrupulous landlord" that killed a young servant boy instead. The bomb should "serve as a warning to the heartless, shameless exploiters of honest Veracruz tenants that the Revolution had indeed arrived in its power" and that workers were determined "to avenge themselves fully for wrongs already done them." An "immense, honorable" funeral is planned for the boy, "a martyr to the great cause of liberty and justice," but since the celebration of the bombing had been planned in advance, it would take place since it would be "inglorious" to disappoint the "merrymaking workers of Veracruz." Here the incredible cynicism of so-called revolutionaries surpasses that in "Flowering Judas" and "Hacienda." More chilling is the response of the merchants, their businesses threatened by labor agitation. One recommends machine guns as a solution, but another assures him, "Don't worry, we'll smash them to pulp. They never win. They're such cattle, they don't even know they are just fighting for a change of masters." He says once more, "They never win" (SF 7–8), punctuating Porter's despair at the possibility of real revolutionary change.

Although she hopes never to see Veracruz again, Jenny Brown has "the tenderest memories" of the city: "I used to walk about there at night, after a rain, with everything washed clean, and the sweet-by-night and jasmine in full bloom and the colors of the pastel walls very pure. I would come on those unexpected squares and corners and fountains, all of them composed, just waiting to be painted. . . . The people seemed so friendly and easy." When David Scott "coldly, doubtfully" protests this memory, Jenny insists, "You must let me remember it in my own way, as beautiful at least once" (SF 42). Her memory, based on Porter's own memory of Veracruz in 1930, and all memories are subjective since they are influenced by feeling. Jenny's view of Veracruz may be as valid as that which the narrator chooses to give us in the first chapter.

Because she is a version of the author in 1931, Jenny Brown is the novel's most fully developed character. Enraptured by Tenerife, she responds as if she were Miranda: "Oh look, look . . . at all the things here we never saw before" (SF 375). Porter, unwilling to include her idealized alter ego among the ship's fools, replaced her with a less flattering version of herself, including all her unresolved inconsistencies, without having to admit it. As in "Flowering Judas," a change of names gave her license to be more truthful about herself, as if she were writing about someone else.

Inconsistencies pop up in Jenny's account of her family background. She tells Freytag that since her mother died young, she was raised by her father's parents, eighteenth-century rationalists—a term Porter applied to her father— and therefore totally free of prejudice "on grounds of nationality or religion." "Negroes came to the back door, of course," but that was "mere observance of local custom." Apparently recognizing the illogic of her family's beliefs, she adds, "Oh . . . what a museum piece of upbringing it was! Yet I loved it, I be-lieved every word of it, I still do . . ." (SF 90). Through Jenny, Porter indirectly admits her own racial prejudice that she never overcame, as Givner points out (451–453), despite her earlier radicalism.

Politically Jenny is made to appear inconsistent and naive. She denies being a radical, but, in response to the captain's treatment of the steerage passengers, is all for picketing him. Claiming that nothing is "incurable, not even human nature"—even though she later despairs at her own human nature—she believes

> warmly and excitedly in strikes, she has been in many of them, they worked; there was nothing more exciting and wonderful than to feel a part of something that worked towards straightening out things—getting decent pay for people, good working conditions, shorter hours—it didn't much matter what. She had picketed dozens of times with just any strikers who happened to need pickets, and she had been to jail several times, it was just a lark! (SF 164)

Drawing from her experiences as a picket during the Sacco-Vanzetti affair, Porter invents Jenny's activism in Mexico through David's memory of her picketing with strikers "without even asking what they were striking for, or even where they worked. 'Tobacco factory, I think,' she said one night . . ." (SF 221). His memory recalls Braggioni's wife, who is a union organizer "among the girls in the cigarette factories, and walks in picket lines . . ." (99). Through Freytag, Porter mocks Jenny's and her own embroidery of their past experiences and casts doubt on the sincerity of their political beliefs:

> She might have been a young girl talking about the gay parties of her debutante season. Freytag could not take her seriously. She did not say where or when these things happened, nor precisely how she had happened to be mixed up in them . . . nor what were the beliefs that led her to such acts. Her light running talk was full of omissions and pauses which she seemed to expect him to fill in from his own experience of such events. (SF 165)

When Porter described May Day celebrations in the 1930s as pretty shows, she herself sounded like a young debutante.

Jenny is equally inconsistent as artist, a combination of aggressive caricaturist and naive romantic with regard to Indian art and culture. A painter rather than writer, like Charles Upton in "The Leaning Tower," she vents her spleen in caricature as in her portrait of David, who finds that "she always recognized revenge for what it was, yet admitted its barbarous justice" (SF 43). In fact, she makes it a moral imperative: "She believed in hitting back, blow for blow and as many extra as you could manage to get in.—Not to resist and punish an injury . . . was to consent to the wrong, plain moral cowardice in her view . . ." (SF 304). Her stand reinforces the novel's main theme, but the phrase "blow for blow" also recalls the couple on the Taxco road avenging themselves on each other unto their death and, as both David and Jenny unhappily learn, characterizes their tit-for-tat relation.

By also making David Scott a painter, unlike Eugene Pressly, Porter created a double of Jenny and, by extension, of herself, the same self with opposing views. David's "favorite palette was a mixture of grays, browns, ochers, and dark blues with a good deal of white" while Jenny used to splash "her little canvases recklessly with geometrical designs in primary colors like fractured rainbows" (SF 76–77). Although David had persuaded her to tone down her palette, her return to primary colors marks her artistic independence and an important step on the way to her predictable separation from him. But David's palette most resembles Porter's in "Hacienda" and "Pale Horse, Pale Rider." During his walking tour with Porter in 1921, Winold Reiss found the landscape resplendent with color, but she saw only darkness and death.

Porter's opposing selves do battle over Indian culture and art. In Veracruz Jenny wears, to David's chagrin, an "outfit, which she had lifted without leave from the workday costume of the town-dwelling Mexican Indian" (SF 13)—an outfit similar to that of Pablo O'Higgins or the journalist in "That Tree." Reflecting Porter's enthusiasm for Indian ways in 1922, Jenny had "a hearty contempt for foreigners who boiled everything they ate or wore, and missed all the lovely fruit and the savory Mexican food from the steaming clay pots in the Indian villages" (SF 399). Regarding Mexican art, she is equally enthusiastic and naive. She wants "good simple people who don't know a thing about art to like [her] work, to come for miles to look at it, the way the Indians do the murals in Mexico City," but David, calling her "you good simple girl," claims that the "good simple Indians were laughing their heads off and making gorgeously dirty remarks" about the murals. He considers Indian art "debased all to hell now" and warns her "not to go fake primitive." When she professes a love for the Indians from whom she has learned something, David retorts, "But they didn't love you. . . . We love their beautiful straw mats because we don't have to sleep on them, and they want our spring mattresses. There's nothing to blame them for, but I'm sick of this sentimental yap about them" (SF 55–56). In this long, bickering exchange Porter's enthusiastic self of 1922, expressed in her *Christian Science Monitor* letter, confronts her jaundiced self of 1930–1931, expressed in "Leaving the Petate" and in her peevish comments over the debasement of Indian art. We are told that Jenny carried on "colloquies" with her "other self" with "real words and a face-to-face encounter" (SF 93). Porter externalized this other self in the person of David. The couple resemble a Siamese fighting fish doing battle with its own mirror image.

Through Jenny, Porter also gives the frankest account of her relationship to her family and to men. Jenny's family suspects that she

> couldn't possibly be up to any good, or she would have stayed at home, where she belonged. That is the sum of it, thought Jenny, and wouldn't their blood run cold if they could only know the facts? Ah well, the family can get under your skin with little needles and scalpels if you venture too near them: they attach suckers to you and draw blood from every pore if you don't watch out. But that didn't stop you from loving them, nor them from loving you, with that strange longing, demanding, hopeless tenderness and bitterness, wound into each other in a net of living nerves. (SF 186)

The passage gives a franker explanation of why Porter left Texas than the one she gave Archer Winsten in 1937. The vampire and net images express the engulfed feelings of one who protects herself through escape and communication at a safe distance. Mrs. Treadwell, in a more advanced stage of rejection, always moves away "from the threat of human nearness" (SF 142).

Family suspicion of the "facts" of Jenny/Porter's sexual life were well founded. Unlike Miranda, Jenny is, as Frau Rittersdorf suspects, "one of these advanced, emancipated young women of the Bohemian world" (SF 84), who admits to David that her past relations with men were "just for the excitement," not love but "foxfire" (SF 149), the term Porter applied to her affair with Francisco Aguilera in 1924. Jenny's finely delineated flirtation with Wilhelm Freytag demonstrates how Porter fell in and out of love despite certain knowledge of its impossibility:

> Maybe I shall fall in love with you, maybe I am in love with you already, the way I fall in love: always with utter strangers and as if I were going under water, and I'll fall out again as if I were falling off a cliff. I'm glad I don't know anything about you, except that you have the kind of looks I like. . . . If we could sleep together without too much trouble and lose ourselves together for a little while, I'd be easy again, I'd be able to see better. (SF 92)

Because David, to whom she is supposedly committed, cannot satisfy her body's "long famine of love" (SF 86), Jenny is attracted to the handsome Freytag; "It had been her ruin, she decided, this weakness for handsome men. If a man were sufficiently good-looking she granted him all desirable qualities without hesitation" (SF 166)—a pattern Porter first expressed in her 1948 "Letters to a Nephew." Freytag's attraction to Jenny is a coarser version of the same response: "Out of his past . . . there rose disturbingly a half dozen faces . . . none of them beautiful before he loved them, none of them beautiful since, some of them hateful even, but each one unbelievably enchanting for that brief time when he was hot after each in turn, bedeviled and blinded with illusion. It was always true love and it was always going to last forever . . ." (SF 165). Freytag's self-delusion reveals the way Porter created characters out of her own personality traits, making them particularly unattractive when projected onto her male characters.

Freytag's talk of love is a "cradlesong" that Jenny's "wishful deluded heart sang to itself . . . echoing not what she knew in her bitter mind, but her feelings." Split between feelings that attract and mind that rejects, Jenny cuts through "his maunderings" to exclaim that love "is a booby trap. . . . I hate it and always did. It makes such filthy liars of everybody. But I keep falling into it just the same" (SF168). She even claims that "David hates love worse than I do, even" (SF 169), a claim that David, in an earlier passage, confirms: "But Jenny was not the wife he wanted if he wanted a wife, which he certainly did not want now: in fact, he faced it coldly, he would never in the world marry Jenny, he did not intend to marry at all; marriage was a bad business, a mug's game" (SF 130). In light of Pressly's persistent efforts to marry Porter, this passage is another example of her projection of her attitudes, in this case to justify her rejection of Pressly. (In another projection we are told that David "had never been anywhere but that he wanted to be somewhere else; never in any kind of fix that he wasn't planning all the time to get out of it" [SF 379]. But this characterization clashes with his complaint that the "whole wild escapade to Europe was Jenny's idea; he had never intended to leave Mexico at all, but he had let her lead him by the nose" [SF 28]—a complaint Pressly could have made about Porter. The two passages point to David's inconsistent character or to Porter's inconsistent creation of it.)

In her fearful rejection of love, Jenny resembles Laura in "Flowering Judas," who feels "betrayed irreparably by the disunion between her way of living and her feeling of what life should be" (91). Similarly Jenny feels "enslaved . . . to her notions of what life *should* be, her wish to shape, to direct, to make of it what she wished it to be" (SF 93). But the difference between the two characters is that Laura struggles between her own principles and the corrupt revolutionary world of Mexico, her despair culminating in her guilt over Eugenio's death, whereas Jenny is little concerned with the world at large but merely with her resolve not to "let [David] spoil Europe for her" and make her "even a greater fool than she feared." So "staring up into the pure blue light of a day fit for the joy of angels, she gave way and despaired quietly and awfully" (SF 93). Jenny's despair is real, but has no clear external cause. Therefore she makes David her psychological scapegoat, finding it "hard to admit to herself that she was a fool" (SF 93) because she cannot free herself from him. The novel's most terrifying image of the male/female relationship, that of the man and woman killing each other on the Taxco road, has lived on in Jenny's memory, but she doesn't realize its significance until, in a dream, she sees that "the faces were David's and her own, and there she was looking up into David's blood-streaming face, a bloody stone in her hand, and David's knife was raised against her pierced bleeding breast" (SF 145). The dream confirms her fear of the mutual destructibility of love.

Not as sexually repressed as Laura, Jenny is fascinated with Amparo, who insultingly slaps her inner thigh and accuses Jenny of having "nothing *here*" for refusing to buy a lottery ticket. Recounting the incident to a horrified David, Jenny imitates Amparo's action, reminding him that he enjoyed seeing two Indian women fighting over a man, each slapping themselves "right in the middle, each one bragging about what she's got that the other hasn't" (SF 352–353). These gestures demeaningly reduce women to sex objects, but they also signal their power to expose male carnality. Porter, awed in 1931 by Pastora Imperio's power to elicit a vast "orgiastic sigh" from her male audience, made her the model for the female Zarzuela dancers, one of whom is named Pastora while another, Amparo, hoped to be a star "like the great Pastora Imperio" (SF 225). But Porter secretly admires them for no other reason than their sexual power. In her essay "A Defense of Circe" (1955), she observes, "Not even a god, having once formed a man, can make a swine of him. That is for him to choose. Circe's honeyed food with the lulling drug in it caused them to reveal themselves" (CE 135). So the drunken Mrs. Treadwell, her face painted in imitation of the dancers, inadvertently deceives the equally drunken Denny into thinking she is Amparo and then punishes him for his attempted assault by lacerating his face with the metal-capped heel of her sandal. Her act is a macabre version of her polite rejection of the young ship's officer, who complains, "Then why did you come with me, why did you encourage me to kiss you?" (SF 461). As Laura does unconsciously in "Flowering Judas," she attracts the male with her sexuality and then punishes him for being attracted, but the potential for swinishness is his.

The root of Mrs. Treadwell's hatred, as William Nance points out, is her resentment at "man's violation of her virginity" (183). Her complaints about her former husband's physical abuse are drawn from Porter's own experience with her first husband, John Koontz, who, according to Givner (249), was the model for Denny. Frau Rittersdorf's belief that American women like Jenny lose "their virginity at puberty or even earlier" (SF 154) further suggests Porter's emotional investment in the assault. After it is over, Mrs. Treadwell smiles "delightedly at her hideous face in the looking glass" and "fold[s] herself into bed like a good little girl who has finished her prayers" (SF 466). Porter makes her grotesque but also shares in her vengeful triumph over Denny and, by extension, over all males who treat women as blatant sex objects or as inferior helpmates.

Such males abound in the novel. For example, David and Freytag shake hands and exchange "a curious expression" that Jenny interprets: "It was the wordless affirmation of pure male complicity, complete understanding from far depths of instinctive being . . . sympathy and a secret alliance, from which she was excluded by natural law, in their unalienable estate of manhood" (SF 496). The most outrageous proponent of the male attitude is Professor Hutton, who indulges in "a vengeful meditation" on "the sex that brought confusion into everything, religion, law, marriage; all its duplicities, its love of secret bypaths, its instinct for darkness and all mischiefs done in darkness" (SF 237). The novel conclusively proves Porter's contention, first learned from her father, that men and women do not like each other, no matter what their sexual attraction at any given moment. In fact, sexual attraction itself seems the source and expression of their hatred.

Identifying their hatred with a place, most passengers on the *Vera*, like Porter herself, leave Mexico with no desire ever to return. Hansen has given up the dairy business there because "they change the rules every day" (SF 100). Hotelkeeper Herr Lutz remembers that official Mexican pamphlets promised "cheap food, cheap labor, cheap rent, cheap taxes, cheap everything except the tourists," but "not a word about politics, not a whisper about revolution." Lutz reflects, "Even now, it sounds like Paradise on earth—well, we all know there is no such place" (SF 101). It was the place where Herr Baumgartner failed and became an alcoholic, although his wife remembers that many Germans who had immigrated to it after World War I considered it "a new land of promise" (SF 49), alluding to the novel's earlier title, *Promised Land*.

In Porter's letters and earlier works, the promised land of Mexico became instead a place of terror, the air full of death and corruption. In *Ship of Fools* the air is also permeated with foul odors. The steerage passengers evoke disgust with their "strange mingled smell of vegetable and animal rot" (SF 73). Frau Rittersdorf fears the "great danger of infectious disease among such creatures" (SF 60) without realizing that she is infected by the disease of her own humanity. For David, the "smell of disinfectant could not drown the other fetid smells of unclean human garments, the rancid smell of Herr Glocken's shoes, the old mildewed smell of the cabin itself" (SF 27). Amparo exudes "from every pore a warm spermy odor" (SF 151) mixed with cheap perfume, causing Frau Schmidt to shun her. When Herr Baumgartner embraces his young son, the boy "stiffened and turned his head rigidly from the stink of the breath blown in his nostrils" (SF 457). Johann literally smells death in his uncle, Herr Graf, and longs to escape "the smothering air of old age" (SF 74), while the "dank air of the passageway stuck upon" Doctor Schumann "as a fresh breeze after the fetid sweetness and rot" of the Condesa's cabin (SF 121). The smell of mortality is everywhere.

Throughout the novel, passengers attempt to escape the smells of the ship. Jenny and the Huttens look "for relief from themselves and from each other in the fresh winds from the sea and the lulling darkness" (SF 218). But, like Miranda in "Pale Horse, Pale Rider" and Herr Graf, they cannot escape the smell of their own mortality or, like Herr Lowenthal, "the airless ghetto" of their souls. At the end of the novel, when the ship shaves the coast of the Isle of Wight, Jenny "believed she was deceived again in her sense of smell, which often brought her strange improbable whiffs of cross currents of air," an experience Porter mentioned in her letter to Caroline Gordon. Elsa Lutz, who had passed the isle four times before, assures Jenny that it always has "that lovely smell," adding that when she was little she "thought maybe heaven would be like that" (SF 493). Apparently the Isle of Wight is uninhabited by humankind.

Conclusion

Mexico in the Sixties

Except for rewriting and proofreading, Porter finished *Ship of Fools* in Rockport, Massachusetts, in June of 1961. In a letter to Mary Doherty of the year before (May 4, 1960), Porter, after making excuses for not seeing her during the latter's visit to New York in 1956, outlined her plan to return to Mexico on a speaking engagement sponsored by the State Department. About Mexico she wrote,

> It will be strange I don't doubt to see Mexico again after all these years. Nearly thirty years since I went to Europe from there, nearly forty since I went there the first time. My memories of the country itself and the people are very good and warm, but my personal life was a real shambles from first to last: I never met anywhere else in my life such destructive people as Retinger, the unspeakable Paca Toor—the fraud who ran the silver-works racket in Taxco, what was his name? Sprat something or other—the awful Peggy Cowley, poor doomed and deviled Hart Crane who wanted somebody to go to hell with him—even Gene, who seemed as good a human being as I knew at least in those times, was a kind of monster of indecision, self-pity, inertia, and gluttony—so you see, I should hate to see any of these people again, or take up in any way any left over shreds of my life there, which could have been so pleasant if I hadn't got so many bloodsuckers at my arteries. If I hadn't this appointment to the University, I should not come back at all.

Her litany of old enemies is curious since only William Spratling, whom she saw little of in 1930–1931, still lived in Mexico. On May 20 Doherty wrote back, not sure "who of the old friends you are going to find here" since many had died and "of course Paca Toor dead for years."

Shortly after her arrival, Porter gave a press conference on May 26, reported on the front page of *El Universal* the next day. In it she blamed communism for exporting ideas that created the "rebel without a cause" and undermined all positive values such as love of family, country, and religion, but she praised the United States for combating such pessimism. She also noted that Lizardi's *The Itching Parrot* was being sold on a scale just below that of the Bible.

Doherty wrote Porter a note on June 6 (proving her own difficulty in contacting the famous author) to inform her, "You are perfectly correct, dear— these Mexican friends of yours are all going to stick at their posts waiting for you to call them!!" After calling around, Doherty found that Adolfo Best Maugard did not answer his phone, Dr. Atl would have to be reached by Porter herself, while Jorge Enciso could not make her lecture but would be delighted to see her at the Museum of Anthropology, where her "beloved 'crystal rabbit' is still in its place," the same rabbit that Anna in a scene from *Thieves' Market* planned to see again. Xavier Guerrero wished to accompany her to the Popular Arts Museum, which grew out of the 1922 art exhibition, but Salomón de la Selva, fearing he might not have money to entertain her "in style," decided to stay away. Doherty thought they would all be flattered if Porter called them, but pride and a tight schedule precluded that possibility.

On August 7, 1962, Doherty congratulated Porter on the success of her novel and on the news that the movie rights amounted to almost half a million dollars, reminding her, "I felt you deserved it from those early days when I would pick out of the wastebasket the pages you would toss away. I knew then they were all good, and merited saving. And now the world really knows." She loved "to think you were coming our way as you promised to *two* Novembers ago." On August 30, 1963, Porter wrote Doherty from Paris, hoping that she had read her "best-seller"; except for the many new readers and "a very nice, solid income for life," "the only thing it did for me . . . was to bring on a million-odd of gourd-heads who either couldn't get through it, or went around asking plaintively, 'WHY did you write such an awful book? Do you really hate humanity?'" She was tempted to reply, "I wrote that awful book because there are certain kinds of humanity that I do really hate." But the purpose of her letter was a request, as most of her letters to Doherty were, to tell her all she knew about David Siqueiros, Tina Modotti, and her lover, Julio Antonio Mella, a Cuban leftist whom Cuban agents assassinated in 1929 while walking in downtown Mexico City with Modotti. The occasion of her request was a petition, presented by prominent intellectuals to Mexican president Adolfo López Mateos on his visit to France, to release Siqueiros from prison where he was held without charge. Porter mentioned her earlier refusal to sign such a petition for "that hardened old murderer and conspirator" who, "besides his other crimes against his society and associates, should have been shot for his paintings alone." She stated that "in Mexico, everybody knew that Siqueiros was a Communist of the real original thug type," but also noted that he "is not really a communist, and never was: no more than Diego Rivera," both hopping "on the bandwagon" for the publicity. Ignoring the fact that in 1931 she had been fond of Siqueiros and his wife, she now complained that he had left Blanca Luz and "their horrid little boy" at her Mixcoac house, where "Cowley left his horrible Peggy . . . while Hart Crane was on my hands, and there were others as you know." To make sure that Doherty responded, Porter flattered her: "You write the kind of letters that make people who read them say, 'But she should have been a *writer!*' and I say, 'But look at her letters,—she *is* a writer.'"

Flattery was unnecessary to encourage Porter's most loyal friend to respond, on December 13, with an eight-page letter, followed by another of February 26, 1964, wondering whether Porter had received the first. There is no record of Porter's response nor of any contact with Doherty during her second speaking engagement in Mexico in the fall of 1964. At this time she granted Enrique Hank Lopez an interview about herself and Mexico, in which she mentioned the funeral of Adolfo Best Maugard, a few days before, although she was unable to attend. The interview was the first of several about her exciting adventures in Mexico, the accuracy of which is questionable, but not the quality of the fiction they inspired her to produce.

Summing Up

Kenneth Durant told Katherine Anne Porter, before her visit to Mexico in 1920, that she wrote like an angel. We do not know what prompted his extravagant praise. If he had read any of her pieces in the Fort Worth and Denver newspapers, he could have identified his friend's angelic prose but could not have predicted the nature and quality of the creative works she would soon create. With the appearance of "The Fiesta of Guadalupe" in December 1920, journalist and artist merged to produce the earliest work in her canon, one that bears the full imprint of her talent and personality.

"The Fiesta of Guadalupe" and "Xochimilco," published within a few months of each other, hold the key to Porter's fascination with Mexico. Both center on the Indian, but one is somber and despairing while the other is full of light and hope. Mexico was—and unfortunately still is—a country of extremes. Xochimilco, the place of perpetually blooming flowers, reminded Porter of an Eden she sought all her life, but Guadalupe was a place where the hopeless vainly sought relief from their afflictions. The two places were not figments of her imagination, but they appeared in stark contrast to each other because they corresponded to the alternating extremes of hope and despair that characterized her chronic depression before she ever entered Mexico. In precisely such terms she reminisced about Mexico to Mary Doherty in 1943; although she remembered those days as "mostly hell," still "they had hope. . . . Mexico was new to us, and beautiful, the very place to be at that moment."

Porter also remembered that her "childlike faith in the Revolution was well over in about six months." Never childlike, it only seemed to end in six months because by then she was threatened with deportation. Close to the revolution's center of power, she received an invaluable political education, but it led her to despair that the poor could ever overcome the Mexican Trinity and to conclude that there was no such thing as a good government. Mexico dashed her political hope, but helped her sharpen her talent at caricature to express her despair in "Flowering Judas" and "Hacienda."

As Porter claimed, Mexico gave her back her past. "The Grave" (1935) is the clearest example of how experiences in Mexico stirred memories of her unhappy childhood in Texas, but her earliest Mexican stories, beginning with "The Dove of Chapacalco," obliquely expose her discontent, rooted in her father's rejection of her and aggravated by her marriage at age sixteen to John Koontz. The solitary narrator of "In a Mexican Patio" is her earliest self-portrait, later amplified in "Flowering Judas," while "Virgin Violeta" is her earliest version of herself as adolescent, revealing, like other early Mexican stories, her obsession with rape and the loss of virginity as well as the victim's determination to gain revenge through the art of caricature. Porter's terror of death, revealed in "Flowering Judas," recalled a similar terror in Denver that later found expression in "Pale Horse, Pale Rider."

Since Porter's self-dramatizations constitute a major part of her canon, it has been necessary to explore the many patterns in her notes, letters, and fiction, Mexican and non-Mexican, in hope of understanding her personality and the causes of her chronic depression since they contributed to the pessimism in her fiction. Although she was aware of disturbing character traits she feared she had inherited from her father, her self-analyses were unsuccessful. In "Pale Horse, Pale Rider" she idealized her alienation, lamenting the loss of love and at the same time revealing its danger. In her early Mexican notes, she had speculated that love was only an illusion. By the 1940s, the idea of hatred as the necessary enemy in the downward path to wisdom became a fearfully attractive defense against or substitute for love. Thus she offered the symptom of her neurosis as its cure. In her correspondence with Charles Shannon in 1945 and with William Goyen in 1951,[1] she used the word "love" as if she believed in its existence, but questioned it while working on *Ship of Fools*. The novel bluntly expresses her darkest view of the human condition, her last revenge against the world that denied her the love and happiness for which she yearned all her life. As she showed in "Letters to a Nephew," she romantically transformed love into something it could never be for long and then mourned its loss, as she had in "Pale Horse, Pale Rider."

Attracted to Mexico in 1920, Porter fled it in 1921, resolving never to return, but she returned three times more in the space of ten years. She made the same resolution in 1931, but on two different occasions in the 1940s she again planned to return and in the 1960s did return for brief visits. Mexico was like a lover who always betrayed her trust, but on some unconscious level she welcomed the betrayal because it always revealed tragic truths that became the subject of her art. Still its Edenic allure persisted. In 1921 it was Xochimilco and Amecameca and in 1931 Oaxtepec, while as late as February 1, 1964, she wrote Robert Penn Warren, "I think of Mexico because I no longer feel at home here anywhere, there is nowhere I wish to go and Mexico is not so far away now. . . . Maybe I will go to Lake Chapala or Cuernavaca or some lovely place near water, and you can come to visit me! I'd like that, and I hope you may!" Perhaps she didn't remember Laura's lament in "Flowering Judas" that she "is not at home in the world" (97), but no matter, the invitation is there to visit Porter in Mexico through her sketches and stories. We may not discover Eden, but the journey will be worth it.

Notes

Introduction

1. The following works, in order of publication, deal with Porter in Mexico: William L. Nance, "Katherine Anne Porter and Mexico," *Southwest Review* 55 (Spring 1970): 277–289; Colin Patridge, "'My Familiar Country': An Image of Mexico in the Work of Katherine Anne Porter," *Studies in Short Fiction* 7 (Fall 1970): 597–614; Dewey Wayne Gunn, "'Second Country': Katherine Anne Porter," *American and British Writers in Mexico, 1556–1973,* 102–122; Bonelyn Lugg, "Mexican Influences on the Work of Katherine Anne Porter" (Ph.D. diss., Pennsylvania State Univ., 1976); Ronald G. Walker, "The Fascination of Mexico," *Infernal Paradise: Mexico and the Modern English Novel;* Joan Givner, *Katherine Anne Porter: A Life;* Darlene Harbour Unrue, *Truth and Vision in Katherine Anne Porter's Fiction;* and Ruth Moore Alvarez, "Katherine Anne Porter and Mexican Art" (Ph.D. diss., Univ. of Maryland, 1990).

2. KAP to Kenneth Durant, November 20, 1954, Papers of Katherine Anne Porter, McKeldin Library, University of Maryland. Subsequent references to Porter's notes and correspondence are to the McKeldin collection excepting letters to Caroline Gordon and Allen Tate (at the Princeton University Library), letters to Malcolm Cowley (at the Newberry Library), letters to Josephine Herbst (at the Princeton University Library) and letters to Carleton Beals (at the Boston University Library). Josephine Herbst's letters are in the Yale Collection of American Literature, Beinecke Rare Book and Manuscript Library, Yale University.

3. Among those who give valuable psychological insights into Porter's personality are William L. Nance, Joan Givner, and Jane Krause DeMouy. Nance finds that Porter's fictional characters who resemble her possess "a principle of rejection so strong that it defines *every* relationship as oppressive" (*Katherine Anne Porter and the Art of Rejection,* 7). Givner points out that "the impetus behind [Porter's] literary work and the recreation of her own image had their root in the same source: her inability to accept the disunion between what life is and what it should be" (*A Life,* 62). Porter's work, according to DeMouy, reveals "a basic psychological conflict" between "a desire, on the one hand, for the independence and freedom to pursue art or principle of social convention, and, on the other hand, a desire for the love and security in the traditional roles of wife and mother" (*Katherine Anne Porter's Women,* 6).

4. On Porter's childhood, see Givner, *A Life,* 62–63.

5. On hereditary depression, see H. I. Kaplan and B. J. Sadok, *Synopsis of Clinical Psychiatry,* 288–303. Karen Horney's *Feminine Psychology* gives valuable insights into

the Oedipus relation between daughter and father. Although no psychological theory can adequately explain the personality of Porter or anyone else, R. D. Laing's profile of the "ontologically insecure person" is also helpful in understanding the character of Miranda in "Pale Horse, Pale Rider" and, by extension, Porter herself. The insecure person's dread of losing "autonomy and identity" helps explain the inability of Porter's characters to form lasting love relations. See R. D. Laing, *The Divided Self: An Existential Study in Sanity and Madness,* 42. Also see Shirley E. Johnson, "Love Attitudes in the Fiction of Katherine Anne Porter," *West Virginia University Philological Papers* 13 (December 1961): 82–93, and Malcom M. Marsden, "Love as Threat in Katherine Anne Porter's Fiction," *Twentieth Century Literature* 13 (March 1967): 29–38.

1. Porter and Mexican Politics

1. Archer Winsten, "Presenting the Portrait of an Artist," *New York Post,* May 6, 1937, reprinted in *Katherine Anne Porter: Conversations,* ed. Joan Givner 10, 12. Other references to interviews in this volume are given in my text and designated by I.

2. Malcolm Cowley, *Exile's Return: A Literary Odyssey of the 1920s,* 291.

3. *The Collected Stories of Katherine Anne Porter,* 210. Subsequent references to this edition appear in the text.

4. See James R. Green, *Grass-Roots Socialism: Radical Movements in the Southwest 1895–1943,* 228–270.

5. Ibid., 296.

6. See Horace C. Peterson, *Opponents of War 1917–1918,* 142–147.

7. David M. Kennedy, *Over Here: The First World War and American Society,* 21.

8. Pauline Naylor, "Katherine Anne Porter's Ft. Worth Days Recalled," *Fort Worth Star-Telegram,* April 10, 1966.

9. See Lawrence H. Chamberlain, *Loyalty and Legislative Action: A Survey of the New York State Legislature 1919–1949,* 31–32.

10. See Kathryn Adam Sexton, "Katherine Anne Porter's Years in Denver" (master's thesis, Univ. of Colorado, 1961), 92–94.

11. *The Collected Essays and Occasional Writings of Katherine Anne Porter,* 470. Subsequent references to this edition appear in the text, designated by CE.

12. KAP to Porter family, January 3, 1920.

13. On Beatty see "Bessie Beatty, 61, Commentator, Dies," *New York Times,* April 7, 1947. On Evans see "Ernestine Evans, Editor-Critic 77," *New York Times,* July 4, 1967; *Who Was Who in America* 19 (July 4, 1967): 2. On 12 St. Luke's Place and Gumberg, see Elinor Langer, *Josephine Herbst,* 53–54. On Dell, see KAP to Delafield Day, undated, 1929. On Evans's visits, see Helen Black to Genevieve Taggard, April 23, 1923, Genevieve Taggard Papers, New York Public Library.

14. On Durant see Theodore E. Kruglak, *The Two Faces of TASS,* 91–98; and Eugene Lyons, *Assignment in Utopia,* 40–48.

15. Porter's defense did not prevent George Whicher from asserting that she "specialized in the evocation of exotic atmospheres." See *The Literature of the American People,* ed. Arthur Hobson Quinn, 925.

16. Porter mentioned both Tata Nacho and Best Maugard in an interview with Hank Lopez in 1965 (I 121). Both arrived in New York in 1919. On their friendship and

Tata Nacho's career as songwriter and musicologist, see Hugo de Grial, *Músicos mexicanos,* 154.

17. *El Heraldo de México,* November 10, 1920, 4. On Best Maugard, see Jean Charlot, *The Mexican Mural Renaissance 1920–1925,* 62–66.

18. See Givner, *A Life,* 147; and Alvarez, "Porter and Mexican Art," 8–9.

19. W. D. Outman, "Current Comment," *Magazine of Mexico* 1 (March 1921): 66.

20. See John Mason Hart, *Revolutionary Mexico: The Coming and Process of the Mexican Revolution,* 96–100, 350–352.

21. See John Womack, *Zapata and the Mexican Revolution,* 45–46; James C. Carey, *The Mexican Revolution in Yucatán, 1915–1924,* 11–12; John Kenneth Turner, *Barbarous Mexico,* chapters 1 and 2.

22. See Friedrich Katz, *The Secret War in Mexico: Europe, the United States, and the Mexican Revolution,* 97–112.

23. On the constitution of 1917 see Charles C. Cumberland, *Mexico: The Struggle for Modernity,* 265–272.

24. See John Mason Hart, *Anarchism and the Mexican Working Class, 1860–1931,* 17–18, 47, 91–98, 108–111.

25. On the Casa del Obrero, see ibid., 118–155.

26. Marie Robinson Wright, *Picturesque Mexico,* 122–124.

27. Luis Araiza, *Historia del Movimiento Obrero Mexicano,* 3:106; Rosendo Salazar and José G. Escobedo, *Las pugnas de la gleba,* 1:150.

28. Araiza, *Historia,* 3:105, 112.

29. Salazar and Escobedo, *Las pugnas,* 1:165–166.

30. On CROM's rise to power see Marjorie Ruth Clark, *Organized Labor in Mexico,* 59–69; on Morones see John W. F. Dulles, *Yesterday in Mexico: A Chronicle of the Revolution, 1919–1936,* 271–279.

31. See Linda B. Hall, *Alvaro Obregón: Power and Revolution in Mexico, 1911–1920,* 188–190, 217, 240–241.

32. See Dulles, *Yesterday in Mexico,* 29–40.

33. Ibid., 73–74.

34. See Womack, *Zapata,* 54–58.

35. See Lorenzo Meyer, *Mexico and the United States in the Oil Controversy, 1917–1942,* 8–9, 22–24.

36. See Robert Freeman Smith, *The United States and Revolutionary Nationalism in Mexico, 1916–1932,* 156–174.

37. Alfonso Taracena, *La verdadera revolución mexicana* 8:150–154.

38. National Archives, Naval Intelligence (NID), 13028 B (August 31, 1920).

39. Robert Haberman, "Mexican Workers Celebrate Labor Day with Great Parades and Demonstrations, *New York Call,* October 18, 1920, 4.

40. George E. Hyde, "Renegade Americans Promoting Bolshevik Movement in Mexico," *New York Tribune,* September 5, 1920, 9.

41. See Barry Carr, *El movimiento obrero y la política en México, 1910–1929,* 1:180.

42. Carey, *Revolution in Yucatán,* 136. On Carrillo Puerto, see Dulles, *Yesterday in Mexico,* 136–140.

43. Smith, *Revolutionary Nationalism,* 178.

44. See Hall, *Alvaro Obregón,* 258, 198.

45. *Mexican Review* 4 (January 1921): 6.

2. Porter in Mexico, 1920–1921

1. See Janice R. MacKinnon and Stephen R. MacKinnon, *Agnes Smedley: The Life and Times of an American Radical,* 19–20, 32–33, 256.

2. On Torres, see National Archives, Military Intelligence (MID), 10058-0-3, 16; 10058–836.

3. On Haberman see "Roberto Haberman Dead at 79; Founder of Mexican Labor Unit," *New York Times,* March 5, 1962, 23; Clark, *Organized Labor,* 63, 202; Dulles, *Yesterday in Mexico,* 122, 138, 140; Carr, *El Movimiento Obrero,* 195–196. On Yúdico in Yucatán, see Jacinto Huitrón, *Orígenes e historia del Movimiento Obrero en México,* 283–284; and Salazar and Escobedo, *Las pugnas,* 1 : 136–137.

4. Vicente Blasco Ibáñez, *Mexico in Revolution,* 2.

5. A comparison of the 1920 and 1970 texts reveals around forty brief stylistic changes. The most serious error in the 1970 version reads, "They have parted a carved bit of wood and plaster, I see the awful hands of faith . . ." (CE 397). The original reads, "Over that painted and carved bit of wood and plaster, I see the awful hands of faith . . ." The 1970 version completely obscures Porter's comment about the Indians' misplaced faith in the Virgin. (I mostly quote from the 1920 version.)

6. "Hacienda," *Virginia Quarterly Review* 8 (October 1932): 565.

7. Georg Simmel, "The Adventure," in *Essays on Sociology, Philosophy and Aesthetics,* ed. Kurt H. Wolff, 249.

8. Porter told Lopez that Turnbull made a movie in which a young man falls in love with a woman whose legs he sees through his basement apartment window. The legs were Porter's (79–80). But no record exists of Turnbull as director, and the films he photographed do not resemble the film Porter described. On Turnbull as photographer, see Cristina Felix Romandia, ed., *Filmografía mexicana de medio y largo metrajes 1906–1940* 18/5, 21/1-5-7, 25/6.

9. William Niven (1850–1937) first came to Mexico in the 1890s. Malcolm Niven allowed me to read his father's diaries. Concerning Niven's escape from hanging, see National Archives, State Department, 312, 112 N64.

10. See John Pomian, ed., *Joseph Retinger: Memoirs of an Eminence Grise.*

11. SD: American Embassy in Mexico, vol. 12 (December 13, 1920), National Archives.

12. On Anderson and Porter, see Givner, *A Life,* 120–122.

13. Doherty's memory of Mother Jones is confirmed by Haberman's letter of April 1921, inviting Jones to Mexico from mid-May until early July. See Dale Fethering, *Mother Jones, the Miner's Daughter: A Portrait,* 176–177, 247.

14. Mary Doherty's correspondence is in my possession.

15. Samuel Gompers, "Pan-American Labor Congress at Mexico City," *American Federationist* 28 (March 1921): 195. On leftist criticism of Gompers, see Salazar and Escobedo, *Las pugnas,* 2 : 85–86. Their suspicions went back to the formation of the Pan-American Federation when Gompers, with Woodrow Wilson's approval, courted Mexican labor to pressure Carranza to abandon Mexico's neutrality during World War I. See Sinclair Snow, *The Pan-American Federation of Labor,* 37.

16. Enrique Hank Lopez, *Conversations with Katherine Anne Porter: Refugee from Indian Creek,* 78. Other references to this work appear in my text.

17. See MacKinnon and MacKinnon, *Agnes Smedley,* 41–48.

18. Edward Schwartz, "Katherine Anne Porter: A Critical Bibliography," *Bulletin of the New York Public Library* 52 (May 1953): 219.

19. "Xochimilco" appeared anonymously in the *Christian Science Monitor,* May 31, 1921, and is reproduced in my "Identifying a Sketch by Katherine Anne Porter," *Journal of Modern Literature* 7 (1979): 555–561.

20. See Mark T. Gilderhus, "Senator Albert B. Fall and 'The Plot against Mexico,'" *New Mexico Historical Review* 48 (Fall 1973): 304–305; Meyer, *Oil Controversy,* 99.

21. The Pablo González archive is part of the Fall Collection at the Huntington Library.

22. On the bombing see Taracena, *La verdadera,* 7: 129–130. On the strike see Salazar and Escobedo, *Las pugnas,* 2: 107–108.

23. Taracena, *La verdadera,* 7: 145, 151–152.

24. Ibid., 159–160.

25. Ibid., 163.

26. Ibid., 170–171.

27. *Mexican Review,* July 18, 1921, 5.

28. Hart, *Anarchism,* 160.

29. SD: Miscellaneous Letters of American Embassy in Mexico, vol. 13 (#3907), National Archives.

30. Taracena, *La verdadera,* 7: 175–176.

31. On the Oaxaca conspiracy, see *Mexican Post,* June 6, 16–20, 24, 26, 29, 1921; Taracena, *La verdadera,* 7: 191.

32. Givner, *A Life,* 157–158.

3. Porter and Mexican Art, 1922 and 1923

1. On Porter's stay in Fort Worth, see Givner, *A Life,* 157–160.

2. See Ernest Greuning, *Mexico and Its Heritage,* 520; Carleton Beals, *Mexican Maze,* 188–190; Frederick C. Turner, *The Dynamic of Mexican Nationalism,* 111.

3. See Leo Deuel, *Conquistadors without Swords: Archaeologists in the Americas,* 188–189; Henry C. Schmidt, *The Roots of lo Mexicano: Self and Society in Mexican Thought, 1900–1934,* 77–79.

4. Manuel Gamio, *Forjando patria,* 52.

5. Manuel Gamio, *La población del Valle de Teotihuacán,* xlvii-xlviii. Although Gamio published this work in 1922, Porter drew ideas contained in it directly from Gamio in 1921.

6. All statistical information about Teotihuacán is derived from ibid., xviii-lxxxvi.

7. Greuning, *Mexico and Its Heritage,* 213; Robert E. Quirk, *The Mexican Revolution and the Catholic Church 1910–1929,* 105.

8. Taracena, *La verdadera,* 7: 158.

9. See Quirk, *Catholic Church,* 105.

10. Porter never accents Spanish words in her typescripts—thus, Angel Gomez.

11. See David C. Bailey, *Viva Cristo Rey!: The Cristero Rebellion and the Church-State Conflict in Mexico,* 37.

12. See Carey, *Revolution in Yucatán,* 40–41; and Gruening, *Mexico and Its Heritage,* 214.

13. Octavio Paz, *The Labyrinth of Solitude,* 83.

14. See José Joaquín Blanco, *Se llamaba Vasconcelos,* 80–87, 92–93; Charlot, *Mural Renaissance,* 135–136, 252–256, 269–279.

15. Katherine Anne Porter, "Old Gods and New Messiahs," *New York Herald Tribune Books,* September 29, 1929, 2.

16. On Mérida, see Charlot, *Mural Renaissance,* 71; on Siqueiros, see 73, 197.

17. Dr. Atl, *Las artes populares en México,* 16.

18. Porfirio Martínez Peñaloza, *Tres notas sobre el arte popular en México,* 52.

19. Katherine Anne Porter, *Outline of Mexican Popular Arts and Crafts,* 9.

20. Adolfo Best Maugard, *A Method for Creative Design,* 107, 111, vi.

21. Diego Rivera, *My Life, My Art,* 130.

22. See Taracena, *La verdadera* 8:13, 87, 121–122.

23. Ibid., 121.

24. See Bernard F. Reilly, "Miguel Covarrubias: An Introduction to His Caricatures," in *Miguel Covarrubias Caricatures,* ed. Beverly J. Cox and Donna Jones Anderson, 23–24, 27.

25. José Juan Tablada, "Orozco, the Mexican Goya," *International Studio* 78 (March 1924): 500.

26. Reilly, "Miguel Covarrubias," 24.

27. Manuel González Ramírez, *La caricatura política,* reproduction 70.

28. Salvador Novo, *New Mexican Grandeur,* 46–47.

29. KAP to Delafield Day, July 17, 1928; Porter's caricature of Stein appeared in "Everybody Is a Real One," *New York Herald Tribune Books,* January 16, 1927, 2.

30. Also see Joan Givner, "Katherine Anne Porter and the Art of Caricature," *Genre* 5 (1972): 51–60.

31. See Smith, *Revolutionary Nationalism,* 204–213; Meyer, *Oil Controversy,* 84–89.

32. On the ill-fated exhibition, see Alvarez, "Porter and Mexican Art," 45–49.

33. Salvador Domínguez, "Atzcapotzalco," in *Mexico en el tiempo: El marco de la capital,* 162.

34. Allen Tate criticized the story's "uncertainty of purpose" in his review "A New Star," *Nation* 131 (October 1930): 352–353. John Edward Hardy finds the "psychological and moral situations" clearer in stories that reflect Porter's own cultural setting (*Katherine Anne Porter,* 63). According to Unrue, the uncertainty in the story may arise from "the multiplicity of threads" woven into it (*Truth and Vision,* 24).

35. James Hafley, in his discussion of the story's journey motif, finds the influence of Wallace Stevens's "The Emperor of Ice-Cream" in the description of the dead María Rosa's protruding feet. See "'María Concepción': Life Among the Ruins," *Four Quarters* 12 (November 1962): 13. However, both works first appeared in July 1922.

36. See Erich Neumann, *The Great Mother: An Analysis of the Archetype.* DeMouy discusses Porter's use of Mexican mythology in the story (*Porter's Women,* 21–27).

37. DeMouy (*Porter's Women,* 26) and Unrue (*Truth and Vision,* 23) find that Juan's upflung arms suggest the posture of the crucifixion.

38. For another view of the two Marías as doubles, see DeMouy, *Porter's Women,* 26–27.

39. Elizabeth (Liza) Anderson had an affair with Retinger in 1922, married John Dallett, played host to Porter in 1924, and visited Porter in Mexico in 1930. In the Porter papers, her letters are listed under Dallett and Monk, her second husband's name.

40. See Givner, *A Life,* 168–170.

41. Bertram D. Wolfe, *The Fabulous Life of Diego Rivera,* 183–187.

42. See Hart, *Revolutionary Mexico,* 342.

43. See John A. Britton, *Carleton Beals: A Radical Journalist in America,* 35.

44. Carleton Beals, *Glass Houses: Ten Years of Free-Lancing,* 181.

45. Charlot, *Mural Renaissance,* 243.

46. Diego Rivera, "The Guild Spirit in Mexican Art," *Survey Graphic* 5 (May 1924): 175. Other references to this essay appear in my text.

47. Stanton L. Catlin, "Mural Census," in *Diego Rivera: A Retrospective,* ed. Cynthia Newman Helms, 244.

48. Brenner papers, in possession of Susannah Glusker, Mexico City.

49. See Roque Armando Sosa Ferreyro, *El crimen del miedo: Reportaje histórico,* 17–21, 115–121.

50. Katherine Anne Porter, Foreword to Regine Pernoud, *The Retrial of Joan of Arc,* vii-viii.

4. Thinking of Mexico 1924–1930

1. On Porter and Aguilera, see Givner, *A Life,* 168–170.

2. Porter wrote Monroe Wheeler (December 27, 1960) that she began "Holiday" when she was thirty and made and rejected three drafts over the years, but, after re-discovering it among her papers, expanded the first draft without disturbing its "tone or pace or direction" (L 579). The manuscript at the University of Texas at Austin consists of a twenty-three-page first draft, which is a shorter version of the published story except for the first five pages, which Porter had destroyed. Substituted in their place are four pages of a 1960 draft and five pages of an undated second draft, giving us a whole story, pieced together. Most quotations in my text are to the manuscript, indicated by the absence of page references.

3. Porter wrote Monroe Wheeler (December 27, 1960) that "Holiday" was based on something that happened to her when she was twenty. In the margin of page 109 of George Hendrick's *Katherine Anne Porter,* she wrote, "Her name was Ottilie Hillendahl," to correct his speculation about the origin of the name. Porter reminded her sister Gay (March 5, 1928) of the time she, Mary Alice, and their father drank too much during a turnverein on the Hillendahl farm. According to Paul Porter, around 1915 Mary Alice married Jules Hillendahl, whose nickname was Kuno, the name Porter gave to the German shepherd in "Holiday." Porter's letter to Wheeler is reproduced in part in *Letters of Katherine Anne Porter,* ed. Isabel Bayley, 579. Other references to this edition appear in my text with the designation L.

4. George Core approaches the story in terms of William Empson's concept of the pastoral. See "'Holiday': A Version of Pastoral," in *Katherine Anne Porter: A Critical Symposium,* ed. Lodwick Hartley and George Core, 149–158.

5. On Porter's close attachment to her niece, see Givner, *A Life,* 123, 138–139.

6. On August 20, 1923, Porter signed a receipt for twelve drawings by Rivera, agreeing to sell or return them by February 20, 1924. In a note of January 21, 1925, Rivera authorized Anita Brenner to recover the drawings. The correspondence is among Brenner's papers.

7. Britton records Beals's work for Kenneth Durant and Tass in 1928 (*Carleton Beals,* 82–83).

8. D. H. Lawrence, *The Plumed Serpent,* 24, 45, 73.

9. Daisy Caden Pettus, ed., *The Rosalie Evans Letters from Mexico,* 55, 85.

10. "Children and Art," *Nation,* 124 (March 2, 1927): 234.

11. See Josephine Herbst, "A Year of Disgrace," *Noble Savage* 3 (Spring 1961): 128–160.

12. Moisés Sáenz and Herbert I. Priestly, *Some Mexican Problems,* 165. Other references to this work appear in my text. The essays of Gamio and Vasconcelos appear in a companion volume, *Aspects of Mexican Civilization* (Chicago: Univ. of Chicago Press, 1926).

13. "Paternalism and the Mexican Problem," *New York Herald Tribune Books,* March 27, 1927, 12.

14. On liberalism vs. radicalism, see Frederick J. Hoffman, *The Twenties: American Writing in the Postwar Decade,* 337–341.

15. Katherine Anne Porter, *The Never-Ending Wrong.* On Gold, Hibben, and Gropper, see 23, 244, 33, 45, 47, and 53. On anarchism, see 7 and 59. On liberalism, see 13–14. On Bessie Beatty, see 15. In a letter of September 11, 1927, Porter promised Isidor Schneider "to make my list for you from our committee mailing list, for it included everybody I know, with their addresses."

16. See Vicente Garrido Alfaro, "Luis Hidalgo: The Cerographer of Satire," *Mexican Life,* October 7, 1931: 26–28. Also see Guillermo Rivas, "Luis Hidalgo: A Satirist in Wax," *Mexican Life,* October 1, 1925: 16–18.

17. Porter did an ink drawing of Hidalgo and a caricature of Gertrude Stein which appeared in "Everybody Is a Real One," her review of *The Making of Americans.*

18. Hoffman, *The Twenties,* 127.

19. William Carlos Williams, *In the American Grain,* 66.

20. "History for Boy and Girl Scouts," *New Republic* 48 (November 10, 1926): 353.

21. Katherine Anne Porter, *Ship of Fools,* 341. Other references to the novel are designated by SF in my text.

22. Dulles, *Yesterday in Mexico,* 377.

23. On Porter's relation to Josephson, see Givner, *A Life,* 204–208.

24. See Joan Givner, "'The Plantation of This Isle': Katherine Anne Porter's Bermuda Base," *Southwest Review* 63 (Autumn 1978): 339–351.

25. Janet Lewis to KAP, January 12, 1930.

26. Hardy finds that the woman's self-love "to the exclusion of all other things and persons" leads to self-contempt (*Porter,* 66). On the other hand, Joan Givner stresses the woman's guilt over allowing others to take advantage of her when she should have resisted them. See "A Re-reading of Porter's 'Theft,'" *Studies in Short Fiction* 6 (Summer 1969): 463–465. Porter wrote Texan friend Lon Tinkle (June 10, 1976) that she completely approved Givner's interpretation. Her approval is unsurprising, but it does not invalidate Hardy's analysis.

27. David Levin, *In Defense of Historical Literature: Essays on American History, Autobiography, Drama, and Fiction,* 41–42.

28. "The Dark Ages of New England—The Puritan Emerges Alive and Softened," *New York Evening Post,* November 3, 1928, 8.

29. Givner, *A Life,* 215.

30. Undated letter from Porter to Brenner; Brenner diary entry, January 24, 1929, Brenner papers, Mexico City. During the twenties Chilean poet Gabriela Mistral served as good-will ambassador. Porter met her in Mexico in 1923. Her uncompleted essay is among her papers.

31. "These Pictures Must Be Seen," *New York Herald Tribune Books,* December 22, 1929, 5–6.

32. *This Is My Best,* ed. Whit Burnet, 539.

33. J. H. Retinger, *The Rise of the Mexican Labor Movement,* 91.

34. About Amezcua, see Womack, *Zapata,* 202–203, 209–210; and Valentín López González, *Los compañeros de Zapata,* 23–24.

35. Robert Penn Warren, "Katherine Anne Porter (Irony with a Center)," *Kenyon Review* 4 (Winter 1942): 34; Givner, *A Life,* 217; Dorothy Redden, "'Flowering Judas': Two Voices," *Studies in Short Fiction* 6 (Winter 1969): 196.

36. Glenway Wescott, *Images of Truth: Remembrances and Criticism,* 31.

37. KAP to Blackmur, November 29, 1929, *Hound & Horn* correspondence, Yale University Library. On Porter's allusions to Eliot's poetry, see Leon Gottfried, "Death's Other Kingdom: Dantesque and Theological Symbolism in 'Flowering Judas,'" *PMLA* 84 (January 1969): 113, 121, 123.

38. Redden in "Two Voices" writes that one narrative voice "concurs in Laura's self condemnation" while another "concurs in her self-acquittal" as she maintains "astonishing self-control" in face of both her fear of life and death (201).

5. Mexico Once More, 1930–1931

1. Day to Caroline Gordon, May 21, 1930; KAP to Gay, May 30, 1930.

2. KAP to Pressly, May 1934.

3. See Wolfe, *Rivera,* 272.

4. Ione Robinson, *A Wall to Paint On,* 125.

5. Kenneth Durant to KAP, February 8, 1952. Durant quotes from Porter's letter to Taggard, which he dates as December 26, 1930.

6. Frances Toor to Carleton Beals, October 22, 1930.

7. KAP to Malcolm Cowley, March 3, 1965.

8. Durant to KAP, February 8, 1952, quoting from her letter to Taggard.

9. KAP to Gordon, January 12, 1931.

10. See Raúl Mejía Zúñiga, *Moisés Sáenz: Educador de México,* 23–49; and Gonzalo Aguirre Beltrán, ed. *Antología de Moisés Sáenz.*

11. Ella Wolfe to Carleton Beals, June 10, 1925; Wolfe, *Rivera,* 229.

12. Katherine Anne Porter, "History on the Wing," *New Republic* 89 (November 18, 1936): 82.

13. Lesley Byrd Simpson, *Many Mexicos,* 316.

14. Anita Brenner, *Idols Behind Altars: The Story of the Mexican Spirit,* 124.

15. John Crawford to KAP, September 25, 1930; Day to KAP, July 1930.

16. Day to KAP, 1929; on McKenna see William D. Miller, *Dorothy Day: A Biography,* 210–211.

17. "Music of the Official Jarabe and Verses," *Mexican Folkways* 6 (1930): 24.

18. On the fatal attraction of Mexico, see Walker, *Infernal Paradise,* 49, 57.

19. Brom Weber, ed., *The Letters of Hart Crane: 1916–1932,* 367.

20. Crane to Malcolm Cowley, June 2, 1931, ibid., 370.

21. See John Unterecker, *Voyager: A Life of Hart Crane,* 670–673.

22. See Philip Horton, *Hart Crane: The Life of an American Poet,* 285–287.

23. Porter, *The Never-Ending Wrong,* 51–52.

24. Cowley to KAP, September 14, 1931; KAP to Cowley, October 3, 1931; KAP to Cowley, March 3, 1965, Newberry Library.

25. Concerning the killing, see Harry M. Geduld and Ronald Gottesman, eds., *Sergei Eisenstein and Upton Sinclair: The Making and Unmaking of "Que Viva Mexico!"*, 112.

26. KAP to Monroe Wheeler, November 13, 1933; KAP to Glenway Wescott, January 10, 1934; KAP to Dad and Gay, January 8, 1935.

27. Geduld and Gottesman, eds., *"Que Viva Mexico!"*, 112–113.

28. See Nance's discussion of the "appearance-reality" theme in *Art of Rejection*, 51–52.

29. Robinson, *Wall*, 70–71.

30. See Alma Reed, *The Mexican Muralists*, 33–34.

31. Adolfo Best Maugard, *The New Knowledge of the Three Principles of Nature*, 9, 76.

32. In "To the Editor of *Close-Up*," *Close-Up* 10 (1933): 256–257, Best Maugard complains that he had the right to exercise censorship.

33. On the function of Rosalita's death, see George Hendrick, "Katherine Anne Porter's 'Hacienda'" *Four Quarters* 12 (November 1962): 27.

34. Robert L. Perry notes that the modernity of the three contributes to the story's theme of the illusion of change. See "Porter's 'Hacienda' and the Theme of Change," *Midwest Quarterly* 6 (Summer 1965): 408–411.

35. James G. Frazer describes Diana as a goddess of fertility whose image in her sanctuary on the Aventine was a copy of "the many-breasted idol of the Ephesian Artemis" (*The Golden Bough*, 141). Robert Briffault describes Dana as mother of the gods; two conical hills in County Derry are called her paps (*The Mothers*, 3:70). Wolfram Eberhard records a Chinese myth in which Kuan Yin saved her people by fertilizing rice with her milk (*Folktales of China*, 9).

36. See Gutierre Tibón, *Historia del nombre y de la fundación de México*, 714; Neumann, *The Great Mother*, 126.

37. Eduard Seler, "Mexicans (Ancient)" in *Encyclopaedia of Religion and Ethics*, ed. James Hastings 8: 614–615; Neumann, *The Great Mother*, 123.

38. The source of the Xochitl's legend is Fernando de Alva Ixtlixochitl; see his collected *Obras históricas*, ed. Edmundo O'Gorman, 274–282. A reproduction of Obregón's painting appears in Vicente Riva Palacio, ed., *México a través de los siglos*, between 212 and 213.

39. George Hendrick compares the "disengagement and isolation" of the narrator with that of Laura in "Flowering Judas" ("Porter's 'Hacienda,'" 26).

40. DeMouy points out that the narrator identifies in Kennerly all her own tendencies: the need for security and certainty (*Porter's Women*, 101). The identity extends, unconsciously, to the fear of the dark-skinned natives.

6. Becoming Miranda

1. Janet Lewis's letter to KAP (September 14, 1931) refers to *How Many Redeemers*.

2. KAP to Caroline Gordon, 1932; KAP to Gordon, August 6, 1932; KAP to Gordon, "First day of Spring," 1935.

3. Mary Titus fully explores the significance of the death of Porter's mother on Miranda. See "'Mingled Sweetness and Corruption': Katherine Anne Porter's 'The Fig Tree' and 'The Grave,'" *South Atlantic Review* 53 (Spring 1988), 111–125. Dale Kramer

argues that Miranda's suppression of her memory of the rabbits indicates that she refuses to confront their significance. See "Notes on Lyricism and Symbols in 'The Grave,'" *Studies in Short Fiction* 2 (Summer 1965): 331–336.

4. Givner compares Mr. Thompson with Harrison Porter and Gene Thompson, a relative on whose farm the Porter children once lived (*A Life*, 73–77).

5. KAP to Malcolm Cowley, November 5, 1931; KAP to Eugene Pressly, January 16, 1932.

6. Laing notes that the insecure person's fear of love causes him "to destroy 'in his mind' the image of anyone . . . he may be in danger of becoming fond of, out of desire to safeguard that person . . . from being destroyed" (*The Divided Self*, 93).

7. Wayne C. Booth, *The Rhetoric of Fiction*, 275–277. For similar views see Harry John Mooney, *The Fiction and Criticism of Katherine Anne Porter*, 25, 31; John V. Hagopian, "Katherine Anne Porter: Feeling, Form, and Truth," *Four Quarters* 12 (November 1962): 6; Daniel Curley, "Katherine Anne Porter: The Larger Plan," *Kenyon Review* 25 (Autumn 1963): 667; Louis Auchincloss, *Pioneers and Caretakers*, 141; and Mark Schorer, Afterword to *Pale Horse, Pale Rider* (New York: Signet, 1965), 174–175. The following do not accept Miranda at her own estimate: S. H. Poss, "Variations on a Theme in Four Stories of Katherine Anne Porter," *Twentieth Century Literature* 4 (April–July 1958): 23–24; Sarah Youngblood, "Structure and Imagery in Katherine Anne Porter's 'Pale Horse, Pale Rider,'" *Modern Fiction Studies* 5 (Winter 1959): 347; Johnson, "Love Attitudes," 86; William Nance, *Art of Rejection*, 133–157; Jean Alexander, "Katherine Anne Porter's Ship in the Jungle," *Twentieth Century Literature* 12 (1966): 181–184; Malcolm M. Marsden, "Love as a Threat in Katherine Anne Porter's Fiction," 23–24; and Philip R. Yanella, "The Problems of Dislocation in 'Pale Horse, Pale Rider,'" *Studies in Short Fiction* 5 (Fall 1969): 637–642.

8. "Rivera's Personal Revolution in Mexico," *New York Herald Tribune Books*, March 21, 1937, 7.

9. Joan Givner, "Katherine Anne Porter: Queen of Texas Letters?" *Texas Libraries* 45 (Winter 1984): 120.

10. On Wheeler and Wescott, see Givner, *A Life*, 274–276.

11. Leone B. Moats, *Thunder in Their Veins*, 154–161, 188–189.

12. Taracena, *La verdadera*, 8:9.

13. Fanny Calderon de la Barca, *Life in Mexico*, 79.

14. On Gaona, see Ernest Hemingway, *Death in the Afternoon*, 348.

15. Givner, *A Life*, 415.

7. Ship of Fools

1. See, for example, Theodore Solotaroff, "*Ship of Fools* and the Critics," *Commentary* 34 (October 1962): 280. Throughout the novel Porter awards her characters flashes of insight about themselves that might have served as Joycean epiphanies to close their short stories. For instance, Dr. Schumann, "who before had been playing the notion of signing up for another voyage, then and there in a flash of insight knew that this voyage was to be his last" (SF 192). While reading a magazine, Mrs. Treadwell thinks about her age "when without any warning at all she felt Time itself as a great spider spinning a thick dusty web around her life . . ." (SF 253). Later Schumann "faced an aspect of his character he had not suspected until that hour. He had lived on

flattering terms with the delusive wickedness of his own nature . . ." (SF 350). Again, Schumann, who has more than his share of epiphanies, "suffered the psychic equivalent of a lightning stroke, which cleared away there and then his emotional fogs and vapors, and he faced his truth . . ." (SF 373). Professor Hutten is "dismayed" by an involuntary idea that "struck him powerfully as revealed truth" (SF 373) while David Scott experiences a "brief flash" of insight about his relation to Jenny Brown (SF 439). And so on. The effect of such flashes is dissipated by their very frequency. Wayne Booth mentions the novels scattered anticlimaxes in "Yes, But Are They Really Novels?" *Yale Review* 51 (Summer 1962): 632.

2. See Hardy, *Porter,* 114–115, 134.

3. On the relation of Porter's letter to Caroline Gordon and *Ship of Fools,* see Willene and George Hendrick, *Katherine Anne Porter,* 104–105.

4. Allen Tate, *Essays of Four Decades,* 394.

5. D. H. Lawrence, *Studies in Classic American Literature,* 79.

6. Solotaroff, "*Ship of Fools* and the Critics," 283.

7. M. M. Liberman argues that Porter establishes the children's humanity by portraying them as victims of their parents' inhumanity. See *Katherine Anne Porter's Fiction,* 18–19.

Conclusion

1. On Shannon and Goyen, see Givner, *A Life,* 341–344 and 384–388.

Bibliography

Works by Katherine Anne Porter

Books

My Chinese Marriage. By M[ae] T[iam] F[ranking]. New York: Duffield, 1921.
Outline of Mexican Popular Arts and Crafts. Los Angeles: Young & M'Callister, 1922.
Ship of Fools. Boston: Little Brown, 1962.
The Collected Stories of Katherine Anne Porter. New York: Harcourt, Brace & World, 1965.
The Collected Essays and Occasional Writings of Katherine Anne Porter. New York: Delacourt Press, 1970.
The Never-Ending Wrong. Boston: Little Brown, 1977.
Katherine Anne Porter: Conversations. Ed. Joan Givner. Jackson: Univ. of Mississippi Press, 1987.
Letters of Katherine Anne Porter. Ed. Isabel Bayley. New York: Atlantic Monthly Press, 1990.

Uncollected Essays and Reviews; Short Stories

Review of *Mexico in Revolution* by Vicente Blasco Ibáñez. *El Heraldo de México,* November 22, 1920, 7.
"The Fiesta of Guadalupe." *El Heraldo de México,* December 13, 1920, 10.
Review of *Caliban* by W. L. George. *El Heraldo de México,* December 15, 1920, 10.
[With Robert Haberman.] "Striking the Lyric Note in Mexico." *New York Call,* January 16, 1921, 1, 3.
"The New Man and the New Order." *Magazine of Mexico* 1 (March 1921): 5–15.
"Xochimilco." *Christian Science Monitor,* May 31, 1921, 10.
"A Letter from Mexico and the Gleam of Montezuma's Golden Roofs." *Christian Science Monitor,* June 5, 1922, 22.
"Two Ancient Mexican Pyramids—The Core of a City Unknown Until a Few Years Ago." *Christian Science Monitor,* September 19, 1922, 7.
"María Concepción." *Century* 105 (December 1922): 224–239.
"Corridos." *Survey Graphic* 5 (May 1924): 157–159.

"To a Portrait of the Poet." *Survey Graphic* 5 (May 1924): 182.

"Mexico." *New York Herald Tribune Books,* November 2, 1924, 9.

"Maya Treasure." *New York Herald Tribune Books,* February 8, 1925, 9.

"The Great Catherine." *New York Herald Tribune Books,* November 29, 1925, 3–4.

"Ay, Que Chamaco." *New Republic* 45 (December 23, 1925): 141–142.

"A Singing Woman." *New York Herald Tribune Books,* April 18, 1926:6.

"History for Boy and Girl Scouts." *New Republic* 48 (November 10, 1926): 353.

"Everybody Is a Real One." *New York Herald Tribune Books,* January 16, 1927, 1–2.

"Enthusiast and Wildcatter." *New York Herald Tribune Books,* February 6, 1927, 14.

"Children and Art." *Nation* 124 (March 2, 1927): 233–234.

"Paternalism and the Mexican Problem." *New York Herald Tribune Books,* March 27, 1927, 12.

"The Dark Ages of New England—The Puritan Emerges Alive and Softened." *New York Evening Post,* November 3, 1928, sec. 3, p. 8.

"Old Gods and New Messiahs." *New York Herald Tribune Books,* September 29, 1929, 1–2.

"'These Pictures Must Be Seen'" *New York Herald Tribune Books,* December 22, 1929, 5–6.

"Music of the Official Jarabe and Verses." *Mexican Folkways* 6 (1930): 24.

"Hacienda." *Virginia Quarterly Review* 8 (October 1932): 556–569.

"History on the Wing." *New Republic* 89 (November 18, 1936): 82.

"Rivera's Personal Revolution in Mexico." *New York Herald Tribune Books,* March 21, 1937, 7.

"Why She Selected Flowering Judas." In *This Is My Best.* Ed. Whit Burnet, 539–540. New York: Dial Press, 1942.

"Mexico's Thirty Long Years of Revolution." *New York Herald Tribune Books,* May 30, 1943, 1–2.

Foreword to *The Retrial of Joan of Arc,* by Regine Pernoud, v–viii. New York: Harcourt, Brace, 1955.

Sources Cited on Porter

Alexander, Jean. "Katherine Anne Porter's Ship in the Jungle." *Twentieth Century Literature* 12 (1966): 179–188.

Alvarez, Ruth Moore. "Katherine Anne Porter and Mexican Art." Ph.D. diss., University of Maryland, 1990.

Auchincloss, Louis. *Pioneers and Caretakers.* Minneapolis: Univ. of Minnesota Press, 1965.

Booth, Wayne C. *The Rhetoric of Fiction.* Chicago: Univ. of Chicago Press, 1961.

———. "Yes, but Are They Really Novels?" *Yale Review* 51 (Summer 1962): 632–634.

Core, George. "'Holiday': A Version of Pastoral." In *Katherine Anne Porter: A Critical Symposium,* ed. Lodwick Hartley and George Core, 149–158. Athens: Univ. of Georgia Press, 1969.

Curley, Daniel. "Katherine Anne Porter: The Larger Plan." *Kenyon Review* 25 (Autumn 1963): 671–695.

DeMouy, Jane Krause. *Katherine Anne Porter's Women: The Eye of Her Fiction*. Austin: Univ. of Texas Press, 1983.

Givner, Joan. "A Re-reading of Porter's 'Theft.'" *Studies in Short Fiction* 6 (Summer 1969): 463–465.

———. "Katherine Anne Porter and the Art of Caricature." *Genre* 5 (1972): 51–60.

———. "'The Plantation of This Isle': Katherine Anne Porter's Bermuda Base." *Southwest Review* 63 (Autumn 1978): 339–351.

———. "Katherine Anne Porter, Journalist." *Southwest Review* 64 (Autumn 1979): 309–322.

———. *Katherine Anne Porter: A Life*. New York: Simon and Schuster, 1982.

———. "Katherine Anne Porter: Queen of Texas Letters?" *Texas Libraries* 45 (Winter 1984): 119–123.

Gottfried, Leon. "Death's Other Kingdom: Dantesque and Theological Symbolism in 'Flowering Judas.'" *PMLA* 84 (January 1969): 112–124.

Gunn, Dewey Wayne. "'Second Country': Katherine Anne Porter." In *American and British Writers in Mexico, 1556–1973*. Austin: Univ. of Texas Press, 1969.

Hafley, James. "'María Concepción': Life among the Ruins." *Four Quarters* 12 (November 1962): 11–17.

Hagopian, John V. "Katherine Anne Porter: Feeling, Form, and Truth." *Four Quarters* 12 (November 1962): 1–10.

Hardy, John Edward. *Katherine Anne Porter*. New York: Frederick Unger, 1973.

Hendrick, George. "Katherine Anne Porter's 'Hacienda.'" *Four Quarters* 12 (November 1962): 24–29.

Hendrick, Willene, and George Hendrick. *Katherine Anne Porter*. Rev. ed. Boston: Twayne Publishers, 1988.

Horton, Philip. *Hart Crane: The Life of an American Poet*. New York: W. W. Norton, 1937.

Johnson, Shirley E. "Love Attitudes in the Fiction of Katherine Anne Porter." *West Virginia University Philological Papers* 13 (December 1961): 82–93.

Kiernan, Robert F. *Katherine Anne Porter and Carson McCullers: A Reference Guide*. Boston: G. K. Hall, 1976.

Kramer, Dale. "Notes on Lyricism and Symbols in 'The Grave.'" *Studies in Short Fiction* 2 (Summer 1965): 331–336.

Langer, Elinor. *Josephine Herbst*. Boston: Little, Brown, 1984.

Levin, David. *In Defense of Historical Literature: Essays on American History, Autobiography, Drama, and Fiction*. New York: Hill and Wang, 1967.

Liberman, M. M. *Katherine Anne Porter's Fiction*. Detroit: Wayne State Univ. Press, 1971.

Lopez, Enrique Hank. "A Country and Some People I Love." *Harper's Magazine* 231 (September 1965): 58–68.

———. *Conversations with Katherine Anne Porter: Refugee from Indian Creek*. Boston: Little, Brown, 1981.

Lugg, Bonelyn. "Mexican Influences on the Work of Katherine Anne Porter." Ph.D. diss., Pennsylvania State Univ., 1976.

Marsden, Malcolm M. "Love as a Threat in Katherine Anne Porter's Fiction." *Twentieth Century Literature* 13 (March 1967): 29–38.

Martínez Peñaloza, Porfirio. *Tres notas sobre el arte popular en México*. Mexico City: Miguel Angel Porrua, 1980.

Medina Ruiz, Fernando. "El comunismo es la causa del 'Rebelde sin Causa,' afirma la escritora Porter." *El Universal,* May 27, 1960, 1, 7, 11.

Mooney, Harry John. *The Fiction and Criticism of Katherine Anne Porter.* Pittsburgh: Univ. of Pittsburgh Press, 1957.

Nance, William L. *Katherine Anne Porter and the Art of Rejection.* Chapel Hill: Univ. of North Carolina Press, 1964.

———. "Katherine Anne Porter and Mexico." *Southwest Review* 55 (Spring 1970): 277–289.

Naylor, Pauline. "Katherine Anne Porter's Ft. Worth Days Recalled." *Fort Worth Star-Telegram,* April 10, 1966, 16.

Partridge, Colin. "'My Familiar Country': An Image of Mexico in the Work of Katherine Anne Porter." *Studies in Short Fiction* 7 (Fall 1970): 597–614.

Perry, Robert L. "Porter's 'Hacienda' and the Theme of Change." *Midwest Quarterly* 6 (Summer 1965): 403–415.

Poss, S. H. "Variations on a Theme in Four Stories of Katherine Anne Porter." *Twentieth Century Literature* 4 (April–July 1958): 21–29.

Redden, Dorothy. "'Flowering Judas': Two Voices." *Studies in Short Fiction* 6 (Winter 1969): 194–204.

Schorer, Mark. Afterword to *Pale Horse, Pale Rider,* by Katherine Anne Porter. New York: Signet, 1965.

Schwartz, Edward. "Katherine Anne Porter: A Critical Bibliography." *Bulletin of the New York Public Library* 52 (May 1953): 211–247.

Sexton, Kathryn Adam. "Katherine Anne Porter's Years in Denver." Master's thesis, Univ. of Colorado, 1961.

Solotaroff, Theodore. "*Ship of Fools* and the Critics." *Commentary* 34 (October 1962): 277–286.

Tate, Allen. "A New Star." *Nation* 131 (October 1930): 352–353.

Titus, Mary. "'Mingled Sweetness and Corruption': Katherine Anne Porter's 'The Fig Tree' and 'The Grave.'" *South Atlantic Review* 53 (Spring 1988): 111–125.

Unrue, Darlene Harbour. *Truth and Vision in Katherine Anne Porter's Fiction.* Athens: Univ. of Georgia Press, 1985.

Unterecker, John. *Voyager: A Life of Hart Crane.* New York: Farrar, Straus and Giroux, 1969.

Walker, Ronald G. *Infernal Paradise: Mexico and the English Novel.* Berkeley: Univ. of California Press, 1978.

Walsh, Thomas F. "Katherine Anne Porter's 'Noon Wine' Devils.'" *Georgia Review* 23 (Spring 1968): 90–96.

———. "Deep Similarities in 'Noon Wine.'" *Mosaic* 11 (1975): 83–91.

———. "Miranda's Ghost in 'Old Mortality.'" *College Literature* 6 (1979–1980): 57–63.

———. "The Dream Self in 'Pale Horse, Pale Rider.'" *Wascana Review* 14 (Fall 1979): 61–79.

———. "Identifying a Sketch by Katherine Anne Porter." *Journal of Modern Literature* 7 (1979): 555–561.

———. "Xochitl, Katherine Anne Porter's Changing Goddess." *American Literature* 52 (May 1980): 183–193.

———. "Braggioni's Jockey Club in 'Flowering Judas.'" *Studies in Short Fiction* 20 (Spring–Summer 1983): 136–138.

————. "The Making of 'Flowering Judas.'" *Journal of Modern Literature* 12 (March 1985): 109–130.

Warren, Robert Penn. "Katherine Anne Porter (Irony with a Center)." *Kenyon Review* 4 (Winter 1942): 29–42.

Weber, Brom, ed. *The Letters of Hart Crane: 1916–1932*. New York: Hermitage House, 1952.

Wescott, Glenway. *Images of Truth: Remembrances and Criticism*. New York: Harcourt Brace, 1964.

Whicher, George. In *The Literature of the American People*. Ed. Arthur Hobson Quinn. New York: Appleton-Century-Crofts, 1951.

Yanella, Philip R. "The Problems of Dislocation in 'Pale Horse, Pale Rider.'" *Studies in Short Fiction* 5 (Fall 1969): 637–642.

Youngblood, Sarah. "Structure and Imagery in Katherine Anne Porter's 'Pale Horse, Pale Rider.'" *Modern Fiction Studies* 5 (Winter 1959): 344–352.

Sources Cited on Mexico and Psychology

Aguirre Beltrán, Gonzalo, ed. *Antología de Moisés Sáenz*. Mexico City: Ediciones Oasis, 1970.

Araiza, Luis. *Historia del Movimiento Obrero Mexicano*. Mexico City: Ediciones Casa del Obrero Mundial, 1975.

Atl, Dr. [Gerardo Murillo]. *Las artes populares en México*. Mexico City: Cultura, 1922.

Bailey, David C. *Viva Cristo Rey!: The Cristero Rebellion and the Church-State Conflict in Mexico*. Austin: Univ. of Texas Press, 1974.

Beals, Carleton. *Glass Houses: Ten Years of Free-Lancing*. Philadelphia: J. B. Lippincott, 1938.

————. *Mexican Maze*. Philadelphia: J. B. Lippincott, 1931.

Best Maugard, Adolfo. *A Method for Creative Design*. New York: Alfred Knopf, 1926.

————. *The New Knowledge of the Three Principles of Nature*. Mexico City: I. I. C. E. E., 1949.

————. "To the Editor of *Close-Up*." *Close-up* 10 (1933): 256–257.

Blanco, José Joaquín. *Se llamaba Vasconcelos*. Mexico City: Fondo de Cultura, 1977.

Blasco Ibáñez, Vicente. *Mexico in Revolution*. New York: E. P. Dutton, 1920.

Brenner, Anita. *Idols Behind Altars: The Story of the Mexican Spirit*. 1929. Reprint. Boston: Beacon Press, 1970.

Briffault, Robert. *The Mothers*. 3 vols. New York: Macmillan, 1927.

Britton, John A. *Carleton Beals: A Radical Journalist in America*. Albuquerque: Univ. of New Mexico Press, 1987.

Calderon de la Barca, Fanny. *Life in Mexico*. New York: E. P. Dutton, 1931.

Carey, James C. *The Mexican Revolution in Yucatán: 1915–1924*. Boulder: Westview Press, 1984.

Carr, Barry. *El movimiento obrero y la política en México, 1910–1929*. 2 vols. Mexico City: SepSetentas, 1976.

Catlin, Stanton L. "Mural Census." In *Diego Rivera: A Retrospective*, ed. Cynthia Newman Helms, 235–335. New York: W. W. Norton, 1986.

Chamberlain, Lawrence H. *Loyalty and Legislative Action: A Survey of the New York State Legislature 1919–1949.* Ithaca: Cornell Univ. Press, 1951.

Charlot, Jean. *The Mexican Mural Renaissance 1920–1925.* New Haven: Yale Univ. Press, 1963.

Clark, Marjorie Ruth. *Organized Labor in Mexico.* New York: Russell & Russell, 1973.

Constantine, Mildred. *Tina Modotti: A Fragile Life.* New York: Paddington Press, 1975.

Cowley, Malcolm. *Exile's Return: A Literary Odyssey of the 1920s.* New York: Viking Press, 1951.

Cumberland, Charles C. *Mexico: The Struggle for Modernity.* New York: Oxford Univ. Press, 1968.

De Grial, Hugo. *Músicos mexicanos.* Mexico City: Editorial Diana, 1965.

Deuel, Leo. *Conquistadors without Swords: Archaeologists in the Americas.* New York: Schocken Books, 1967.

Domínguez, Salvador. "Azcapotzalco." In *Mexico en el tiempo: El marco de la capital,* 162–163. Mexico City: Talleres de Excelsior, 1946.

Dulles, John W. F. *Yesterday in Mexico: A Chronicle of the Revolution, 1919–1936.* Austin: Univ. of Texas Press, 1961.

Eberhard, Wolfram. *Folktales of China.* Chicago: Univ. of Chicago Press, 1965.

Félix Romandía, Cristina, ed. *Filmografía mexicana de medio y largo metrajes, 1906–1940.* Mexico City: Cineteca Nacional, 1988.

Fethering, Dale. *Mother Jones, the Miner's Daughter: A Portrait.* Carbondale: Southern Illinois Univ. Press, 1974.

Frazer, James G. *The Golden Bough.* New York: Macmillan, 1947.

Gamio, Manuel. *Forjando patria.* Mexico City: Editorial Porrua, 1982.

———. *La población del Valle de Teotihuacán.* Mexico City: Talleres Gráficos, 1922.

Garrido Alfaro, Vicente. "Luis Hidalgo: The Cerographer of Satire." *Mexican Life,* October 7, 1931, 26–28.

Geduld, Harry M., and Ronald Gottesman, eds. *Sergei Eisenstein and Upton Sinclair: The Making and Unmaking of "Que Viva Mexico!"* Bloomington: Indiana Univ. Press, 1970.

Gilderhus, Mark T. "Senator Albert B. Fall and 'The Plot against Mexico.'" *New Mexico Historical Review* 48 (Fall 1973): 299–311.

Gompers, Samuel. "Pan-American Labor Congress at Mexico City," *American Federationist* 28 (March 1921): 193–200.

González Ramírez, Manuel. *La caricatura política.* Mexico City: Fondo de Cultura Económica, 1955.

Green, James R. *Grass-Roots Socialism: Radical Movements in the Southwest 1895–1943.* Baton Rouge: Louisiana State Univ. Press, 1978.

Greuning, Ernest. *Mexico and Its Heritage.* New York: D. Appleton Century, 1936.

Haberman, Robert. "Mexican Workers Celebrate Labor Day with Great Parades and Demonstrations." *New York Call,* October 18, 1920, 4–5.

Hall, Linda B. *Alvaro Obregón: Power and Revolution in Mexico, 1911–1920.* College Station: Texas A&M Univ. Press, 1981.

Hanna, Paul. "Mexico—1921: V. Relations with the United States." *Nation* 112 (April 27, 1921): 614–617.

Hart, John Mason. *Anarchism and the Mexican Working Class, 1860–1931.* Austin: Univ. of Texas Press, 1978.

————. *Revolutionary Mexico: The Coming and Process of the Mexican Revolution.* Berkeley: Univ. of California Press, 1947.

Hemingway, Ernest. *Death in the Afternoon.* London: Jonathan Cape, 1932.

Herbst, Josephine. "Man of Steel." *American Mercury* 31 (January 1934): 32–40.

————. "A Year of Disgrace." *Noble Savage* 3 (Spring 1961): 128–160.

Hoffman, Frederick J. *The Twenties: American Writing in the Postwar Decade.* New York: Viking Press, 1955.

Horney, Karen. *Feminine Psychology.* Ed. Harold Kelman. New York: W. W. Norton, 1973.

Huitrón, Jacinto. *Orígenes e historia del Movimiento Obrero en México.* Mexico City: Editores Mexicanos Unidos, 1974.

Hyde, George E. "Renegade Americans Promoting Bolshevik Movement in Mexico." *New York Tribune,* September 5, 1920, 9.

Ixtlixochitl, Fernando de Alva. *Obras históricas.* Ed. Edmundo O'Gorman. Mexico City: UNAM, 1975.

Kaplan, H. I., and B. J. Sadok. *Synopsis of Clinical Psychiatry.* Baltimore: Williams and Wilkins, 1988.

Katz, Friedrich. *The Secret War in Mexico: Europe, the United States, and the Mexican Revolution.* Chicago: Univ. of Chicago Press, 1981.

Kennedy, David M. *Over Here: The First World War and American Society.* New York: Oxford Univ. Press, 1980.

Kruglak, Theodore E. *The Two Faces of TASS.* Minneapolis: Univ. of Minnesota Press, 1962.

Laing, R. D. *The Divided Self: An Existential Study in Sanity and Madness.* Baltimore: Penguin Books, 1965.

Lawrence, D. H. *The Plumed Serpent.* New York: Alfred A. Knopf, 1926.

————. *Studies in Classic American Literature.* New York: Doubleday Anchor Books, 1953.

López González, Valentín. *Los compañeros de Zapata.* [Cuernavaca]: Gobierno del Estado de Morelos, 1980.

Lyons, Eugene. *Assignment in Utopia.* London: George C. Harrop, 1938.

MacKinnon, Janice R., and Stephen R. MacKinnon. *Agnes Smedley: The Life and Times of an American Radical.* Berkeley: Univ. of California Press, 1988.

Mejía Zúñiga, Raúl. *Moisés Sáenz: Educador de México.* Mexico City: Federación Editorial Mexicana, 1970.

Meyer, Lorenzo. *Mexico and the United States in the Oil Controversy 1917–1942.* Austin: Univ. of Texas Press, 1977.

Miller, William D. *Dorothy Day: A Biography.* New York: Harper & Row, 1982.

Moats, Leone B. *Thunder in Their Veins.* New York: Century, 1932.

Neumann, Erich. *The Great Mother: An Analysis of the Archetype.* Princeton: Princeton Univ. Press, 1972.

Niven, William. "Omitlan, a Prehistoric City in Mexico." *Bulletin of the American Geographical Society* 29 (1987): 217–222.

Novo, Salvador. *New Mexican Grandeur.* Mexico City: Ediciones Era, 1967.

Orozco, José Clemente. *An Autobiography.* Austin: Univ. of Texas Press, 1962.

Outman, W. D. "Current Comment." *Magazine of Mexico* 1 (March 1921): 66.

Paz, Octavio, *The Labyrinth of Solitude.* New York: Grove Press, 1985.

Peterson, Horace C. *Opponents of War, 1917–1918.* Madison: Univ. of Wisconsin Press, 1957.

Pettus, Daisy Cadden, ed. *The Rosalie Evans Letters from Mexico.* Indianapolis: Bobbs-Merrill, 1926.

Pomian, John, ed. *Joseph Retinger: Memoirs of an Eminence Grise.* Sussex: Univ. Press, 1972.

Prescott, William. *History of the Conquest of Mexico.* Philadelphia: J. B. Lippincott, 1904.

Quirk, Robert E. *The Mexican Revolution and the Catholic Church 1910–1929.* Bloomington: Indiana Univ. Press, 1973.

Reed, Alma. *The Mexican Muralists.* New York: Crown, 1960.

Reilly, Bernard F. "Miguel Covarrubias: An Introduction to His Caricatures." In *Miguel Covarrubias Caricatures,* ed. Beverly J. Cox and Donna Jones Anderson, 23–39. Washington, D.C.: Smithsonian Institution Press, 1985.

Retinger, J. H. *The Rise of the Mexican Labor Movement.* Reprint of *Morones of Mexico* (1926). Washington, D.C.: Documentary Publications, 1976.

Riva Palacio, Vicente, ed. *México a través de los siglos.* 5 vols. Mexico City: Publicaciones Herrerías, 1887–1889.

Rivas, Guillermo. "Luis Hidalgo: A Satirist in Wax." *Mexican Life,* October 1, 1925, 16–18.

Rivera, Diego. "The Guild Spirit in Mexican Art (as told to Katherine Anne Porter)." *Survey Graphic* 5 (May 1924): 174–178.

———. *My Life, My Art.* New York: Citadel Press, 1960.

Robinson, Ione. *A Wall to Paint On.* New York: E. P. Dutton, 1946.

Sáenz, Moisés, and Herbert I. Priestly. *Some Mexican Problems.* Chicago: Univ. of Chicago Press, 1926.

Salazar, Rosendo, and José G. Escobedo. *Las pugnas de la gleba.* Mexico City: Editorial Avante, 1922.

Sánchez, George I. *Mexico: A Revolution by Education.* New York: Viking Press, 1936.

Schmidt, Henry C. *The Roots of lo Mexicano: Self and Society in Mexican Thought, 1900–1934.* College Station: Texas A&M Univ. Press, 1978.

Seler, Eduard, "Mexicans (Ancient)." In *Encyclopaedia of Religion and Ethics.* Vol. 8. Ed. James Hastings, 612–617. New York: Charles Scribner's Sons, 1916.

Simmel, Georg. "The Adventure." In *Essays on Sociology, Philosophy and Aesthetics,* ed. Kurt H. Wolff, 243–258. New York: Harper Torchbooks, 1968.

Simpson, Lesley Byrd. *Many Mexicos.* Berkeley: Univ. of California, 1967.

Smith, Robert Freeman. *The United States and Revolutionary Nationalism in Mexico, 1916–1932.* Chicago: Univ. of Chicago Press, 1972.

Snow, Sinclair. *The Pan-American Federation of Labor.* Durham: Duke Univ. Press, 1964.

Sosa Ferreyro, Roque Armando. *El crimen del miedo: Reportaje histórico.* Mexico City: B. Costa-Amic, [1969].

Tablada, José Juan. "Orozco, the Mexican Goya." *International Studio* 78 (March 1924): 492–500.

Taracena, Alfonso. *La verdadera revolución mexicana.* 18 vols. Mexico City: Editorial Jus, 1962.

Tate, Allen. *Essays of Four Decades.* Chicago: Swallow Press, 1968.

Tibón, Gutierre. *Historia del nombre y de la fundación de México.* Mexico City: Fondo de Cultura Económica, 1975.

Turner, John Kenneth. *Barbarous Mexico.* Chicago: Charles H. Kerr, 1910.

Turner, Frederick C. *The Dynamic of Mexican Nationalism*. Chapel Hill: Univ. of North Carolina Press, 1968.

Williams, William Carlos. *In the American Grain*. New York: New Directions, 1956.

Wolfe, Bertram D. *The Fabulous Life of Diego Rivera*. New York: Stein and Day, 1963.

Womack, John. *Zapata and the Mexican Revolution*. New York: Vintage Books, 1970.

Wright, Marie Robinson. *Picturesque Mexico*. Philadelphia: J. B. Lippincott, 1897.

Index

Permissions
Acknowledgments

Grateful acknowledgment is made for permission to include exerpts from manuscript and previously unpublished material as follows:

From unpublished fiction, notes, and letters of Katherine Anne Porter, by permission of Isabel Bayley, literary trustee for the estste of Katherine Anne Porter.

From letters of Katherine Anne Porter and Ernestine Evans to Carleton Beals, by permission of Boston University Libraries.

From Katherine Anne Porter's correspondence with Malcolm Cowley Papers, by permission of the Newberry Library.

From the letters of Katherine Anne Porter to Caroline Gordon and Allen Tate, from the Caroline Gordon Papers and the Allen Tate Papers, published with permission of Princeton University Library.

From the letters of Katherine Anne Porter to Josephine Herbst, Robert McAlmon, and Robert Penn Warren, published with permission of the Yale Collection of American Literature, Beinecke Rare Book and Manuscript Library, Yale University.

From Porter's typescript of "Holiday" by permission of the Harry Ransom Humanities Research Center, The University of Texas at Austin.

From the book *The Collected Essays and Occasional Writings of Katherine Anne Porter* by Katherine Anne Porter, published by Houghton Mifflin Co./Seymour Lawrence, Boston. Copyright © 1970 by Katherine Anne Porter. Reprinted by permission.

Exerpts from the book, *The Letters of Katherine Anne Porter,* Selected and Editied and with an Introduction by Isabel Bayley. Copyright © 1990 by Isabel Bayley. Used with permission of Atlantic Monthly Press.

From *Katherine Anne Porter: Conversations,* ed. Joan Givner, 1987, by permission of University Press of Mississippi.

From Katherine Anne Porter, "Ay, Que Chamaco," © 1925, The New Republic, Inc., and "History on the Wing," © 1936, The New Republic. Reprinted by permission of *The New Republic.*

From Wayne C. Booth, *The Rhetoric of Fiction,* © 1961 by The University of Chicago, reprinted by permission of the University of Chicago Press.

From Harry M. Geduld and Ronald Gottesman, eds., *Sergei Eisenstein and Upton Sinclair,* by permission of Indiana University Press, publisher.

From Paul Hanna, "Mexico—1921", *The Nation* Magazine/The Nation Company, Inc., copyright 1921, and Katherine Anne Porter, "Children and Art," *The Nation* Magazine/The NationCompany, Inc., copyright 1927, by permission of The Nation.

From Karen Horney, *Feminine Psychology,* 1967, by permission of W.W. Norton & Company, Inc., publisher

From D.H. Lawrence, *The Plumed Serpent,* Copyright 1926, 1951, by Alfred A. Knopf, Inc., by permission of the publisher.

From Erich Neumann, *The Great Nation: An Analysis of the Archetype,* 1972, by permission of Princeton University Press.

From Georg Simmel, "The Adventure," in *Essays on Sociology, Philosophy, and Aesthetics,* ed. Kurt H. Wolff, copyright 1968, by permission of Harper & Row, Publishers, Inc.

From William Carlos Williams, *In the American Grain.* Copyright 1933 by William Carlos Williams. Reprinted by permission of New Directions Pub. Corp.